RHS

WHAT
PLANT
WHEN

LONDON, NEW YORK, MUNICH, MELBOURNE, DELHI

WRITERS Martin Page, with Andrea Loom
NEW EDITION REVISED AND UPDATED BY Simon Maughan

DK LONDON
SENIOR EDITOR Helen Fewster
SENIOR ART EDITOR Elaine Hewson
DATABASE MANAGER David Roberts
MANAGING EDITOR Esther Ripley
MANAGING ART EDITOR Alison Donovan
PRODUCTION EDITOR Joanna Byrne
PRODUCTION CONTROLLER Mandy Inness
ASSOCIATE PUBLISHER Liz Wheeler
ART DIRECTOR Peter Luff
PUBLISHER Jonathan Metcalf

DK INDIA
EDITOR Nidhilekha Mathur
DESIGNER Nitu Singh
DTP OPERATOR Anurag Trivedi
MANAGING EDITOR Suchismita Banerjee
MANAGING ART EDITOR Romi Chakraborty
DTP MANAGER Sunil Sharma

First edition published in Great Britain in 2002 as *Plants for Every Season* by
Dorling Kindersley Limited, 80 Strand, London WC2R 0RL
A Penguin Company

New edition published in 2011

Copyright © 2002, 2006, 2009, 2011 Dorling Kindersley Limited, London
2 4 6 8 10 9 7 5 3
001 – 180269 – June 2011

A CIP catalogue record for this book is available from the British Library.

ISBN 978-1-4053-6297-9

Printed and bound by Star Standard Industries Pte Ltd, Singapore

To find out more about RHS membership visit our website
www.rhs.org.uk or call 0845 062 1111

Discover more at
www.dk.com

CONTENTS

USING THE GUIDE

The aim of this book is to help you to select plants for your garden that will provide colour and interest throughout the year. There are seven chapters, based on the six seasons of the gardening year, plus a final section suggesting plants that offer year-round interest. This "All Seasons" chapter will help you to choose some plants that give shape and structure to the garden, or that have evergreen foliage. They may be used to create a permanent framework, into which other flowering plants can be introduced.

It will come as no surprise to learn that the largest chapters relate to late spring, and to early and late summer, but you may be interested to discover how many plants are in flower at other times of year. Use this book to plan ahead so your garden has autumn interest as well as colour in winter and early spring.

In each chapter the plants have been divided into colour categories – white, pink, red, purple, blue, green, yellow, and orange – and then presented in alphabetical order. Some may flower over a long period or have several seasons of interest, but here they are placed in the season in which they make the

most significant impact. Thus a flowering cherry may have found its way into "Autumn" due to its attractive foliage, while pyracanthas may be grown for their early summer flowers as well as their bright clusters of winter berries.

SYMBOLS USED

♥ The RHS Award of Garden Merit

Sun or shade preferences/tolerances
☼ Full sun
◗ Partial shade; either dappled shade or shade for part of the day
● Full shade

Soil moisture preferences/tolerances
◊ Well-drained soil
◐ Moist soil
● Wet soil
NB Where two or more symbols appear from the same category, the plant is suitable for a range of conditions.

Hardiness ratings
❄ Plants requiring the protection of a heated glasshouse over winter but may be placed outdoors in sheltered sites in summer.
❄❄ Plants that survive outside in mild regions or in favoured sites, or those that, in temperate countries, are usually grown outside in summer but need frost-protection over winter.
❄❄❄ Fully hardy plants.

f Fragrant flowers or aromatic leaves.

PLANNING YOUR GARDEN

It is a good idea to plan before you plant by making a rough drawing of your existing garden and plotting in various permanent plants and features like paths, patio, or shed. Computer programs are available to help you visualise how your garden will look, but a sheet of squared paper and a pencil can perform the same task, at a much lower cost. Hard landscaping in the form of paths and patios, should be done before the garden is planted. It is also important to take into account your garden's use: whether you need space for entertaining, or areas for pets and children to play. Once your priorities are established, you can turn to the plants.

SELECT IN ORDER

Start by choosing trees and shrubs. These provide the permanent backbone of the garden. Boundary hedges or mixed shrub screens give shelter from wind, privacy, and buffer noise. Specimen shrubs and especially trees need enough room to develop unhindered. They can grow to a considerable size, so it is usually better to plant one or two modest specimens and allow them to grow naturally rather than spoil

their appearance by heavy pruning, or removing them after a few years.

Once these long-term plants are in place you can turn your attention to the small shrubs and herbaceous perennials. Often simplicity is the key to achieving a harmonious garden. Rather than using lots of different plants it is better to plant groups of three or five of the same variety, which will merge together and create more impact. The final elements are the bulbs and annuals, all of which give instant colour in their first year, and are invaluable for filling gaps. Hardy annuals can be sown *in situ* and bulbs can be naturalized under trees and in grass.

YEAR-ROUND INTEREST

There are no set times when the seasons begin and end. It depends on the climate where you live, your garden situation, and the weather. In mild years, flowers start to open between one and two weeks earlier than in others; summers can be brought to an abrupt halt by severe drought or an unseasonable frost.

To achieve year-round interest in the garden, start by choosing a few plants for winter, when the choice is most limited: perhaps a tree with

Dual purpose
Bergenias are easy-going good ground cover plants for sun or light shade. This one has bright pink spring flowers and the foliage colours in winter.

interesting bark, or a cluster of winter-flowering shrubs and some early bulbs. Then select for early spring and autumn; some plants will double up with spring flowers and bright autumn tints. Move on to make your selection for late spring, before looking through the summer sections. Consider planting up a few containers for each season; again there is a huge choice for summer, but different varieties of plants like pansies go throughout the year.

COLOUR

Many people enjoy lots of colour, but some of the most appealing beds, borders, or containers have a colour theme. You might choose shades of one colour, although this can be dull, or use a limited palette. White and pastel colours are cool and show up well at dusk – good near a patio or path. Blues and mauves are hazy and give a sense of distance, whereas hot reds, oranges and yellows appear closer.

ASSESSING YOUR SITE

Planting a new garden can be an exciting prospect, but before you rush to the garden centre it is wise to assess your site by testing the soil and identifying areas of sun and shade. If your site is bare, one way of finding out what grows well in your locality is to look at what succeeds in neighbouring gardens, or ask at the garden centre. Try to select plants that suit the conditions rather than fighting against nature;

this helps to prevent expensive disappointments, and generally your plants will be healthier and need less attention.

If you have acquired a garden that is well established, try to stem your enthusiasm and observe it for

Focal points
The variegated *Yucca gloriosa* is a superb architectural plant, and provides a strong focus in a border in well-drained sunny gardens. It may also be grown in containers.

a year. In doing so, you discover its hidden delights, such as bulbs, and see how plants perform through the seasons. Only then should you consider changes. If possible, keep established trees for the maturity they give, but smaller plants can be moved, ideally in early spring.

TESTING THE SOIL

The soil is critical in determining which plants will grow well in your garden and you need to establish its characteristics. Sandy soil is free-draining, low in nutrients and feels gritty as you rub it between your fingers. At the other extreme is clay soil, which is smooth and malleable when handled. It is nutrient rich, but sticky when wet, becomes rock hard when dry and often has poor drainage. The ideal soil is moist and well-drained, retaining water, but without becoming waterlogged. Much can be done to ameliorate soil conditions. Sandy soils can be improved by adding plenty of well-rotted manure or garden compost on a regular basis. Clay soil may be lightened by deep digging, adding grit and organic matter such as garden compost or leafmould.

To test whether your soil has poor drainage dig a hole about 1m (3ft) square and fill it with water.

If the water has not drained away within a few hours the site is badly drained. You then have the option of growing moisture-loving plants and perhaps creating a bog garden or installing sub-surface drainage.

You should also test the pH of your soil to find out whether it is acid or alkaline. Soil-testing kits are available from most garden centres and this simple test can save you money in the long term, as some plants, like rhododendrons and many heathers, will only thrive on acid or neutral soil.

ASPECT

The orientation of your house and garden is another important factor that determines which plants grow best. In a north-facing garden the area close to the house will always be in shadow, and it is likely to be cold and windy in winter. This limits the choice of plants to those that are hardy and tolerate shade. South-facing gardens are more sheltered but can be hot in summer, so unless you plant shading trees, confine your choice to sun-lovers. South-west-facing gardens are ideal because they offer full sun and some shade throughout the year. In windy situations it advisable to plant a sheltering hedge or screen.

CARING FOR PLANTS

All perennials, especially trees and shrubs, need well-prepared sites. Dig over the ground, remove all traces of perennial weeds and incorporate plenty of well-rotted organic matter. Although most plants are sold in containers throughout the year, deciduous trees and shrubs, including roses, are best planted in the dormant season between late autumn and early spring, when the soil is neither frozen or sodden. Conifers and evergreens are best left until spring. Plant herbaceous perennials in autumn, while the soil is still warm, or (better for plants of borderline hardiness) in spring.

PLANTING

Water plants in containers an hour or two before transplanting them; after planting, water again. Then cover the root area, particularly around shrubs and trees, with a thick mulch of organic matter or composted bark to conserve soil moisture and suppress weeds. Make sure they never go short of water in dry periods during the first year, or two or three years for shrubs and trees. Bulbs are normally planted in autumn, but some are planted in spring. They need a well-drained site and, as a rule of thumb, plant them at twice their depth.

AFTERCARE

In spring remove winter debris, clearing away the dead growth of perennials and cutting back ornamental grasses as new shoots begin to show. Weed and prick over the bare soil of beds and borders with a fork to aerate it, taking care not to pierce emerging bulbs. Rake in balanced fertilizer and then, when the soil is moist and temperatures rising, mulch with organic matter. Insert stakes and supports so they will be covered by the new foliage of perennials.

Once frosts are over, bedding and tender plants, such as dahlias, gladiolus, begonias, and cannas can be put out, but be prepared to drape them with fleece in case temperatures fall at night.

Deadheading is the main job for summer: it keeps plants tidy and stimulates the development of new buds and more flowers. Containers and hanging baskets will need daily watering and feeding every 10–14 days unless a slow-release fertilizer was mixed in at the time of planting. Water plants in borders, particularly those recently planted. Irrigate thoroughly to encourage deep roots; watering little and often results in surface roots, and exposes plants to drought and damage.

In autumn the remains of annuals can be cleared away and perennials tidied for the winter. Perennials with hollow stems like delphiniums and lupins should be cut down to the ground but others including grasses and those not entirely hardy, like kniphofias, are better left intact for protection. These and shrubs of borderline hardiness benefit from a protective mulch of straw or bracken in all but mild areas; keep it in position throughout winter. Move tender plants under glass for winter and lift dahlias, begonias, cannas, and gladiolus to store in a cool frost-free place over winter.

Repeat performance

Large herbaceous borders are glorious during the summer. Deadhead plants regularly to extend the display.

EARLY SPRING

Winter's cold grip seems to loosen as the bulbs begin to flower. Their growth initially can be quite slow, but the first warm day stirs them from their slumber. It is often very cold at night and some early flowers, like magnolias and camellias, may be damaged in exposed areas. Keep newspaper and fleece at hand to protect plants from overnight frost.

The flowers opening beneath deciduous trees and shrubs are a feature of early spring. Bulbs, hellebores, primroses and starry blue hepaticas in mixed and woodland borders take advantage of the light before the leaves on overhanging branches unfurl. In more open sites and lawns, naturalized crocuses and daffodils make drifts of mauve, white, or sunny yellow. Allow the foliage of bulbs to die down naturally wherever they grow to ensure they flower well in future.

Magnolias are the monarchs of the spring garden, but not all are large or slow to flower; 'Star Wars' blooms from a very young age, and the smaller *M. stellata*, is ideal in an urban garden. Other trees and shrubs in blossom at this time are fragrant corylopsis and daphnes, early-flowering apricots and cherries (*Prunus*), and the tangled shoots of Japanese quince (*Chaenomeles*).

FOLIAGE FOUNDATIONS

Dramatic foliage is always an asset. The bright purple-red leaves of *Photinia x fraseri* 'Red Robin' stand out like beacons in spring sunshine, and it makes an unusual hedge. Many pieris, such as 'Wakehurst', also boast brilliant red leaves but they turn shades of pink and cream before maturing to green.

Hellebores have flowers in a wide range of subtle colours, but *Helleborus foetidus* also makes a valuable foliage plant, adding height and structure to the garden at the start of the year.

Anemone blanda 'White Splendour' ♀

PERENNIAL

A spreading plant, with knobbly tubers and irregularly lobed leaves, the petals of the flowers are white, with a pink tint underneath. It enjoys a sunny site and well-drained soil, and will quickly spread to form a large clump. Plant the tubers in autumn, at a depth of about 8cm (3in), and then leave undisturbed to naturalize.

☼ ◊ ❀ ❀ ❀

‡ to 10cm (4in) ↔ to 15cm (6in)

Erica arborea var. *alpina* ♀

EVERGREEN SHRUB

This attractive tree heather bears masses of fragrant flowers from the end of the winter to mid-spring. Perfect for adding height to a rock or heather garden, this variety prefers to be grown in full sun in well-drained, slightly acid (lime-free) soil, but will tolerate mildly alkaline conditions. The first year after planting, prune back by about two-thirds after flowering to form a bushy plant. After that, further pruning is not necessary.

☼ ◊ ❀ ❀ ❀ *f*

‡ to 2m (6ft) ↔ to 85cm (34in)

Erica x *darleyensis* 'White Glow'

EVERGREEN SHRUB

The Darley Dale heath is compact and bushy with fine, lance-shaped leaves. Masses of white flowers with reddish-brown tips appear in late winter and early spring. It benefits from a sunny position and well-drained, preferably acid (lime-free) soil, although slightly alkaline soils are acceptable. Trim off the previous season's growth after it has flowered to keep the plant neat.

☼ ◊ ❊❊❊

‡ to 25cm (10in) ↔ to 50cm (20in)

Helleborus x *hybridus*

PERENNIAL

These hybrid hellebores have leathery, green leaves. The nodding flowers are white, pink, green, or purple and are often covered with small red spots. Vigorous, variable plants, they prefer heavy, moist, neutral, or alkaline soil that is rich in organic matter. They will tolerate full sun, but are best planted in the dappled shade of a woodland border, or beneath the branches of deciduous trees or shrubs. Although they regularly self seed, the best plants are purchased from specialist nurseries.

☼ ◑ ◊ ❊❊❊

‡↔ to 45cm (18in)

Hyacinthus orientalis '*White Pearl*'

PERENNIAL BULB

The large pure white, rather waxy, bell-shaped flowers of this bulbous plant are intensely fragrant, and emerge in early spring on stiff stems among bright green leaves. Plant the bulbs at a depth of 10cm (4in), about 8cm (3in) apart, in sun or partial shade in deep, well-drained fertile soil, and group them in clumps or use in a bedding scheme. Bulbs planted in pots of bulb fibre can be forced into flower early to create an indoor show for the winter months.

☼ ☀ ◊ ❋❋❋ *f*
‡ to 25cm (10in) ↔ to 8cm (3in)

Leucojum vernum ♀

PERENNIAL BULB

The spring snowflake is one of the earliest bulbs to bloom. Leafless stalks produce one or two green-tipped white flowers amid clumps of strap-shaped glossy green leaves. For the greatest impact, plant groups of bulbs in moist soil, rich in organic matter, in the partial shade below deciduous trees or shrubs. Propagate by division in the spring, or sow seed in the autumn.

☀ ◊ ❋❋❋
‡ to 15cm (6in) ↔ to 10cm (4in)

Lysichiton camtschatcensis ♀

PERENNIAL

The white skunk cabbage bears large, white, hooded flowerheads in the early spring. Large, dark green leaves follow shortly after, which eventually grow taller than the flowers. The thick roots require deep, permanently moist, fertile soil, so it is not suitable for growing in containers, but it can be used beside a pond as a marginal plant, or planted in a bog garden. Allow space for clumps to develop and the leaves to expand.

☼ ◐ ◊ ◊ ❀ ❀ ❀

‡ to 75cm (30in) ↔ to 60cm (24in)

Magnolia stellata ♀

DECIDUOUS SHRUB

The star magnolia is a vigorous and free-flowering shrub or tree, suitable for even the smallest of gardens. Left to its own devices it forms a broad-spreading shrub, covered in winter with fat, silky-haired flower buds. The star-shaped spring flowers open on bare branches and are composed of numerous narrow white petals. Plant this magnolia in a sheltered position in sun or light shade, and moist, well-drained, fertile soil. It requires no pruning.

☼ ◐ ◊ ◊ ❀ ❀ ❀

‡ to 3m (10ft) ↔ to 4m (12ft)

Magnolia stellata 'Waterlily' ♀

DECIDUOUS TREE

The star magnolia is a fairly compact tree that is suitable for smaller gardens. Just ensure it has sufficient space to spread its branches. 'Waterlily' bears an abundance of pure white, slightly fragrant flowers in late spring. These are made up of numerous strap-like petals. This magnolia needs a sunny or partially shaded spot, and moist, well-drained soil.

☼ ◑ ◊ ◊ ✽✽✽ *f*

↕ to 3m (10ft) ↔ to 4m (12ft)

Narcissus 'Cheerfulness' ♀

PERENNIAL BULB

An attractive, early-flowering daffodil with white outer petals that surround clusters of smaller petals in the centre. The long-lasting blooms have a strong fragrance and are good for cutting. For maximum visual impact, plant the bulbs in bold groups in late summer to early autumn in well-drained, fertile soil. The bulbs should be planted at one and a half times their depth below the soil surface.

☼ ◊ ✽✽✽ *f*

↕ to 40cm (16in) ↔ to 15cm (6in)

Narcissus 'Merlin' ♥

PERENNIAL BULB

The blooms of this dainty daffodil are good for cutting and have pure white, rounded petals and a flat, cup-shaped, yellow trumpet with a reddish-orange rim. It prefers a sunny site and well-drained soil, and flowers in the middle of spring. The bulbs should be planted as for 'Cheerfulness' (*see opposite*) in a herbaceous border, or it can be grown in grass and left to naturalize.

☼ ◊ ❀ ❀ ❀
‡ to 45cm (18in) ↔ to 15cm (6in)

Narcissus 'Thalia'

PERENNIAL BULB

This vigorous daffodil will form large clumps, and is suitable for naturalizing in the border or rock garden. Deep, long-lasting, funnel-shaped flowers with milky-white petals, often with three or more blooms per stem, are produced in early to mid-spring. They also make excellent cut flowers. Plant the bulbs as for 'Cheerfulness' (*see opposite*) in a sunny position, and well-drained, fertile soil.

☼ ◊ ❀ ❀ ❀
‡ to 35cm (14in) ↔ to 15cm (6in)

Narcissus triandrus ♀
PERENNIAL BULB

Angel's tears is a dwarf narcissus that bears nodding, pale cream flowers with reflexed petals and rounded cups. The leaves are green and strap-shaped. A small-growing plant, it performs well in containers, and will naturalize, if the conditions are right, in a sunny rock garden or raised bed in well-drained soil. There is also a white-flowered variety, *albus*. Plant the bulbs as for 'Cheerfulness' (*see p.18*).

☼ ◊ ❋❋

‡ to 25cm (10in) ↔ to 8cm (3in)

Prunus 'Snow Goose'
DECIDUOUS TREE

This smallish, flowering cherry tree bears a white to very pale pink blossom from early to mid-spring. At other times of year it makes a narrowly upright, deciduous tree. This type of cherry is not grown for its fruit, but the autumn leaf colour can be spectacular when the leaves turn from green to orange and yellow before they fall. Its compact size and narrow habit make it good for small gardens, suitable for most soil types, including clay and chalk.

☼ ◊ ◊ ❋❋❋

‡ to 6m (20ft) ↔ to 3m (10ft)

Prunus spinosa

DECIDUOUS TREE

Blackthorn is nature's answer to the barbed wire fence. A vigorous shrub or small tree, it bears star-shaped, white flowers that open on bare branches in early and mid-spring. The branches are armed with sharp thorns, and it makes a superb impenetrable hedge. It bears purple fruits, or sloes, in autumn, which can be used to make a comforting liquor. It grows happily in full sun on moist, well-drained soils, and can be cut back hard in early spring. Hedges can be pruned at anytime.

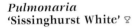

‡ to 5m (15ft) ↔ to 4m (12ft)

Pulmonaria 'Sissinghurst White' ♀

PERENNIAL

The leaves of this lungwort are elliptic and covered with small white spots. The flowers are pale pink when in bud and open in spring to form pure white funnel-shaped blooms. It makes good ground cover and is ideal for planting beneath deciduous trees in humus-rich, moist, but well-drained soil. Clip over after it has flowered to encourage fresh foliage. To keep the plant vigorous it is a good idea to divide and replant it every few years.

‡ to 30cm (12in) ↔ to 60cm (24in)

Sanguinaria canadensis 'Plena' ♀

PERENNIAL

Bloodroot is aptly named, as its fleshy roots exude a red sap when cut. The white spring flowers, often tinted pink on the reverse, are succeeded by waxy, heart- or kidney-shaped, greyish-green leaves that provide excellent ground cover in damp, shaded sites. Divide large clumps after flowering.

‡ to 15cm (6in) ↔ to 30cm (12in)

Tulipa biflora

PERENNIAL BULB

Well suited to a sunny site in a rock garden, the fragrant, star-shaped flowers of this dwarf tulip are creamy-white, or ivory, with bright yellow centres. The blooms are produced from late winter and persist through early spring. Plant the bulbs in groups in late autumn in a light, fertile, well-drained soil, and leave undisturbed so clumps can develop. The bulbs like to be dry in the summer, so do not plant where neighbours may need watering.

☼ ◊ ❉ ❉ ❉ *f*

‡ to 10cm (4in) ↔ to 13cm (5in)

Tulipa 'Schoonoord'
PERENNIAL BULB

This is a relatively small tulip, ideal for an urban garden where space is at a premium. The wide-spreading, double, pure white flowers open in the middle of spring. The bulbs need a sunny site, and should be planted in late autumn in a well-drained, fertile soil. *Tulipa* 'Peach Blossom', which grows to the same height, has double deep rose-pink flowers and makes a complementary planting companion for displays in tubs and bedding schemes.

☼ ◊ ❀❀❀
‡ to 30cm (12in)

Tulipa turkestanica ♀
PERENNIAL BULB

A tulip with star-shaped white flowers and a yellow or occasionally orange centre. The flowers have an unpleasant aroma, and are produced in early or mid-spring. Choose a sunny site that is dry in summer, such as a hot border or by a sunny wall, and plant the bulbs in autumn in groups in well-drained, light, reasonably fertile soil.

☼ ◊ ❀❀❀ *f*
‡ to 30cm (12in)

Alnus incana 'Aurea'
DECIDUOUS TREE

This attractively pale-leaved variety of the grey alder will grow into a large, broad, conical tree over time, but it can be trimmed to size, or even grown as a hedge. Alders are ideal for damp or wet ground, where they thrive, but they tolerate a range of soil types. Pinkish brown catkins appear in late winter and early spring, and small woody fruits resembling cones hang from the tree for much of the year. When the tree is bare in winter, the golden winter shoots are an attractive feature.

☼ ◑ ◆ ❀ ❀ ❀
‡ to 20m (70ft) ↔ to 10m (30ft)

Anemone blanda 'Radar' ♀
PERENNIAL

The leaves of this spreading perennial are deeply divided, and in early spring it produces star-shaped, deep magenta flowers with white centres. It grows best on very well-drained sandy soil, in full sunshine. Plant the small, knobbly tubers in autumn in groups and leave undisturbed to naturalize.

☼ ◊ ❀ ❀ ❀
‡ to 10cm (4in) ↔ to 15cm (6in)

Bergenia 'Sunningdale'

EVERGREEN PERENNIAL

An early flowering plant, the deep pink spring blooms of which are borne on stiff red stems. The rounded, leathery leaves become bronze-coloured in the autumn. It should be grown in full sun or partial shade, and is suitable for planting beneath shrubs and deciduous trees. Propagate it by division in the spring after the flowers have finished, and remove tatty leaves at this time too.

☼ ☽ ◐ ◊ ◖ ❀ ❀ ❀

‡ to 45cm (18in) ↔ to 60cm (24in)

Camellia x *williamsii* 'Donation' ♀

EVERGREEN SHRUB

This camellia is valued for its deep pink, double flowers which appear in late winter and persist through spring. A vigorous, free-flowering shrub, it also boasts glossy, dark green foliage. Plant it in partial shade, away from the early morning sun, in moist, but well-drained neutral or acid (lime-free) soil, mixed with plenty of organic matter, or grow it in containers of ericaceous compost. For perfect blooms, stand pots in an unheated greenhouse or conservatory.

☽ ◊ ◖ ❀ ❀ ❀

‡ to 5m (15ft) ↔ to 2.5m (8ft)

Chaenomeles speciosa 'Moerloosei' ♀

DECIDUOUS SHRUB

This flowering quince can be used as a free-standing shrub or trained along a wall. It produces a tangle of spiny stems, covered with glossy, dark green leaves, while clusters of saucer-shaped, white and pink flowers appear in early spring. The blooms are followed in the autumn by edible greenish-yellow fruits that can be made into jelly. Cut back after flowering if grown against a wall.

☀ ☽ ◊ ❀❀❀

‡ to 2.5m (8ft) ↔ to 5m (15ft)

Chionodoxa 'Pink Giant'

PERENNIAL BULB

This medium-sized bulbous perennial produces soft pink, star-shaped flowers with white centres in early spring. It is ideal for a rock garden or for planting beneath shrubs where the bulbs can be left to naturalize. It prefers a sunny site and well-drained soil. Plant bulbs in the autumn in groups, and propagate by dividing established clumps or by seed.

☀ ◊ ❀❀❀

‡ to 25cm (10in) ↔ to 5cm (2in)

Clematis 'Apple Blossom' ♀

CLIMBER

The glossy, dark, evergreen leaves of this
vigorous climber are accompanied in
spring by large clusters of pink-tinged,
scented white flowers with deeper pink
undersides that pale to pinkish-white.
It is fairly hardy but should be planted
in a sunny position against a south- or
west-facing wall in a well-drained soil.
Purchase plants from a reputable source
as there are a lot of inferior seedlings
available. It can be pruned back after
flowering, but not into old dark wood.

☼ ◊ ❀❀❀ *f*
‡ to 5m (15ft)

Daphne cneorum 'Eximia' ♀

EVERGREEN SHRUB

A prostrate shrub with small oval, dark
green leaves. The rose pink flowers are
highly fragrant and borne in clusters at
the end of the branches. To grow well
it needs a rich soil, which should be
mixed with well-rotted garden compost
or leafmould when planting. All parts
of the plant are harmful if ingested, and
the sap can irritate the skin on contact.

☼ ◊ ❀❀❀ *f*
‡ to 10cm (4in) ↔ to 50cm (20in)

Erica x *darleyensis* 'Kramer's Rote' ♥

EVERGREEN SHRUB

Bronze-tinted green foliage and bright magenta spring flowers are features of this bushy heather. It should be grown in moist, but well-drained, humus-rich or peaty soil. It prefers acid (lime-free) conditions but tolerates slightly alkaline soil, and is a useful ground-cover plant. Trim off the previous season's growth after flowering to keep the plant neat. 'Archie Graham' is similar heather, but with mauve-pink flowers.

☼ ◊ ◖ ❀ ❀ ❀

‡ to 30cm (12in) ↔ to 60cm (24in)

Hyacinthus orientalis 'Queen of the Pinks'

PERENNIAL BULB

This is one of the best pink hyacinths, with bright green leaves and highly fragrant flowers borne on robust stems in spring. Plant the bulbs outside in the autumn where they should flower the following year, in fertile, well-drained soil at a depth of 10cm (4in), and about 8cm (3in) apart. They can be grown in informal clumps, used in a bedding scheme, or grown in pots. Feed after flowering to help the bulbs build up their strength.

☼ ◖ ◊ ❀ ❀ ❀ ❀ *f*

‡ to 30cm (12in) ↔ to 8cm (3in)

Magnolia x *loebneri* 'Leonard Messel' ♀
DECIDUOUS SHRUB

A substantial shrub or small tree with large, rounded leaves, in spring it bears fragrant flowers, which boast a dozen lilac-pink, strap-shaped petals, the colour of which is most intense during warm springs. It grows happily on most soils and tolerates alkaline conditions. Plant where it has adequate space to spread, as magnolias resent disturbance. It needs no pruning.

☼ ☀ ◊ ◊ ❀ ❀ ❀ *f*
‡ to 8m (25ft) ↔ to 6m (20ft)

Magnolia 'Star Wars' ♀
DECIDUOUS TREE

This recently introduced magnolia bears massive deep pink blooms at a very early age. It was named after the shape of the flowers, which can measure up to 30cm (12in) across, and have petals pointing in many different directions. 'Star Wars' suits most soils and, in time, this vigorous plant may grow to form a medium-sized, pyramid-shaped tree. Plant where it has plenty of space to develop unhindered.

☼ ☀ ◊ ◊ ❀ ❀ ❀
‡ to 10m (30ft) ↔ to 8m (25ft)

Narcissus 'Passionale' ♀

PERENNIAL BULB

This vigorous spring-flowering daffodil has milky-white petals and a large pink cup, and makes a superb cut flower. In late summer or early autumn, plant the bulbs in well-drained, fertile soil at one and a half times their depth. They will perform well in a sunny situation, and can be used in a border planting, or a formal bedding scheme. Deadhead the plants after flowering, and divide large clumps after 3–5 years.

☼ ◊ ❀❀❀

‡ to 40cm (16in) ↔ to 15cm (6in)

Paeonia cambessedesii ♀

PERENNIAL

The Majorcan peony is one of the first to bloom in early spring. It has greyish-green leaves, with deep red undersides and wavy margins, while the flowers have five pale magenta-pink petals and deeper pink veins. Plant it in full sun in a well-drained soil. It needs protection from late frosts, and is best grown in the shelter of a south-facing wall, or under a cloche in winter.

☼ ◊ ❀❀

‡↔ to 55cm (22in)

Prunus 'Accolade' ♀

DECIDUOUS TREE

A beautiful flowering cherry, 'Accolade'
has mid-green leaves that turn orange-
red in autumn before they fall. Its wide-
spreading branches produce clusters of
three semi-double, pale pink flowers in
early spring, which emerge from deep
pink buds. It needs a sunny situation
and should be planted in deep, well-
drained, fertile soil. This tree does not
require pruning.

☼ ◊ ❀❀❀
‡↔ to 8m (25ft)

Prunus mume 'Beni-chidori'

DECIDUOUS TREE

Japanese apricots are spreading trees,
suitable for small gardens. The almond-
scented, double, deep pink flowers of
'Beni-chidori' appear in late winter or
early spring and become paler as they
age. The tree may also later produce
small orange fruit, which look a little
like apricots, but are very bitter. Plant
it in a sunny, sheltered position, where
frost is unlikely to damage the blooms,
in deep, well-drained, fertile soil. No
pruning is required.

☼ ◊ ❀❀❀ *f*
‡↔ to 9m (28ft)

Prunus 'Okame' ♀
DECIDUOUS TREE

The toothed, oval, dark green leaves of this flowering cherry in autumn turn brilliant shades of orange and red. The cup-shaped, single, deep pink flowers are produced in early spring. It is best planted in a sunny position, in a deep, moist, well-drained, fertile soil, and will not need to be pruned.

☼ ◊ ◖ ❀❀❀
‡ to 10m (30ft) ↔ to 8m (25ft)

Prunus x *yedoensis*
DECIDUOUS TREE

The beautiful Yoshino cherry grows to form a medium-sized, round-headed tree with gently arching branches. In early spring it bears clusters of five or six single, pale pink flowers, which gradually fade to white in the sun. It should be planted in deep, fertile, well-drained soil. No pruning is required.

☼ ◊ ❀❀❀
‡ to 15m (50ft) ↔ to 10m (30ft)

Tulipa 'Pink Beauty'

PERENNIAL BULB

Tulips are an invaluable addition to the spring border, and are used to create a spectrum of colour relatively early in the year. There is plenty of choice, with different varieties bursting into flower throughout spring and early summer, providing a range of sizes, colours, and flower shapes. The deep pink petals, with a brush stroke of white, and cup-shaped flowers of 'Pink Beauty' appear early, and it makes a particularly eye-catching bedding plant.

☼ ◊ ❀ ❀ ❀

‡ to 60cm (24in) ↔ to 13cm (5in)

Viola x *wittrockiana* Ultima Series

PERENNIAL

These violets, more commonly known as pansies, have been widely hybridised to produce a range of long-flowering plants. The Ultima Series start to flower in winter and continue through spring. They are available in a range of bright colours, including pink, and make a superb choice for brightening up the garden during early spring. Use them as bedding, and in tubs and window boxes, and grow them in a sunny site in fertile, well-drained soil.

☼ ◊ ❀ ❀ ❀

‡ to 23cm (9in) ↔ to 30cm (12in)

Camellia japonica 'Coquettii' ♀

EVERGREEN SHRUB

In early to mid-spring the arching stems of this slow-growing shrub are covered with deep red, semi-double or double flowers. It makes an elegant addition to a border and will complement plantings in a woodland garden, but it can also be grown as a specimen in containers or in open ground. Choose a partially shaded site, out of the early morning sun, in moist, but well-drained, humus-rich acid soil. Use an ericaceous (lime-free) compost in containers.

☼ ◑ ◊ ◊ ❀ ❀ ❀

‡ to 9m (28ft) ↔ to 8m (25ft)

Chaenomeles x *superba* 'Crimson and Gold' ♀

DECIDUOUS SHRUB

The deep crimson flowers with golden yellow anthers are produced by this Japanese quince from spring to early summer, and are often followed in the autumn by yellow-green fruit. Its wide, spreading habit makes it a useful shrub for ground cover, planting against walls or in a border, or it can be grown as an informal, low flowering hedge. Quinces trained against walls or used as hedges should be cut back after flowering.

☼ ◊ ❀ ❀ ❀

‡ to 1m (3ft) ↔ to 2m (6ft)

Corydalis solida 'George Baker' ♀

PERENNIAL

This attractive tuberous perennial has deeply dissected greyish-green leaves. In spring, it produces bright red, with a hint of orange, tubular flowers. Plant it in a rock or gravel garden in full sun or partial shade, in well-drained fertile soil. 'George Baker' can be divided in the autumn if clumps become too large.

☼ ◑ ◊ ❋ ❋ ❋
‡ to 25cm (10in) ↔ to 20cm (8in)

Erysimum 'Blood Red'

PERENNIAL

Although perennial, wallflowers are often grown as biennial bedding plants, and planted in combination with tall-stemmed tulips. Left alone, they will live for several years, but can become woody and leggy with age. This variety has vivid, deep red flowers in spring, and is ideal for growing against a dry wall, or to brighten up the front of a sunny border or raised bed. Plant it in autumn in very well-drained, neutral to alkaline soil.

☼ ◊ ❋ ❋ ❋
‡↔ to 30cm (12in)

Helleborus orientalis
Early Purple Group

PERENNIAL

Often sold under its former name of
H. atrorubens, this variable hellebore
flowers very early in the year. It has
deep maroon, saucer-shaped, pendent
flowers that emerge from late winter
to early spring. The deciduous, palm-
shaped leaves are mid-green, flushed
with purple. It thrives on rich, moist,
well-drained soil, and its preference for
partial shade makes it a good choice
for a shrub border or a woodland garden.

☀ ◐ ◊ ◊ ❀ ❀ ❀

↕ to 30cm (12in) ↔ to 45cm (18in)

Paeonia tenuifolia

PERENNIAL

Fern-leaf peonies are among the earliest
species to flower, producing beautiful
deep red, single flowers in spring, amid
dark green ferny leaves. There are also
other forms with double white, red, and
pink flowers. Plant it in a sunny site, in
well-drained, sandy soil. This delicate-
looking plant may be grown in rock or
gravel gardens or a herbaceous border.

☼ ◊ ❀ ❀ ❀

↕↔ to 70cm (28in)

Photinia x *fraseri* 'Red Robin' ♀

EVERGREEN SHRUB

The glossy young leaves of this shrub are bright purplish-red, and turn dark bronze-green as the season progresses. From mid-spring it produces clusters of small white flowers. It prefers fertile, well-drained soil; the foliage is easily damaged by cold winds, so plant it in a sunny, sheltered position. It can be used as a hedging plant or free-standing shrub. Trim hedges two to three times a year to keep up the show of bright young foliage.

‡↔ to 5m (15ft)

Pieris formosa 'Wakehurst' ♀

EVERGREEN SHRUB

The brilliant red young foliage of this beautiful shrub gradually turns various shades of pink and creamy-white, and then finally goes dark green. Small, urn-shaped, white flowers are borne in mid-spring and hang in pendent clusters. 'Wakehurst' does best in semi-shade, and needs protection from cold winds and frost. Plant it in moist, slightly acid (lime-free), humus-rich soil in a shrub or woodland border. Prune lightly after it has flowered to maintain its shape.

‡ to 5m (15ft) ↔ to 4m (12ft)

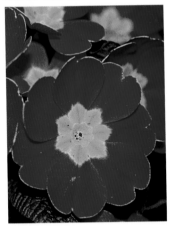

Primula 'Crescendo Bright Red' ♀

EVERGREEN PERENNIAL

Polyanthus are vigorous primulas which should be planted in the autumn for a spring bedding display. They produce rosettes of evergreen leaves and often start flowering at the end of winter. The Crescendo Series is available in a range of bright colours, including vivid red. Polyanthus prefer a sunny position, but will tolerate some shade, and should be planted in reasonably fertile, moist but well-drained, soil.

☀ ☀ ◊ ◊ ❀ ❀ ❀
↕ to 15cm (6in) ↔ to 30cm (12in)

Pulmonaria rubra 'Redstart'

PERENNIAL

This attractive herbaceous perennial has bright green, hairy leaves and funnel-shaped, coral-red flowers. It begins to flower early in the year, with blooms often appearing in the middle of winter and continuing into spring. It forms a loose clump, and provides excellent ground cover for damp shady positions. Young plants are vigorous, and should be divided after four or five years. Clip over after flowering to encourage a flush of bright new foliage.

☀ ☀ ◊ ❀ ❀ ❀
↕ to 40cm (16in) ↔ to 90cm (36in)

Tulipa 'Red Riding Hood' ♀

PERENNIAL BULB

The bright red flowers of this striking tulip have black marks at the base of the petals, and its lance-shaped leaves are strongly marked with purple stripes. Plant bulbs in late autumn in a sunny situation in well-drained, fertile soil, in a border, or rock garden, where they can be left for years. Alternatively, plant them in containers and move the bulbs out into the garden after flowering. For a bold bedding display, plant with a deep-yellow tulip, such as 'Yokahama'.

☼ ◊ ❀❀❀
‡ to 20cm (8in) ↔ to 15cm (6in)

Tulipa 'Apeldoorn'

PERENNIAL BULB

Darwin tulips, such as 'Apeldoorn', are easy to grow and their rounded flowers look equally at home in spring bedding displays as they do when used as cut flowers. 'Apeldoorn' has scarlet-red flowers with black centres, surrounded by yellow. Plant bulbs in late autumn, in a sunny site in well-drained, fertile soil. It looks superb when partnered with a yellow tulip, such as 'Daydream'.

☼ ◊ ❀❀❀
‡ to 60cm (24in) ↔ to 13cm (5in)

Anemone blanda 'Violet Star'

PERENNIAL

Spring-flowering anemones make superb border plants, particularly for partially shaded areas under shrubs and trees. Their sunny, many-petalled flowers are a welcome sight, and if planted in groups of three or five, they soon spread and naturalize. 'Violet Star' has purple-blue flowers, but consider mixing with other types, such as 'White Splendour' or the magenta 'Radar', to vary the display. Choose a reasonably drained site, and enrich the soil with humus.

☼ ◑ ○ ◊ ✳ ✳ ✳
↕↔ to 15cm (6in)

Crocus tommasinianus ♀

PERENNIAL CORM

This crocus gives the impression of being rather delicate, but its slender appearance is deceptive. It produces purple, violet, or lilac flowers from late winter to early spring, and grows easily from seed. Choose a sunny site with well-drained soil, and in autumn plant the corms in groups to create drifts of colour at the front of a border, or to naturalize in short grass.

☼ ◊ ✳ ✳ ✳
↕ to 10cm (4in) ↔ to 2.5cm (1in)

Iris 'George'
PERENNIAL BULB

Dwarf irises are often overlooked when
it comes to the early spring garden, but
clumps of these bulbs are well worth
planting every autumn in borders, pots,
containers, or windowboxes – anywhere
where they will be noticed in the garden
in late winter and early spring. 'George'
is a rich purple, but try mixing different
varieties: colours vary from pale blue to
deep, velvety purple, often with yellow
crests on the petals. They are ideal
underneath larger plants, tolerant of
the dry, partially shaded conditions.

‡ to 10cm (4in) ↔ to 1m (3ft)

Primula auricula 'Adrian'
EVERGREEN PERENNIAL

A rosette-forming perennial, this alpine
auricula has fleshy pale green leaves,
and in spring bears beautiful flowers
with purple-blue petals, slightly paler
edges, and a white eye. Alpine auriculas
are extremely hardy plants, but will
do best in a sunny or partially shaded
site in moist, well-drained soil. Grow
them in a rock or gravel garden, raised
beds, an unheated greenhouse, or in
pots of gritty, loam-based compost.

‡↔ to 10cm (4in)

Rhododendron dauricum
EVERGREEN SHRUB

The leaves of this semi-evergreen shrub are green with a dark brown underside. It starts flowering in late winter when the funnel-shaped, bright pinkish-purple blooms bring a dramatic burst of colour to an otherwise gloomy garden. Plant it in a sunny site, in well-drained, humus-rich, acid (lime-free) soil, and mulch it annually with leafmould or chipped bark. This very hardy rhododendron is suitable for exposed sites, and may be used to create an informal screen.

☼ ◑ ◊ ◐ ✽ ✽ ✽
↕↔ to 1.5m (5ft)

Rhododendron 'Praecox' ♥
EVERGREEN SHRUB

This is among the first rhododendrons to bloom, flowering from late winter and continuing into early spring. It is normally evergreen, but sheds some of its leaves during winter. The flowers are pinkish-purple, and appear in clusters of two or three. Although generally hardy, the flowers may be damaged by severe frost. It makes a spectacular flowering hedge, but is equally at home in the border. Plant in full sun or partial shade, in moist, well-drained, acid soil.

☼ ◑ ◊ ◐ ✽ ✽ ✽
↕↔ to 1.3m (4½ft)

Tulipa humilis
Violacea Group

PERENNIAL BULB

This early, spring-flowering tulip has
large purple star-shaped flowers with
a bright yellow blotch at the base of the
petals, and narrow greyish-green leaves.
Plant bulbs in late autumn, in a sunny
position in light, well-drained soil. It
is ideal for the rock garden, or makes a
colourful display in raised beds. Leave
undisturbed so clumps can build up *in
situ*; they like to be dry during summer.

☼ ◊ ✿ ✿ ✿

‡ to 25cm (10in) ↔ to 13cm (5in)

Viola odorata

PERENNIAL

Sweet violets may be small, but their
very aromatic bluey-purple or white
flowers will perfume the garden from
late winter and throughout early spring.
They self-seed, and will quickly become
established, particularly when allowed
to naturalize in a woodland setting or
by deciduous shrubs. Plant in a sunny
position or in dappled shade, in well-
drained, humus-rich soil. They can also
be divided and replanted in spring.

☼ ☽ ◊ ✿ ✿ ✿ *f*

‡ to 20cm (8in) ↔ to 30cm (12in)

Ajuga reptans 'Multicolor'

EVERGREEN PERENNIAL

This technicolour version of the blue bugle is an excellent evergreen perennial for ground cover, spreading freely by means of rooting stems. Dark blue flowers appear in whorls atop upright stems. While these are a key feature from spring to early summer, the glossy leaves extend the interest much further, particularly early in the year. In colour, the foliage is an unusual mix of purple, green, brown and white. It is invaluable for border edging under shrubs and robust perennials.

☼ ☀ ◊ ◖ ❁ ❁ ❁

↕ to 12cm (5in) ↔ to 45cm (18in)

Anemone blanda 'Atrocaerulea'

PERENNIAL

The deep-blue, daisy-like flowers of this anemone are striking when naturalized in grass or beneath the bare branches of deciduous trees. It has a low, clump-forming habit which also makes it a suitable plant for the front of a border. Plant the knobbly tubers in autumn, in full sun or partial shade and humus-rich, well-drained soil.

☼ ☀ ◊ ❁ ❁ ❁

↕ to 10cm (4in) ↔ to 15cm (6in)

Anemone nemorosa '*Robinsoniana*' ♥

PERENNIAL

This wood anemone bears numerous
pale lavender-blue flowers with a light
grey reverse to the petals. The mid-
green leaves die back after flowering.
It is a low, creeping plant, useful for
underplanting or naturalizing. A native
of European woods, it does best in a
woodland situation, but it will grow in
most positions, given dappled or partial
shade and a moist, but well-drained,
humus-rich soil.

☀ ◊ ◑ ❀ ❀ ❀
‡ to 15cm (6in) ↔ to 30cm (12in)

Aubrieta '*Cobalt Violet*'

PERENNIAL

A mat-forming perennial with masses of
small hairy leaves. In spring it produces
profuse quantities of small, violet-blue
flowers, and is ideal for trailing over the
edge of a raised bed or stone wall, or for
growing in a rock garden. Plant it in
fertile, well-drained, neutral or alkaline
soil, and trim it over with secateurs
after flowering to keep it neat and tidy.

☼ ◊ ❀ ❀ ❀
‡ to 10cm (4in) ↔ to 20cm (8in)

Chionodoxa luciliae ♀

PERENNIAL BULB

In spring, glory-of-the-snow bears up to three violet-blue, star-shaped flowers, each with a small white eye. It comes from the stony slopes of Turkey, and is most at home in a rock garden, raised bed, or naturalized under deciduous trees or at the front of a border. Plant the bulbs in autumn, in a sunny site in well-drained soil. Established clumps benefit from a mulch with well-rotted compost in autumn.

☼ ◊ ❋ ❋ ❋

‡ to 10cm (4in) ↔ to 5cm (2in)

Clematis 'Frances Rivis' ♀

CLIMBER

A deciduous, early flowering climber with mid-blue, bell-shaped flowers in spring to early summer, and feathery seedheads in autumn. It is very hardy and tolerates fairly exposed situations. Prune it back after flowering. Provide support in the form of wires or trellis attached to a wall or fence, or train it over an arch or tripod. Grow it in well-drained, fertile, preferably alkaline soil, with the roots in shade and its head in the sun.

☼ ◑ ◊ ❋ ❋ ❋

‡ to 3m (10ft) ↔ to 1.5m (5ft)

Hepatica nobilis var. *japonica*

PERENNIAL

This is a slow-growing perennial which retains its leathery leaves during most winters. The star-shaped flowers, with blue-purple, pink or white petals that open in spring, sit above three small dark green leaves. It requires partial shade and moist, humus-rich soil, and is well suited to a woodland setting or a shady border.

☼ ◊ ❋❋❋

‡ to 8cm (3in) ↔ to 12cm (5in)

Hyacinthus orientalis 'Blue Jacket' ♀

PERENNIAL BULB

This is one of the best blue flowered hyacinths, with wonderfully fragrant, navy-blue blooms. The petals have a waxy texture and purple veins. Plant it in autumn, in deep, well-drained, fertile soil in sun or partial shade. Hyacinths are perfect for creating colourful spring bedding displays, and are also useful container or window box plants. Grow them either outside, or forced in bowls of bulb fibre for display in the home.

☼ ☀ ◊ ❋❋❋ *f*

‡ to 25cm (10in) ↔ to 8cm (3in)

Iris histrioides 'Major'

PERENNIAL BULB

The vivid blue flowers of this vigorous
dwarf iris open in early spring. Its lower
petals are marked with a bright yellow
ridge, which is surrounded by dark blue
lines, and the square leaves are very
short at the beginning of the year, but
extend to 30cm (12in) after flowering.
Plant it in a sunny location, in well-
drained, fertile soil. Dwarf irises are
an excellent choice for the rock garden,
raised beds or containers.

☼ ◊ ❀❀❀
‡ to 10cm (4in) ↔ to 7cm (3in)

Iris 'Joyce'

PERENNIAL BULB

A superb plant for a rock garden, this
is a reticulata iris which flowers very
early in the spring. It bears sky blue
flowers with a bold yellow flare down
the centre of the petals. Plant bulbs in
autumn, in a sunny situation and well-
drained, neutral or alkaline soil. 'Joyce'
will also grow happily in containers or
troughs of gritty, loam-based compost.
Keep the bulbs on the dry side during
the summer.

☼ ◊ ❀❀❀
‡ to 12cm (5in) ↔ to 7cm (3in)

Iris 'Katharine Hodgkin' ♀
PERENNIAL BULB

This vigorous dwarf iris flowers from late winter. Its upper petals are covered with fine, deep blue veins, while the broad lower petals have a yellow centre and are heavily marked with blue lines and speckles. Plant the bulbs in autumn and grow this iris on a sunny bank or in other well-drained situations, making sure the bulbs are kept on the dry side during the summer. It enjoys neutral or slightly alkaline soil.

☼ ◊ ❀❀❀
‡ to 12cm (5in) ↔ to 7cm (3in)

Iris reticulata 'Cantab'
PERENNIAL BULB

Another reticulata iris (*see* 'Joyce'), this one has pale blue flowers with slightly darker lower petals, marked by a deep yellow crest. The blooms start to appear in late winter. These iris are vigorous but the bulbs often divide after it has flowered and then take a couple of years to grow large enough to bloom again. Plant the bulbs in autumn in a sunny situation and fertile, well-drained soil, such as in a rock garden or trough filled with gritty loam-based compost.

☼ ◊ ❀❀❀
‡ to 12cm (5in) ↔ to 7cm (3in)

Muscari armeniacum ♀
PERENNIAL BULB

The grape hyacinth is one of the most widely grown spring-flowering bulbs, used to create spectacular bedding displays and in the border. Each stem carries a dense spike of small, deep blue flowers above narrow, bright green leaves. In the right conditions, it spreads quickly and may occasionally be invasive. The bulbs can become overcrowded and will benefit from division in summer every few years. Plant bulbs in autumn, in full sun, in fertile, moist but well-drained soil.

☼ ◐ ◊ ❀ ❀ ❀

‡ to 20cm (8in) ↔ to 10cm (4in)

Omphalodes cappadocica ♀
EVERGREEN PERENNIAL

The forget-me-not-like flowers of this evergreen are azure blue with white eyes, and borne on slender stems from early spring. It has creeping roots and forms clumps of heart-shaped, slightly hairy leaves, and makes ideal ground cover for shady places. Grow it in full or partial shade and slightly moist, well-drained, humus-rich fertile soil.

◐ ◑ ◊ ❀ ❀ ❀

‡ to 20cm (8in) ↔ to 25cm (10in)

Pulmonaria '**Lewis Palmer**' ♀

PERENNIAL

This deciduous ground-cover plant has slightly hairy, lance-shaped leaves with greenish-white spots and small funnel-shaped flowers that are pink when they open in spring and then turn a vibrant blue. Lungwort should be grown in humus-rich, moist soil in partial or full shade. It attracts bees, and makes an excellent choice for a wildlife garden, or use it to enhance a shady woodland or shrub border. Clip it over after it has flowered to refresh the foliage.

☀ ☀ ◊ ❀ ❀ ❀

‡ to 35cm (14in) ↔ to 45cm (18in)

Puschkinia scilloides

PERENNIAL BULB

The pale blue, bell-like flowers of this bulbous perennial are set off by a fine blue line down the centre of each petal. Its compact spikes make an attractive addition to the rock garden or a shrub border. Plant it in a sunny or partially shaded site, in well-drained, fertile soil.

☀ ☀ ◊ ❀ ❀ ❀

‡ to 15cm (6in) ↔ to 5cm (2in)

Rhododendron Blue Tit Group

EVERGREEN SHRUB

A remarkably compact rhododendron, which in early spring bears abundant small, funnel-shaped greyish-blue flowers. Its leaves are initially yellow-green but darken to a mid-green colour as the plant matures. Like many dwarf rhododendrons, 'Blue Tit' will bloom happily in a container or in a rock or gravel garden, given full sunshine and moist, well-drained, acid soil or ericaceous (lime-free) compost.

☼ ◐ ◊ ◊ ❊ ❊ ❊
↔ to 1m (3ft)

Scilla bifolia ♀

PERENNIAL BULB

This is a distinctive early spring flowering bulb that looks wonderful naturalized in grass or under deciduous shrubs and trees. It has narrow strap-shaped, bright green leaves and star-shaped flowers, borne on one side of the stem. This species has blue or violet-blue flowers, but there are also varieties with white ('Alba') and pink ('Rosea') blooms. Plant it in fertile, humus-rich, well-drained soil, in full sunshine or partial shade.

☼ ◊ ❊ ❊ ❊
↔ to 15cm (6in)

Scilla mischtschenkoana ♀

PERENNIAL BULB

The pale blue, bell-shaped flowers of this bulbous perennial have a dark blue stripe down the centre of each petal. They are carried above broad, strap-shaped arching leaves on rather short stems, which grow longer as the flowers open in early spring. Naturalize it in grass or plant in a rock or gravel garden or raised bed in a sunny position with well-drained soil. Plant bulbs in autumn.

☼ ◊ ❀❀❀
‡ to 10cm (4in) ↔ to 5cm (2in)

Scilla siberica 'Spring Beauty'

PERENNIAL BULB

This bulbous perennial has small spikes of bell-shaped, violet-tinted, deep blue flowers arranged on one side of the stem. Ideal for a rock garden or a mixed herbaceous border beneath deciduous shrubs or trees, it prefers sandy, well-drained, fertile soil in slight shade or full sun. Divide large clumps after flowering during the summer. Plant bulbs in autumn.

☼ ◑ ◊ ❀❀❀
‡ to 20cm (8in) ↔ to 5cm (2in)

Euphorbia characias subsp. *wulfenii* ♀

EVERGREEN SHRUB

A large rounded bush with greyish-green leaves. The huge, globe-shaped heads packed with small yellow-green flowers appear from early spring. It is ideal for the back of a border, gravel garden, or gaps in paving, but needs a sunny site and well-drained soil. Buy young plants from a reliable source to avoid inferior, less brightly coloured seedlings. Cut out the old flowerheads in autumn, and wear gloves as the sap may cause an allergic skin reaction.

☼ ◊ ❀❀❀
‡↔ to 1.2m (4ft)

Euphorbia myrsinites ♀

EVERGREEN PERENNIAL

This is a sprawling evergreen perennial, suitable for planting in a rock or gravel garden, gaps in paving, or at the edge of a raised bed or on a stone wall. The fleshy, blue-green leaves are arranged in a spiral around the stems. In spring, the stems are topped with clusters of yellowish-green flowers, which turn a greyish-pink as they fade. Plant it in full sun, in well-drained soil. It may self-seed if the dead heads are not removed after flowering.

☼ ◊ ❀❀❀
‡ to 8cm (3in) ↔ to 20cm (8in)

Helleborus argutifolius ♀
EVERGREEN PERENNIAL

The Corsican hellebore bears bright
green, slightly nodding, cup-shaped
flowers from late winter to early spring.
Its evergreen leaves are divided into
three toothed, greyish-green leaflets.
One of the largest hellebores, it grows
best on moist, well-drained, alkaline or
neutral soil, in full sun or partial shade.
Choose it for a mixed border or allow
to naturalize in a woodland setting as
it self-seeds freely.

‡ to 60cm (24in) ↔ to 45cm (18in)

Helleborus foetidus ♀
EVERGREEN PERENNIAL

The stinking hellebore is a vigorous,
clump-forming perennial with dark
evergreen, deeply divided, somewhat
leathery leaves; it is named for the
unpleasant smell that emanates from
them when they are crushed. The bell-
shaped, slightly fragrant, green flowers
are produced in clusters on tall, erect
stems from late winter to early spring.
Equally at home in full sunshine or
partial shade, it can be planted in a
variety of situations in the garden
and is happy on moist, alkaline soils.

‡↔ to 45cm (18in)

Acacia dealbata ♀
EVERGREEN TREE

The silver wattle is a fast-growing tree that brings a bit of Australian sunshine into the garden when it is most needed, by way of its bright yellow, scented, pompom flowers. The grey, evergreen leaves are also remarkable, as they are very finely divided into scores of tiny leaflets. It is slightly tender, so choose a warm and sheltered site. The subspecies *subalpina* is more shrub-like but hardier, with paler flowers, and the compact, but very free-flowering variety 'Gaulois Astier' is ideal for a container in sun.

☀ ◊ ❀❀ *f*
‡ to 15m (50ft) ↔ to 15m (50ft)

Anemone x *lipsiensis*
PERENNIAL

The pale, sulphur-yellow flowers of this carpet-forming wood anemone appear in spring. Its dark green leaves are deeply toothed and lie close to the soil surface. Best grown in partially shaded situations beneath deciduous trees or shrubs, this natural hybrid prefers a humus-rich, well-drained soil, and will tolerate chalky conditions.

☀ ◊ ◊ ❀❀❀
‡ to 15cm (6in) ↔ to 30cm (12in)

Anemone ranunculoides ♀

PERENNIAL

This spreading perennial received its name because of its similarity to the buttercup. It has deeply divided mid-green leaves and bright yellow flowers with five or six petals. It enjoys a site in partial shade and is ideal for a mixed border or naturalizing in a woodland or wild garden. Plant it in moist, but well-drained, humus-rich soil.

☼ ◊ ◑ ❁ ❁ ❁
↕↔ to 20cm (8in)

Caltha palustris ♀

PERENNIAL

The kingcup, or marsh marigold, is a vigorous clump-forming perennial with serrated glossy green leaves. It is one of the earliest aquatic plants to come into bloom, and has large bright golden yellow flowers. Thriving in full sun in wet soil, it makes an excellent choice for a bog garden, but may also be grown in a permanently moist border, or shallow water at the edge of a pond, contained in a perforated basket. 'Flore Pleno' is slightly less vigorous, and has double yellow flowers.

☼ ◊ ◑ ❁ ❁ ❁
↕ to 60cm (24in) ↔ to 45cm (18in)

Corylopsis pauciflora ♀
DECIDUOUS SHRUB

This bushy, deciduous plant produces small, very fragrant, pale yellow, bell-shaped flowers in spring. The young leaves appear after the flowers, and are pink when they open, but turn green as they age. Although other corylopsis species tolerate alkaline conditions, *C. pauciflora* requires acid soil. Given plenty of room, it will grow into a pleasing, spreading shape, and enhance a woodland garden or a shrub border in dappled shade. The flowers can be damaged by hard frosts.

☀ ◊ ◊ ❀ ❀ ❀ *f*

‡ to 1.5m (5ft) ↔ to 2.5m (8ft)

Corylus avellana 'Aurea'
DECIDUOUS SHRUB

In late winter and early spring this decorative hazel bears dangling yellow catkins. It forms a broad, spreading shrub or small tree, with bright yellow-green, sharply toothed leaves, and in late summer the rounded hazelnuts are favoured by squirrels. A relatively small variety, it is suitable for a shrub border, and contrasts well with the purple-leaved hazel, *C. avellana* 'Purpurea'.

☀ ☀ ◊ ❀ ❀ ❀

‡↔ to 5m (15ft)

Crocus chrysanthus 'E.A. Bowles' ♀

PERENNIAL CORM

This dainty crocus has deep lemon-yellow, goblet-shaped flowers, with purple feathering on the outer petals. The leaves are dark green with a white stripe. Plant the corms in groups in the autumn in well-drained soil at the front of a sunny border for an early splash of spring colour, or grow in raised beds and containers.

☼ ◊ ❀❀❀
‡ to 7cm (3in) ↔ to 5cm (2in)

Crocus 'Cream Beauty' ♀

PERENNIAL CORM

A compact, spring-flowering crocus with rich cream-coloured flowers that darken at the base to a greenish-gold, and have a golden throat. Plant the bulbs as for 'E.A Bowles' (*above*) in a sunny position in well-drained, gritty soil. It suits a rock garden, and may also be naturalized in grass.

☼ ◊ ❀❀❀
‡ to 7cm (3in) ↔ to 5cm (2in)

Edgeworthia chrysantha
DECIDUOUS SHRUB

The paper bush never fails to impress passers-by in early spring, who always pause to admire its unusual bunches of small yellow flowers that appear on the branch tips. Resembling daphne flowers, they are also scented, which makes them attractive to winter insects. The bark is reddish brown and the leaves pale green. It must be sheltered to thrive, with moist but well-drained, humus-rich, loamy soil. The leaves will drop in hot weather if the soil gets too dry, and late frosts can be damaging.

☼ ◊ ◊ ✻ ✻ ✻ *f*
‡↔ to 1.5m (5ft)

Eranthis hyemalis ♀
PERENNIAL

The winter aconite begins flowering in late winter and continues into early spring. Its bright yellow blooms perch on a ruff of deeply divided, leaf-like bracts. Ideal for naturalizing in grass and woodland borders, it will create a colourful carpet beneath deciduous trees and shrubs. Plant the tubers in autumn in fertile, moist, well-drained soil that does not dry out in summer. Large clumps can be divided after it has flowered.

☀ ◊ ◊ ✻ ✻ ✻
‡↔ to 10cm (4in)

Erythronium 'Pagoda' ♀

PERENNIAL BULB

This dog's-tooth violet bears drooping clusters of up to five sulphur-yellow flowers in spring. A vigorous plant with mottled, glossy green leaves, it is suitable for planting beneath shrubs or in the dappled shade of a woodland garden in moist, humus-rich, well-drained soil. Plant the bulbs in autumn. Large clumps can be divided after the leaves have died; replant immediately to prevent the bulbs from drying out.

‡ to 35cm (14in) ↔ to 20cm (8in)

Forsythia x *intermedia* 'Lynwood' ♀

DECIDUOUS SHRUB

Forsythias are free flowering, medium-sized shrubs, the upright branches of which are covered with large bright yellow flowers during spring before the leaves unfurl. Plant them in a row to create a spectacular hedge, or grow one as a freestanding shrub in a border. Cut hedges and prune back the shoots of shrubs after flowering to promote new growth and flowers the following year. Choose a site in full sun or light shade in fertile, well-drained soil.

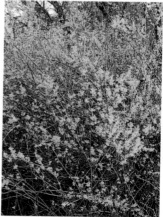

‡↔ to 3m (10ft)

Hyacinthus orientalis **'City of Haarlem'** ♀
PERENNIAL BULB

With spikes of primrose-yellow, waxy, bell-shaped flowers, this is one of only a few yellow hyacinths. Its intense scent makes it an appealing houseplant when forced into bloom early in the winter months. Outdoors, it looks wonderful in spring bedding displays, and needs full sun and free-draining soil. Forced bulbs grown for indoor display should be fed regularly after flowering, and then planted outside. The flowers will be smaller in subsequent years.

☼ ◊ ❀❀❀ *f*
‡ to 25cm (10in) ↔ to 8cm (3in)

Iris danfordiae
PERENNIAL BULB

This is an extremely attractive dwarf iris with bright yellow spring flowers. It is best considered as a disposable plant, because although it flowers well in the first season, the bulb then splits into tiny bulblets which rarely bloom again. Ideal for containers, troughs or raised beds, the bulbs should be planted in late summer or early autumn in a sunny position and well-drained soil.

☼ ◊ ❀❀❀
‡ to 10cm (4in) ↔ to 5cm (2in)

Iris winogradowii ♀
PERENNIAL BULB

The pale yellow flowers of this dwarf iris emerge in early spring. Its leaves are very short at flowering time, but lengthen afterwards. Suitable for a rock or gravel garden or a raised bed, grow it in full sunshine, in well-drained, moisture-retentive soil. Do not allow the bulbs to dry out during summer.

☼ ◊ ◑ ✸✸✸

‡ to 10cm (4in) ↔ to 7cm (3in)

Mahonia aquifolium 'Apollo' ♀
EVERGREEN SHRUB

This suckering shrub has large leaves, divided into spiny leaflets, with red stalks. Its bright yellow flowers are carried in compact clusters, which are succeeded by bluish-black berries. The Oregon grape will thrive in the dry soil beneath trees; grown in sun or shade, it provides superb ground cover and should be clipped to the ground after flowering every other year. The leaves take on coppery tones in autumn.

☼ ◑ ◊ ◑ ✸✸✸

‡ to 60cm (24in) ↔ to 1.2m (4ft)

Narcissus 'Ambergate'

PERENNIAL BULB

This striking daffodil bears flowers with a large, deep orange cup, surrounded by warm yellow petals from mid-spring. The flowers can measure as much as 10cm (4in) across, making it a dramatic choice for a display of cut flowers. It may also be planted in groups in a mixed border or naturalized in grass. Plant bulbs in late summer to one and a half times their depth in a sunny site in well-drained, reasonably fertile soil.

☼ ◊ ❀ ❀ ❀
‡ to 40cm (16in) ↔ to 15cm (6in)

Narcissus bulbocodium ♀

PERENNIAL BULB

The diminutive hoop-petticoat daffodil produces dark green, almost cylindrical leaves, and yellow, funnel-shaped early spring flowers. Tiny, pointed petals appear halfway down the flower funnel, so that it looks rather like a lady wearing a long yellow ball gown. It grows best in a sunny position, and can be planted among fine-leaved grasses or in a raised bed. The variety *N. conspicuus* bears deep golden-yellow flowers. Plant bulbs as for 'Ambergate' (*see above*).

☼ ◊ ❀ ❀ ❀
‡ to 15cm (6in) ↔ to 5cm (2in)

Narcissus cyclamineus ♀

PERENNIAL BULB

This early-flowering daffodil produces deep yellow, vase-shaped flowers, with strongly swept-back petals, and bright green leaves. Grow in a sunny position, in well-drained neutral to acid (lime-free) soil. It makes an excellent choice for containers, a woodland border, or for naturalizing in grass. Plant bulbs as for 'Ambergate' (*see opposite*).

☼ ◊ ❀❀❀

‡ to 20cm (8in) ↔ to 8cm (3in)

Narcissus 'February Gold' ♀

PERENNIAL BULB

A widely grown daffodil, 'February Gold' is extremely vigorous and in the early spring produces nodding, large golden-yellow flowers with slightly swept-back petals. The flowers are set off by mid-green, strap-shaped leaves. It is suitable for planting in borders or for naturalizing in grass. Plant bulbs as for 'Ambergate' (*see opposite*).

☼ ◊ ❀❀❀

‡ to 30cm (12in) ↔ to 8cm (3in)

Primula palinuri
EVERGREEN PERENNIAL

This is an attractive rosette-forming primula with rather fleshy, spoon-shaped leaves. In early spring it bears often large, cowslip-like clusters of slightly fragrant yellow flowers. Grow it in a sunny site in reasonably fertile, moist, well-drained, preferably alkaline soil, and mulch with grit. It suffers in cold, wet winters, so it is best to grow it in pots of gritty loam-based compost.

☼ ◊ ◊ ❀ ❀ ❀ *f*
‡↔ to 30cm (12in)

Primula vulgaris ♀
EVERGREEN PERENNIAL

The primrose is often regarded as the true harbinger of spring. Each stem of this rosette-forming perennial carries up to 25 single, pale yellow flowers with an orange spot at the base of each petal. It prefers a position in partial shade and moist, well-drained, humus-rich soil. An excellent plant for growing in containers, it will also be happy in woodland and shrub borders, and rock gardens. Propagate it from seed, or divide during early spring or autumn; never collect bulbs from the wild.

☼ ◊ ◊ ❀ ❀ ❀
‡ to 20cm (8in) ↔ to 35cm (14in)

Ranunculus ficaria 'Brazen Hussy'

PERENNIAL

This celandine boasts glossy, bronze-coloured, heart-shaped leaves that lie close to the ground, and bright yellow flowers which emerge in spring. Given wet soil in winter it can be invasive, but it is easy to remove unwanted portions, and it dies back completely during the summer. It will thrive in partial shade and moist soil in a shrub border, at the base of a hedge, or in a woodland setting. The variety *R. aurantiacus* bears single orange flowers.

‡ to 5cm (2in) ↔ to 20cm (8in)

Rhododendron lutescens

SEMI-EVERGREEN SHRUB

An attractive medium-to-large semi-evergreen shrub, with bronzy-green leaves, its clusters of primrose-yellow flowers start to open in late winter and continue into early spring. Ideal for brightening up a shady woodland situation, it should be protected from cold winds and planted in moist, well-drained, humus-rich, acid (lime-free) soil. Mulch it annually with leafmould or chipped bark.

‡↔ to 5m (15ft)

Salix caprea 'Kilmarnock'
DECIDUOUS TREE

Salix caprea is usually a tall, vigorous tree, but the Kilmarnock willow rarely exceeds a height of 2m (6ft), making it ideal for planting in small gardens or large containers. It has a weeping habit and bears numerous rounded yellow catkins in late winter and early spring. Plant it in deep, moist, well-drained soil in a sunny site. The branches can become congested; in late winter prune out surplus ones, and removing shoots that appear on the trunk.

☼ ◊ ◉ ❋ ❋ ❋
↕↔ to 2m (6ft)

Tulipa kaufmanniana
PERENNIAL BULB

The flowers of the water-lily tulip have narrow, pointed, yellow or cream petals, that are tinted orange or pink on the outside. Its tall stems bear up to five blooms, carried above lance-shaped greyish-green leaves. A long-lived bulb, it is best grown in a rock garden. Plant the bulbs in late autumn in full sun, in fertile, well-drained soil at a depth of at least 10cm (4in).

☼ ◊ ❋ ❋ ❋
↕ to 25cm (10in) ↔ to 15cm (6in)

Tulipa urumiensis ♀
PERENNIAL BULB

The cheerful golden yellow star-shaped flowers of this low-growing tulip appear in early spring above a rosette of waxy green leaves; much of its stem remains below ground. Its petals are flushed with green and red on the outside. Grow it in a raised bed or rock garden where clumps can develop undisturbed and the soil is well-drained and fairly dry in summer. Plant the bulbs in late autumn at a depth of about 10cm (4in).

☼ ◊ ❀❀❀
‡ to 15cm (6in) ↔ to 13cm (5in)

Valeriana phu 'Aurea'
PERENNIAL

The main feature of valerian is its bright butter-yellow foliage, which appears in early spring. The leaves turn lime-green after a few weeks and then mature to mid-green. After these exciting foliage effects, its small white summer flowers are rather unimpressive. It provides the perfect foil for blue spring flowers in the herbaceous border. Plant it in full sun in any reasonably fertile, well-drained soil, and divide it in autumn.

☼ ◊ ❀❀❀
‡↔ to 38cm (15in)

LATE SPRING

As temperatures rise and light levels increase, the garden seems to burst into life. Blossom buds open, and spring-flowering shrubs with bright new foliage add colour and scent to borders and beds. As the bulbs continue their seasonal show, leaves of perennials pushing through the soil hint at the drama to come.

However, new growth can be damaged by late frosts, so keep fleece handy to protect young plants, and do not be tempted to put out tender bedding or summer displays in containers too early. Slugs and snails are about in the damp conditions and the succulent shoots of many perennials are vulnerable to their attentions. You can entice birds, toads, and hedgehogs to help control the pests by providing a pond; with candelabra primulas and other moisture-loving plants in bloom there is plenty for the gardener to enjoy too.

Easy-growing, blossoming ornamental cherries (*Prunus*) and crab apples (*Malus*) are great value; many will reward you with autumn interest. The massive blooms of tree peonies make real impact, but the rhododendrons, with hundreds to choose from, and flowers in almost every shade provide the most excitement. If you lack the acid conditions they enjoy, try early-flowering clematis and fragrant lilacs (*Syringa*).

ALPINES AND BULBS

The rock garden is at its best as the season begins, studded with jewel-like flowers of arabis, gold dust (*Aurinia*), spring gentians and small species tulips. Tulips also dominate late spring bulb displays with larger-flowered varieties creating bold swathes of colour in beds, borders and containers. Clumps of quamash (*Camassia*), and tall, stately crown imperials (*Fritillaria imperialis*) make imposing centrepieces in the border, while the delicate snake's head fritillary (*Fritillaria meleagris*) is superb naturalized in grass.

Arabis alpina subsp. *caucasica* 'Variegata'
EVERGREEN PERENNIAL

This mat-forming plant has rosettes of greyish-green, spoon-shaped leaves. The white fragrant flowers are produced in loose clusters over a long period from late spring to early autumn. It is very hardy and will flower well when grown in poor, well-drained soil in full sun, making it ideal for a rock or scree garden. 'Variegata' has the added bonus of green leaves with pale yellow margins.

☼ ◊ ❀❀❀ *f*
↕↔ to 15cm (6in)

Camassia leichtlinii ♀
PERENNIAL BULB

The white form of quamash flowers from late spring to early summer. The tall flowering stems make a striking addition to the herbaceous border. The bulbs should be planted at a depth of 10cm (4in) in autumn. Plant quamash in groups in deep, moist but well-drained soil in a sunny or slightly shaded position. In areas prone to long periods of frost, place a thick mulch over the area where the bulbs have been planted.

☼ ◑ ◊ ◔ ❀❀
↕ to 1.5m (5ft) ↔ to 30cm (12in)

Cassiope 'Edinburgh' ♀
EVERGREEN SHRUB

This compact plant has small, slightly hairy, dark green leaves, and in late spring produces nodding white bell-shaped flowers with swept-back tips, similar to those of lily-of-the-valley. It is closely related to heathers and needs a moist, fertile, acid soil in a sunny or partially shaded spot. Cassiopes are fairly demanding plants, requiring the right growing conditions to flourish; 'Edinburgh' is the least fussy.

☼ ◑ ◊ ❋ ❋ ❋
‡↔ to 20cm (8in)

Choisya ternata ♀
EVERGREEN SHRUB

The Mexican orange blossom is a fast-growing shrub with dark green, glossy foliage. The leaves are aromatic when crushed. It produces a profusion of fragrant, star-shaped, white flowers in late spring – a light pruning after these have faded can often stimulate a second flush of blooms in autumn. Grow in fertile, well-drained soil in full sun. SUNDANCE has bright yellow-green leaves.

☼ ◊ ❋ ❋ ❋ *f*
‡↔ to 2.5m (8ft)

Convallaria majalis ♀
PERENNIAL BULB

Lily-of-the-valley is a delightful spring-flowering plant with arching stems of white, sweetly scented, bell-shaped flowers that appear between the dark green leaves. It makes an ideal ground-cover plant for shady, damp situations and spreads very quickly by means of creeping roots. 'Albostriata' has gold-striped leaves, and 'Fortin's Giant' is slightly taller, growing to a height of 30cm (12in).

☼ ☽ ◑ ◊ ❀❀❀ *f*

↕ to 15cm (6in) ↔ indefinite

Cornus florida 'White Cloud'
DECIDUOUS TREE

The flowering dogwood forms an attractive spreading tree that looks as if it is adorned with large white flowers in late spring. In fact, these "blooms" comprise four creamy-white, petal-like bracts surrounding a cluster of tiny green flowers. An additional feature of this beautiful plant is the slightly twisted green leaves which, in autumn, turn bright orange and red.

☼ ◊ ❀❀❀

↕ to 6m (20ft) ↔ to 8m (25ft)

Davidia involucrata ♀

DECIDUOUS TREE

In late spring, the branches of the
pocket handkerchief tree are hung
with what look like hundreds of crisp,
white linen squares. These are, in fact,
showy bracts that surround the tiny
flowerheads. Although fully hardy,
it needs shelter from strong winds. It
will grow in most situations but prefers
moist but well-drained, fertile soil
and a sunny position. When mature
it can become quite large, making it
less suitable for small gardens.

☼ ◊ ◊ ❀❀❀
‡ to 15m (50ft) ↔ to 10m (30ft)

Erythronium oregonum

PERENNIAL BULB

This dog's-tooth violet forms a clump
of unusual dark green leaves with paler
mottling. In spring, it produces stems
bearing two or three pendent flowers
with creamy-white reflexed petals and
yellow anthers. Suitable for a woodland
garden or beneath deciduous shrubs,
grow it in fertile, moist but well-drained
soil. Divide clumps in summer after the
flowers have faded.

◐ ◊ ◊ ❀❀❀
‡ to 35cm (14in) ↔ to 12cm (5in)

Fraxinus ornus ♀

DECIDUOUS TREE

The manna ash makes a very good specimen tree for a medium to large garden, valued for its fluffy clusters of tiny, fragrant, creamy white flowers that cover the tree in late spring. It has a rounded crown of divided, dark green leaves that turn dark purple before falling in autumn. The tree thrives in most fertile, well-drained soils, and will tolerate hot, dry sites. Little pruning is required; cut out any badly placed, dead, diseased or crossing shoots in winter.

☼ ◊ ◑ ❀❀❀ *f*
↕↔ to 15m (50ft)

Halesia monticola

DECIDUOUS TREE

The fast-growing snowdrop tree forms an attractive cone shape. In late spring, often before the leaves emerge, white, bell-shaped blooms appear in clusters along the branches. These are followed in summer by green, winged fruit, measuring up to 5cm (2in) long. In autumn the leaves take on a strong yellow colour before falling. Plant in moist but well-drained, neutral or slightly acid (lime-free) soil, in a sunny or partially shaded, sheltered position.

☼ ☀ ◊ ◑ ❀❀❀
↕ to 12m (40ft) ↔ to 8m (25ft)

Iris confusa ♀

PERENNIAL

This is one of the crested irises with flattened flowers. The leaves, which are green and sword-shaped, are held in fans on bamboo-like stems. In late spring and early summer, it bears abundant small white flowers, measuring just 5cm (2in) across. *Iris confusa* is not entirely hardy and should be grown in a sunny or slightly shaded, sheltered position. Soil should be moist and fertile. Every year mulch after flowering.

☼ ☀ ◌ ❄❄

‡ to 1m (3ft) ↔ indefinite

Magnolia wilsonii ♀

DECIDUOUS TREE

This elegant magnolia forms a large shrub or small tree, and in late spring and early summer produces fragrant, white flowers with a ring of crimson-red in the centre. It can be damaged by frost and needs a sheltered spot in full sun or light shade. It also requires a moist, well-drained soil. As with all magnolias, give it plenty of space to develop unhindered.

☼ ☀ ◌◌ ◌ ❄❄❄ *f*

‡↔ to 8m (20ft)

Malus toringo subsp. *sargentii*

DECIDUOUS TREE

This crab apple produces a profusion of white flowers in spring, giving rise in the autumn to bright red fruit. It has dark green, three-lobed leaves. Give it a spot in full sun or light shade and, although tolerant of a wide range of soil types, it prefers moderately fertile, moist, well-drained soil.

☼ ☼ ◐ ◊ ✿✿✿

‡ to 4m (12ft) ↔ to 5m (15ft)

Narcissus poeticus var. *recurvus* ♀

PERENNIAL BULB

The old pheasant's eye narcissus obtained its common name from the short, red-rimmed, yellow cup in the centre of the flower. This particular variety has fragrant, long-lasting flowers with swept-back, pure white petals, and greenish-yellow throats. It flowers slightly later in spring than many other daffodils, and can be grown in borders, large containers, or naturalized in grass. Plant it in well-drained soil in full sun or dappled shade.

☼ ☼ ◊ ✿✿✿ *f*

‡ to 35cm (14in) ↔ to 10cm (4in)

Osmanthus x *burkwoodii* ♀
EVERGREEN SHRUB

This slow-growing shrub has oval, dark green, slightly glossy, leathery leaves. In mid-spring it produces small clusters of fragrant white flowers which, on a still sunny day, will fill the garden with a sweet scent. Plant this shrub in full sun or partial shade in fertile, well-drained soil. It can be used as a hedging plant, which will need clipping once a year in the summer.

☼ ☀ ◊ ❄❄❄ *f*
↕↔ to 3m (10ft)

Osmanthus delavayi ♀
EVERGREEN SHRUB

A large, rounded, evergreen, this plant has arching stems from which hang clusters of tubular flowers in mid- to late spring. The highly fragrant white blooms are set off by dark green, glossy, toothed foliage. Later in the year, small blue-black berries appear. Grow this bush in well-drained soil in full sun or partial shade, and protect it from drying winds. Prune it after the flowers have faded.

☼ ☀ ◊ ❄❄❄ *f*
↕ to 6m (20ft) ↔ to 4m (12ft)

Paeonia suffruticosa '**Godaishu**'

PERENNIAL

This decorative white tree peony is well worth searching for. It has dark green, slightly waxy leaves, and large semi-double flowers with pure white soft petals that surround yellow stamens. For the best results, plant it in well-drained soil in full sun or partial shade.

☼ ◐ ◊ ❀❀❀
↕↔to 2m (6ft)

Polygonatum x *hybridum* ♀

PERENNIAL

Solomon's seal is an elegant plant, with small tubular white flowers that hang gracefully from arching green stems. It adds a touch of class to late spring herbaceous borders and woodland gardens, and needs a cool, shaded position, and fertile, well-drained soil. Solomon's seal may be attacked by sawfly caterpillars, which can quickly reduce the leaves to a skeleton. 'Striatum' has variegated leaves. Divide clumps in spring.

☼ ◊ ❀❀❀
↕ to 1.2m (4ft) ↔to 1m (3ft)

Primula denticulata var. *alba*

PERENNIAL

Drumstick primulas have neat, globe-shaped flowerheads composed of many small blooms. This variety has white flowers, each with a bright yellow eye, although drumstick primulas also come in shades of pale lilac, pink, and deep purple. All thrive in moist, well-drained, neutral to slightly acid soil, and fare best if the soil dries out a little in the summer months. They are ideal for use in a herbaceous border or among shrubs, and are easy to raise from seed.

☀ ◑ ◊ ◐ ❀❀❀

‡↔ to 45cm (18in)

Prunus padus 'Watereri' ♀

DECIDUOUS TREE

The bird cherry has a decorative habit, with spreading branches that carry pendent stems of cup-shaped, almond-scented, white flowers in late spring. These are then followed by small black fruits, which are loved by birds. This vigorous tree should be grown in full sun or light shade, in a well-drained, moist soil. The bird cherry makes an excellent specimen for the middle of a lawn or in a mixed border.

☀ ◑ ◊ ◐ ❀❀❀ *f*

‡ to 15m (50ft) ↔ to 10m (30ft)

Prunus 'Shirofugen' ♥

DECIDUOUS TREE

One of the best flowering cherries, 'Shirofugen' would make a fine, fast-growing specimen tree for a medium to large garden. Its wide-spreading branches are covered in white blossom in late spring. Each flower is "double", meaning that is packed with petals, guaranteeing a massive shower of white as they fall. The flowers fade to a very pale pink as they age, contrasting nicely with the fresh, copper-coloured foliage.

☼ ◑ ◊ ◗ ✿ ✿ ✿
‡ to 8m (25ft) ↔ to 10m (30ft)

Pyrus salicifolia 'Pendula' ♥

DECIDUOUS TREE

An ornamental pear, 'Pendula' has attractive weeping branches covered with oval, silvery leaves. These are accompanied in mid- to late spring by clusters of creamy-white flowers. Small, green, inedible fruit may also appear in late summer. It needs full sun and well-drained soil and makes a decorative specimen for a lawn or a mixed border.

☼ ◊ ✿ ✿ ✿
‡ to 8m (25ft) ↔ to 6m (20ft)

Rhododendron '**Fragrantissimum**' ♀

EVERGREEN SHRUB

This rhododendron has highly fragrant, white, funnel-shaped spring flowers that contrast beautifully with the slightly hairy evergreen foliage. It is suitable for mild gardens and warm sheltered sites; where frost is likely it is better grown in a container and taken under cover for winter. Grow it in sun or partial shade in a well-drained, acid (lime-free) to neutral soil, or ericaceous compost. Outdoors, mulch generously with bark or leafmould.

☼ ❋ ◊ ◖ ❁ *f*
↔ to 2m (6ft)

Rhododendron '**Loderi King George**' ♀

EVERGREEN SHRUB

One of the best white rhododendrons, this slow-growing plant can grow to 4m (12ft) in height. The pale pink flower buds open in late spring to form large trusses of white, fragrant flowers with green markings. It is best planted in a woodland garden, and, like most rhododendrons, needs a moist, well-drained acid (lime-free) soil. Mulch it every year with bark or leafmould, especially when young.

☼ ❋ ◊ ◖ ❁ ❁ ❁ *f*
↔ to 4m (12ft)

Saxifraga '**Southside Seedling**' ♥
PERENNIAL

This saxifrage bears densely packed rosettes of pale green, spoon-shaped leaves. It flowers freely, and in late spring produces branched stems of red centred white blooms. The leaf rosettes die after flowering. 'Southside Seedling' requires a very well-drained, slightly alkaline soil, preferably with grit added to it, and prefers a sunny position.

☼ ◊ ❀❀❀

‡ to 30cm (12in) ↔ to 20cm (8in)

Smilacina racemosa
PERENNIAL

The false spikenard is a slow-spreading plant with tall stems topped in late spring with conical clusters of small, slightly scented white flowers. The large leaves are also an attractive feature. To grow well, false spikenard requires a shady site, and suits a woodland garden setting or a moist shady border. It will perform well in a moist, slightly acid (lime-free) soil. Divide large clumps in the spring.

☀ ◑ ◊ ❀❀❀ *f*

‡ to 90cm (36in) ↔ to 45cm (18in)

Spiraea 'Arguta' ✀
DECIDUOUS SHRUB

Known as bridal wreath because of its arching stems that are covered in late spring with small, white flowers that create a light, delicate effect. The blooms are borne among lance-shaped, bright green leaves. Bridal wreath is perfect for a low hedge or in a mixed shrub border, and needs a moist, well-drained soil in full sun. The flowers are produced on the previous year's wood, and the stems should be pruned back in early summer after flowering.

☼ ◊ ◑ ❀ ❀ ❀
‡ to 2m (6ft) ↔ to 1.5m (5ft)

Syringa vulgaris 'Madame Lemoine' ✀
DECIDUOUS SHRUB

Lilacs are large shrubs with branched, upright stems, covered with dark green, heart-shaped leaves. 'Madame Lemoine' has large, cone-shaped clusters of pure white, highly scented flowers, which are produced in abundance during the spring. Tolerant of pollution and most soils, except very acid soil, it is ideal for growing in an urban garden. If lilacs become leggy, cut them back hard to 1m (3ft) above the ground after they have flowered.

☼ ◊ ◑ ◑ ❀ ❀ ❀ *f*
‡↔ to 7m (22ft)

Trillium grandiflorum ♀

PERENNIAL

Wake-robin produces large flowers with three distinctive clear white petals and bright yellow stamens, which turn pale pink as they age. The blooms contrast beautifully with the deep green leaves that will eventually form a large clump. Trilliums need moist, well-drained soil and a slightly shaded position. They are best suited to deciduous woodland, but can also be used in a rock garden.

☼ ◐ ◊ ♦ ❀ ❀ ❀
‡ to 38cm (15in) ↔ to 30cm (12in)

Trollius x *cultorum* 'Alabaster'

PERENNIAL

Most globeflowers have bright yellow or orange flowers, but those of 'Alabaster' are much paler. It has bowl-shaped, deep cream-coloured flowers, held on slim, upright stems. It will grow happily in wet soil, as long as it dries out slightly in summer, and is suitable for waterside plantings or bog gardens. Large clumps can be divided in early summer, immediately after flowering.

☼ ☼ ◊ ◊ ♦ ❀ ❀ ❀
‡ to 60cm (24in) ↔ to 45cm (18in)

Tulipa 'White Triumphator' ♀

PERENNIAL BULB

This elegant lily-flowered tulip blooms in the late spring and has pure white flowers. Plant *en masse* in a mixed herbaceous border, or use in bedding schemes. Alternatively, plant a few in large containers for a sophisticated patio display. The bulbs should be planted in late autumn in full sun and fertile, well-drained soil. In bedding displays it is often easier to lift bulbs and discard them after flowering rather than letting the foliage die naturally.

 ☼ ◊ ❋ ❋ ❋

‡ to 70cm (28in)

Viburnum plicatum 'Mariesii' ♀

DECIDUOUS SHRUB

The broad-spreading branches of this viburnum are held in several layers, one above the other. In late spring it bears clusters of small, fertile flowers surrounded by sterile, saucer-shaped flowers with large white petals. The flowers are followed by small red fruits, which turn black in the autumn. Plant it in a shrub border or woodland garden, in full sun or partial shade, and moist, well-drained soil.

 ☼ ◐ ◊ ◊ ❋ ❋ ❋

‡ to 3m (10ft) ↔ to 4m (12ft)

Aesculus x *neglecta* 'Erythroblastos' ♀

DECIDUOUS TREE

The emerging spring foliage of the aptly named sunrise horse chestnut is bright pink, and later turns pale green. Just after the leaves have unfurled in late spring, 'Erythroblastos' produces cones of pink or peach flowers. This slow-growing tree also puts on an impressive autumn display with bright yellow and orange leaves. Grow it in deep, moist, well-drained soil in full sun or partial shade.

☼ ◐ ◊ ◖ ❋ ❋ ❋
‡ to 10m (30ft) ↔ to 8m (25ft)

Anagallis tenella 'Studland'

PERENNIAL

This bog pimpernel forms a low mat of bright green leaves, and in late spring is covered with small, lightly scented, deep pink flowers. It requires a moist, free-draining soil to survive and will die if it is allowed to dry out in summer. Suitable for a rock garden where the soil is moist, this dainty plant can also be used as ground cover. A short-lived plant, it can be propagated by taking cuttings in late summer.

☼ ◖ ❋ ❋ ❋ *f*
‡ to 1cm (½in) ↔ to 15cm (6in)

Aquilegia vulgaris 'Nora Barlow' ♀

PERENNIAL

This unusual aquilegia has double pink and white flowers, with pale green-tipped petals, which are slightly swept back when the flower is fully open. It needs a well-drained, moist soil in full sun, and makes a stunning addition to a spring herbaceous border. Plant it in bold groups of at least 3–5 plants for the best effect.

☼ ◊ ◑ ❀ ❀ ❀

↕ to 75cm (30in) ↔ to 50cm (20in)

Armeria maritima 'Vindictive' ♀

EVERGREEN PERENNIAL

Thrift is a seaside plant, and will grow happily in a rock garden. It forms a rounded cushion of deep green, grass-like leaves, and bears large numbers of bright pink flowers in the spring. Its deep taproot allows it to survive the driest of summers, and care should be taken when weeding to avoid damage to this root, which may kill the plant. Thrift is suitable for either coastal or inland gardens, as long as it is given a sunny site and well-drained soil.

☼ ◊ ❀ ❀ ❀

↕ to 10cm (4in) ↔ to 15cm (6in)

Bellis perennis Pomponette Series

PERENNIAL

A selected form of the common daisy, this perennial is frequently grown as a biennial for spring bedding. The double pink, white, or red flowers have quill-like petals, and measure up to 4cm (1½in) across. Grow in a sunny position, in a well drained, fertile soil, in spring bedding schemes, as edging, or in pots or window boxes. Deadhead regularly to extend the flowering period.

‡↔ to 20cm (8in)

Clematis 'Elizabeth'

CLIMBER

This vigorous plant is perfect for growing up a large, sturdy trellis, a large, mature tree, or up wires fixed to a house or boundary wall. In late spring, just as the lobed leaves unfurl, it produces masses of fragrant pink blooms along its climbing stems. It needs a sheltered situation in full sun, and a well-drained soil. It may need pruning after it has flowered to keep it under control.

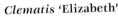

‡ to 7m (22ft)

Clematis 'Markham's Pink' ♀

CLIMBER

Deep pink, semi-double flowers adorn this beautiful plant in late spring and early summer. Not as vigorous as many early-flowering clematis, it is ideal for a small urban garden. It blooms on the previous year's wood, and if necessary should be pruned after flowering to remove any dead wood and to keep it within bounds. This clematis is very hardy and will tolerate an exposed site in sun or partial shade. It prefers well-drained soil.

☼ ☽ ◊ ❊❊❊

↕ to 3m (10ft)

Clematis montana var. *rubens*

CLIMBER

This vigorous plant will soon cover an ugly wall or scramble up a large mature tree. In late spring, it produces a huge number of single, pale pink flowers with creamy-yellow anthers. Grow it in free-draining soil in a sunny or partially shaded site, and prune it after flowering to keep it in check.

☼ ☽ ◊ ❊❊❊

↕ to 10m (30ft)

Darmera peltata ♀

PERENNIAL

The umbrella plant is a waterside plant that flowers before the large umbrella-shaped leaves emerge. Clusters of tiny, pale pink blooms, held on stout stems, are produced in late spring. Grow it in permanently wet soil, beside a pool or in a bog garden, in a sunny or partially shaded position. In time, it will spread to cover a large area.

☼ ☀ ◊ ◖ ❉ ❉ ❉

‡ to 1.2m (4ft) ↔ to 60cm (24in)

Dicentra spectabilis

PERENNIAL

This elegant plant has many common names, including bleeding heart, lady's locket, and lady-in-the-bath. The leaves are pale green and deeply-lobed, and delicate pink and white heart-shaped flowers hang from long arching stems. For the best results plant it in a partially shaded position, in moist, well-drained, fertile soil. In hot, dry summers it may die down early.

☼ ◊ ◖ ❉ ❉ ❉

‡ to 75cm (30in) ↔ to 50cm (20in)

Epimedium x *rubrum* ♀

PERENNIAL

This carpet-forming plant has attractive, heart-shaped leaves tinted reddish brown in spring as they unfurl, which then colour yellow in the autumn. In late spring it bears small crimson-pink, star-shaped flowers with long yellow spurs. Epimediums need a partially shaded position, and moist, but well-drained, fertile soil. Propagate clumps by division in early spring or autumn.

☀ ◐ ◊ ❀❀❀
↔ to 30cm (12in)

Erica australis ♀

EVERGREEN SHRUB

The Spanish heath produces small, bell-shaped, purple-pink flowers from mid-spring to the beginning of summer, and has dark green, needle-like foliage. It is not completely hardy so plant it in a sheltered position. Young plants benefit from some winter protection until they are established. Although tolerant of alkaline conditions, it prefers slightly moist acid (lime-free) or neutral soil, and full sun.

☀ ◊ ❀❀
↕ to 2m (6ft) ↔ to 1m (3ft)

Erythronium dens-canis ♀
PERENNIAL BULB

The dog's-tooth violet has distinctive purple, pink or white pendent flowers, with reflexed petals. The decorative oval-shaped, green leaves have pinkish-brown mottling on the upper surface. Dog's-tooth violets can be planted in woodland or grass, and grow best in well-drained, fertile soil in partial shade. To propagate, lift and divide the clumps of bulbs after flowering and replant them immediately in fertile soil.

☀ ◊ ❀ ❀ ❀
‡ to 25cm (10in) ↔ to 10cm (4in)

Geranium cinereum 'Ballerina' ♀
PERENNIAL

This semi-evergreen, mound-forming hardy geranium, or cranesbill, has deeply divided grey-green leaves. One of the first cranesbills to bloom in late spring, it bears many cup-shaped, pinkish-purple flowers, with distinctive purple veins and dark eyes. It makes a good rock- or gravel-garden plant, and flowers over a long period. Plant it in full sun in well-drained soil, and divide plants in the spring.

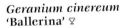

☀ ◊ ❀ ❀ ❀
‡ to 10cm (4in) ↔ to 30cm (12in)

Kolkwitzia amabilis 'Pink Cloud' ♀

DECIDUOUS SHRUB

One of the prettiest of the spring flowering shrubs, *Kolkwitzia* deserves its common name – the beauty bush. It has arching branches, clothed with tapering, dark green leaves. In late spring, it bears clusters of bell-shaped deep pink flowers with yellow-tinted throats. Plant it in a sunny site in fertile, well-drained soil. Although hardy, the new leaves may be damaged by late frosts, so it is best to choose a sheltered site in cold or exposed gardens.

☼ ◊ ❀ ❀ ❀

‡ to 3m (10ft) ↔ to 4m (12ft)

Lamium orvala

PERENNIAL

This pretty variety of dead nettle forms clumps of triangular, mid-green leaves. The hooded flowers are bronzy-pink, and borne in tiers around the stem. It needs shade and a moist, well-drained soil to do well, and is never invasive, unlike other dead nettles. There is also an attractive white-flowered form called 'Album'.

☼ ◊ ◐ ❀ ❀ ❀

‡↔ to 30cm (12in)

Lewisia cotyledon ♀
EVERGREEN PERENNIAL

Lewisias are rosette-forming alpines from the mountains of North America. The funnel-shaped flowers of this species are produced in vivid pink, white, red, apricot, or yellow, and are borne from late spring to early summer. Unlike many lewisias, which need to be grown under glass, *L. cotyledon* can be planted outside in crevices, a dry-stone wall, or a rock garden. Plant it in full sun and a very well-drained, fertile soil.

☼ ◊ ❀❀❀
↕ to 30cm (12in) ↔ to 15cm (6in)

Magnolia x *soulangeana*
DECIDUOUS TREE

This is probably the most widely grown of all magnolias. Fast growing, it will quickly form a small tree with wide spreading branches. The goblet-shaped flowers are pink to pinkish-purple, but there are also forms with white and reddish-purple blooms. The flowers appear from mid-spring, before the leaves. Select a planting position in full sun or partial shade, where the tree has plenty of space to develop its spreading shape. It also needs a moist, well-drained soil.

☼ ◐ ◊ ◑ ❀❀❀
↕↔ to 6m (20ft)

Malus floribunda ♀
DECIDUOUS TREE

The Japanese crab apple grows to form
a large shrub or small, spreading tree
with graceful, pendent branches. The
flower buds are red, opening in mid-
spring to a very pale pink, with small
fruits ripening yellow in autumn. It is
not fussy about the soil conditions, as
long as the site is not waterlogged. Grow
this crab apple in sun or partial shade,
and use it as a specimen tree in a lawn
or in a mixed border.

☼ ☀ ◊ ❀ ❀ ❀

‡↔to 10m (30ft)

Oxalis adenophylla ♀
PERENNIAL

This mat-forming, tuberous perennial
has greyish-green leaves, divided into
heart-shaped leaflets. In late spring it
produces purplish-pink flowers with
conspicuous purple veins. Plant the
tubers in a rock or gravel garden, or in
troughs, in well-drained, gritty soil,
in full sun. It is easily propagated by
division in the autumn or early spring.

☼ ◊ ❀ ❀ ❀

‡ to 5cm (2in) ↔ to 10cm (4in)

Paulownia tomentosa ♀
DECIDUOUS TREE

The foxglove tree has extremely large, rounded leaves. In late spring, the lilac, foxglove-like, scented flowers appear. The tree is not entirely hardy, and the flowers may be damaged by frost. In cold areas, it can be treated as a foliage plant by cutting it down to ground level in late winter or early spring, which stimulates growth of even larger leaves the following spring. If this is done annually, apply a balanced fertilizer and mulch after pruning. Plant it in well-drained soil in a sunny, sheltered site.

☼ ◊ ❀ ❀ *f*

‡ to 12m (40ft) ↔ to 10m (30ft)

Phlox subulata 'Marjorie'
PERENNIAL

A pretty cushion-forming plant with narrow green leaves, the rose-pink flowers of this moss phlox have five notched petals and a dark eye. It is ideal for a spring display in a rock or gravel garden or raised bed, and will perform well when planted in well-drained, fertile soil, in a sunny position.

☼ ◊ ❀ ❀ ❀

‡ to 10cm (4in) ↔ to 20cm (8in)

Primula rosea ♀

PERENNIAL

This primula forms a rosette of toothed, bronze-green leaves, and produces clusters of beautiful clear pink flowers in late spring. It needs moist, neutral to acid, fertile soil, and will suit a bog garden or the damp soil beside a pond. It can be grown in full sun, as long as the soil is permanently wet.

☼ ☀ ◐ ◆ ❀ ❀ ❀
‡↔ to 20cm (8in)

Primula sieboldii ♀

PERENNIAL

This primula has long been cultivated in Japan, and there are many different forms from which to choose. The wild plant has pinkish-purple flowers with white eyes, but there are also cultivars with pink or white flowers. The blooms are held above a rosette of bright green leaves. Plant it in a moist, fertile soil, preferably in partial shade, or full sun if the soil remains moist all summer.

☼ ☀ ◆ ❀ ❀ ❀
‡ to 30cm (12in) ↔ to 45cm (18in)

Prunus 'Kanzan' ♀

DECIDUOUS TREE

This pretty flowering cherry has upright branches when young, which spread more widely as the tree matures, and this habit must be considered before planting. Double, deep pink flowers are produced just before the reddish-brown leaves appear in mid- to late spring. Grow it in moist, fertile, well-drained soil in full sun.

☀ ◊ ◊ ❀ ❀ ❀
↨↔ to 10m (30ft)

Prunus 'Kiku-shidare-zakura' ♀

DECIDUOUS TREE

Often sold as 'Cheal's Weeping', the graceful, weeping branches of this flowering cherry are covered in spring with clusters of double, bright pink flowers. It is quite tolerant of pollution, and is often planted in avenues along urban roads. Pruning should be avoided to prevent peach leaf curl disease from entering through the wounds. Where pruning has to be carried out, it should be performed in the summer when the sap is rising.

☀ ◊ ◊ ❀ ❀ ❀
↨↔ to 3m (12ft)

Rhododendron 'Pink Pearl'
EVERGREEN SHRUB

This is a very popular rhododendron, grown for its large trusses of pale pink spring flowers. While the plant is generally very vigorous, the branches are rather weak and have a tendency to droop. Plant it among other shrubs or in a woodland garden. It should be grown in a sunny or partially shaded position in deep, moist, well-drained, acid soil. Mulch annually with chipped bark or leafmould.

☼ ☀ ◊ ◊ ❀ ❀ ❀
‡↔ to 4m (12ft)

Rhododendron yakushimanum
EVERGREEN SHRUB

A compact, hardy rhododendron, this variety forms a domed bush of dark green, glossy leaves. In late spring, it is covered with funnel-shaped, rose-pink flowers, which fade to pale pink and then white. Plant it in full sun or partial shade, in moist, well-drained, fertile, acid soil, and mulch annually with chipped bark or leafmould. This shrub is suitable for containers if grown in ericaceous compost.

☼ ☀ ◊ ◊ ❀ ❀ ❀
‡↔ to 2m (6ft)

Sambucus nigra 'Guincho Purple'

DECIDUOUS SHRUB

This popular cultivar of the common elder is an upright shrub with dark green, divided leaves, which turn black-purple then red in autumn. In late spring to early summer, fragrant, pink-tinged white flowers are borne in large, flattened clusters, followed by small black berries. Elders are ideal in new gardens, because they establish quickly. For the best foliage, cut all stems to the ground in winter, or prune out some of the older stems annually.

☼ ◑ ◊ ❁❁❁ *f*
‡↔ to 6m (20ft)

Syringa meyeri 'Palibin' ♀

DECIDUOUS SHRUB

This slow-growing lilac is the perfect choice for a small garden, where the common form (*Syringa vulgaris*) may grow too large. It forms a compact bush, which is covered from late spring to early summer with clusters of very fragrant, pale lavender-pink flowers. Plant it in full sun in well-drained soil, or in a large container of loam-based potting compost.

☼ ◊ ❁❁❁ *f*
‡↔ to 1.5m (5ft)

Tulipa 'Don Quichotte' ♀

PERENNIAL BULB

This bright cherry-pink tulip makes
a dramatic statement when planted
in large groups and used as a bedding
plant. Its vivid colour combines well
with cream or white tulips, such as
'White Triumphator' (*see p.87*), or
forget-me-nots. Plant the bulbs in late
autumn in well-drained soil in full sun.

☼ ◊ ❀ ❀ ❀
‡ to 45cm (18in)

Tulipa 'Groenland'

PERENNIAL BULB

The viridiflora tulips are named for
the bright green stripe in the middle
of the outer petals. 'Groenland' has soft
pink petals marked with a triangular
green brush stroke. It can be used in
groups in a herbaceous border, or as a
bedding plant. Like all tulips, the bulbs
need to be planted in late autumn in
a sunny position, in well-drained soil.

☼ ◊ ❀ ❀ ❀
‡ to 45cm (18in)

Acer palmatum '**Corallinum**'

DECIDUOUS TREE

A compact form of *Acer palmatum* that grows slowly to form a bushy shrub or small tree. It is particularly dramatic in spring when young bright red shoots appear, together with vivid shrimp-pink leaves, which gradually turn pale green. In autumn the leaves turn orange, red and yellow. It is best planted in sun or partial shade in moist, well-drained acid (lime-free) soil.

☀ ◊ ◊ ❀ ❀ ❀
‡ to 1.2m (4ft) ↔ to 1m (3ft)

Anemone x *fulgens*

PERENNIAL

This striking tuberous plant bears vivid scarlet flowers with black centres that resemble poppies. The late spring flowers are held on stout stems above deeply-lobed leaves. For the best effect, plant it in groups in sandy, well-drained soil and a sunny position, as it can be damaged while dormant in summer by persistent rain and wet soil conditions.

☀ ◊ ❀ ❀ ❀
‡ to 30cm (12in) ↔ to 10cm (4in)

Camellia japonica 'Rubescens Major' ♀

EVERGREEN SHRUB

This is a very old form of the Japanese camellia, and produces double crimson-red flowers with darker veins from mid-spring. It forms a compact bush, with glossy, rounded dark green leaves. There are several other good camellias with red flowers, such as the semi-double 'Paul's Apollo' and 'R. L. Wheeler'. Plant 'Rubescens Major' in a slightly shaded site, away from early morning sun, in deep, moist, well-drained, acid (lime-free) soil.

☀ ◊ ◕ ❀❀❀
‡↔to 10m (30ft)

Crataegus laevigata 'Paul's Scarlet' ♀

DECIDUOUS TREE

Similar in shape to the common native hawthorn, this small tree is covered in late spring with double, deep pink flowers. These are sometimes followed in the late summer by small red fruits. The leaves are shiny and deeply lobed. It will grow well in most soils, as long as they are not waterlogged, in a sunny or lightly shaded location. Mature trees are particularly attractive.

☼ ☀ ◊ ◕ ❀❀❀
‡↔to 8m (25ft)

Dicentra 'Bacchanal'

PERENNIAL

Bleeding hearts are perennial herbs with finely divided leaves. 'Bacchanal' bears its dangling, deep crimson-red flowers on arching stems in late spring. Plant it in fertile soil in partial shade below shrubs or in a mixed border. Try to combine it with plants that will hide its dying foliage in the summer.

☀ ◗ ◖ ❋ ❋ ❋
↕ to 35cm (14in) ↔ to 45cm (18in)

Geum rivale

PERENNIAL

Water avens grows naturally beside rivers and streams, making them ideal for bog gardens and pool-sides. This species produces clumps of hairy, dark green divided leaves and, in late spring, it bears single, nodding, bell-shaped flowers on arching stems. Plant it in damp soil in full sunshine, and divide clumps in autumn.

☼ ◗ ◖ ❋ ❋ ❋
↕↔ to 60cm (24in)

Paeonia 'Buckeye Belle'

PERENNIAL

'Buckeye Belle' is a spring-flowering peony with semi-double, deep red flowers. It is a vigorous plant, and will eventually form a large clump. Peonies need to be grown in well-drained, fertile soil, but require relatively little aftercare. They are generally pest free, but may be attacked by the fungal disease, peony blight. *Paeonia* 'Belle Center' is very similar to 'Buckeye Belle', but flowers two weeks later, making them good companions.

☼ ☀ ◊ ◑ ❀ ❀ ❀

↕↔ to 85cm (34in)

Primula japonica

PERENNIAL

The Japanese primrose is a robust perennial with a rosette of spoon-shaped, pale green leaves. In spring it produces a stout stem with up to six tiers of as many as 25 white, pink, red or purplish-red flowers. It needs humus-rich, damp soil and is ideally suited to the bog garden and areas of damp woodland or waterside plantings.

☼ ☀ ◑ ◑ ❀ ❀ ❀

↕↔ to 45cm (18in)

Primula japonica 'Miller's Crimson' ♀

PERENNIAL

Candelabra primulas are ideal for a bog garden or planting by a pool, and are grown for their colourful flowers which are arranged in tiers up the stem. The leaves of *Primula japonica* are rounded with finely serrated edges, and in late spring 'Miller's Crimson' bears striking crimson-red flowers. It prefers a shaded spot in moist soil, and looks best when planted in a group. Divide candelabra primulas in early spring.

☀ ◑ ◊ ◖ ❀ ❀ ❀
‡↔ to 45cm (18in)

Rhododendron 'Elizabeth'

EVERGREEN SHRUB

'Elizabeth' is a dwarf rhododendron, making it an excellent choice for small gardens. In late spring, it bears trumpet-shaped, bright red flowers that measure up to 7.5cm (3in) across. These large blooms are borne in clusters of five or six, and create an eye-catching display. Grow this shrub in sun or partial shade in moist, well-drained, acid (lime-free) soil, and mulch annually with leafmould or chipped bark.

☀ ☀ ◊ ◖ ❀ ❀ ❀
‡↔ to 1.5m (5ft)

Rhododendron 'Hotspur'

DECIDUOUS SHRUB

Deciduous azaleas are unsurpassed for vivid spring colour, and 'Hotspur' is no exception, with its clusters of flame-red flowers. The brightly coloured autumn foliage adds to this plant's decorative qualities. Plant it in full sun or partial shade, in moist, fertile, acid (lime-free) soil and mulch annually with leafmould or chipped bark. 'Silver Slipper' is a similar azalea, but bears white flowers.

☼ ◐ ◊ ✿✿✿
‡↔ to 2m (6ft)

Rhododendron prunifolium

SEMI-EVERGREEN SHRUB

One of the latest native azaleas to bloom, plumleaf azalea's orange or crimson flower clusters appear in July and August. Though rare and threatened in its native Georgia and Alabama range, it is readily available at nurseries because it grows easily from seed and cuttings. Several cultivars are available such as 'Apricot Glow' with orange flowers and 'Pine Prunifolium' with bright red flowers. Plant in a woodland or naturalized setting. Grow in partial shade in moist, sandy, acidic soil.

◐ ◊ ✿✿
‡ to 5m (15ft) ↔ to 3m (10ft)

Ribes sanguineum '*Pulborough Scarlet*' ♀

DECIDUOUS SHRUB

The flowering currants create a dazzling display in late spring when their stems are clothed in masses of tiny flowers, arranged in clusters. This variety has an upright habit, dark green, aromatic leaves, and dark red pendent flowers with white centres. It is suitable for an informal hedge that needs only a light trim after flowering. Flowering currants will grow almost anywhere, but prefer a sunny site and moderately fertile soil.

☼ ☀ ◊ ◊ ❀ ❀ ❀ *f*
‡ to 2m (6ft) ↔ to 2.5m (8ft)

Schisandra rubriflora

CLIMBER

This climber has red shoots and lance-shaped or oval dark green leaves. In late spring, it produces striking deep red flowers, measuring up to 2.5cm (1in) across, followed on female plants by red fleshy fruits. Contrary to appearances, it is also fully hardy, and grows well in moist, well-drained soil, in sun or partial shade.

☀ ◊ ◊ ❀ ❀ ❀
‡ to 6m (20ft)

Trillium sessile
PERENNIAL

Wake robin is a clump-forming plant, with three large, irregularly marked leaves. The flowers are borne in late spring and consist of three upright, narrow, maroon-red petals, surrounded by three smaller spreading sepals. It will do well when grown in dappled shade or woodland, in moist, fertile, well-drained soil. It benefits from an annual mulch of leafmould or well-rotted compost. Divide it after the leaves have died.

☀ ◊ ◊ ❁ ❁ ❁
‡ to 38cm (15in) ↔ to 45cm (18in)

Tulipa sprengeri ♀
PERENNIAL BULB

The species tulips are very underrated, with a simplicity and elegance that is hard to beat. This species is one of the latest to flower in spring and has single, bright red flowers with sharply pointed petals. It self seeds and will naturalize if planted in deciduous woodland, and prefers a sunny or lightly shaded site and well-drained, acid (lime-free) soil.

☀ ◊ ◊ ❁ ❁ ❁
‡ to 50cm (20in)

Acer palmatum '**Bloodgood**' ♀

DECIDUOUS TREE

'Bloodgood' is a strong-growing Japanese maple with lobed, finger-like, purple foliage. The colour is particularly vibrant in spring, when the leaves emerge, and intensifies to a rich scarlet in autumn, before the leaves fall. Red-winged seeds appear during summer, which contrast well with the foliage. It makes a good specimen tree for a medium-sized garden, but choose a site sheltered from cold or drying winds or the leaf tips might shrivel. Very little pruning is required.

☼ ☀ ◊ ◑ ❀ ❀ ❀
‡↔ to 5m (15ft)

Allium unifolium ♀

PERENNIAL BULB

This is a decorative ornamental onion from Oregon, in the USA. Each small bulb produces a single greyish-green leaf, which dies before bright pinkish-purple, six-petalled flowers appear in late spring. Plant the bulbs in autumn in a sheltered, sunny position, in well-drained, fertile soil. It suits a rock or gravel garden, and should be grown in bold groups for the best effect.

☼ ◊ ❀ ❀
‡ to 30cm (12in) ↔ to 10cm (4in)

Fritillaria graeca
PERENNIAL BULB

This unusual fritillary is a native of Southern Greece. It has a delicate habit, bearing slim flower stems from which hang pendent, brownish-purple, bell-shaped flowers with a bold green stripe down the centre of the petals. Despite its place of origin, it is very hardy, but needs to be planted in a sunny site and in soil with very good drainage. It will add interest to a rock garden or raised bed, and the bulbs should be planted in groups in the autumn.

☼ ◊ ❀❀❀
‡ to 20cm (8in) ↔ to 5cm (2in)

Fritillaria meleagris
PERENNIAL BULB

In late spring, the snake's head fritillary produces pendent, bell-shaped, purple or white flowers, with a distinctive checkerboard pattern on the petals. It grows well when naturalized in grass, and will often self seed. Take care when mowing, as the young seedlings look very much like grasses. It should be planted in a moist, well-drained soil, and prefers slightly alkaline conditions. If the bulbs become congested, mark the position and they can be lifted in the autumn and replanted elsewhere.

☼ ◔ ◊ ◊ ❀❀❀
‡ to 30cm (12in) ↔ to 8cm (3in)

Ipheion uniflorum

PERENNIAL BULB

In the late spring, this vigorous clump-forming plant produces violet, blue, or white star-shaped flowers. The narrow leaves smell of onions when bruised. Plant bulbs in autumn in a sheltered spot where they can naturalize. They prefer a fertile, moist, well-drained soil, in a sunny situation. In cold gardens, mulch in winter, as plants may be killed by hard frost.

☼ ◊ ◗ ❀❀

‡ to 20cm (8in) ↔ to 2cm (8in)

Lunaria annua

BIENNIAL

Honesty is a fast-growing biennial that will often flower in its first year. It has tall stems, and toothed, heart-shaped, dark green leaves. Small spring flowers with four petals are borne in late spring and come in shades of either purple or white. It often self seeds and will thrive in a woodland garden or at the bottom of a hedge, preferring a site in partial shade or sun, and moist, well-drained soil. Honesty is frequently grown for its round, silvery seed pods, used in dried flower arrangements.

☼ ☀ ◊ ◗ ❀❀❀

‡ to 75cm (30in) ↔ to 30cm (12in)

Phlox douglasii 'Crackerjack' ♀

PERENNIAL

A reliable plant, this dwarf phlox forms a mound of narrow dark green leaves, and in spring is covered with small, bright purplish-magenta flowers. Grow this variety in full sun, in well-drained, fertile soil. It is ideally suited to a rock garden, the cracks of a dry stone wall, or between the slabs of a stone path.

☼ ◊ ✿✿✿

‡ to 8cm (3in) ↔ to 20cm (8in)

Primula pulverulenta ♀

PERENNIAL

This species is one of the most striking of the candelabra primulas. In late spring it bears tiers of deep reddish-purple flowers with a bright red or purple eye. The plants form rosettes of toothed, mid-green leaves, and their stems are covered with a greyish-green downy material called "farina". Plant it in partial shade, in fertile, moist soil. It will tolerate full sun, as long as the soil remains damp throughout the summer. Candelabra primulas look best when they are planted in a group near water.

☼ ◑ ◊ ✿✿✿

‡ to 1m (3ft) ↔ to 60cm (24in)

Pulsatilla vulgaris ♀
PERENNIAL

This is an extremely beautiful clump-forming pasque flower, with attractive divided, feathery foliage. The pendent, bell-shaped flowers have bright purple petals and golden yellow stamens. Ideal for a rock garden, it needs gritty, very well-drained soil and a sunny position, and grows best on alkaline soil. Pasque flowers do not like to have their roots disturbed and are best left undisturbed after planting. Propagate by seed.

☼ ◊ ✿✿✿
‡↔ to 23cm (9in)

Rhododendron 'Hatsugiri'
EVERGREEN SHRUB

This small, compact evergreen azalea in late spring produces a profusion of bright reddish-purple flowers, borne in clusters of three blooms. It is suitable for a container on a patio, or the front of a border, and will tolerate full sun, unlike many of its cousins. Plant it in a free-draining, humus-rich, acid (lime-free) soil or ericaceous compost. In the open garden mulch it generously with leafmould or bark.

☼ ◑ ◊ ✿✿✿
‡↔ to 60cm (24in)

Tulipa 'Blue Parrot'

PERENNIAL BULB

This robust tulip is not truly blue but more violet. It has single flowers with slightly twisted petals, and blooms in late spring. Use it in borders and as a cut flower. *Tulipa* 'Greuze' also has violet-purple flowers, but they are more uniform in shape. The bulbs of both should be planted in late autumn in free-draining soil in full sun.

☼ ◊ ❀❀❀
↕ to 60cm (24in)

Tulipa 'Queen of Night'

PERENNIAL BULB

'Queen of Night' is an elegant hybrid tulip with large, dark maroon-purple flowers. The single cup-shaped blooms are borne on elegant long green stems above lance-shaped, greyish-green leaves. It looks particularly effective when planted with an ivory-coloured variety, such as 'Maureen'. Plant bulbs of this reliably perennial tulip in late autumn in a sunny position and free-draining soil.

☼ ◊ ❀❀❀
↕ to 60cm (24in)

Anemone coronaria '*Lord Lieutenant*'

PERENNIAL

This striking plant originates from the Mediterranean region. The cultivar 'Lord Lieutenant' bears superb, velvety semi-double, deep blue flowers with black eyes, which open in mid- to late spring and are good for cutting. The divided foliage adds to this plant's charms. Plant the small tubers in autumn, preferably in light, sandy soil in full sun.

☼ ◊ ✿ ✿ ✿
‡ to 45cm (18in) ↔ to 15cm (6in)

Brunnera macrophylla ♀

PERENNIAL

This spreading perennial has coarse, long-stalked, heart-shaped leaves and bright blue flowers in spring. It will eventually form a large clump and is good for providing ground cover in semi-shaded situations. It needs moist, well-drained, humus-rich soil. 'Hadspen Cream' has partially variegated leaves with creamy-white margins, which brighten a dull corner. Propagate it by seed in autumn, or division in spring.

☀ ◊ ◊ ✿ ✿ ✿
‡ to 45cm (18in) ↔ to 60cm (24in)

Ceanothus 'Joyce Coulter'

EVERGREEN SHRUB

Tolerant of drought and clay soils, this California lilac attracts birds, bees, and butterflies with its profusion of fragrant blue blossoms from mid- to late spring. Left unpruned, the seedheads dry to a russet colour for added autumn interest. This plant works well in a mixed shrub border or foundation planting. Avoid overwatering. Grow in full sun in very well drained soil.

☼ ◊ ❀❀ *f*

‡ to 1.2m (4ft) ↔ to 3m (10ft)

Corydalis flexuosa ♀

PERENNIAL

This plant has waxy, light green, ferny leaves, and produces clusters of long, tubular, bright blue flowers in late spring. The growing position should be marked to avoid damaging the delicate rootstock during cultivations in autumn and winter. It needs partial shade and should be grown in fertile, moist, well-drained soil.

☼ ◊ ◊ ❀❀❀

‡ to 30cm (12in) ↔ to 20cm (8in)

Gentiana acaulis ♀
EVERGREEN PERENNIAL

The trumpet gentian is a beautiful rock plant that bears vivid, trumpet-shaped, deep blue flowers with green spotted throats. The late spring blooms appear above rosettes of evergreen, glossy leaves that form a slightly raised mound. 'Coelestina' has Cambridge-blue blooms. The trumpet gentian needs to be planted in moist, very well-drained, acid soil in a partly shaded situation.

☼ ◌ ◊ ❀❀❀

‡ to 8cm (3in) ↔ to 30cm (12in)

Hyacinthoides non-scripta
PERENNIAL BULB

In late spring, few sights compare with the beauty of a deciduous woodland carpeted with the fragrant flowers of English bluebells. Replicate these shady conditions, and bluebells will self seed and spread throughout the garden. For the best results, plant the bulbs in the autumn in moist, acid (lime-free), fertile soil, although they will tolerate slightly alkaline conditions. Cultivars with white and mauve flowers are also available.

☼ ☼ ◊ ❀❀❀ *f*

‡ to 40cm (16in) ↔ to 8cm (3in)

Muscari latifolium ♀

PERENNIAL BULB

This is an unusual grape hyacinth, with a spike of tiny, bicoloured, urn-shaped flowers. The lower flowers are purplish-black, while the upper, smaller, infertile flowers are pale blue. The lance-shaped leaves are broader than those of most other muscaris. Plant the small bulbs in a sunny, sheltered site in a well-drained soil, and use at the front of a border or in a rock garden. Established clumps can be divided, or sow seed in summer. This variety is not fully hardy and may be killed by prolonged, hard frosts.

☼ ◊ ❀❀

‡ to 25cm (10in) ↔ to 8cm (3in)

Rosmarinus officinalis 'Sissinghurst Blue' ♀

EVERGREEN SHRUB

Widely grown as a culinary herb and for its aromatic foliage, rosemary makes a decorative shrub, and can be grown as a low hedge. 'Sissinghurst Blue' is a dwarf variety that bears small, pale blue flowers in late spring. It suits a sunny, sheltered location and well-drained soil. Rosemary will respond well to pruning, and old straggly plants can be cut back hard in the spring. Propagate by semi-ripe cuttings in the summer.

☼ ◊ ❀❀ *f*

‡↔ to 50cm (20in)

Symphytum x *uplandicum* 'Variegatum' ♥

PERENNIAL

Russian comfrey is a vigorous, clump-forming perennial, ideal for ground cover in wild gardens. 'Variegatum' has rather coarse, hairy green leaves, with a broad cream margin. The small, pink, tubular flowers are borne on tall stems and eventually turn blue. 'Variegatum' is far less vigorous than the normal green form, and will flourish in moist soil in sun or partial shade. It can be divided in the early spring.

☼ ☼ ◊ ❀ ❀ ❀

‡ to 1m (3ft) ↔ to 60cm (24in)

Syringa vulgaris 'Katherine Havemeyer' ♥

DECIDUOUS SHRUB

A double-flowered form of the common lilac that produces clusters of pink buds that develop into lavender-blue, sweetly perfumed flowers. It grows quickly to form a spreading shrub or small tree, and will perform well when planted in a moist, well-drained fertile soil in full sun or partial shade. Young plants do not need pruning, but rejuvenate old lilac bushes by cutting them back hard after they have flowered. Lilacs are also tolerant of pollution.

☼ ☼ ◊ ◊ ❀ ❀ ❀ *f*

‡↔ to 7m (22ft)

Veronica peduncularis
PERENNIAL

Masses of small, saucer-shaped, deep blue flowers open over a long period from spring to early summer on this mat-forming, low-growing veronica. The glossy, purple-tinted green leaves are also an attractive feature. Grow it in a well-drained soil in a sunny location, such as a rock garden or raised bed. Stocks can be increased by dividing it in the autumn.

☼ ◊ ❀❀❀

‡ to 10cm (4in) ↔ to 60cm (24in)

Wisteria frutescens
CLIMBER

American wisteria is a vigorous twining vine with long, hanging racemes of fragrant, pale blue flowers in summer. Native to the southeastern United States, it thrives in wet woodland settings. Train it on a sturdy trellis or arbour near a patio or pond. Avoid high nitrogen fertilizer. Notable cultivars include 'Amethyst Falls', which has fragrant, lavender-blue flowers, 'Nivea', which produces white flowers, and 'Kate's Dwarf', which has finer foliage and compact purple flower clusters.

☀ ☼ ◊ ◆ ❀❀❀ *f*

‡ to 10m (30ft)

Adonis vernalis

PERENNIAL

This hardy clump-forming perennial originates from Europe, where it is often found in rocky, exposed sites. In spring it produces golden yellow flowers above deeply dissected bright green leaves. Grow it in a raised bed, rock or gravel garden in full sun and well-drained, preferably alkaline soil.

☼ ◊ ❋❋❋

‡↔ to 30cm (12in)

Aurinia saxatilis ♀

EVERGREEN PERENNIAL

Gold dust, formerly known as *Alyssum saxatile*, is an evergreen with greyish-green leaves. In early spring it produces masses of small, bright yellow flowers. Other gold dusts include 'Citrina', which bears bright lemon-yellow flowers, and 'Compacta', a small variety with golden-yellow blooms. It needs a sunny, well-drained situation, and can be grown on a wall, to spill over the front of a raised bed, or in a rock garden.

☼ ◊ ❋❋❋

‡ to 23cm (9in) ↔ to 30cm (12in)

Berberis x *stenophylla* ❦
EVERGREEN SHRUB

This vigorous, spiny plant forms an elegant, spreading bush with arching branches covered with clusters of deep yellow flowers. The blooms appear in late spring, and are followed in summer by waxy black fruit. Plant it in full sun in a well-drained, fertile soil. It is most useful when grown as a dense intruder-proof hedge, which should be clipped after flowering has finished.

☼ ◊ ✿ ✿ ✿
‡ to 3m (10ft) ↔ to 5m (15ft)

Berberis thunbergii 'Aurea'
DECIDUOUS SHRUB

A beautiful barberry with bright golden-yellow leaves, it is much shorter than other varieties, and is suitable for small gardens. In late spring it bears clusters of pink-tinged, pale yellow flowers, which are followed in autumn by bright red berries. While it needs good light, bright sun can scorch the yellow leaves, but in dense shade the foliage will turn green. It grows happily in most soils.

☼ ◐ ◊ ◊ ✿ ✿ ✿
‡ to 1.5m (5ft) ↔ to 2m (6ft)

Colchicum luteum
PERENNIAL CORM

Colchicums are best known for their bright pink flowers, produced in the autumn, but this species is different. It has golden-yellow, goblet-shaped flowers that appear from mid-spring. It needs very good drainage and should be planted in gritty, fertile soil in full sun. It can be quite difficult to grow outdoors because the corms need to be kept completely dry when they are dormant. In wet climates, grow it in pots in a cold frame and take it outside in the spring.

☼ ◊ ❀❀❀

‡ to 10cm (4in) ↔ to 8cm (3in)

Cytisus x praecox '**Allgold**' ♀
EVERGREEN SHRUB

This small, free-flowering broom bears a profusion of dark yellow blooms from mid- to late spring. Ideal for growing in a sunny mixed border, it needs a deep, slightly fertile, well-drained soil. After flowering, it can be trimmed back to keep it in shape, although pruning is not essential. 'Warminster' has a similar habit to 'Allgold', but produces creamy-yellow flowers.

☼ ◊ ❀❀❀

‡ to 1.2m (4ft) ↔ to 1.5m (5ft)

Dionysia tapetodes

EVERGREEN PERENNIAL

This alpine plant forms a tight cushion of small, greyish-green leaves, and in the late spring and early summer bright yellow, upward facing flowers appear above the foliage. It is hardy, but needs dry, very well-drained soil and full sun to succeed. In its natural environment, it grows in the crevices of rocks, and is best suited to growing in pots of alpine compost under glass to protect it from a damp environment and winter rains.

☼ ◊ ❀❀❀

‡ to 1cm (½in) ↔ to 15cm (6in)

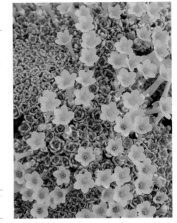

Doronicum x *excelsum* 'Harpur Crewe'

PERENNIAL

Bright, golden-yellow, daisy-like flowers adorn this leopard's bane in late spring. The blooms are held on tall erect stems above decorative, heart-shaped, basal leaves. Plant it in a moist, fertile soil in partial shade, and grow it in groups to enliven an early herbaceous border or woodland garden with dazzling colour. Leopard's bane can be propagated by division in autumn.

☼ ◊ ❀❀❀

‡↔ to 60cm (24in)

Epimedium pinnatum subsp. *colchicum* ♀
EVERGREEN PERENNIAL

An attractive clump-former, this plant produces rounded leaves divided into five leaflets, and golden-yellow single flowers, which are relatively large for an epimedium, measuring up to 18mm (¾in) across. It prefers a semi-shaded situation and heavy, moisture-retentive, fertile soil. Although slower to spread than the species, the leaves still make excellent ground cover. The appearance of the plant will be improved if the old foliage is clipped over in late winter.

☀ ◊ ❀❀❀
‡↔ to 30cm (12in)

Erysimum 'Bredon' ♀
EVERGREEN PERENNIAL

The bright, chrome-yellow flowers of this shrubby evergreen perennial appear from late spring above a mound of grey-green foliage. It will suit position near the front of a mixed or herbaceous border in poor or not-too-fertile, well-drained soil. Alternatively, try mixing different varieties, such as orange-yellow 'Butterscotch', with tulips to create colourful spring displays in beds or containers. Trim after flowering to keep compact. Erysimums are ideal for hot, dry sites.

☀ ◊ ❀❀❀
‡↔ to 45cm (18in)

Erysimum 'Moonlight'
EVERGREEN PERENNIAL

A mat-forming perennial wallflower
with evergreen, greyish-green, lance-
shaped leaves. Throughout spring and
early summer it produces clusters of
slightly fragrant, pale sulphur-yellow
flowers. It is rather short-lived, but it
makes an excellent subject for a dry
wall, gravel or raised bed, or a rock
garden. Plant it in full sunshine, in
poor, gritty, very well-drained soil.

☼ ◐ ◊ ❀❀❀ *f*
‡ to 25cm (10in) ↔ to 45cm (18in)

Euphorbia polychroma ♀
PERENNIAL

This plant is guaranteed to brighten up
a dull spring morning. The stems are
clothed in bright green leaves, which
form a rounded clump, and from late
spring and well into summer it bears
acid yellow flowers, surrounded by a
collar of striking greenish-yellow bracts.
A tolerant plant, it will grow on most
well-drained soils, and can be used at
the front of a border or in a woodland
garden. Care should be taken when
pruning the stems, because the latex
they exude can irritate the skin.

☼ ◊ ◗ ❀❀❀
‡↔ to 50cm (20in)

Fritillaria imperialis '**Maxima Lutea**' ♀

PERENNIAL BULB

The value of crown imperials in the late spring garden is beyond question. The tall stems carry a tuft of shiny, green leafy bracts at the top, beneath which hang a number of bright yellow, bell-shaped flowers. The bulbs should be planted in late summer in full sun and a deep, well-drained soil, where they will not be disturbed. 'Rubra' is more robust, with orange-red flowers and purple stems.

☼ ◊ ❀❀❀

↕ to 1.5m (5ft) ↔ to 30cm (12in)

Genista hispanica

DECIDUOUS SHRUB

A mound-forming shrub, Spanish gorse produces a profusion of golden-yellow, pea-like, small flowers on green prickly stems in late spring and early summer. Plant it in a well-drained soil and sunny position, such as the front of a raised bed. Spanish gorse is not totally hardy and may be killed by severe frosts, so in colder gardens, plant it in a sheltered position by a warm wall to prevent it from being damaged.

☼ ◊ ❀❀

↕ to 75cm (30in) ↔ to 1.5m (5ft)

Genista tinctoria
DECIDUOUS SHRUB

Dyer's greenweed is a small and spreading bush that freely bears clusters of bright yellow pea flowers from spring and into summer. The narrow, mid-green foliage is a good foil to the flowers. Flat seedpods follow the flowers. 'Royal Gold' and 'Flore Pleno' are both notable garden varieties that flower profusely. Trim after flowering, but not into old wood as this may not grow back. Good planted in a raised bed or rock garden, or near the front of a border.

☼ ☀ ◊ ◊ ❀ ❀ ❀
‡↔ to 50cm (20in)

Iris 'Golden Harvest'
PERENNIAL BULB

This iris produces pure golden-yellow flowers that are good for cutting from the middle of spring to early summer. It requires a very well-drained neutral or slightly alkaline soil and a sunny site, as bulbs may not survive wet conditions while they are dormant. Large clumps should be divided as soon as possible after flowering.

☼ ◊ ❀ ❀ ❀
‡ to 80cm (32in) ↔ to 15cm (6in)

Kerria japonica '**Golden Guinea**' ♀
DECIDUOUS SHRUB

Kerria is an easy-to-grow and vigorous shrub, with graceful, arching green stems. One of the most popular forms is 'Pleniflora', which has double, deep yellow flowers. 'Golden Guinea' is less vigorous, with single yellow blooms. It grows best in free-draining soil and full sun, but can tolerate light shade. Kerria spreads by suckers, which can be dug up in the autumn to propagate it. Cut back the stems after flowering to keep it within bounds.

☼ ☼ ◊ ❀ ❀ ❀
↕ to 2m (6ft) ↔ to 2.5m (8ft)

Laburnum anagyroides
DECIDUOUS TREE

The laburnum is a widely-grown garden plant and in late spring produces long, pendent clusters of pea-like, bright yellow flowers. Laburnums will grow in almost any soil, as long as it is not waterlogged, but they need full sun to flourish. They are easily propagated from seed sown in the autumn – but remember that laburnum seeds are very poisonous. *L. x watereri* 'Vossii' has larger blooms held in longer clusters.

☼ ◊ ◊ ❀ ❀ ❀
↕↔ to 8m (25ft)

Meconopsis cambrica
PERENNIAL

The Welsh poppy has single lemon-yellow or orange flowers, and blooms from late spring to the autumn. The flowers are borne on long stems above fern-like, greyish-green foliage. 'Flore Pleno' has double yellow flowers, and comes true from seed. Welsh poppies are happiest in partial shade and moist, acid (lime-free) soil, although they will tolerate alkaline conditions. They have a tendency to self seed and will spread quickly, unless the seedheads are cut off before they ripen.

to 45cm (18in) ↔ to 30cm (12in)

Narcissus jonquilla ♀
PERENNIAL BULB

Wild jonquils are valued for their sweet fragrance and small yellow blooms that appear in spring. Each stem produces five or six bright yellow, single flowers above linear, almost cylindrical leaves. These narcissi look lovely naturalized in grass or beneath deciduous trees, and also make wonderful container plants for a patio, where their fragrance can be enjoyed at close range. Plant the bulbs in free-draining soil in sun for the best results.

to 30cm (12in) ↔ to 8cm (3in)

Paeonia delavayi var. *ludlowii*
DECIDUOUS SHRUB

When given the correct conditions, the Tibetan tree peony will eventually form a broad, spreading bush. In late spring, it bears bright yellow flowers, and has decorative, lobed, deeply-cut foliage, borne on graceful arching stems. Grow this tree peony in a full sun or light shade on moist, well-drained soil. It is easily propagated from seed. Cut out one or two of the older stems in late winter to rejuvenate established plants.

☼ ☽ ◊ ◊ ✿ ✿ ✿
‡ to 2m (6ft) ↔ to 3m (9ft)

Paeonia mlokosewitschii ♀
PERENNIAL

There are few more desirable plants than "Molly-the-Witch", with its large primrose-yellow flowers and glaucous green divided foliage. The stems are tinted pink or red. Slow-growing at first it can eventually form a wide-spreading clump. It grows happily in full sun or dappled shade, although a well-drained soil is essential. Propagate it from seed. Although peonies tend to resent being disturbed, large clumps can be divided in the autumn.

☼ ☽ ◊ ✿ ✿ ✿
‡↔ to 75cm (30in)

Primula prolifera ♀

EVERGREEN PERENNIAL

This candelabra primula forms rosettes of pale evergreen leaves with serrated edges. The fragrant, golden-yellow flowers appear in late spring. Like all candelabra primulas, it requires deep, fertile, neutral or slightly acid (lime-free) soil, which does not dry out in summer. It looks particularly striking when planted in a large group near water. Divide congested clumps in the early spring, or grow plants from seed.

☀ ◊ ❄❄❄ *f*
‡↔ to 60cm (24in)

Primula veris ♀

EVERGREEN PERENNIAL

The cowslip is one of the best loved spring flowers, and produces clusters of pale yellow, fragrant blooms throughout the season. The erect flower stems are surrounded by a rosette of evergreen, deeply-veined leaves. Cowslips should be planted in a partly shaded site, in well-drained, moist soil. They can be grown in full sun, as long as the soil remains permanently moist. Grow it from seed in spring, or divide large clumps in the autumn or early spring.

☀ ☀ ◊ ◊ ❄❄❄ *f*
‡↔ to 25cm (10in)

Quercus rubra 'Aurea'
DECIDUOUS TREE

This yellow-leaved variety of the red oak makes a striking landscape tree when the leaves emerge in spring, and their colour is at its most intense. The leaves fade to yellow-green in summer, and become yellow-orange in autumn before they fall. Red oaks need little in the way of maintenance, but any dead, diseased or crossing branches can be removed in winter. They are ideal for medium to large gardens, and cope well in urban environments. There is a more compact golden form called 'Magic Fire'.

☼ ☀ ◊ ◉ ✻ ✻ ✻
‡ to 8m (25ft) ↔ to 4m (12ft)

Rhododendron luteum ♀
DECIDUOUS SHRUB

This widely-grown deciduous azalea in spring bears large numbers of strongly fragrant, funnel-shaped, bright yellow flowers. The lance-shaped leaves turn shades of purple, red, and orange in the autumn. This azalea prefers full sun, but will tolerate a little shade. Plant it with the root ball just proud of the surface in moist, well-drained acid (lime-free) soil, and mulch annually with leafmould or chipped bark.

☼ ☀ ◊ ◉ ✻ ✻ ✻ *f*
‡↔ to 4m (12ft)

Rhododendron macabeanum ♀

EVERGREEN TREE

Many people consider this to be the best of all the yellow rhododendrons. In mid- to late spring it produces large trusses of deep yellow flowers with purple spots on the inside. Very hardy, it eventually grows into a substantial tree, making it only really suitable for large gardens, where it is best planted in dappled shade beneath deciduous trees. It enjoys moist, well-drained acid (lime-free) soil. Mulch annually with leafmould or chipped bark.

☼ ◐ ◊ ❄❄❄
‡ to 15m (50ft) ↔ to 6m (20ft)

Ribes odoratum

DECIDUOUS SHRUB

The buffalo currant is an upright shrub with attractive three-lobed, bright green leaves. From mid- to late spring clusters of small fragrant, tubular, golden-yellow flowers with bright red anthers appear, followed in summer by black berries. In autumn its foliage turns various shades of red and purple. Plant it in full sun or light shade in well-drained soil. It is easy to propagate by taking hardwood cuttings during the winter.

☼ ◑ ◊ ❄❄❄ *f*
‡↔ to 2m (6ft)

Trillium luteum ♥

PERENNIAL

This clump-forming plant has silver-green mottled leaves with pointed tips. Its yellow, fragrant flowers appear in late spring and are composed of three narrow green sepals and three upright, pale yellow petals. It is a good choice for a woodland garden, and should be grown in a shaded position in moist, well-drained, acid (lime-free) soil. In the autumn, mulch it with well-rotted leafmould.

☼ ☀ ◊ ◖ ❀ ❀ ❀ *f*

‡ to 40cm (16in) ↔ to 30cm (12in)

Trollius europaeus

PERENNIAL

The European globeflower is a reliable plant for moist soils. Resembling a large buttercup, the spherical, lemon-yellow flowers appear in late spring and early summer. It also has attractive, glossy, divided foliage. This globeflower can be planted in full sun or partial shade and is suitable for bog gardens, as it does particularly well in fertile soil that never dries out. 'Canary Bird' is one of the best cultivars. European globeflowers can be grown from seed, or divided in the autumn.

☼ ☀ ◖ ❀ ❀ ❀

‡ to 60cm (24in) ↔ to 45cm (18in)

Tulipa 'Golden Apeldoorn'

PERENNIAL BULB

A widely grown single-flowered tulip
with bright golden-yellow flowers. The
base of the inner petals is marked with
a large black patch that disguises the
black stamens. Plant it in well-drained,
fertile soil in a sunny position. Most
tulips look best when grown with a
contrasting colour; this yellow variety
would look good with the cherry-red
'Apeldoorn', or scarlet 'Oxford' in a
bedding scheme.

☼ ◊ ❀ ❀ ❀
‡ to 60cm (24in)

Tulipa 'West Point' ♀

PERENNIAL BULB

This is a striking lily-flowered tulip, the
late spring primrose-yellow flowers of
which have pointed petals that curve
slightly outwards at the tips. It should
be planted in a sunny situation in well-
drained, fertile soil, and looks stunning
when combined with a bright red tulip,
such as the lily-flowered 'Mariette'. It is
particularly suitable for containers.

☼ ◊ ❀ ❀ ❀
‡ to 50cm (20in)

Uvularia grandiflora ♀
PERENNIAL

An unusual spreading plant, the large merrybells has erect stems that droop at the tip, and in late spring carry narrow, bell-shaped, yellow flowers. It should be planted in deep, moist, well-drained soil. Merrybells is a hardy plant, and will perform well when grown in a shady border, or in the dappled shade of a woodland garden. It is vulnerable to slug and snail damage and will need to be protected from these pests during the growing season.

☀ ◐ ◊ ◊ ✽✽✽

↕ to 60cm (24in) ↔ to 30cm (12in)

Vancouveria chrysantha
PERENNIAL

Golden inside-out flower is a semi-evergreen perennial native to California and Oregon. From late spring to early summer, loose panicles of dainty yellow flowers appear above the thick, dark green, diamond-shaped leaves. Best planted as a ground cover in a woodland or naturalized setting. Grow in partial shade in moist soil.

☀ ◊ ✽✽✽

↕ to 30cm (12in) ↔ to 60cm (24in)

Viola biflora
PERENNIAL

A dwarf violet with attractive kidney- or heart-shaped leaves, this plant spreads slowly by creeping roots. In the spring and early summer it produces solitary or pairs of small, deep lemon-yellow flowers, the lower petals of which have purple-brown streaks that radiate out from the centre. It performs well when planted in well-drained, moist soil in a partially shaded situation, and is suitable for a woodland garden.

☀ ◊ ◊ ❀❀❀
‡ to 8cm (3in) ↔ to 20cm (8in)

Viola 'Jackanapes' ♥
EVERGREEN PERENNIAL

This violet has toothed, bright green leaves, and spreading stems that bear bicoloured flowers in late spring and throughout the summer. The small blooms are deep maroon-purple at the top, and bright yellow at the base, with purple streaks radiating from the centre. 'Jackanapes' should be grown in moist, well-drained soil in full sun or partial shade. It is short-lived and needs to be propagated regularly by taking stem-tip cuttings in late summer.

☼ ☀ ◊ ◊ ❀❀❀
‡ to 12cm (5in) ↔ to 20cm (8in)

Berberis linearifolia 'Orange King'

EVERGREEN SHRUB

This attractive barberry has glossy, dark green leaves, and strong, upright, spiny stems. The cup-shaped, bright orange flowers, borne in small clusters, appear in late spring, and are then followed in late summer by waxy black fruit. It will grow well in full sun and deep, moist, well-drained soil. To propagate it, take softwood cuttings in late summer.

☼ ◊ ◖ ◗ ❀ ❀ ❀
‡↔ to 2.5m (8ft)

Primula x *bulleesiana*

EVERGREEN PERENNIAL

This beautiful candelabra primula is a hybrid between *P. bulleyana* and *P. beesiana*. Plants may have orange, yellow, pink, red, and purple flowers, borne in tiers around stout stems. Plant it in a slightly shaded situation in moist, neutral or slightly acid (lime-free) soil. The plant overwinters as a rosette of mid-green leaves, and can be divided, or grown from seed, in the spring.

◑ ◗ ❀ ❀ ❀
‡↔ to 60cm (24in)

Primula bulleyana ♀

PERENNIAL

Clusters of crimson flowers that quickly fade to bright orange are borne on this striking candelabra primula in the late spring. The toothed, rounded, lance-shaped, mid-green leaves form a tight rosette at the base of the plant. It suits waterside plantings and bog gardens as it enjoys partial shade and deep, moist, fertile, neutral or slightly acid soil that does not dry out in summer. It can be propagated by division in spring.

☼ ◊ ❄❄❄

↔ to 60cm (24in)

Rhododendron 'Frome'

DECIDUOUS SHRUB

A medium-sized deciduous azalea, this form has orangy-yellow, frilly, funnel-shaped flowers with red marks on their throats. It forms a large, dome-shaped bush, and is suitable for the middle or back of a mixed border, or beneath deciduous trees. It needs a moist, well-drained, fertile, acid (lime-free) soil in partial shade. Mulch it annually with leafmould or chipped bark.

☼ ◊ ◊ ❄❄❄

↔ to 1.5m (5ft)

EARLY SUMMER

Not a day goes by without more flowers opening somewhere in the garden. Hanging baskets and containers, brimming with pelargoniums, verbenas, and other tender bedding, can be put out now all danger of frost has passed. The herbaceous border reaches a peak of perfection: peonies and delphiniums surround their supports, holding their flowers up against the weather for pure enjoyment, while bearded irises, daylilies, starry alliums, and hardy geraniums bloom in profusion and dazzling shades.

In the light shade of trees, making cool leafy ground cover, grow hostas, heucheras, and bugle (*Ajuga*). Monkshood (*Aconitum*) and the feathery clumps of goatsbeard (*Aruncus*) will thrive in moist conditions, but for permanently wet soil and pond margins the beauty of the Japanese iris is without peer.

Mediterranean shrubs such as genistas, thymes, and phlomis revel in the hot dry conditions.

More dramatic bursts of colour are provided by sun-loving annuals, especially those sown in autumn, like eschscholzia. Half-hardy salvias can be used for bedding or to fill gaps, perhaps replacing oriental poppies after their flowers have gone. All will flower into autumn if they are deadheaded – the key to extending the display of many annuals and, of course, roses.

SUMMER ROMANCE

Most evocative of summer are the roses, gracing many garden situations with fragrance and colour throughout the season. Modern shrub roses are easier going than hybrid teas, often having the characteristics of old roses but flowering for longer. Ground cover roses are healthy and very versatile; for example, SURREY trails over sunny banks or walls, but is also at home in a large pot or hanging basket, while 'Madame Knorr' makes a spectacular thorny hedge.

Achillea ptarmica 'The Pearl' ♀

PERENNIAL

Sneezewort is a slender perennial with narrow, serrated, dark green leaves. From early to late summer, 'The Pearl' bears abundant small, pompon-shaped flowers with tiny, white petals. It is happiest when planted in a sunny position, in well-drained fertile soil. Propagate it by division in autumn. The flowerheads dry well.

☼ ◊ ❀❀❀
↔ to 75cm (30in)

Actinidia kolomikta ♀

CLIMBER

This deciduous, woody-stemmed climber, with its green, white, and purple-red variegated leaves, is ideal for clothing a pergola or a wall. Fragrant white flowers are borne in clusters in early summer, and are sometimes followed by yellow-green fruits. Plant in fertile, well-drained soil and provide shelter from strong winds. It will grow in partial shade but full sun will give the best leaf colour. Propagate by semi-ripe cuttings in late summer. Prune lightly in early spring to keep it within bounds.

☼ ☀ ◊ ❀❀❀ *f*
↕ to 4m (12ft)

Aesculus parviflora ♀
DECIDUOUS SHRUB

A close relative of the horse chestnut, the bottlebrush buckeye has similar leaves, which are divided into several long, slightly waxy, bronze-green leaflets. From early summer it produces tall spikes of white flowers. In the autumn the leaves turn bright yellow. It is a very tolerant plant, and can be grown in full sun or partial shade, preferring fertile, slightly moist but well-drained soil. The bush spreads by suckers, which can be separated and replanted, or removed to control the spread.

☼ ☀ ◐ ◊ ❀ ❀ ❀
‡ to 3m (10ft) ↔ to 5m (15ft)

Aruncus dioicus ♀
PERENNIAL

Goatsbeard forms large clumps of fern-like, mid-green foliage. From early to midsummer, tiny, star-shaped, white flowers appear on fluffy plumes up to 50cm (20in) long. An easy-going plant, it is tolerant of sun or shade, and moist or dry, reasonably fertile soil. It suits a sunny border or damp ground by water, or a woodland border. Divide plants in early spring or autumn.

☼ ☀ ◐ ◊ ❀ ❀ ❀
‡ to 2m (6ft) ↔ to 1.2m (4ft)

Cardiocrinum giganteum

PERENNIAL BULB

The giant lily is an impressive plant, with up to 20 fragrant, trumpet-shaped blooms on top of a tall, stout stem that does not require staking. It forms a rosette of dark green, glossy leaves at the base. For the best results, give it a shady, sheltered position in moist, humus-rich soil. Although the lily dies after flowering, the bulb forms plenty of small bulblets that can be dug up and replanted immediately. They will be ready to flower in three to five years. Protect new growth over winter with a dry mulch.

☼ ◊ ✿✿✿ *f*

‡ to 3m (10ft) ↔ to 1.1m (3½ft)

Cistus ladanifer ♀

EVERGREEN SHRUB

This is a substantial, though often short-lived, upright shrub. The branches are covered with aromatic leaves, and from early summer, it bears large quantities of white, saucer-shaped flowers with yellow centres. Each papery petal carries a crimson spot at its base. A native of the Mediterranean, this shrub thrives in full sun and well-drained soil, and suits a gravel garden or a site close to a sunny wall. It also grows well in coastal gardens. Established plants will not tolerate being moved.

☼ ◊ ✿✿ *f*

‡ to 2m (6ft) ↔ to 1.5m (5ft)

Clematis florida var. *sieboldiana*
CLIMBER

This clematis is widely grown for its striking early summer flowers, with their creamy-white petals and rich purple stamens. Severe winters may damage early top growth, so plant it in a sheltered spot in humus-rich, well-drained soil, or in a container of loam-based potting compost. In early spring, prune stems back to a strong pair of buds, approximately 20cm (8in) above the ground. Train it along supporting wires, trellis, or over a tripod.

☼ ◑ ◊ ❋ ❋
↕ to 2.5m (8ft)

Clematis 'Silver Moon'
CLIMBER

Large, silvery-white flowers, with a hint of mauve, make this among the most attractive of the early summer-flowering clematis. Rarely growing taller than 2m (6ft), it is ideal for a small garden. It needs a sheltered spot in sun or partial shade, with its roots in shade, and well-drained, humus-rich, fertile soil. Provide it with a support or allow it to scramble through shrubs. In early spring, remove dead stems and prune back the other shoots to a couple of strong buds.

☼ ◑ ◊ ❋ ❋ ❋
↕ to 2m (6ft)

Cornus canadensis ♀
PERENNIAL

Spreading by means of underground stems, the creeping dogwood will provide a low-growing carpet of lush greenery beneath shrubs or trees. The bright green, oval leaves, which grow in opposite pairs, are a perfect foil for the creamy white, petal-like bracts that surround the tiny green-red flowers. It does best on moist but well-drained, slightly acid (lime-free) soil in partial shade. Divide established plants in early spring or autumn.

☀ ◐ ❀❀❀
‡ to 15cm (6in) ↔ to 30cm (12in)

Cornus 'Norman Hadden' ♀
DECIDUOUS TREE

'Norman Hadden' bears masses of large, creamy white, petal-like bracts in early summer which, after a few weeks, turn a deep shade of pink. The blooms are followed in autumn by strawberry-like fruits. Yet another of its attractions is that, with age, its bark will start to peel, creating a handsome effect. For best results, plant in a sunny or partially shaded position, protected from strong winds, in well-drained, neutral to acid (lime-free), fertile soil.

☀ ☀ ◐ ❀❀❀
‡↔ to 8m (25ft)

Crambe cordifolia ♀

PERENNIAL

This extremely vigorous perennial has large, dark green, crinkled leaves. In wonderful contrast, small, highly fragrant, star-shaped flowers are borne in a white froth on stiffly branching, slender stems. To accommodate its sprawling habit, provide it with plenty of space. Although it will tolerate poor soil, it prefers a sunny position in well-drained fertile soil. Plant it in a gravel garden or herbaceous border.

☼ ☽ ◊ ❀ ❀ ❀ *f*
‡ to 2m (6ft) ↔ to 1.2m (4ft)

Delphinium 'Butterball'

PERENNIAL

In summer, this vigorous perennial bears tall spikes of white, semi-double flowers with deep yellow eyes. For the greatest impact, plant in groups of up to ten in well-drained, fertile soil in full sun. The stems will need supporting with canes from a young age to prevent them snapping in strong winds. Feed the plants in spring and remove the faded flowerheads, and you may be rewarded with a second burst of flowers.

☼ ◊ ❀ ❀ ❀
‡ to 1.5m (5ft) ↔ to 90cm (36in)

Deutzia gracilis
DECIDUOUS SHRUB

An upright, spreading shrub, it bears clusters of fragrant, pure white flowers in early summer. Plant it in a sunny site in fertile, well-drained soil, and provide protection from late-spring frosts which can damage the flowers. Prune back the old shoots after flowering has finished. Take softwood cuttings in summer and hardwood cuttings in autumn.

☼ ◊ ❀❀❀ *f*
↕↔ to 1m (3ft)

Dianthus 'Haytor White' ♀
PERENNIAL

This white, modern pink is widely grown for cutting, and will fill a room with its delicious clove scent. The double flowers have deeply serrated petals. Pinks do best in a sunny position at the front of a border or by paving, and should be planted in reasonably fertile, well-drained soil. In spring, pinch out the growing tips to promote bushy growth. Deadheading will help prolong flowering. Take cuttings from non-flowering stems in early spring.

☼ ◊ ❀❀❀ *f*
↕ to 45cm (18in) ↔ to 40cm (16in)

Digitalis purpurea
f. *albiflora* ♀

BIENNIAL

This foxglove will grow easily in most gardens, provided you give it moist but well-drained soil and a little shade. In the first year it produces a large rosette of oval-shaped, deep green leaves, followed, in early summer of the next year, by a tall spire of pure white flowers. Sow seed in spring, and plant out the young seedlings in autumn. Foxgloves look best when planted in groups in front of a dark background by shrubs or in a dappled woodland.

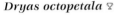

☀ ◐ ◊ ❀ ❀ ❀

‡ to 1.5m (5ft) ↔ to 45cm (18in)

Dryas octopetala ♀

EVERGREEN SHRUB

The dainty flowers of the mountain avens belie its tough nature – this plant can cope with the harsh conditions on top of windswept, stony slopes and cliffs. What it lacks in height it more than makes up for in spread; its glossy, dark green leaves will quickly fill crevices between rocks, gaps in dry-stone walls, or form large mats in a gravel garden. Grow it in well-drained, gritty soil in sun or partial shade.

☀ ◐ ◊ ❀ ❀ ❀

‡ to 6cm (2½in) ↔ indefinite

Erica carnea 'Springwood White' ♀

EVERGREEN PERENNIAL

Early-flowering heathers can bring a beautiful carpet of colour to the garden in spring and early summer, sometimes flowering as early as late winter. This vigorous, trailing variety gives a profusion of white flowers for up to two months above bright, evergreen foliage. It tolerates acid soils and can be grown in a container or trough. The flowers are good for cutting. Trim as soon as the flowers begin to fade to ensure that next year's flower buds are not damaged.

☼ ◐ ◊ ◑ ✿✿✿

↕ to 25cm (10in) ↔ to 55cm (22in)

Galega officinalis 'Alba' ♀

PERENNIAL

An ideal plant for the back of a sunny border, this goat's rue bears small, pea-like, white flowers in early summer. For the best results, plant it in sun or partial shade in moist, well-drained soil. If the soil is rich the stems will be floppy and the plant will need supporting, either with canes inserted in late spring, or by allowing it to grow through other open, sturdy shrubs. Propagate by dividing established plants between late autumn and spring.

☼ ◑ ◊ ◑ ✿✿✿

↕ to 1.5m (5ft) ↔ to 90cm (36in)

Gillenia trifoliata

PERENNIAL

This is an upright, herbaceous perennial with red-tinted, branched stems and small, single, white to pinkish-white flowers which are good for cutting. Plant it in a well-drained, fertile soil. Originally from the woods of North America, it enjoys the light or dappled shade of a woodland garden or shady border beneath deciduous trees. In exposed sites the tall, wiry stems will need supporting early in the year. Divide large clumps in spring or autumn.

☀ ◐ ◊ ❀❀❀
‡ to 1.2m (4ft) ↔ to 60cm (24in)

Gladiolus callianthus

PERENNIAL CORM

This half-hardy gladiolus may be sold under its former name of acidanthera. The fragrant white flowers, borne on tall, arching stems, have deep red or purple throats, and are good for cutting. Plant the corms in a sunny border, in well-drained, fertile soil. They will rot quickly in wet conditions, and it is advisable to mix grit with heavier soil when planting. They will not survive a cold winter, so dig up the corms in early autumn, dry them and store in a frost-free place until planting in spring.

☀ ◊ ❀❀ *f*
‡ to 1m (3ft) ↔ to 5cm (2in)

x *Halimiocistus sahucii* ♀
EVERGREEN SHRUB

A spreading shrub with narrow, dark green, downy leaves, this species bears a profusion of saucer-shaped, white flowers from early summer to autumn. It makes a welcome addition to a gravel or rock garden, or a raised bed, where it will enjoy basking in the full heat of the sun. It does well in poor soils and very well-drained conditions are a must. If in doubt, improve drainage by adding grit to the soil.

☀ ◊ ✽✽✽

↕ to 45cm (18in) ↔ to 90cm (36in)

Hebe 'Pewter Dome' ♀
EVERGREEN SHRUB

A rounded, spreading shrub, it bears greyish-green leaves and spikes of small, white flowers for several weeks from early summer. Grow in reasonably fertile, well-drained soil in sun or partial shade. Provide some shade from strong sun, which can burn the leaves. It is suitable for a rock garden or a mixed border, and is good for seaside gardens. In mild areas it can be used as a low hedge. It needs no pruning, but hedges can be clipped lightly after flowering.

☀ ☀ ◊ ✽✽

↕ to 40cm (16in) ↔ to 60cm (24in)

Helianthemum 'Wisley White'

EVERGREEN SHRUB

Rock roses are attractive dwarf shrubs that bear an abundance of small, saucer-shaped flowers all summer. The papery flowers of 'Wisley White' are pure white with yellow stamens, offset by greyish-green leaves. Rock roses thrive in well-drained soil on sun-baked banks, cracks in paving, and in gravel gardens. Trim after flowering to keep the shape of the bush neat. Propagate by semi-ripe cuttings in early summer.

☼ ◊ ❀❀❀

‡ to 23cm (9in) ↔ to 30cm (12in)

Hesperis matronalis var. *albiflora*

PERENNIAL

The tall flower spikes of sweet rocket are a favourite with butterflies. Make the most of the heavenly scent – which, incidentally, grows stronger after dusk – by planting it alongside a path or patio. It is short-lived and best grown as a biennial. Plants are easy to raise from seed sown *in situ* outdoors. Grow in full sun, in fertile, moist, well-drained soil. It is also tolerant of poor soil.

☼ ◊ ◊ ❀❀❀ *f*

‡ to 75cm (30in) ↔ to 60cm (24in)

Hydrangea petiolaris

CLIMBER

The climbing hydrangea is a woody-stemmed, deciduous, self-clinging climber. It is a useful flowering plant for shady walls, where it bears large and attractive, lacecap-like heads of creamy white flowers in summer. The mid-green leaves are oval and coarsely toothed. Plants can sometimes be slow to establish, but once the space is filled, trim back overlong shoots after flowering. Grow in any reliably moist, fertile soil, and in areas with very cold winters, choose a sheltered site.

☼ ☀ ◐ ◊ ❀ ❀
‡ to 15m (50ft)

Iberis amara

ANNUAL

In summer, this fast-growing annual produces masses of white to purplish-white scented flowers which are borne in dense, flattish clusters. Enjoying a sunny site and well-drained soil, it is perfect for edging a path or planting in a gravel garden or raised bed. Sow seed *in situ*, in spring or autumn.

☼ ◊ ❀ ❀ ❀ *f*
‡ to 30cm (12in) ↔ to 15cm (6in)

Iris 'Bold Print'

PERENNIAL

Bearded iris come in a huge range of colours and subtle colour combinations. 'Bold Print' has striking white flowers that are edged and lightly veined with deep purple. Grow it in full sun, in a well-drained, neutral to slightly acid soil. Divide congested clumps in late summer. When planting, make sure that the tops of the rhizomes are exposed to the sun.

☼ ◊ ❀ ❀ ❀

‡ to 55cm (22in) ↔ indefinite

Lamium maculatum 'White Nancy' ♥

PERENNIAL

Ideal as ground cover in shady areas, and beneath trees and shrubs, this attractive dead nettle retains its green-edged, silver leaves throughout most winters. In early summer, it produces dainty spikes of hooded, white flowers. Plant it in moist but well-drained soil in full or partial shade. Divide large clumps in autumn or early spring.

☀ ◑ ◊ ◊ ❀ ❀ ❀

‡ to 15cm (6in) ↔ to 1m (3ft)

Lavandula angustifolia '**Nana Alba**' ♀

EVERGREEN SHRUB

This is a compact white-flowering variety of the classic English lavender – well known for its spikes of fragrant flowers in early summer. English lavenders establish easily in most well-drained soils and 'Nana Alba' makes a fine low hedge or border edge. Clip lavenders back hard each year to sideshoots in late winter, or they will grow leggy and bare in the middle. After flowering, trim off dead flowerheads, but save hard pruning until later.

☼ ◊ ❊❊❊ *f*
‡↔ to 30cm (12in)

Lavatera x *clementii* '**Barnsley**'

SEMI-EVERGREEN SHRUB

The tree mallow is a vigorous, free-flowering, semi-evergreen shrub with lobed green leaves. From early summer until the first frosts, 'Barnsley' steadily produces clusters of funnel-shaped, white flowers with distinctive red eyes. Choose a spot for it in full sun, in well-drained, ideally light, fertile soil. Provide shelter from strong winds as the branches are brittle. Propagate by softwood cuttings in summer. It is suitable for gardens in coastal areas.

☼ ◊ ❊❊❊
‡↔ to 2m (6ft)

Leucanthemum x *superbum* 'Wirral Supreme' ♀
PERENNIAL

A stalwart of the herbaceous border, this vigorous plant produces masses of double, daisy-like flowers on stiff, erect stems held above dark green, lance-shaped leaves. The blooms make good cut flowers. In exposed sites, the tall stems may need support. Happiest in fairly fertile, well-drained but moist soil, in full sun or partial shade, it will eventually spread to form a large clump. Divide established plants in early spring or late summer.

☼ ☀ ◊ ◊ ❀❀❀

‡ to 90cm (36in) ↔ to 75cm (30in)

Leucojum aestivum 'Gravetye Giant' ♀
PERENNIAL BULB

If left undisturbed in a lightly shaded spot in damp, fertile soil, the summer snowflake will quickly spread to form a large clump of glossy, dark green leaves. From spring to early summer, 'Gravetye Giant' produces up to eight slightly pendent, white flowers tipped with green that have a faint chocolate scent. Plant the bulbs in autumn, preferably in a waterside setting.

☀ ◊ ❀❀❀ *f*

‡ to 90cm (36in) ↔ to 8cm (3in)

Lilium 'Mont Blanc'

PERENNIAL BULB

From early to midsummer, this sturdy Asiatic lily produces bunches of ivory-white flowers with brown-spotted throats. Its compact stems make it ideal for growing in containers or in a raised bed. Plant bulbs in full sun, in fertile, well-drained soil from late autumn to early spring. The flowers are good for cutting, but care must be taken because the pollen stains clothing and damages polished surfaces.

☼ ◊ ❋❋❋

‡ to 70cm (28in)

Matthiola 'Hansens Park'

PERENNIAL

Their sweet fragrance makes stocks a popular bedding plant and cut flower. Most have narrow, greyish-green leaves and erect stems. Sow seed in spring in pots of loam-based seed compost, and overwinter young plants in a cold frame before planting out the following spring in moist but well-drained, slightly fertile soil. There are a few white-flowering forms available. *M. fructiculosa* 'Alba' is compact and ideal for containers.

☼ ◊ ◊ ❋❋❋ *f*

‡ to 45cm (18in) ↔ to 30cm (12in)

Paeonia lactiflora 'Baroness Schröder'

PERENNIAL

This superb Chinese peony produces a bold clump of dark green leaves and very large, almost globe-shaped flowers. The petals are blushed pink when they first open but turn snow-white as they mature. Plant in fertile, moist but well-drained soil, in full sun or partial shade. The blooms are heavy so provide support for them before they open. The fragrant flowers are excellent for cutting, although they are best left undisturbed in a border.

☼ ◑ ◊ ◊ ❀❀❀ *f*

↔to 90cm (36in)

Papaver orientale 'Black and White' ♀

PERENNIAL

This white-flowered, oriental poppy has crimson-black markings at the petal bases. The flowers are borne above the mid-green foliage at the tips of white-bristly, upright stems during early summer; they are followed by distinctive seed pods, which should be cut back at the base to encourage further flowering. Like other oriental poppies, it is a mainstay of the cottage garden border, and its colouring suits a border made up of cooler shades.

☼ ◊ ◊ ❀❀❀

↔to 90cm (36in)

Philadelphus 'Belle Etoile' ♀

DECIDUOUS SHRUB

Mock orange is a superb free-flowering shrub with sprays of large, white fragrant flowers. When weighted down with blossom the branches arch over, giving the shrub a graceful spreading outline. Plant it in full sun or partial shade, in reasonably fertile, well-drained soil. Each year, when it has finished flowering, prune some of the older branches down to the ground to encourage new, young shoots.

☼ ◑ ◊ ❀❀❀ *f*
‡ to 1.2m (4ft) ↔ to 2.5m (8ft)

Potentilla fruticosa 'Groneland'

DECIDUOUS SHRUB

Shrubby cinquefoils produce an abundance of charming small flowers over a long period from late spring to mid-autumn. This variety has white flowers, but there are other varieties available with flowers of red, yellow, or pink. The dark green leaves are composed of several leaflets, and they fall in winter. This is a dependable, undemanding shrub that makes a useful addition to a mixed or shrub border, or as a low flowering hedge.

☼ ◊ ◑ ❀❀❀
‡ to 1m (3ft) ↔ to 1.5m (5ft)

Prunus lusitanica subsp. azorica

EVERGREEN TREE

This vigorous Portugal laurel forms an evergreen shrub or small tree, and bears large glossy leaves. It produces free-flowering spikes of small, white, scented blooms in late spring and early summer. In autumn, it bears red cherry-like fruits that turn black when ripe. This plant grows well even on shallow chalky soil, and will flourish when planted in a sheltered position in full sun. It makes a good specimen plant, but it is often trimmed as a hedge.

☼ ◊ ◆ ❄❄ *f*

↕↔ to 20m (70ft)

Pyracantha 'Watereri'

EVERGREEN SHRUB

This upright shrub combines glossy, dark green leaves with an abundance of small, white, early-summer flowers. These are followed in autumn and winter by shiny red berries. It is a good choice for a boundary hedge as its sharp spines will deter intruders; alternatively, train it against a wall. Plant it in a sheltered position, in well-drained, fertile soil in full sun or shade. Shorten side shoots to two or three leaves after flowering, and trim hedges in spring and summer.

☼ ◐ ● ◊ ❄❄❄

↕↔ to 2.5m (8ft)

Romneya coulteri ♀
DECIDUOUS SHRUB

The Californian tree poppy is a vigorous shrub with large, poppy-like, fragrant flowers, and grey-green leaves. It can be difficult to establish but in the right conditions will spread extensively. Plant it in a sunny site, in deep, well-drained soil, and provide protection during cold winters – in frost-prone areas, grow plants in the shelter of a sunny wall or fence. It usually dies down each year, but should reshoot in spring. Mature plants resent disturbance and are best left to grow unhindered.

☼ ◊ ❀❀ *f*
↔ to 2m (6ft)

Rosa 'Blanche Double de Coubert' ♀
DECIDUOUS SHRUB

This shrub rose flowers from early summer to early autumn, producing semi-double, fragrant, white blooms. Occasionally it will go on to develop bright red hips in autumn. Suitable for a mixed border, it can also be used as a hedge. It tolerates a wide range of conditions but prefers full sun and an open site on fairly fertile, moist but well-drained soil. In early spring, cut out a few of the oldest stems, and lightly trim back flowering shoots.

☼ ◊ ◊ ❀❀❀ *f*
‡ to 1.5m (5ft) ↔ to 1.2m (4ft)

Rosa 'Madame Hardy' ♀
DECIDUOUS SHRUB

Ideal for a mixed border, this extremely attractive shrub rose has vibrant green, leathery foliage and forms a rounded shape. It flowers only once, producing rosette-shaped blooms that have a green button eye and carry a spicy fragrance. A sunny site and fairly fertile, moist but well-drained soil is ideal, although it will tolerate a wide range of growing conditions. Prune it in early spring, removing only the old stems, or lightly trimming it into shape.

☼ ◑ ◊ ✿✿✿ *f*
‡to 1.5m (5ft) ↔to 1.2m (4ft)

Styrax hemsleyanus ♀
DECIDUOUS TREE

The snowbell tree is a small and graceful deciduous tree grown for both its white flowers and its autumn foliage colour. In early to midsummer, the delicate bell-shaped flowers, for which this tree is best known, hang in clusters from the branches. In autumn, the leaves turn to red and yellow. Snowbells are good trees for small to medium gardens and grow best in a well-drained, neutral to acid soil, with shelter from cold winds. *S. japonicus*, the Japanese snowbell, is similar.

☼ ☀ ◊ ✿✿✿
‡to 5m (15ft) ↔to 4m (12ft)

Tanacetum parthenium 'Aureum'

PERENNIAL

In summer, feverfew produces clusters of daisy-like, white flowers with dark yellow centres borne on upright stems above aromatic golden-yellow leaves. Grow in a sunny border, herb or gravel garden in well-drained soil. Deadhead regularly as it will self-seed liberally around the garden.

☼ ◊ ❀❀❀ *f*
↕↔ to 45cm (18in)

Veratrum album ♀

PERENNIAL

A statuesque plant with large, pleated, green leaves, in early summer it throws up a tall spike of small, star-shaped, white flowers lightly tinged with green. Tolerant of shade and happy in humus-rich, moist but well-drained soil, it is ideal for a woodland garden or shady border. Provided the soil never dries out, it will also cope in full sun. Protect it from cold, drying winds, and divide congested clumps in autumn or early spring. All parts of this plant are toxic.

☼ ◐ ● ◊ ❀❀❀
↕ to 2m (6ft) ↔ to 60cm (24in)

Zantedeschia aethiopica '**Crowborough**' ♀

PERENNIAL BULB

The arum lily has shapely flowers held on stiff stems above luxuriant, dark green leaves. 'Crowborough' is hardy and can be planted in shallow water at the edge of a pond, or in a border in deep, moist, fertile soil in sun or dappled shade. In the latter situation, protect the root area over winter with a thick layer of mulch. When grown in a container, move under cover when frost threatens.

☼ ☀ ◊ ♦ ❈ ❈ ❈
‡ to 1m (3ft) ↔ to 45cm (18in)

Zenobia pulverulenta

DECIDUOUS SHRUB

From early to midsummer, this attractive shrub produces aniseed-scented, bell-shaped, white flowers that are similar to those of lily-of-the-valley. Its leaves are glossy green above and waxy beneath. Give it a sheltered spot and it may retain some leaves in winter. It prefers a humus-rich, acid (lime-free), moist soil, preferably in partial shade. It will grow in a sunny situation provided the soil never dries out.

☼ ☀ ◊ ❈ ❈ ❈ *f*
‡ to 2m (6ft) ↔ to 1.5m (5ft)

Acer negundo 'Flamingo'
DECIDUOUS TREE

This round-headed maple is renowned for its pink-tinted, white-margined oval leaflets, which appear in spring and early summer. The effect is exaggerated if the tree is pruned to a shrub-sized framework every one or two years in winter; this results in larger, more exotic-looking leaves with intensified colour. Kept in this way, the tree will suit a small garden or mixed border. The bare stems in winter are also attractive. Remove any branches with all-green leaves. Best on an acid to neutral soil.

☼ ◊ ◊ ❀ ❀ ❀

‡ to 15m (50ft) ↔ to 10m (30ft)

Allium schoenoprasum
PERENNIAL BULB

Chives are widely grown as a kitchen herb but the plant is pretty enough to use in a herbaceous border or edge a bed. In summer, small, dark pink, or occasionally lavender-white flowers appear on the top of narrow stems among the greyish-green leaves. Cut back after flowering to encourage fresh leaves to sprout. Chives prefer full sun and well-drained soil. Large clumps may be divided in spring.

☼ ◊ ❀ ❀ ❀

‡ to 25cm (10in) ↔ to 10cm (4in)

Argyranthemum 'Vancouver' ♀

PERENNIAL

With its fern-like foliage and unusual, rose-pink blooms, 'Vancouver' is a particularly striking argyranthemum. It has a long flowering period, from early summer until early autumn, making it excellent for borders, bedding and container displays. Pinching out the growing tips will help maintain a neat, bushy habit. It is not fully hardy and is best in a sheltered spot in well-drained soil and full sun. If potted up it is easily moved under glass for winter.

☼ ◊ ❀❀

‡ to 90cm (36in) ↔ to 80cm (32in)

Astilbe 'Straussenfeder' ♀

PERENNIAL

The dark green leaves of this astilbe, which are tinted bronze when young, will provide attractive ground cover for a permanently moist border by water or in a bog garden. Sprays of coral-pink flowers are produced in summer, but the faded flowerheads remain attractive through to autumn. Astilbes prefer wet, fertile soil in full sun. Plant in groups of four or five for maximum impact. A fast grower, clumps will need dividing every few years in early spring to maintain vigour.

☼ ☀ ◊ ◖ ❀❀❀

‡↔ to 1m (3ft)

Astilbe 'Venus'

PERENNIAL

The limited spread of this astilbe makes it ideal for a small garden. In early summer tall sprays of bright pink flowers are borne above vibrant green foliage. It grows best in moist, fertile soil in full sun and is excellent for a bog garden or damp soil beside a pond. In drier soils, grow in partial shade. Divide clumps every few years in early spring to keep plants strong and to encourage more flowers. The bleached flowerheads dry well and continue to look attractive on the plants through to autumn.

☼ ☀ ◑ ◐ ❀ ❀ ❀
↕↔ to 1m (3ft)

Astrantia major

PERENNIAL

Hattie's pincushion is a clump-forming plant with toothed, mid-green leaves. The tiny, early summer flowers are pink or green and surrounded by a pinkish-white, papery collar. Astrantias prefer moist, fertile soil in full sun or light shade. They are good for a slightly shaded herbaceous border, a woodland garden, or damp ground beside a pond or stream. Deadhead to prevent self-seeding. Large clumps may be divided in spring.

☼ ☀ ◑ ❀ ❀ ❀
↕ to 60cm (24in) ↔ to 45cm (18in)

Campanula lactiflora 'Loddon Anna' ♀

PERENNIAL

The milky bellflower is a tall herbaceous plant, which bears large clusters of bell-shaped, lilac-pink flowers throughout the summer. They may need staking as they are inclined to fall over in strong winds. It enjoys full sun or dappled shade in a fertile, neutral to alkaline, moist, well-drained soil. It self-seeds, and can be divided in spring or autumn. 'Prichard's Variety' is not as tall and has violet-blue flowers.

☼ ☀ ◊ ◖ ❀❀❀
‡ to 1.2m (4ft) ↔ to 60cm (24in)

Campanula punctata

PERENNIAL

This low-growing bellflower thrives in moist but well-drained, fertile, fairly light soil, particularly if it gets plenty of sun. In early summer, dusky- to shell-pink flowers hang from erect stems. Their inner surfaces are freckled red and covered in a fuzz of soft hairs. The dark green, semi-evergreen leaves are heart-shaped at the base. To encourage a second flush of blooms, and prevent self-seeding, cut back after flowering.

☼ ☀ ◊ ◖ ❀❀❀
‡ to 30cm (12in) ↔ to 40cm (16in)

Centaurea hypoleuca '**John Coutts**'

PERENNIAL

This upright plant has greyish-green, wavy-edged leaves. The long-lasting, fragrant flowers are borne singly on long stems throughout early summer. The outer florets are star-shaped, with bright pink thistle-like centres. Plant in a border or rock garden, in full sunshine and well-drained soil. Divide big clumps in spring or autumn.

☼ ◊ ❀❀❀ *f*

‡ to 60cm (24in) ↔ to 45cm (18in)

Centranthus ruber

PERENNIAL

Red valerian will grow in some of the most exposed places, on cliffs, walls, and at the edge of roads. It is also grown successfully as a border perennial, where it is valued for its long flowering season. It has fleshy, bright-green leaves and, throughout summer, branching stems covered with small, star-shaped, pink, red, or white flowers. Plant in poor, well-drained soil in full sun and deadhead regularly. Suitable for coastal gardens.

☼ ◊ ❀❀❀

‡ to 90cm (36in) ↔ to 60cm (24in)

Cistus x *argenteus* 'Peggy Sammons' ♥

EVERGREEN SHRUB

Each bloom on a rock rose lasts for only one day, but they are produced constantly from early to late summer. 'Peggy Sammons' has large, purplish-pink flowers and greyish-green leaves. It thrives on well-drained soil, even poor, in full sun and will survive most winters in a sheltered position. Grow in containers, around paved areas, on sunny banks, in a border, or in coastal gardens.

☼ ◊ ❀❀

 ‡↔ to 1m (3ft)

Clematis 'Comtesse de Bouchaud' ♥

CLIMBER

A vigorous, deciduous clematis with pale green leaves. In summer many pinkish-mauve flowers are produced, with dark lines radiating out from their yellow centres. Grow in well-drained, fertile soil, in sun or partial shade, with the roots in shade. Cut back in early spring to a pair of strong buds 20cm (8in) above soil level, as this will encourage flowers. Clematis are often grown through roses and other shrubs or trees, or used to clothe trellis, walls, or arches.

☼ ◐ ◊ ❀❀❀

 ‡↔ to 3m (10ft)

Clematis 'Nelly Moser' ♀

CLIMBER

In early summer this deciduous clematis bears large, pinkish-purple flowers, with a reddish stripe down the centre of each petal. The foliage is a pretty pale green. It is best grown in well-drained fertile soil, in a slightly shaded position as the blooms fade in strong sun. Scramble it through a tree or shrub, or over a trellis or an arch. To encourage lots of flowers, remove any dead stems in early spring and prune remaining shoots back to a pair of strong buds.

☀ ◊ ❀ ❀ ❀
‡ to 3m (10ft)

Cordyline 'Southern Splendour'

PERENNIAL

This cultivar of the New Zealand cabbage palm features an upright, arching habit with pink, grey-green, and bronze-striped, sword-shaped, evergreen leaves. It is a great choice for containers – inside or out – and is also suitable as a specimen plant in a mixed or shrub border, or a courtyard garden. Apply a balanced fertilizer when planting. Grow in full sun to partial shade in well drained soil.

☀ ☀ ◊ ❀ ❀
‡ to 3m (10ft) ↔ to 60cm (24in)

Cornus kousa 'Miss Satomi' ♀

DECIDUOUS TREE

This dramatic dogwood has many attractions, including decorative bark, deep purplish-red leaves in autumn, and a handsome shape. Perhaps most striking is the early summer display of masses of dark pink bracts against the dark green foliage. The bracts surround a cluster of tiny flowers. Plant in a sunny or partially shaded situation, in soil that is neutral or acid (lime free), well-drained and humus-rich.

☀ ◑ ◊ ❀ ❀ ❀

‡ to 7m (22ft) ↔ to 5m (15ft)

Daboecia cantabrica 'Bicolor' ♀

EVERGREEN SHRUB

The leaves of the Cantabrian heath are larger than other heathers. The urn-shaped flowers are borne over a long period from early summer to mid-autumn, and 'Bicolor' produces blooms in purple-pink, white or striped on the same flower spike. Plant it in full sun or light shade, in neutral or acid (lime-free), well-drained soil. It is suitable for a rock or heather garden, and forms a colourful carpet when used as ground cover.

☀ ◑ ◊ ❀ ❀ ❀
‡ to 45cm (18in) ↔ to 60cm (24in)

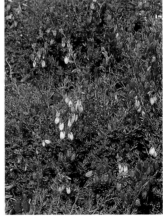

Deutzia x *elegantissima* 'Rosealind' ♀

DECIDUOUS SHRUB

Deutzias are stunning when grown in the border or as a specimen plant; choose a position in full sun and fertile, well-drained soil. Thousands of star-shaped, pale pink flowers are borne in early summer. Maintain this shrub's neat shape by pruning out old and flowered shoots when the blooms have faded.

☼ ◊ ❀ ❀ ❀
↕ to 1.2m (4ft) ↔ to 1.5m (5ft)

Dianthus alpinus 'Joan's Blood' ♀

PERENNIAL

Alpine pinks are compact, tuft-forming evergreens with narrow, shiny, dark green leaves. In summer, 'Joan's Blood' is almost completely covered by large, deep pink flowers with toothed petals. This decorative plant is ideal for planting at the front of borders, in raised beds, rock gardens, and between paving slabs. Choose a sunny spot in humus-rich, well-drained soil.

☼ ◊ ❀ ❀ ❀
↕ to 8cm (3in) ↔ to 10cm (4in)

Dianthus 'Doris' ♀

PERENNIAL

With its pale pink, wavy-edged petals
and raspberry coloured centre, this is
one of the prettiest pinks. Often two
or three flushes of clove-scented blooms
will be borne from early summer to
autumn, above a mound of grey-green
leaves. The flowers are decorative in
a border and very long lasting when
cut. Pinks thrive in well-drained soil
and full sun.

☀ ◊ ❀❀❀ *f*
‡to 45cm (18in) ↔to 40cm (16in)

Dianthus 'Houndspool Ruby' ♀

PERENNIAL

This bold pink has double, rose-pink
flowers, with a splash of red at their
centre, and delicately fringed petals.
Modern pinks bloom throughout
summer, are good in a border and
excellent for cutting. They also form
dense mounds of narrow, grey-green,
evergreen leaves. Choose a position
in full sun with well-drained soil.

☀ ◊ ❀❀❀
‡to 45cm (18in) ↔to 30cm (12in)

Dictamnus albus var. *purpureus* ♀

PERENNIAL

The burning bush produces aromatic oils that can, very occasionally, ignite on a hot summer's day. Long spikes of large pink flowers with dark purple veins are produced in early summer. The foliage is lemon-scented, but take care as contact with its leaves may irritate the skin. Plant in well-drained soil, in sun or partial shade, and avoid transplanting as it resents disturbance.

☼ ◑ ◊ ❀❀❀ *f*

‡ to 90cm (36in) ↔ to 60cm (24in)

Dierama pulcherrimum

PERENNIAL BULB

Angel's fishing rod is so named because the bright pink, bell-shaped flowers hang from graceful, arching stems in summer. The narrow leaves are greyish green and grass-like. It is especially pretty grown beside a pond, where the water will reflect its slender form, or in a border. Choose a sunny situation in reliably moist but well-drained soil, planting the bulbs 5–7cm (2–3in) deep, in spring.

☼ ◊ ◊ ❀❀

‡ to 1.5m (5ft) ↔ to 60cm (24in)

Digitalis x mertonensis ☙

PERENNIAL

This foxglove has large, strawberry-coloured, funnel-shaped flowers borne on sturdy spikes in early summer. It forms clumps of handsome, glossy green leaves. Foxgloves prefer moist, well-drained soil in partial shade, but will tolerate a wide range of conditions. They are equally happy in a border or naturalized beneath deciduous trees. Allow plants to self-seed or sow seed in late spring.

to 90cm (36in) ↔ to 30cm (12in)

Eremurus robustus ☙

PERENNIAL

From a clump of strappy, bluish-green leaves, this impressive plant produces a tower of pale pink flowers on top of a tall, leafless stem. Foxtail lilies are effective when several are grouped together in a border. Grow in a sunny position, in sandy, very well-drained soil, as the roots will die if they get too wet in winter. The flower spikes may need support, especially in exposed areas. In late winter and spring, if frost threatens, mulch with bracken, straw, or fleece to protect emerging shoots.

to 3m (10ft) ↔ to 1.2m (4ft)

Escallonia 'Apple Blossom' ♀

EVERGREEN SHRUB

A bushy shrub with rounded, glossy green leaves, this escallonia bears small, clear pink flowers with white centres in early summer. Grow it in a border, against a wall, or as a hedge or windbreak. If the wind is not too cold, it will also thrive in coastal areas. To help retain a neat shape, trim lightly in mid- to late spring.

☼ ◊ ❊❊❊
‡↔ to 2.5m (8ft)

Filipendula rubra 'Venusta' ♀

PERENNIAL

Queen of the prairies is a spreading perennial with architectural, deeply-cut, mid-green foliage. In summer it produces branched stems bearing clusters of tiny, fragrant, deep rose-pink flowers. It is a bog plant and needs to be sited in partial shade, although it tolerates full sun in permanently moist soil. Grow close to a pond margin, or in damp ground beneath deciduous trees; it will only thrive in a herbaceous border if the soil never dries out.

☼ ☀ ◊ ❉ ❊❊❊ *f*
‡ to 2.5m (8ft) ↔ to 1.2m (4ft)

Fragaria PINK PANDA ('Frel')

PERENNIAL

This vigorous ground-cover plant is related to the strawberry but rarely fruits. Deep pink flowers are produced for a long period during summer. The leaves are bright green, deeply veined, and almost evergreen. It does well in full sun or partial shade and prefers moist but well-drained, fertile soil. Ideal for the front of a herbaceous border, if it threatens to spread out of bounds, control it by removing unwanted runners (the horizontal stems).

‡ to 15cm (6in) ↔ indefinite

Geranium endressii ♀

PERENNIAL

A clump-forming hardy geranium, or cranesbill, with trumpet-shaped, pale pink flowers with notched petals. The evergreen leaves are hairy and wrinkly. Cranesbills tolerate a wide range of soil types and growing conditions, coping well in full sun or partial shade – a rock garden, the front of a mixed border, or a wild garden are ideal. Clip over after flowering to encourage fresh growth and more flowers. *G. endressii* combines well with a blue-flowering geranium such as *G. ibericum*.

‡ to 45cm (18in) ↔ to 60cm (24in)

Geranium x *riversleaianum* 'Russell Prichard' ♀

PERENNIAL

This hardy geranium, or cranesbill, has trailing, creeping stems, making it a good ground-cover plant. In summer it has deeply divided, slightly hairy, greyish green leaves and deep magenta flowers. It prefers to be planted in full sun in well-drained, slightly fertile soil, but will tolerate a wide range of conditions. Clip over after flowering to encourage fresh growth and more flowers.

☼ ◊ ✿ ✿ ✿
‡ to 30cm (12in) ↔ to 1m (3ft)

Gladiolus 'Rose Supreme'

PERENNIAL CORM

This is one of the largest gladioli available; the tall spikes can hold as many as 24 flowers above a fan of sword-shaped leaves. Each rose-pink bloom has a cream throat and dark pink edges. Plant it in full sun, in fertile, well-drained soil and support with a cane. Gladioli are superb for adding height to a border and make excellent cut flowers. Lift corms in autumn, store dry over winter and replant in spring in soil enriched with organic matter.

☼ ◊ ✿
‡ to 1.7m (5½ft) ↔ to 25cm (10in)

Helianthemum 'Rhodanthe Carneum' ♀

EVERGREEN SHRUB

A wide-spreading rock rose with silver-grey leaves. In summer it produces numerous flat pale pink flowers marked with yellow in the centre. Grow it at the front of a border, in a raised bed, alongside paving, or in a rock or gravel garden. Choose a position in fertile, well-drained soil and full sun. Prune after flowering to keep the bush neat and tidy and prevent it from becoming leggy.

☼ ◊ ❀ ❀ ❀
↕↔ to 30cm (12in)

Iberis umbellata Fairy Series

ANNUAL

The abundant and colourful flowers of this candytuft are invaluable in spring and summer. They flower freely in an interesting mix of pink shades, from almost white to lilac-purple or reddish pink. They are hardy annuals so will grow from seed each year, but they are also readily available as bedding plants. Useful for containers, large gaps in patio paving, and the fronts of borders, they are best in poor to moderately fertile soil that is moist but well drained.

☼ ◊ ◊ ❀ ❀ ❀
↕↔ to 20cm (8in)

Impatiens walleriana 'Tempo Lavender'

PERENNIAL

With its vivid, lavender-pink, long-lasting flowers and light green leaves, 'Tempo Lavender' is a particularly pretty summer bedding plant. Available in a wide range of colours, busy lizzies are tender perennials that are usually grown as annuals. For the best flowers, choose a spot in partial shade, in moist but well-drained soil. They also make good container plants.

☀ ◊ ◊ ❀❀
‡↔ to 25cm (10in)

Incarvillea delavayi

PERENNIAL

An exotic-looking plant with large flowers held on strong stems above a rosette of lush, mid-green leaves. The flowerhead consists of up to 10 trumpet-shaped, rose-pink or purple blooms. Grow it in fertile, moist, well-drained soil in a bright, sunny position but, preferably, one that avoids direct midday sun. A good choice for a gravel garden or mixed or herbaceous border.

☼ ◊ ◊ ❀❀❀
‡ to 60cm (24in) ↔ to 30cm (12in)

Indigofera amblyantha

DECIDUOUS SHRUB

A medium-sized, spreading shrub grown for its long display of lovely pea-like flowers and elegant foliage. The small, purple-pink flowers begin to appear in dense clusters in early summer and continue into autumn. Its arching stems carry grey-green leaves made up of many leaflets. It suits most well-drained soils, but train it against a warm wall in cold climates. Prune established plants in early spring, cutting back to just above ground level. *I. heterantha* is similar, and also recommended.

☼ ◊ ❀❀
‡↔ to 2m (6ft)

Iris 'Carnaby'

PERENNIAL

Bearded irises are mostly grown for their flamboyant flowers that come in a huge range of colours; however, their sword-shaped leaves are attractive too. This variety has large flowers with peach-pink upper petals and pink-purple lower petals that are furred with an orange "beard". Divide congested clumps after flowering, replanting only plump sections of rhizome in a sunny spot in well-drained fertile soil, ensuring their tops are exposed to the sun.

☼ ◊ ❀❀❀
‡ to 1m (3ft) ↔ indefinite

Kalmia latifolia ♀
EVERGREEN SHRUB

The calico bush is an excellent choice for slightly acid soil, where your reward will be large heads of pink or white flowers. It forms a nicely rounded bush, with oval, dark green leaves. Kalmias prefer humus-rich, moist but well-drained, acid (lime-free) soil in partial shade, although they will tolerate full sun where the ground remains damp in summer. Deadhead regularly and lightly trim after flowering to maintain a neat shape. Mulch annually with leafmould or chipped bark.

☼ ☀ ◐ ◊ ✽ ✽ ✽
↕↔ to 3m (10ft)

Lupinus 'The Chatelaine'
PERENNIAL

The stately, pink-and-white flowered spires of this lupin are excellent for lending height and colour to a border from early to midsummer. They are also good for cutting. The palm-like, mid-green leaves are beautiful in their own right, and after rain droplets of water collect on their surface. Lupins are generally short-lived, but last longer in slightly acid to neutral soils with good drainage. Protect the young growth from slugs and snails. Varieties are available in a range of colours.

☼ ◊ ✽ ✽ ✽
↕ to 1.2m (4ft) ↔ to 45cm (18in)

Lychnis flos-jovis ♀

PERENNIAL

The upright stems of the flower of Jove are covered with white hairs, giving them a silvery appearance, while the spoon-shaped, soft basal leaves are also silver-grey. From early to late summer, clusters of pink, scarlet or white flowers with deeply divided petals appear. This species is a good choice for the front of a sunny border or a gravel garden. Plant it in well-drained, slightly fertile soil, and sow seed in spring.

☼ ◊ ❀❀❀
‡↔ to 45cm (18in)

Matthiola incana **Cinderella Series**

PERENNIAL

Stocks are extremely fragrant flowers that, despite being perennial, are usually grown as a biennial or annual. The Cinderella Series has double, white, deep pink, purple, or lavender flowers, produced from early summer. Plant in a sunny position, in fertile, well-drained, neutral or slightly alkaline soil. Stocks are excellent as annual bedding and as cut flowers.

☼ ◊ ❀❀❀ *f*
‡↔ to 25cm (10in)

Nectaroscordum siculum subsp. *bulgaricum*
PERENNIAL BULB

An elegant perennial with pendulous, pink-flushed, bell-shaped flowers that are borne on tall stems. These emerge from a clump of garlic-smelling, linear leaves. It can be grown in full sun, or partial shade, and prefers a slightly fertile, well-drained soil. This bulb is ideal for a wild garden, where it may freely self-seed. In a herbaceous border, to help control its spread, simply deadhead regularly.

☼ ☀ ◊ ❀❀❀

‡ to 1.2m (4ft) ↔ to 45cm (18in)

Neillia thibetica
DECIDUOUS SHRUB

This shrub grows well in a border or beneath deciduous trees, spreading by suckers to form a dense thicket. The arching branches have glossy green leaves and long clusters of bright pink, bell-shaped flowers. Grow in full sun or partial shade, in fertile, well-drained soil. To encourage strong new growth the following year, prune after flowering by cutting branches back to a strong pair of buds, and removing a quarter of the stems right to the base of the plant.

☼ ◊ ❀❀❀

‡↔ to 2m (6ft)

Onopordum acanthium
BIENNIAL

The Scotch thistle is an architectural
plant that is good for a large border or
a wild or gravel garden. In its first year,
an impressive rosette of spiny, greyish-
green leaves is formed. During the
second year, a strong, prickly stem,
which is covered with white hairs, is
produced. The stem is crowned with
thistle-like flowerheads, composed of
many small deep pink, or occasionally
white, flowers. Grow in full sun, in
fertile, well-drained, neutral or alkaline
soil. It will readily self-seed.

☼ ◊ ❀ ❀ ❀
‡ to 1.8m (6ft) ↔ to 1m (3ft)

Osteospermum jucundum ♀
PERENNIAL

Free-flowering and extremely decorative,
this is a superb perennial for any border.
It has pretty mauvish-pink or magenta,
daisy-like blooms that are produced
throughout summer above a clump
of greyish-green leaves. Grow in well-
drained, fertile soil in full sun. Regular
deadheading will help extend the
flowering period.

☼ ◊ ❀ ❀ ❀
‡↔ to 30cm (12in)

Paeonia lactiflora 'Monsieur Jules Elie' ♀

PERENNIAL

A large, herbaceous peony, forming bold clumps of glossy, dark green leaves. In early summer it produces deep pink, double flowers that are good for cutting. Grow in a border, in sun or partial shade, in deep, fertile, well-drained soil. For the best blooms, mulch generously with organic matter in autumn. The blooms, which reach over 20cm (8in) across, may need some support – encircling stakes are ideal. Clumps are best left undisturbed.

☀ ☼ ◊ ◊ ❀ ❀ ❀
↕↔ to 1m (3ft)

Papaver orientale 'Cedric Morris' ♀

PERENNIAL

The Oriental poppy is a vigorous plant that will provide a spectacular splash of colour in any border. It forms a large clump of lobed, grey-haired leaves and, in summer, tall stems bear very large, soft-pink flowers with a black mark at the base of each petal. After the decorative seed pods appear, the plant dies down – make sure it is masked by other plants during this unattractive phase. Plant in full sun, in fertile, well-drained soil; sow seed in spring.

☀ ◊ ❀ ❀ ❀
↕↔ to 90cm (36in)

Papaver somniferum
'Paeony Flowered'
ANNUAL

Although grown mainly for its beautiful
flowers, the opium poppy also has
handsome blue-green leaves and
decorative pepper-pot seed pods. In
summer, the 'Peony Flowered' type
bears huge, rounded, frilly blooms in
shades of pink or purple. Sow *in situ*
in spring in a sunny situation, in very
well-drained soil in an annual border or
in gaps in a herbaceous or mixed border.

☼ ◊ ❀ ❀ ❀
‡ to 1.2m (4ft) ↔ to 30cm (12in)

Persicaria bistorta
'Superba' ♀
PERENNIAL

Bistort is a vigorous plant that is often
used in a border or wild garden, or as
ground cover. Numerous flower spikes
are held well above clumps of broad,
mid-green leaves in early summer.
They are made up of many tiny, densely
packed, soft-pink flowers. It prefers
moist ground, although it will tolerate
dry soil, in full sun or partial shade.
Divide large clumps in spring or autumn.

☼ ☼ ◊ ◊ ❀ ❀ ❀
‡ to 75cm (30in) ↔ to 60cm (24in)

Petunia SURFINIA PINK VEIN
('Suntosol') ♀
PERENNIAL

The Surfinia Series is well-known for its large summer flowers and vigorous growth. Their trailing habit makes them ideal for containers and hanging baskets. They can also be grown in beds but the flowers may be damaged by heavy rain. In a border, provide a sunny position and well-drained soil. Deadhead regularly and feed those in containers with a tomato feed every 10–14 days to prolong flowering. Petunias are usually grown as annuals.

☼ ◊ ❀

‡ to 40cm (16in) ↔ to 90cm (36in)

Primula vialii ♀
PERENNIAL

Grow this unusual-looking primula beside a pond or in any moist site in sun or, preferably, partial shade. In summer, from a rosette of hairy leaves, it produces a stout stem topped with a tight spike of small pink flowers that emerge from crimson buds. *P. vialii* is happiest in humus-rich, neutral or acid soil. Although perennial it can be rather short-lived; sow, or allow to self-seed, in spring to renew your stock.

☼ ◑ ◊ ❀❀❀

‡ to 60cm (24in) ↔ to 30cm (12in)

Robinia 'Idaho'

DECIDUOUS TREE

The Idaho locust is a beautiful fast-growing, deciduous tree grown for its wisteria-like clusters of pale pinkish purple flowers. These appear in early summer while the foliage is still a lovely fresh green, and their fragrance is very attractive to pollinating insects. The fern-like foliage only casts light shade, which allows for planting beneath this tough, drought-tolerant tree. The loosely columnar canopy retains its elegance even after flowering. Choose a site sheltered from strong winds.

☼ ◊ ◐ ✳ ✳ ✳ *f*

‡ to 15m (50ft) ↔ to 8m (25ft)

Rosa 'Blessings' ♀

DECIDUOUS SHRUB

If deadheaded regularly, this hybrid tea rose will produce many urn-shaped, pink, scented blooms through to autumn. Prune the main stems to 25cm (10in) above ground in early spring, then apply a balanced fertilizer and mulch generously with well-rotted manure to encourage the production of lots of flowers. Roses should be planted in a sunny situation, in fertile, humus-rich, well-drained, and preferably slightly acid or neutral soil.

☼ ◊ ◐ ✳ ✳ ✳ *f*

‡ to 1m (3ft) ↔ to 75cm (30in)

Rosa 'Frühlingsmorgen'
DECIDUOUS SHRUB

A healthy, upright shrub rose with dark, greyish-green leaves. The single, blossom-pink, hay-scented flowers are produced in early summer. It can be grown up a pillar, in mixed borders, or as hedging and will even tolerate light shade. It needs less rich conditions than hybrid teas and other bush roses. To maintain a neat shape, lightly trim the bush after flowering.

☀ ◐ ◊ ❀ ❀ ❀ *f*
‡ to 2m (6ft) ↔ to 1.5m (5ft)

Rosa GERTRUDE JEKYLL ('Ausbord') ♀
DECIDUOUS SHRUB

Named after the famous Edwardian garden designer, this is a slender, large-flowered shrub rose. It is grown for its deep pink flowers, which are extremely fragrant and start to appear in early summer. With regular deadheading, flowering may continue into early autumn. This disease-resistant rose needs rich growing conditions, so mulch deeply in early spring with well-rotted manure after lightly pruning it to shape – although this is not essential.

☀ ◐ ◊ ❀ ❀ ❀ *f*
‡ to 2m (6ft) ↔ to 1.2m (4ft)

Rosa 'Madame Knorr' ♀
DECIDUOUS SHRUB

An old variety of Portland rose with large, lilac-pink, very fragrant flowers throughout the summer months. It is an easy-going rose with mid-green foliage and thorny stems. It does well on most well-drained soils, and even in poor conditions. When used as hedging, trim it back in late winter or early spring.

☼ ◊ ◑ ✿✿✿ *f*
‡ to 1.2m (4ft) ↔ to 1m (3ft)

Rosa SURREY ('Korlanum') ♀
DECIDUOUS SHRUB

Ground-cover roses are chosen for their low, spreading habit and abundant, healthy foliage. They can be used in many situations: in a border, trailing down a bank or over a wall, and in a container or large hanging basket. Surrey is disease resistant, grows quickly and is very free flowering, with double, soft-pink blooms. Grow in moist but well-drained, fertile soil in full sun. Trim in late winter or early spring to keep it within bounds.

☼ ◊ ◑ ✿✿✿
‡ to 80cm (32in) ↔ to 1.2m (4ft)

Salvia viridis
Claryssa Series

ANNUAL

Clary is an aromatic plant with upright, branching stems. Seed is available in single shades or in rainbow mixtures. The bracts of 'Claryssa Pink' are a particularly bright, rose-pink hue and appear from early summer. Sow seeds *in situ* in mid-spring, in well-drained soil. It can be used as a long-lasting cut or dried flower.

☼ ☀ ◊ ◖ ❀❀❀ *f*

‡ to 40cm (16in) ↔ to 23cm (9in)

Sidalcea 'Elsie Heugh' ♀

PERENNIAL

This false mallow forms clumps of rounded, basal leaves. In early summer upright stems hold purple-pink, fringed flowers that have the texture of satin. They are excellent for cutting. Grow in a sunny border, in well-drained, neutral to slightly acid, fertile soil.

☼ ☀ ◊ ◖ ❀❀❀

‡ to 90cm (36in) ↔ to 45cm (18in)

Spiraea japonica var. *albiflora*

DECIDUOUS SHRUB

This compact, deciduous shrub would suit a mixed or shrub border, but could also be grown as a low, informal flowering hedge. The strongly bronze-tinted new leaves emerge in spring. As they fade to mid-green in early summer, dense clusters of tiny pale pink flowers gradually emerge, with the full display in midsummer. Grow in well-drained soil, and prune established plants back to a framework before the leaves emerge in spring.

☼ ◊ ◑ ❀ ❀ ❀

↕↔ to 1m (3ft)

Tanacetum coccineum 'Eileen May Robinson' ♀

PERENNIAL

The painted daisy is a bushy plant with silver-haired, balsam-scented leaves, which can be used as a cut flower and to make pot-pourri. In early summer it produces an abundance of soft-pink flowers. Cut back after flowers fade to encourage a second flush. It will tolerate any light, well-drained soil in full sun.

☼ ◊ ❀ ❀ ❀ *f*

↕ to 75cm (30in) ↔ to 45cm (18in)

Thymus serpyllum 'Annie Hall'

EVERGREEN SHRUB

This thyme forms a mat of creeping branches covered, in summer, with numerous, tiny, pale pink flowers. Its small dark green leaves are highly aromatic when crushed, making it ideal for planting in paving crevices where its pungent oils are released each time it is trodden on. Alternatively, plant it in a herb or rock garden, or in containers, choosing a sunny position and very well-drained soil.

☼ ◊ ✽✽✽ *f*

↕ to 25cm (10in) ↔ to 45cm (18in)

Verbascum 'Helen Johnson'

PERENNIAL

This mullein produces tall spikes of pinkish-brown, saucer-shaped flowers in early to midsummer. They emerge from an evergreen rosette of downy, greyish-green leaves. Plant in a border or gravel garden in a sunny position, in well-drained soil. 'Helen Johnson' can be short-lived, so propagate new plants by division in autumn.

☼ ◊ ✽✽✽

↕ to 90cm (36in) ↔ to 30cm (12in)

Verbena 'Sissinghurst' ♥

PERENNIAL

This sprawling verbena is ideal for containers and especially hanging baskets. It has dark green leaves and, during summer and into autumn, large round clusters of bright, magenta-pink flowers. Usually grown as an annual in cooler countries, it can be potted up and taken into a greenhouse over winter. It is easily raised from semi-ripe cuttings of non-flowering shoots taken in late summer.

☼ ◊ ◗ ❀ ❀

‡ to 20cm (8in) ↔ to 1m (3ft)

Veronica spicata 'Rotfuchs'

PERENNIAL

Also known as 'Red Fox', this clump-forming perennial a valuable plant for the herbaceous border as it bears striking spires of rich rose-pink flowers for many weeks in summer. In full bloom, it has a spiky appearance, so it would be useful mixed in with plants of other shapes and textures to create interest. The lance-shaped, deciduous leaves are deep green. Choose a moist but well-drained site and cut back after flowering.

☼ ◊ ◗ ❀ ❀ ❀

‡↔ to 50cm (22in)

Aesculus x *carnea* 'Briotii' ♧
DECIDUOUS TREE

This red-flowered horse chestnut is a spreading, rounded tree admired in early summer for its large, upright cones of dark rose-red flowers, which are followed by spiny fruits. The dark green, palm-like leaves are divided into 5–7 leaflets. It is a large tree for big gardens only, but its resistance to horse chestnut leaf miner makes it a good alternative to the increasingly affected common horse chestnut. For a smaller tree, look for the yellow horse chestnut, *A.* x *neglecta* 'Autumn Fire'.

☼ ☀ ◐ ◑ ✽ ✽ ✽
‡ to 20m (70ft) ↔ to 15m (50ft)

Astilbe 'Fanal' ♧
PERENNIAL

This dramatic herbaceous plant bears plumes of tiny red flowers in early summer. Its divided, toothed, deep green foliage contrasts well with the blooms and is a feature in its own right. Astilbes flourish in humus-rich, fertile soil, in a permanently damp border, at the edge of a woodland garden, in a bog garden or by water. They prefer a position in partial shade, although they will grow in full sun, as long as the soil never dries out.

☼ ☀ ◐ ◑ ✽ ✽ ✽
‡ to 60cm (24in) ↔ to 90cm (36in)

Astrantia 'Hadspen Blood'
PERENNIAL

This plant forms a clump of deeply
lobed green leaves, and bears sprays
of tiny dark red flowers, surrounded by
petal-like bracts, for many months from
early to midsummer. Plant astrantias
beside a stream, in a damp border or
a deciduous woodland garden, in moist,
fertile soil in full sun or partial shade.
Large clumps can be divided in spring.

☼ ☀ ◊ ❀❀❀

‡ to 90cm (36in) ↔ to 45cm (18in)

Cirsium rivulare 'Atropurpureum'
PERENNIAL

The thistle-like flowers and informal
habit of this plant make it ideal for
growing in a wild garden, a damp
meadow, or in association with
ornamental grasses. It forms clumps
of narrow, lance-shaped leaves, covered
beneath with soft hairs, and in early
summer produces tall stems of reddish-
purple blooms. It needs to be planted
in a sunny situation, in moist, well-
drained soil. To increase stocks, divide
in the autumn or early spring.

☼ ◊ ❀❀❀

‡ to 1.2m (4ft) ↔ to 60cm (24in)

Clematis 'Jackmanii Rubra'

CLIMBER

Mid-season clematis come in many shapes and colours, with a flowering season that is concentrated during the early part of summer. They look very attractive trained through shrubs like roses, or along a trellis, especially if they bloom just before or after their hosts or neighbours. 'Jackmanii Rubra' has crimson, velvety blooms approximately 10cm (4in) across. Mulch around the roots in late winter and tie in young growth carefully. Trim lightly in late winter.

☼ ◑ ◊ ❀ ❀ ❀
↕ to 3m (10ft)

Clematis 'Niobe' ♀

CLIMBER

Possibly the best of all the red clematis, 'Niobe' has single, velvety, deep ruby-red flowers with yellow stamens, and blooms for a long period in summer. It will brighten up a trellis, or train it over an arch, or up a post. Plant 'Niobe' in a fertile, well-drained soil in sun or partial shade, with the roots in shade. It does particularly well in alkaline soil. In early spring remove any dead or damaged growth, and cut the rest of the stems back to a strong pair of buds.

☼ ◑ ◊ ❀ ❀ ❀
↕ to 3m (10ft)

Dianthus barbatus 'Dunnet's Dark Crimson'

BIENNIAL

Sweet Williams are valued for their early summer flowers and wonderful perfume, and 'Dunnet's Dark Crimson' is a particularly decorative variety. Its dark bronzy-green leaves contrast well with the dense clusters of deep red flowers. Sweet Williams will grow well in a sunny herbaceous border in fertile, well-drained, neutral to alkaline soil. The flowers are good for cutting.

☼ ◊ ❀❀❀

‡ to 60cm (24in) ↔ to 30cm (12in)

Embothrium coccineum Lanceolatum Group

EVERGREEN SHRUB

The Chilean firebush is a very eye-catching shrub in early summer, when it bears clusters of showy, tubular, flaming scarlet flowers that stand out brilliantly against the shiny, dark green, narrow leaves. If allowed to grow, it can make a large shrub for a medium to large garden – either as a free-standing specimen on its own or as part of a border. Choose a sheltered site with moist but well-drained, acid to neutral soil. Needs minimal pruning.

☼ ☼ ◊◊ ❀❀❀

‡ to 10m (30ft) ↔ to 5m (15ft)

Geum 'Red Wings'

PERENNIAL

'Red Wings' is considered to be one of the best geums available. It is a herbaceous perennial, forming clumps of hairy, fresh green, divided leaves. In early and midsummer, bowl-shaped, semi-double, bright scarlet flowers rise up on long, branching stems; these last well when cut. Geums are best suited to mixed or herbaceous borders, in most fertile, moist but well-drained soils. Varieties with yellow and orange flowers are also available. Cut back after flowering.

☼ ◐ ◊ ✿ ✿ ✿

‡ to 60cm (24in) ↔ to 40cm (16in)

Helianthemum 'Fire Dragon' ♀

EVERGREEN SHRUB

This rock rose flowers for many months from early summer and quickly spreads to form a dense mound of linear, grey-green leaves, which set off the bright orange-red, cup-shaped blooms. It will inject colour into a sunny bank, rock or gravel garden, or a raised bed. It will flourish in full sun and a well-drained, alkaline soil, and should be trimmed after flowering to maintain its shape.

☼ ◊ ✿ ✿ ✿

‡ to 30cm (12in) ↔ to 45cm (18in)

Heuchera 'Cherries Jubilee'

EVERGREEN PERENNIAL

Heucheras are invaluable little plants
with their neat mounds of foliage and
long-lasting flowers. While there are
now many varieties to choose from
with brilliant leaf colours and pretty
flowers, 'Cherries Jubilee' is notable
for its dark, chocolatey green foliage.
Spires of coral red flowers appear in
early summer. Heucheras are ideal for
containers and for the shady border.
They tolerate most soils, but perform
best in slightly acid conditions.

✿ ◐ ❀❀❀

‡ to 20cm (8in) ↔ to 40cm (16in)

Leptospermum scoparium 'Kiwi' ♥

EVERGREEN SHRUB

This New Zealand tea tree has aromatic,
lance-shaped, purple-tinged leaves,
and produces masses of dark, crimson-
red flowers from the late spring to early
summer. It is not hardy and may need
to be overwintered in a container in a
cool greenhouse. In mild areas, grow it
outside in well-drained soil next to a
sunny, south-facing wall, ideally on
a sheltered patio or terrace where the
flowers can be fully appreciated.
Suitable for coastal gardens.

✿ ◊ ❀❀ *f*

‡↔ to 3m (10ft)

Lilium chalcedonicum
PERENNIAL BULB

The scarlet turkscap lily is a tall plant with deep green leaves, arranged in a spiral up the stem. It flowers from early to midsummer and has bright scarlet petals, which are strongly swept back, while the long stamens with bright red anthers drop down from the centre of the flower. This unusual lily makes a valuable addition to a sunny or partially shaded herbaceous border, and will grow in almost any well-drained soil.

☼ ◊ ✿✿✿
‡ to 1.5m (5ft)

Lupinus 'Inverewe Red'
PERENNIAL

Bold spikes of deep red flowers appear on this lupin in early summer above clumps of palmate leaves. Planted in groups in a herbaceous border, or as a superb addition to a cottage-style garden. Encourage a second flush of flowers by deadheading. Lupins need a site in full sun or partial shade, and should be planted in well-drained, fertile soil. They usually benefit from staking and the succulent new growth is favoured by slugs and snails.

☼ ☼ ◊ ✿✿✿
‡ to 1.2m (4ft) ↔ to 45cm (18in)

Lychnis x *arkwrightii* 'Vesuvius'

PERENNIAL

This dramatic, but often short-lived perennial has lance-shaped, dark maroon leaves that form a perfect foil for the cross-shaped, brilliant scarlet flowers. These are borne freely from early to midsummer. Good for a sunny, mixed or herbaceous border, especially those with a hot-coloured theme. The plants are fairly low-maintenance and drought tolerant, and they will grow in coastal conditions.

☼ ☀ ◊ ◊ ❀ ❀ ❀

‡ to 45cm (18in) ↔ to 30cm (12in)

Meconopsis napaulensis

PERENNIAL

The satin poppy is a very large plant which can take several years to grow to flowering size. When mature, it will produce clusters of large, red, purple or pink bowl-shaped flowers from early to midsummer, after which the plant will die. It is suited to a woodland garden or the back or a wild area. Plant it in semi-shade, in neutral or acid, moist soil. Sow new seed annually in autumn or spring to provide a continual supply of mature plants that will be ready to bloom in the summer.

☀ ◊ ◊ ❀ ❀ ❀

‡ to 2.5m (8ft) ↔ to 90cm (36in)

Paeonia delavayi ♀
DECIDUOUS SHRUB

The flowers of this tree peony are
borne in early summer, and have dark
red petals and yellow stamens. The
handsome, deeply-dissected, blue-green
foliage provides colour and structure
long after the flowers have faded. It
is perfect for the back of a herbaceous
or mixed border, and prefers a sunny or
partially shaded situation in moist, well
drained soil. Best left alone, apart from
occasionally cutting out one or two of
the oldest stems in autumn.

☼ ☀ ◊ ◊ ❀ ❀ ❀ *f*
‡↔ to 2m (6ft)

Papaver commutatum 'Ladybird' ♀
ANNUAL

A distinctive hardy annual poppy, with
numerous glossy brilliant-red flowers.
Grow it in groups in a gravel garden,
or a border with a fiery colour theme,
in full sun and well-drained soil. It
does not need staking. It will self-seed
naturally, or seed can be collected and
sown in spring where it is to flower.
Alternatively, remove the dead heads
to prevent seed setting and prolong
the flowering season.

☼ ◊ ❀ ❀ ❀
‡ to 45cm (18in) ↔ to 15cm (6in)

Papaver orientale 'Beauty of Livermere'

PERENNIAL

Large scarlet blooms with black centres are borne on the long, sturdy stems of this poppy from early to midsummer. Its vibrant colours contrast well with gravel, or plant it in a sunny border, where it can help to disguise the dying foliage of spring bulbs. It dies back early after flowering, and should be grown close to late-flowering perennials that will fill the gap later in the year. Plant it in well-drained soil.

☼ ◊ ✿✿✿
‡ to 1.2m (4ft) ↔ to 1m (3ft)

Papaver rhoeas

ANNUAL

Field poppies are well-known summer-flowering annuals, ideal for creating a splash of colour in any sunny part of the garden. They are easily grown from seed if sown in spring onto a prepared seedbed, with poor to moderately fertile soil. Various flower colours are available, from white to pink and mauve, or mixed shades. Once established, the plants may self-seed in successive years. Alternatively, collect the ripe "pepper pot" seedheads and save the seed for the next season.

☼ ◊ ✿✿✿
‡ to 60cm (24in) ↔ to 15cm (6in)

Pelargonium 'Caligula'

PERENNIAL

This miniature zonal pelargonium bears dark green leaves, and double, bright scarlet flowers, which are produced from early summer up to the first frosts, if they are deadheaded regularly. Its compact size and long flowering season combine to make it an excellent plant for containers, although it can also be used as bedding in the garden planted in full sun, in free-draining soil. It is tender, and must be kept in a frost-free place in winter.

☼ ◊ ❀

‡ to 12cm (5in) ↔ to 10cm (4in)

Potentilla fruticosa 'Red Ace'

EVERGREEN SHRUB

This shrubby cinquefoil bears orange-red, saucer-shaped, single flowers, which contrast well with the small, divided leaves. It blooms from late spring to mid-autumn, and makes a wonderful low informal hedging or gravel garden plant. Grow it in a sunny position, in well-drained, poor to moderately fertile soil, and trim after flowering, removing weak shoots and cutting dead wood back to the base.

☼ ◊ ❀ ❀ ❀

‡ to 1m (3ft) ↔ to 1.5cm (5ft)

Potentilla
'Gibson's Scarlet' ♀

PERENNIAL

A profusion of single, bright scarlet flowers appear on this cinquefoil from early to late summer. The blooms are produced on long stems above clumps of soft green, palmate foliage. It is an excellent plant for the front of a sunny border, or use it in a raised bed or gravel garden. It needs a sunny position, in poor or moderately fertile, well-drained soil.

☼ ◊ ❋ ❋ ❋

‡ to 45cm (18in) ↔ to 60cm (24in)

Rheum palmatum
'Atrosanguineum' ♀

PERENNIAL

Chinese rhubarb is a large, spreading plant with huge, deeply-cut, rough-textured, green leaves that are crimson-purple when young. In early summer the spectacular foliage is accompanied by tall stems of feathery, pinky-red flowers that provide a focal point in a damp border, or beneath deciduous trees. This plant is happy in full sun or partial shade, in moist soil. Mulch plants annually in spring with well-rotted compost.

☼ ◑ ◊ ❋ ❋ ❋

‡↔ to 2m (6ft)

Rhododendron **'Spek's Brilliant'**

DECIDUOUS SHRUB

Mollis-type deciduous azaleas like 'Spek's Brilliant' are tough plants, and are popular not only for their late flowers, which can be used to extend the rhododendron season, but also for their autumn leaf colour. This variety bears full trusses of funnel-shaped, bright scarlet-orange flowers, with deeper-coloured flares inside. It tolerates full sun, but must have humus-rich, neutral to acid soil. Similar varieties include 'Fireball' and 'Dracula'.

☀ ◐ ◐ ❀❀❀
↕↔to 2.5m (8ft)

Rosa gallica **var. *officinalis* ♥**

DECIDUOUS SHRUB

The crimson damask rose produces lightly scented, pinky-red flowers from early summer. These are followed in autumn by orange-red hips. Plant this compact rose with other old-fashioned roses, or in a shrub or mixed border, alongside hardy geraniums. Alternatively, use it as a low hedge which can be clipped over lightly in early spring. Plant it in full sun in fertile, moist, well-drained soil.

☀ ◇ ◐ ❀❀❀ *f*
↕ to 80cm (32in) ↔ to 1m (3ft)

Rosa KNOCK OUT ('RadRazz')

DECIDUOUS SHRUB

This easy-to-grow deciduous shrub rose can form an informal hedge or work well in a mixed perennial or shrub border. The fragrant cherry red flowers appear from late spring to frost and attract butterflies. In autumn, orange-red hips develop as the dark green foliage turns burgundy. Drought tolerant once established, this rose features excellent disease resistance. Grow in full sun to partial shade in moist, well-drained soil.

☼ ☀ ◊ ◊ ✿✿✿ *f*

↕↔ to 1.2m (4ft)

Rosa L.D. BRAITHWAITE ('Auscrim') ♥

DECIDUOUS SHRUB

A superb modern shrub rose, this form is covered from early summer to autumn with crimson flowers. The blooms are slightly scented when they first open, but develop a stronger fragrance as they age. This rose has a compact habit, and is ideally suited to small gardens, where it can be planted as a specimen or in a border. It will do best when grown in full sun in fertile, moist, well-drained soil. Lightly trim to shape in late winter or early spring.

☼ ◊ ◊ ✿✿✿ *f*

↕ to 90cm (36in) ↔ to 1.2m (4ft)

Rosa 'Roseraie de l'Haÿ' ♀

DECIDUOUS SHRUB

A rugosa shrub rose with heavily scented, purple-red flowers from early summer through to the autumn. The blooms are complemented by the light green, healthy foliage. It makes a prickly-stemmed hedge, ideal for a house boundary, or it can be used as a specimen plant or grown in a mixed border. It prefers full sun, and a deep, fertile, moist but well-drained soil. Clip hedges to shape in early spring, otherwise little pruning is required.

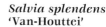

☼ ◊ ◐ ❋ ❋ ❋ *f*
‡ to 2.2m (7ft) ↔ to 2m (6ft)

Salvia splendens 'Van-Houttei'

PERENNIAL

Throughout summer, this variety of scarlet sage bears long spires of vibrant, tubular red flowers above the dark green, toothed foliage. Its long-lasting, brilliant flowers are an invaluable addition to any summer bedding or container display, but they will not survive winter unless overwintered in a frost-free place. The flowers are also good for cutting. 'Scarlet King' is similar, and varieties with pink, white, or bicoloured flowers are available.

☼ ◊ ❋ ❋
‡ to 1m (3ft) ↔ to 75cm (30in)

Sempervivum tectorum ♀
PERENNIAL

Often overlooked as a garden plant, the common houseleek forms rosettes of pointed, bristle-tipped, blue-green leaves, which often turn a rich purple-red in summer. The star-shaped, reddish-purple flowers appear in early summer, after which the leafy rosettes die, but are quickly replaced by new growth. Plant houseleeks in a sunny situation in a rock garden or a trough, or on a dry-stone wall. Good drainage is also essential, and they should be grown in gritty, well-drained compost.

☼ ◊ ❁ ❁ ❁

‡ to 15cm (6in) ↔ to 20cm (8in)

Tropaeolum speciosum ♀
CLIMBER

The flame nasturtium has beautiful rounded leaves that resemble flower petals. Throughout the summer and into autumn, it bears long-spurred, vermilion flowers, which are followed by round, blue fruit. It looks best grown against a trellis, or through an evergreen shrub, which has the benefit of providing some winter protection as it is not totally hardy. Otherwise use a thick winter mulch. Plant it in moist, but well-drained, fertile, neutral to acid soil in full sun or dappled shade.

☼ ☀ ◊ ◊ ❁ ❁

‡ to 3m (10ft)

Acanthus spinosus ♀

PERENNIAL

The distinctive, purple-hooded, white tubular flowers of bear's breeches are held on tall spikes. Its deeply divided leaves are a glossy dark green. Grow it in fertile, well-drained soil, close to a warm wall or in a herbaceous border in full sun. In partial shade it will produce lusher foliage. Divide clumps in spring or autumn. When given plenty of space, this clump-forming perennial makes a striking architectural plant. The flowers dry well when left on the plant or cut.

☼ ◑ ◊ ❀ ❀ ❀
‡ to 1.2m (4ft) ↔ to 60cm (24in)

Allium 'Globemaster' ♀

PERENNIAL BULB

The large flowerheads of this ornamental onion are made up of numerous small, intense-purple flowers grouped together in a huge globe that can reach 20cm (8in) across. The grey basal leaves are slightly hairy and arch over at the tips. For maximum impact, plant the bulbs in the autumn in groups of at least five, in a sunny border, in well-drained, fertile soil. Although good for cutting fresh, the globes look most dramatic when left to dry on the plant.

☼ ◊ ❀ ❀ ❀
‡ to 80cm (32in) ↔ to 20cm (8in)

Allium 'Purple Sensation' ♥
PERENNIAL BULB

This is a superb, ornamental flowering onion, with long strap-shaped greyish-green leaves. In late spring and early summer it produces large flowerheads that are good for cutting, comprised of 50 or more tiny, star- shaped, deep violet florets. The decorative seedheads last well into late summer, although any self-sown plants that result may be inferior to the original. Plant the bulbs in autumn in a sunny position in fertile, well-drained soil.

☼ ◊ ❀❀❀
 ‡ to 80cm (32in) ↔ to 7cm (3in)

Brassica oleracea 'Azur Star'
BIENNIAL

The purple kohl rabi makes a fabulous early summer foliage plant, useful for temporarily filling gaps in border displays. They mix well with blue and purple flowering plants, such as alliums and lupins, due to their richly purple-tinted leaves and stems. Kohl rabi is best known as a vegetable with an oddly swollen, yet pleasantly flavoured stem. When this reaches the size of a tennis ball, the plants can be uprooted and the round stems peeled and cooked.

☼ ◊ ❀❀❀
 ‡↔ to 60cm (24in)

Buddleja alternifolia ♀
DECIDUOUS SHRUB

Clusters of sweetly scented, pale lilac
flowers wreath the arching branches
of this shrub in early summer. So many
are produced that they nearly hide the
silvery-green, lance-shaped leaves. It
flowers on the previous year's wood
and should be pruned back to a strong
bud after flowering. Cut out around a
quarter of the old branches each year
to stimulate new growth. It can be also
be trained as a standard tree, as shown
here. Grow in fertile, well-drained,
preferably alkaline soil in full sun.

☼ ◊ ✽✽✽ *f*
↕↔ to 4m (12ft)

Campanula carpatica 'Jewel'
PERENNIAL

Forming low, dome-shaped mounds of
heart-shaped leaves, this very pretty
plant bears masses of bright blue-purple,
upward-facing bellflowers in summer.
The greatest concentration of flowers
appear in early summer, but the display
often continues or repeats into late
summer. This bellflower grows well
on dry-stone walls, in paving crevices
or rock gardens, in containers, or as
ground cover. It tolerates chalky soils.

☼ ◐ ◊ ◑ ✽✽✽
↕↔ to 15cm (6in)

Campanula glomerata 'Superba' ♀

PERENNIAL

The clustered bellflower is a fast-growing, clump-forming perennial carrying beautiful, dense heads of large, bell-shaped, purple-violet flowers from early summer. The lance-shaped to oval, mid-green leaves are arranged in rosettes at the base of the plant and along the stems. This super plant suits both herbaceous borders or informal, cottage-style gardens; it prefers neutral to alkaline soil. Cut back after flowering to encourage a second flush of flowers.

‡ to 75cm (30in) ↔ to 1m (3ft)

Clematis 'The President' ♀

PERENNIAL

This free-flowering clematis deserves a prominent spot on a pergola or decorative trellis where it can show off its amazing silver-backed, deep purple-blue blooms. These can measure up to 15cm (6in) across. It should be planted in fertile, well-drained soil in full sun or partial shade. Clematis grow best when their roots are in the shade. Remove any dead shoots in early spring and prune the others back to a strong pair of buds.

☼ ☽ ◊ ❀ ❀ ❀

‡ to 3m (10ft)

Corylus maxima '**Purpurea**' ♀
DECIDUOUS SHRUB

This filbert forms a large, upright shrub or small tree, with dangling purple catkins in winter. In spring the dark purple leaves appear. Later, in summer and early autumn there are edible, purple-husked nuts. It makes an attractive specimen tree. Grow in full sun for good foliage colour and abundant nuts. It is best in fertile, well-drained soil and grows well in chalk soil.

☼ ◊ ❀❀❀
‡ to 6m (20ft) ↔ to 5m (15ft)

Cotinus '**Royal Purple**'
DECIDUOUS SHRUB

This purple-leaved smoke bush is grown for its rounded leaves. The fresh foliage looks good right from the outset, but this is heightened in late summer with the appearance of cloud-like plumes of tiny pink-purple flowers. In autumn, its appearance changes again as the leaves turn a brilliant scarlet. 'Royal Purple' is excellent in a shrub border or at the back of a mixed border, or as a specimen tree; where space permits, plant in groups. Prune to size in spring, before the leaves emerge.

☼ ◑ ◊ ◊ ❀❀❀
‡↔ to 5m (15ft)

Delphinium 'Bruce' ♀

PERENNIAL

A mixed summer border would be incomplete without delphiniums. 'Bruce' produces deep violet-purple flowers on tall spires in early summer. An autumn flowering can often be encouraged if the faded flowering stems are cut back. Easily damaged by winds and rain, the plants should be staked when young with a strong cane and the tall stems tied in as they grow. Plant in a well-drained, fertile soil in full sun. Protect emerging foliage from slugs and snails.

☼ ◊ ❁❁❁

‡ to 2.2m (7ft) ↔ to 90cm (36in)

Echium vulgare

PERENNIAL

Viper's bugloss is a bushy, short-lived perennial with bristly hairy leaves, stems, and flowers. It is grown for its early summer flowers, which are borne in short, curved spikes amid and above the narrow leaves. The flowers are purple in bud, opening to broadly bell-shaped, purple-blue, sometimes pink or white flowers. They are attractive to bees. Vipers bugloss can be grown as temporary bedding or in containers.

☼ ◊ ❁❁❁

‡ to 30cm (12in) ↔ to 20cm (8in)

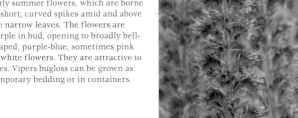

Erodium manescavii
PERENNIAL

The delicate magenta-purple, saucer-shaped blooms of this clump-forming plant are very similar to those of the hardy geranium. Throughout summer, they are borne on long stalks in profuse clusters of up to 20. The top two petals of each flower are darkly freckled. The leaves are attractive, too, being deeply divided, lance-shaped and slightly hairy. Plant it in gritty, very well-drained soil, in full sun. A rock garden would suit it well, or plant it at the front of the herbaceous border. It self-seeds freely.

☼ ◊ ✿✿✿
‡ to 45cm (18in) ↔ to 60cm (24in)

Erysimum 'Bowles's Mauve' ♡
EVERGREEN PERENNIAL

A long-flowering wallflower, 'Bowles Mauve' produces tall spikes of mauve blooms throughout the year; but early summer is when they are most profuse. The flowers are set off by narrow, grey-green leaves. Plant it in well-drained, poor to moderately fertile, preferably alkaline soil in full sun. A lovely border plant, in cold areas give it the shelter of a warm wall. Trim after flowering and take cuttings to make more plants as it tends to be short lived.

☼ ◊ ✿✿✿
‡ to 75cm (30in) ↔ to 60cm (24in)

Geranium psilostemon ♀

PERENNIAL

One of the largest hardy geraniums, this fast-growing plant has deep magenta-purple flowers with an almost black eye. The toothed, mid-green leaves are infused with crimson in spring and autumn. A useful ground-covering plant to infill around shrubs in a border, it grows well in most well-drained soils, in sun or partial shade. Trim it over after flowering to encourage new growth. In the right conditions it will self-seed freely; alternatively divide large clumps in spring.

☼ ☀ ◊ ❀ ❀ ❀
‡↔ to 1.2m (4ft)

Geranium sylvaticum 'Mayflower' ♀

PERENNIAL

With its white-centred, rich violet-blue, upward-facing flowers, 'Mayflower' is one of the most attractive geraniums available. Its deeply lobed, mid-green leaves form a shapely mound. It is a good naturalizer in open ground or under trees and shrubs. Plant it in moist, but well-drained, soil; although it tolerates shade it would prefer full sun. Trim the plant over after flowering to encourage new growth.

☼ ☀ ◊ ◊ ❀ ❀ ❀
‡ to 1m (3ft) ↔ to 60cm (24in)

Gladiolus communis subsp. *byzantinus* ♀

PERENNIAL CORM

The tall flower spikes of this gladiolus carry up to 20 magenta flowers that add zest to an early summer border, and are good for cutting. The rich-green, strappy leaves reach 70cm (28in) long. Unless you want huge swathes of these plants, take care if disturbing the soil around them as small corms will break off and spread. Plant in full sun, in fertile, well-drained soil. Corms do not need to be lifted in winter, but in cold gardens cover the soil with a mulch.

☼ ◊ ✿ ✿ ✿

↕ to 70cm (28in) ↔ to 15cm (6in)

Heliotropium arborescens 'Marine'

EVERGREEN SHRUB

The heliotrope is a tender, short-lived shrub often grown as annual bedding. With its clusters of fragrant, violet-blue flowers, it looks good in pots and window boxes or as front-of-the-border edging. Plant it in full sun in moist, but well-drained, fertile soil. Take softwood cuttings in summer and overwinter them in a cool greenhouse. You can also grow heliotropes as conservatory plants. Use a loam-based compost and provide shading from strong sunlight.

☼ ◊ ◑ ✿ *f*

↕↔ to 45cm (18in)

Heuchera 'Palace Purple'

EVERGREEN PERENNIAL

Heucheras are evergreen, or nearly evergreen, clump-forming plants, which are grown primarily for their attractive foliage. 'Palace Purple' has glossy, deeply lobed, purplish-red leaves and airy spikes of tiny greenish-cream flowers. It makes a sumptuous ground-cover plant in a herbaceous or shrub border. Plant in full sun or partial shade, in moist, but well-drained, neutral fertile soil.

☼ ☀ ◐ ◊ ◖ ❀ ❀ ❀
↕↔to 45cm (18in)

Iris ensata 'Hue and Cry' ♀

PERENNIAL

The Japanese iris is a beautiful aquatic marginal plant. The purple 'Hue and Cry' has flat flowers with six large, white-veined, lower petals, each with a yellow stripe down the centre. Short periods of flooding are tolerated but rather than total immersion, this plant prefers permanently moist or wet, acid soil, and is suitable for a bog garden. There are many other attractive varieties to choose from.

☼ ☀ ◐ ◊ ◖ ❀ ❀ ❀
↕ to 90cm (36in)

Iris x *robusta* 'Gerald Darby' ♀
PERENNIAL

Another stunning water iris, 'Gerald Darby' has narrow, sword-shaped leaves that are covered at the base with purple spots. Its stems, which are dark violet, produce four bluish-purple flowers, each marked with a patch of yellow. Plant it in a moist border or at the edge of a pond. Given the right conditions, this vigorous clump-former can reach the spectacular height of 1.8m (6ft); however, it usually measures just under half that.

☼ ☼ ◊ ◐ ◑ ❈ ❈ ❈
‡ to 75cm (30in)

Iris versicolor ♀
PERENNIAL

The richly coloured petals of the blue flag iris have beautiful markings, with heavy purple veining and a large white patch at their base. Together with the vibrant green, sword-shaped leaves, this is an attractive plant for a bog garden, the shallow margins of a natural pond, or a moisture-retentive border. Plant the rhizomes in permanently moist or wet soil, but not underwater.

☼ ☼ ◊ ◐ ◑ ❈ ❈ ❈
‡ to 80cm (32in)

Lavandula angustifolia '*Hidcote*' ♀

EVERGREEN SHRUB

This English lavender has narrow, silver-grey, aromatic leaves, and in mid- to late summer it produces spikes of highly fragrant, small purple flowers, loved by bees. 'Hidcote' makes a good low hedge, or is suitable for planting in a gravel garden. It needs a site in full sun, and a slightly fertile, well-drained soil. Lavenders are easily propagated by taking semi-ripe cuttings in summer. Trim hedges in spring and lightly after flowering to remove the dead heads.

☼ ◊ ❀❀❀ *f*
‡ to 60cm (24in) ↔ to 75cm (30in)

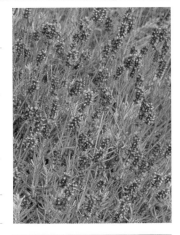

Lavandula stoechas ♀

EVERGREEN SHRUB

French lavender forms an attractive rounded shrub, with branching stems covered with narrow greyish-green, slightly fragrant leaves. It is smaller and flowers slightly earlier than English lavender, but the blooms are not as fragrant. The small purple flowers, each topped by a tuft of pinky-mauve, petal-like bracts, are produced throughout the summer. It is not completely hardy, and should be grown in a warm, sheltered position in slightly fertile, well-drained soil, or in containers.

☼ ◊ ❀❀ *f*
‡↔ to 60cm (24in)

Polemonium **'Lambrook Mauve'** ♀

PERENNIAL

Jacob's ladder is a free-flowering plant that produces clusters of lilac-blue flowers on upright, branched stems. A neat, mound-forming perennial, it is ideally suited to the front of a mixed or herbaceous border. It also makes a lovely feature plant in formal planting, or among low-growing grasses. Give it a spot in full sun or partial shade, in a moist, but well-drained, fertile soil. Deadhead regularly and divide large clumps during the spring.

☀ ☀ ◊ ◊ ❀ ❀ ❀
↕↔ to 45cm (18in)

Roscoea humeana ♀

PERENNIAL

This unusual tuberous plant has orchid-like flowers with a prominent, hooded upper petal. The lush, deep-green, rounded leaves set the blooms off perfectly. A sheltered woodland garden would be the ideal home for this plant, as it grows best in damp shade in a cool climate. It is not fully hardy, so where frosts are likely in winter, cover the root area with a deep mulch, such as leafmould.

☀ ◊ ❀ ❀
↕ to 25cm (10in) ↔ to 20cm (8in)

Stachys macrantha 'Superba'

PERENNIAL

Erect spikes of pinky-purple, hooded flowers are held above rosettes of wrinkled, dark green, heart-shaped leaves. An easy going plant for the front of a herbaceous border, it flowers over a long period from early summer until early autumn. Plant it in well-drained, fertile soil. It is best in full sun, but will tolerate a certain amount of shade.

☼ ◐ ◊ ❀ ❀ ❀
‡ to 45cm (18in) ↔ to 60cm (24in)

Thalictrum aquilegiifolium 'Thundercloud' ♀

PERENNIAL

Meadow rues are clump-forming plants with fern-like foliage, composed of small, rounded leaflets. 'Thundercloud' has erect, waxy stems, and clusters of tiny flowers are borne in the summer. The outer part of the flower quickly falls away to leave the colourful, dark purple stamens that give the blooms a frothy appearance. It may take some time to become established, and prefers partial shade and deep, moist soil.

◐ ◊ ❀ ❀ ❀
‡ to 1m (3ft) ↔ to 30cm (12in)

Aconitum napellus
PERENNIAL

Monkshood is a strongly upright plant, much like a delphinium, with spires of very attractive, hooded, violet-blue flowers that begin to appear from early to midsummer. Behind this beauty lies a dark secret: all parts of this plant are highly poisonous. This makes them ideal for the back of a border where they won't be disturbed. Plant in groups of five or more for the best display, in humus-rich, moist but well-drained soil. The plants will not need staking. When handling the plants, wear gloves.

☼ ☀ ◐ ◗ ❀ ❀ ❀

↕ to 1.5m (5ft) ↔ to 30cm (12in)

Ageratum houstonianum 'Adriatic'
ANNUAL

The floss flower forms a mound of downy, oval, green leaves, above which frothy-looking heads of tiny mid-blue flowers are borne in summer and up to the first frosts. It is widely grown as a bedding plant and complements low-growing annuals with bright yellow flowers, such as calceolarias. It is also suitable for containers and hanging baskets. Plant it in full sun, in a moist, well-drained soil. In containers, keep it well watered when in flower.

☼ ◐ ◗ ❀

↕ to 20cm (8in) ↔ to 30cm (12in)

Ajuga reptans 'Variegata'
EVERGREEN PERENNIAL

Bugle is a useful, easy going ground-cover plant which forms a carpet of evergreen leaves, borne on spreading stems. 'Variegata' has grey-green leaves with a cream edge and cream markings. From late spring to early summer, bugle produces upright stems of small, dark blue tubular flowers. Plant it in any moist soil in partial shade. It will also tolerate full sun if the soil does not dry out during the summer.

☼ ◑ ◐ ◊ ❋ ❋ ❋
‡ to 15cm (6in) ↔ to 90cm (36in)

Allium caeruleum ♀
PERENNIAL BULB

A beautiful onion, this variety produces spherical heads of tiny bright blue, star-shaped flowers in early summer. The blooms are produced after the narrow leaves have died down on triangular, stiff green stems. Plant groups of bulbs in the autumn in a herbaceous border, gravel garden, or a large container, in full sun and well-drained, fertile soil.

☼ ◊ ❋ ❋
‡ to 80cm (32in) ↔ to 15cm (6in)

Anchusa azurea '**Loddon Royalist**' ♀

PERENNIAL

This beautiful, early summer-flowering plant forms a clump of lance-shaped leaves, and robust branched stems of deep blue flowers. The blooms are attractive to bees, making it a good candidate for a wild garden, or a herbaceous border. Plant it in groups in full sun and moist, well-drained soil. Young plants should be cut back after flowering to promote the growth of basal leaves. Deadhead mature plants to encourage a second flush of flowers.

☼ ◊ ◖ ❋ ❋ ❋

‡ to 1.2m (4ft) ↔ to 60cm (24in)

Aquilegia alpina

PERENNIAL

The alpine columbine has an upright habit, and is suitable for planting in a herbaceous border, rock garden or raised bed. It blooms in late spring and early summer and produces long stems that bear slightly nodding, deep blue flowers. The stems thrust up above finely-divided, bluish-green, ferny foliage. Grow it in a sunny or partially shaded position, in fertile, moist, well-drained, gritty soil.

☼ ☀ ◊ ◖ ❋ ❋ ❋

‡ to 45cm (18in) ↔ to 30cm (12in)

Baptisia australis ♀
PERENNIAL

False indigo is a spreading plant with mid-green leaves divided into three egg-shaped leaflets. In the summer it bears tall spikes of dark-blue pea-like flowers, which are often marked with white or cream. The flowers are followed in autumn by large seed pods, suitable for drying. Plant it in an open, sunny site in deep, very free-draining, neutral to acid soil. It is suitable for a herbaceous border, but once planted it is best left undisturbed. Stake tall plants unless the planting site is sheltered.

☼ ◊ ❀❀❀

‡ to 75cm (30in) ↔ to 60cm (24in)

Borago officinalis
ANNUAL

This important herb produces intensely blue, star-shaped early summer flowers, borne in drooping clusters. When in full bloom, it is not uncommon to see bumblebees busying themselves around the bristly oval foliage in search of nectar. Borage is a useful plant for the kitchen garden, as the flowers can be added to salads, or frozen in ice cubes and used in drinks. It will need to be sown from seed each year, but established clumps may self-sow. A white-flowered form, 'Alba' is available.

☼ ☀ ◊ ◗ ❀❀❀

‡ to 90cm (36in) ↔ to 30cm (12in)

Brachyscome iberidifolia
ANNUAL

The Swan River daisy is a bushy, sprawling plant, with deeply divided, greyish-green, ferny foliage. In summer it produces blue, violet, or white, slightly scented, daisy-like flowers. An excellent plant for edging summer containers, including hanging baskets, it will also bring colour to the front of a herbaceous border. The seed should be sown under glass in the spring, and young plants moved out after the last frost, in a sunny position and well-drained, fertile soil.

☼ ◊ ◐ ❀ *f*
‡↔ to 45cm (18in)

Campanula barbata
PERENNIAL

The bearded bellflower is so named because of the unusual hairs that edge the pendent, lavender-blue flowers that appear in early summer. A short-lived perennial, it forms rosettes of hairy, lance-shaped, mid-green leaves beneath the erect flower stems. It is a suitable plant for a rock or gravel garden and should be planted in full sun or partial shade, in moist, but well-drained soil.

☼ ❁ ◊ ◐ ❀❀❀
‡ to 20cm (8in) ↔ to 12cm (5in)

Campanula persicifolia 'Telham Beauty'

PERENNIAL

One of the most vigorous bellflowers, this form bears rosettes of evergreen lance-shaped, bright green leaves. In early summer pale-blue, bell-shaped flowers appear for many weeks on tall stems. Flowering can be prolonged by regular deadheading. It is best planted in groups in a herbaceous or mixed border, or in a woodland or wild-flower garden. Grow it in full sun or partial shade, in fertile, well-drained, neutral or slightly alkaline soil.

☼ ☽ ◊ ❀ ❀ ❀
‡ to 1m (3ft) ↔ to 30cm (12in)

Ceanothus 'Gloire de Versailles' ♀

DECIDUOUS SHRUB

Hardier than many other Californian lilacs, 'Gloire de Versailles' has oval dark green leaves, and clusters of tiny, deep sky-blue flowers, held in open spikes at the end of the stems. It flowers in early summer and again in the autumn. A good shrub for a mixed border or a Mediterranean-style garden, it prefers a position in full sun and a well-drained soil. Overgrown specimens can be cut back hard in spring.

☼ ◊ ❀ ❀ ❀
‡↔ to 1.5m (5ft)

Centaurea montana

PERENNIAL

This perennial cornflower is a vigorous plant that is easy to grow on most soils. It looks very pretty in early summer with its vivid, purple-blue flowers from late spring to midsummer. They have a spidery, thistle-like appearance and are attractive to butterflies and bees. This is a creeping plant that forms soft, woolly mats or clumps of broad and pointed, mid-green leaves. In exposed sites, stakes may be needed to support the stems.

☼ ☀ ◊ ◑ ❀ ❀ ❀

‡ to 50cm (20in) ↔ to 60cm (24in)

Clematis 'H.F. Young'

CLIMBER

This purple-blue, mid-season clematis is reliable and freely produces very big, pale yellow-centred flowers in early summer. A second, less profuse flowering may occur in late summer. Its compact size makes it a good choice for containers, as long as the roots are in shade, or it can be trained up a support or encouraged to grow through shrubs, such as roses. Mulch in late winter and tie in young growth carefully, ideally to fill gaps in the display. Trim lightly in late winter or early spring.

☼ ◊ ◑ ❀ ❀ ❀

‡ to 2m (6ft)

Consolida ajacis

ANNUAL

The annual delphiniums, otherwise
known as larkspurs, are fast-growing
herbaceous plants, with deeply divided,
feathery leaves. They look similar to
perennial delphiniums but tend to have
shorter flowering stems. In the summer
they produce spikes of violet-blue, pink,
or white flowers, with long spurs, and
are good for cutting. Ideal for filling
gaps left by spring bulbs in a border,
they grow best in full sun in light, well-
drained soil. Sow the seed *in situ* in
spring, or autumn in mild gardens.

‡ to 1.2m (4ft) ↔ to 30cm (12in)

Cynoglossum nervosum

PERENNIAL

Hounds tongue is a herbaceous
perennial closely related to borage,
admired for its bright blue, forget-me-
not flowers that are carried in small
clusters on upright stems. They are good
for supplying colour to early summer
beds and borders, and they are good for
cutting. The plant gets its name from
the narrow, mid-green, hairy leaves.

‡↔ to 60cm (24in)

Delphinium grandiflorum 'Blue Butterfly'

PERENNIAL

A short-lived plant, this delphinium is often grown as an annual. It has deeply divided leaves, and in summer it bears spikes of bright blue flowers. Grow it in a bedding scheme, or at the front of a herbaceous border. It also makes a good cut flower. Plant this delphinium in well-drained, fertile soil in full sun. It is less demanding than the large-flowered varieties, such as 'Blue Nile'.

☼ ◊ ✲✲✲
‡↔ to 30cm (12in)

Echium vulgare 'Blue Bedder'

BIENNIAL

The dwarf form of viper's bugloss has an upright habit, and produces bristly, lance-shaped, dark-green leaves. In the early summer it bears an abundance of blue flowers, which turn pink as they age. Plant it in a wild-flower garden or use it as bedding. Viper's bugloss likes a sunny situation and reasonably fertile, well-drained soil.

☼ ◊ ✲✲✲
‡ to 40cm (16in) ↔ to 30cm (12in)

Erigeron 'Dunkelste Aller' ♀

PERENNIAL

Daisy-like flowers always look so cheerful and the blooms of the fleabane are no exception. This one has a sunny yellow centre, fringed with violet blue, semi-double petals. A clump-forming plant with lance-shaped, greyish-green leaves, it would do well in a mixed herbaceous border or rock garden. It will also thrive in a coastal garden but will need staking on exposed sites. As a cut flower, it also has great lasting qualities. Plant in fertile soil that does not dry out in summer.

☼ ◊ ❋ ❋ ❋

‡ to 80cm (32in) ↔ to 60cm (24in)

Festuca glauca 'Blaufuchs'

PERENNIAL

This bright blue fescue is a densely tufted, evergreen, perennial grass. It is excellent in a border or rock garden as a foil to other cool-coloured plants, or for providing a contrast in shape and form. Spikes of not particularly striking, violet-flushed flowers are borne in early summer, above the foliage. The narrow, bright blue leaves are its chief attraction. Grow in any dry, well-drained soil. For the best foliage colour, divide and replant clumps every three years.

☼ ◊ ❋ ❋ ❋

‡ to 30cm (12in) ↔ to 25cm (10in)

Geranium clarkei 'Kashmir Blue'

PERENNIAL

This tough geranium makes useful, herbaceous ground cover for a sunny site, flowering profusely in early summer. The flowers are a lovely dark blue, but varieties in white, purple, and pink are also available. It thrives in most garden soils. Grown in a border, either as edging or mixed in with other low plants, it will need occasional cutting back after flowering to keep it within bounds. To establish as ground cover, plant in groups of five or more.

☼ ☀ ◊ ◑ ❀ ❀ ❀

↕ to 45cm (18in) ↔ indefinite

Geranium 'Johnson's Blue' ♡

PERENNIAL

This is one of the most widely-grown geraniums, favoured for its deeply lobed, mid-green leaves, and long flowering season in summer. It bears deep lavender-blue, saucer-shaped flowers with pink centres. Plant it at the front of a herbaceous border or use it as underplanting in a rose bed. It will grow in most soils, but does best in well-drained, fertile soil in a sunny or partially shaded situation. Divide large clumps in autumn.

☼ ☀ ◊ ◑ ❀ ❀ ❀

↕ to 30cm (12in) ↔ to 60cm (24in)

Geranium pratense 'Mrs Kendall Clark' ♀

PERENNIAL

The meadow cranesbill is a clump-forming plant, with deeply lobed, mid-green leaves. The single flowers appear from early to midsummer and are bluey-grey flushed with pale pink, or sometimes violet-blue with delicate white veining. The meadow cranesbill is a beautiful plant for the front of a border, or use it as ground cover. It grows well in most soils, but prefers a well-drained, fertile soil in full sun or partial shade.

☼ ☀ ◊ ◊ ❀ ❀ ❀
‡ to 90cm (36in) ↔ to 60cm (24in)

Hosta 'Halcyon' ♀

PERENNIAL

The thick, heart-shaped, blue-green leaves of this hosta may be slightly less susceptible to slug damage than some other varieties. In the summer it bears spikes of greyish-lavender funnel-shaped flowers. The colour of the foliage may fade in bright sun, so it is advisable to plant it in partial shade, beneath shrubs or trees, in moist, well-drained soil. In spring, mulch hostas with organic matter, such as composted bark, to conserve moisture in summer.

☀ ◊ ◊ ❀ ❀ ❀
‡ to 40cm (16in) ↔ to 70cm (28in)

Hosta 'Krossa Regal' ♀
PERENNIAL

'Krossa Regal' lives up to its royal name, having both a grand habit and an RHS Award of Garden Merit. It is tall and vigorous, bearing lovely blue-green, heavily veined leaves that emerge rapidly from underground buds in spring. As with all hostas, protect from slugs and snails, although this variety shows greater resistance than others. Long stems that bear beautiful, short-lived, pale violet flowers emerge from the centre of each clump in summer. Remove the flowers once they fade.

☼ ☀ ◐ ◊ ❀ ❀ ❀

‡ to 45cm (18in) ↔ to 60cm (24in)

Iris ensata 'Flying Tiger' ♀
PERENNIAL

Japanese irises are beautiful plants with striking, large flat blooms. The flowers of 'Flying Tiger' measure up to 30cm (12in) across and have rounded petals, marked with bold violet-blue veins and a splash of yellow radiating from the centre. Although it is an aquatic plant, it will grow in a bog garden or moist border, as long as the roots do not dry out in the summer. When grown in a border, it prefers a rich, moist, acid soil.

☼ ☀ ◐ ◊ ♦ ❀ ❀ ❀

‡ to 90cm (36in) ↔ indefinite

Iris 'Jane Phillips' ♀
PERENNIAL

An elegant, tall bearded iris, this variety has bluish-green, sword-shaped leaves, and mid-blue, fragrant flowers. To ensure a good show of flowers year after year, plant it in front of a sunny wall, or in a hot border where its rhizomes can enjoy the summer sun. It also grows well in neutral or slightly alkaline, fertile, well-drained soil. Divide large clumps after flowering and replant plump sections so that the top of the rhizomes are exposed to the sun.

☼ ◊ ❀❀❀ *f*

‡ to 90cm (36in) ↔ to 60cm (24in)

Iris laevigata ♀
PERENNIAL

The deep purple-blue flowers of this beardless water iris appear in early summer, and make a superb addition to a sunny or partially shaded bog garden, or the margins of a pond in acid (lime-free) soil. The blooms are set off by broad, mid-green, strap-like leaves. This is a vigorous iris and large clumps can be divided in the spring. 'Variegata' is an attractive cultivar with white- and green-striped leaves.

☼ ◑ ◊ ◉ ❀❀❀

‡ to 90cm (36in) ↔ indefinite

Iris pallida 'Variegata' ♀
PERENNIAL

The dramatic, variegated sword-shaped leaves of this iris provide structure, colour, and form in a sunny herbaceous border from spring to autumn. The beautiful bearded, mid-blue flowers, which appear in early summer, are a bonus and magnify this plant's charms. For the best results, plant it in groups in well-drained, neutral or alkaline soil.

☼ ◊ ❀❀❀

‡ to 1.2m (4ft) ↔ indefinite

Linum perenne
PERENNIAL

The perennial flax is a clump-forming plant, with narrow, bluish-green, lance-shaped leaves and slender flower stems. Although each pale blue flower lasts for just one day and fades before evening, the blooms are produced in succession from early to midsummer. Grow it in groups in full sun and a well-drained, fertile soil, and use it in a flower garden or herbaceous border. It can be raised from seed sown in pots in a cold frame in autumn or early spring.

☼ ◊ ❀❀❀

‡ to 30cm (12in) ↔ to 15cm (6in)

Lithodora diffusa 'Heavenly Blue' ♥

EVERGREEN SHRUB

This prostrate plant produces trailing branches, covered with small, elliptic, deep green leaves. In the summer it bears large numbers of rich azure-blue flowers. It can be planted in a raised bed, or a rock or gravel garden, and to grow well it needs an acid (lime-free), fertile soil and a sunny situation.

☼ ◊ ❀ ❀ ❀
‡ to 30cm (12in) ↔ to 45cm (18in)

Lobelia erinus 'Sapphire'

PERENNIAL

This dainty plant is usually treated as an annual and raised from seed each year. It is grown for its trailing stems of small, mid-green leaves and abundant bright blue flowers with striking white eyes. It flowers through summer and is an excellent plant for containers, hanging baskets, and edging borders. It should be planted in full sun or partial shade in moist, well-drained soil. When grown in containers, feed it every fortnight with a liquid fertilizer.

☼ ☀ ◊ ◊ ❀
‡ to 20cm (8in) ↔ to 15cm (6in)

Lupinus albifrons
EVERGREEN SHRUB

A decorative tree-lupin, this variety has a rounded habit and attractive foliage covered with silvery hairs. Throughout the summer it produces spikes of pea-like, blue or reddish-purple flowers. Although reasonably hardy, to survive the winter it needs to be planted in a sunny position in very well-drained soil, such as by a wall, in a sheltered raised bed, or gravel garden. Mulch generously with gravel.

☼ ◊ ❀❀

‡↔ to 75cm (30in)

Malva sylvestris 'Primley Blue'
PERENNIAL

This spreading, almost ground-hugging perennial produces very fetching, upright spires of funnel-shaped, pale blue-violet flowers with darker veins. They appear from late spring to mid-autumn, which gives many opportunities for interesting associations with cut flowers from different times in the season. It is useful in a mixed or herbaceous border, tolerating most garden soils.

☼ ◊ ◐ ❀❀❀

‡ to 20cm (8in) ↔ to 60cm (24in)

Nepeta 'Six Hills Giant'
PERENNIAL

This imposing catmint forms large clumps of strongly aromatic, greyish green foliage and spires of vivid blue flowers that cover the plant through summer. It is a good, drought-tolerant plant for the middle of a sunny border, or near paths where its lemony scent can be enjoyed. Cats, bees, and butterflies find the plant irresistible. Cut back in autumn when the foliage is looking tired.

☼ ◑ ◊ ❀❀❀ *f*
‡ to 1m (3ft) ↔ to 1.2m (4ft)

Nigella damascena 'Miss Jekyll' ♀
ANNUAL

A widely-grown, self-seeding annual, love-in-a-mist has highly decorative, finely divided green leaves and early summer blooms. 'Miss Jekyll' bears sky-blue flowers, surrounded by a "ruff" of thread-like leaves, which are followed by attractive seedheads. In spring or autumn, sow the seed *in situ* in bold groups at the front of a mixed border, or with other annuals in a wild-flower meadow. It needs to be grown in full sun and a well-drained soil.

☼ ◊ ❀❀❀
‡ to 45cm (18in) ↔ to 20cm (8in)

Polemonium caeruleum

PERENNIAL

Jacob's ladder has decorative, divided foliage, and in early summer bears erect stems of clear blue, bell-shaped flowers. It is very adaptable and can be grown in an informal planting among low-growing grasses, or at the front of a herbaceous border, where it can help to disguise the dying foliage of early spring bulbs. Plant it in full sunshine or partial shade, in fertile, moist, well-drained soil. Deadhead regularly and divide large clumps in spring.

☼ ☀ ◊ ◑ ✽ ✽ ✽
‡↔ to 60cm (24in)

Salvia x *sylvestris* 'Mainacht' ♔

PERENNIAL

This enigmatic, deep-coloured herbaceous perennial forms neat clumps of pleasantly aromatic, softly hairy, mid-green foliage; it provides strong contrast for silver-leaved plants in a border. It is highly valued for its tall and dense, upright spikes of vibrant, indigo-blue flowers that appear early and midsummer. It grows well in most garden soils, and copes well with drought. Cut back after the first flush of flowers to encourage further blooms.

☼ ◊ ✽ ✽ ✽ *f*
‡ to 70cm (28in) ↔ to 45cm (18in)

Solanum crispum '*Glasnevin*' ♀

CLIMBER

The Chilean potato vine is a fast-growing, woody-stemmed, evergreen climbing shrub. It is grown for its lightly fragrant, deep purple-blue flowers, which are borne in clusters at the tips of the stems during early and midsummer, and are followed by small, yellow-white fruits. The leaves are oval and dark green. Prune after flowering, or in spring, tying in any new shoots. In areas with cold winters, grow it against a sheltered, warm, and sunny wall.

☼ ☀ ◊ ◑ ❋ ❋ *f*
‡ to 6m (20ft)

Veronica prostrata ♀

PERENNIAL

The prostrate speedwell forms a low-growing mat of small, toothed leaves, and in late summer short, upright stems are clothed with tiny pale or deep blue blooms. It is ideally suited to a rock garden or raised bed, but will also add interest to a gravel garden or a dry-stone wall. Plant it in full sun in slightly fertile, well-drained soil. To propagate, divide it in the autumn or spring.

☼ ◊ ❋ ❋ ❋
‡ to 30cm (12in) ↔ indefinite

Carex pendula
PERENNIAL

The weeping sedge forms substantial clumps of relatively wide, strap-like, mid-green leaves that are blue-green underneath. In early summer arching, triangular stems bear pendent, catkin-like flower spikes, which look attractive when hanging over water at the edge of a pool, or in a damp border or woodland setting. Grow this sedge in permanently moist or wet soil in partial shade or sun. It can self seed profusely.

☼ ☀ ◐ ◑ ❄❄❄
‡ to 1m (3ft) ↔ to 30cm (12in)

Dryopteris affinis
PERENNIAL FERN

The golden male fern is a useful foliage plant for shady or partially shady sites, where its upright plumes of feathery fronds are a welcome sight when they begin to unfurl from coppery brown fiddleheads in spring. The young fronds are a delightful fresh green in early summer, maturing to a darker green. They persist through winter and should be cut back in early spring to allow for the new growth. There are several varieties available, such as 'Cristata' and the shorter 'Crispa Gracilis'.

☼ ☀ ◐ ❄❄❄
‡↔ to 90cm (36in)

Hosta 'Frances Williams' ♚

PERENNIAL

A widely-grown hosta, this variety is favoured for its large, thick, blue-green, heart-shaped leaves with yellow-green margins. It has very pale lavender-grey flowers, borne in clusters on tall stems in early summer. It is best to grow it in moist soil in a partially shaded situation because the leaves have a tendency to scorch in bright sun. Plant it to provide interest beneath deciduous trees, or in a mixed or herbaceous border. Take measures to prevent slug damage.

☀ ◊ ❀❀❀

‡ to 60cm (24in) ↔ to 1m (3ft)

Hosta plantaginea var. *japonica* ♚

PERENNIAL

The large oval, light green leaves of this hosta have a glossy texture and distinctive raised veins. It grows well in sun or partial shade, in moist but well-drained soil, and it can be used in a herbaceous or mixed border, or in the light shade underneath deciduous trees. The majority of hostas are grown for their foliage, but this also has attractive, trumpet-shaped, fragrant white flowers, borne on long stems in midsummer. Slugs may cause leaf damage.

☼ ☀ ◊ ◊ ❀❀❀ *f*

‡ to 60cm (24in) ↔ to 1m (3ft)

Hosta undulata var. albomarginata
PERENNIAL

The clumps of relatively small, bright green leaves of this hosta are enlivened with creamy-white margins that define their elliptic shape. Lavender, funnel-shaped flowers are borne on long stems from early to midsummer. This hosta will lighten up a partially shaded site in a herbaceous or mixed border or use it in deciduous woodland. It prefers a moist, well-drained soil. Grow it in loam-based compost in a pot to reduce the chance of slug damage.

☼ ◐ ◑ ❀ ❀ ❀
↕ to 55cm (22in) ↔ to 60cm (24in)

Liriodendron tulipifera ♀
DECIDUOUS TREE

The tulip tree has a conical shape and bears unusual lobed, square leaves, which appear as though they have been chopped off at the tips. The tulip-shaped flowers are yellowish-green with a hint of orange at the base of the petals, but are only produced on mature trees. In the autumn the foliage turns wonderful shades of golden-yellow. Grow the tulip tree in a large garden where it can reach its full size unhindered, in full sun or partial shade, and fertile, moist, well-drained soil.

☼ ◐ ◌ ◑ ❀ ❀ ❀
↕ to 30m (100ft) ↔ to 15m (50ft)

Matteuccia struthiopteris ♀

PERENNIAL

In spring, the shuttlecock fern produces a cluster of brilliant green fronds arranged in a tight funnel. In late summer, dark brown, fertile fronds appear at the centre of the shuttlecock. Plant in partial shade, in moist, neutral to acid (lime-free), humus-rich soil, particularly in woodland or near water. It spreads by underground stems to form large colonies. It can be increased by lifting and separating young plants from the parent plant in spring.

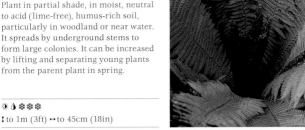

☀ ◊ ❀❀❀

↕ to 1m (3ft) ↔ to 45cm (18in)

Osmunda regalis ♀

PERENNIAL

The elegant royal fern forms a substantial clump of upright, finely divided, bright green fronds that turn shades of apricot-yellow before they die down. In summer, distinctive rusty brown, tassel-like fronds rise from the centre of the clump. Grow in partial shade, in moist, humus-rich, preferably acid (lime-free) soil. It can be planted in full sun in permanently damp soils. The royal fern makes a beautiful specimen in damp woodland or beside a stream or pond.

☀ ◊ ◆ ❀❀❀

↕ to 2m (6ft) ↔ to 1m (3ft)

Acer shirasawanum 'Aureum' ♀

DECIDUOUS TREE

Japanese maples are a very varied group of deciduous trees, but they all have beautiful foliage that turns to fiery shades in autumn. 'Aureum' also has wonderful spring colour as the foliage emerges almost neon yellow and then fades to a golden green. The handsomely rounded, but prominently toothed leaves may shrivel at the tips in dry conditions, so keep the soil moist in hot weather. The varieties 'Autumn Moon' and 'Palmatifolium' are also notable.

☀ ◐ ❀❀❀
↕↔ to 6m (20ft)

Achillea 'Coronation Gold' ♀

PERENNIAL

The bright-yellow flowerheads of yarrow are made up of numerous tiny flowers gathered together in broad, flat clusters. The grey-green, deeply cut leaves provide a perfect foil for them. This vigorous plant tolerates a wide range of growing conditions but does best in a sunny situation, in well-drained, fertile soil. It is a lovely plant for a wild-flower garden. When cut and dried, the flowerheads retain their colour well. Propagate by division in autumn.

☀ ◐ ◐ ❀❀❀
↕ to 1m (3ft) ↔ to 60cm (24in)

Alchemilla mollis ♀
PERENNIAL

After rain or heavy dew, the downy leaves of lady's mantle glisten with water droplets captured in the hairs on their surface. From early summer to early autumn large, airy sprays of tiny yellow-green flowers are produced, which are good for cutting. Fairly drought resistant, it is tolerant of most soil conditions, and although it prefers full sun it will also grow in partial shade. Plant it along the edge of a path or in a wild-flower border, where it will self-seed freely.

☼ ☀ ◊ ◑ ✳ ✳ ✳
↕↔to 50cm (20in)

Allium flavum ♀
PERENNIAL BULB

A large clump of these alliums would look wonderful at the front of a border. A satisfyingly fast-growing bulb, it produces stems topped with up to 60 delicately scented, bright yellow flowers. These dangle on slender stalks but turn upwards when the seed is developing. The bluey-green leaves are waxy and cylindrical. Plant bulbs in autumn in a sunny position, in well-drained soil.

☼ ◊ ✳ ✳ ✳ *f*
↕ to 35cm (14in) ↔ to 8cm (3in)

Allium moly

PERENNIAL BULB

The golden garlic produces clusters of up to 30 golden-yellow, star-shaped flowers on slender stems. Its waxy, lance-shaped leaves are usually produced in pairs. Plant in a sunny situation, in fertile, well-drained soil. It often self-seeds freely and can become invasive, which, if grown in a wild garden or naturalized in woodland, is more of an asset than a problem. Plant bulbs and, if necessary, divide large clumps in autumn.

☼ ◊ ❀ ❀ ❀
‡ to 35cm (14in) ↔ to 12cm (5in)

Anthemis tinctoria 'E.C. Buxton'

PERENNIAL

Filigree foliage and a long-flowering season make the golden marguerite a great-value border plant. A clump-forming evergreen, it produces masses of lemon-yellow, daisy-like flowers with deep yellow centres. The leaves are mid-green above and a soft downy-grey on the reverse. Cut back hard after flowering to reinvigorate the plant and encourage it to produce a neat clump of leaves for next spring. Plant it in a sunny position, in well-drained soil.

☼ ◊ ❀ ❀ ❀
‡↔ to 1m (3ft)

Argyranthemum '**Jamaica Primrose**' ♀

PERENNIAL

In frost-free areas, this plant will just keep on flowering; elsewhere it is usually grown as summer bedding or in containers. Beautiful, soft-yellow, daisy-like flowers and deeply divided, fern-like, mid-green leaves are a winning combination. Grow in moderately fertile, well-drained soil in full sun. Pot up the whole plant and move under glass for winter, or take stem cuttings in early autumn and grow under cover for next year. Easy to train as a standard.

☼ ◊ ❀

‡↔ to 1m (3ft)

Bidens ferulifolia ♀

PERENNIAL

The trailing stems of this plant can be best appreciated when tumbling over the edges of a window box or used to plump up the planting in a hanging basket. It has large, daisy-like, golden-yellow flowers and bright green, filigree foliage and stems. A short-lived perennial, it is usually grown as an annual and is best propagated by taking cuttings at the end of the year. It needs moist, but well-drained, fertile soil. Plants grown in a conservatory or heated greenhouse may flower until winter.

☼ ◊ ❀ ❀

‡ to 30cm (12in) ↔ indefinite

Brachyglottis 'Sunshine' ♀
EVERGREEN SHRUB

A free-flowering habit and attractive silvery-grey, slightly woolly foliage make this mound-forming plant a useful addition to any shrub border. From early to midsummer it produces a profusion of bright yellow, daisy-like flowers. Plant it in a sunny situation, in well-drained fertile soil. It does well in coastal areas but needs to be protected from strong cold winds inland. Prune in the early spring to keep the bush tidy and well shaped.

☼ ◊ ❉ ❉ ❉
↕ to 1.5m (5ft) ↔ to 2m (6ft)

Buddleja globosa ♀
DECIDUOUS SHRUB

The orange ball tree forms a large shrub or small tree, with spherical clusters of dark orange or yellow, fragrant flowers. It has lance-shaped leaves, which may be semi-evergreen in sheltered areas. It can be used in a shrub border or makes a good specimen plant, although it tends to get leggy with age. It prefers a sunny site in well-drained, preferably chalky soil. Pruning is unecessary.

☼ ◊ ❉ ❉ ❉ *f*
↕↔ to 5m (15ft)

Buphthalmum salicifolium
PERENNIAL

Yellow ox-eye has dark green, narrow
leaves and deep yellow, daisy-like
flowers held on long, willowy stems.
In late spring, insert supports so they
are in place before the flowers open.
When cut, the flowers are long lasting.
It is best grown in full sun in well-
drained, poor soil. If given richer soil
it may become invasive, in which case,
divide plants regularly to keep them in
check. In certain situations, however,
its spreading habit would be useful,
such as on a bank or in a wild garden.

☀ ◊ ✿✿✿

‡ to 60cm (24in) ↔ to 90cm (36in)

Calceolaria 'John Innes'
PERENNIAL

Curiously pouch-shaped and often
beautifully marked, the flowers of the
slipper flower are a delight. 'John Innes'
has intense yellow flowers with red-
brown spots. It is a vigorous, clump-
forming plant that needs a well-drained,
moderately fertile, acid soil in sun or
partial shade; it is best grown as a
container plant. It is not fully hardy, so
pot up and take under glass in winter,
or take softwood cuttings in summer
and keep the plants in a cold frame
during winter as an insurance policy.

☀ ☼ ◊ ✿✿

‡ to 20cm (8in) ↔ to 30cm (12in)

Callistemon pallidus
EVERGREEN SHRUB

Aptly named, the yellow bottle brush bristles with stiff-stemmed, greenish-yellow flowers. Its graceful arching branches are covered with greyish-green leaves that are tinged with pink when they are young. Plant in full sun, in well-drained, neutral to acid soil. Not entirely hardy, it needs a sheltered spot against a south- or west-facing wall. Alternatively, plant it in a container of loam-based compost and overwinter in a cool greenhouse.

☼ ◊ ❄

‡↔ to 4m (12ft)

Carex elata 'Aurea' ♀
PERENNIAL

A vibrantly coloured, ornamental sedge-like plant, Bowles' golden sedge is an evergreen that is grown for its gently arching, green-margined, bright yellow leaves. In early summer, it may throw up long, brown, male flower spikes. It requires a site in full sun, in a fertile, moist, but well-drained, soil. To keep the tufts neat and tidy, cut out dead leaves in summer. Plant in a container, or in groups near water or in a mixed border.

☼ ◑ ◊ ◆ ❄❄❄

‡ to 40cm (16in) ↔ to 15cm (6in)

Cephalaria gigantea
PERENNIAL

The giant scabious is a clump-forming perennial with large green leaves, divided into many small lance-shaped leaflets. In the summer it produces tall, branched, erect stems that hold large primrose-yellow flowers, the outer petals of which surround a pincushion of smaller blooms. Plant this scabious in full sun and fertile, moist, well-drained soil. It makes a superb plant for the back of a herbaceous border, but unlike other scabious it needs plenty of space to grow to its full potential.

☼ ◊ ◊ ❀❀❀
‡ to 2.5m (8ft) ↔ to 60cm (24in)

Coreopsis grandiflora 'Badengold'
PERENNIAL

Bees love the daisy-like flowers of tickseeds, as do flower arrangers who value them for their long life after cutting. 'Badengold', is a short-lived perennial that is most often grown as an annual. Sow seed *in situ* from early spring to early summer. Its orange-centred, yellow blooms are held aloft on tall stems above bright green, lance-shaped leaves. It needs a sunny spot, in well-drained, fertile soil. Deadheading helps prolong flowering.

☼ ◊ ❀❀❀
‡ to 75cm (30in) ↔ to 60cm (24in)

Coreopsis verticillata '**Grandiflora**' ♛

PERENNIAL

A good choice for a sunny herbaceous border, and a good cut flower and bee plant, this cheerful tickseed bears masses of single, yellow flowers in early summer; deadheading helps prolong the flowering period. Plants raised from seed sown in early to mid-spring in a seedbed will flower the same year – the feathery, mid-green leaves quickly knit together to form a good-sized clump. Plant in fertile, well-drained soil in full sun or light shade.

☼ ◊ ❀ ❀ ❀

‡ to 60cm (24in) ↔ to 30cm (12in)

Delphinium '**Sungleam**' ♛

PERENNIAL

In early summer, this stunning delphinium sends up tall, tapering spires of creamy-yellow flowers with strong yellow eyes. A second flush of flowers can be encouraged by cutting down the flower spikes as soon as they fade. Plant it in groups in a sunny position in well-drained, humus-rich, fertile soil. To prevent wind damage, especially on exposed sites, insert strong canes when planting and tie in the flower stems as they grow.

☼ ◊ ❀ ❀ ❀

‡ to 2m (6ft) ↔ to 90cm (36in)

Dicentra scandens

CLIMBER

Very pretty yellow locket flowers
hang freely from the scrambling stems
of this herbaceous climber from early
summer. The flowers sometimes have
white, purple, or pink tips. Each winter
it dies back to ground level, when the
old growth should be cleared. New
growth soon appears again in spring,
climbing quite high in a good year.
Best in humus-rich soil in a cool position
in a neutral to slightly alkaline soil.
Provide support.

☀ ◊ ❀ ❀ ❀
‡↔ to 1m (3ft)

Digitalis grandiflora ♀

PERENNIAL

Overwintering as a rosette of deep
green leaves, the yellow foxglove is
an upright, short-lived, perennial that
produces its spikes of pale lemon,
tubular flowers in early summer. It
prefers a semi-shaded situation and
damp, well-drained soil, where it will
happily self-seed. Deadheading after
flowering will check its spread. Grow
the slightly smaller *D. lutea* if you have
an alkaline soil. Both varieties would
suit a wild garden or a less formal
mixed border.

☀ ◊ ◊ ❀ ❀ ❀
‡ to 1m (3ft) ↔ to 45cm (18in)

Eremurus stenophyllus ♀

PERENNIAL

The foxtail lily produces canary-yellow flowers, fading to copper, on spikes that soar above other early summer border plants. Although fairly hardy, they start to grow early in the year and the young buds are prone to frost damage. Cover the crowns in winter and spring with fleece, straw, or bracken to protect the emerging shoots. The bent, strappy leaves will die down when the flower spike starts to emerge. Plant in very well-drained, sandy soil in full sun. An excellent cut flower.

☼ ◊ ✿✿✿

‡ to 1m (3ft) ↔ to 60cm (24in)

Eriophyllum lanatum

PERENNIAL

The woolly sunflower has silvery-green, slightly furry, deeply divided leaves that knit together to form a dense mat. The deep yellow, daisy-like flowers are produced right through summer. Plant in full sun, in well-drained, light soil. Fairly drought tolerant, it is a good plant for rock gardens and crevices in walls and paving. To keep it compact, trim back after flowering has finished. Divide plants in spring.

☼ ◊ ✿✿✿

‡↔ to 30cm (12in)

Eschscholzia californica ♀

ANNUAL

Perfect for a sun-drenched situation in a Mediterranean-style or gravel garden, the Californian poppy has decorative finely-divided, feathery, blue-green foliage, and bright yellow-orange cup-shaped flowers. The blooms open in full sun and close as the light dims at the end of the day, and appear from early to midsummer. Sow them *in situ* in spring, or autumn where winters are mild in poor, free-draining soil, and deadhead them regularly to stimulate new flowers to develop.

☼ ◊ ✿ ✿ ✿

‡ to 30cm (12in) ↔ to 15cm (6in)

Euphorbia palustris ♀

PERENNIAL

Needing soil that is permanently moist, this spurge would make an unusual waterside plant for an informal pond. The strong stems are covered with narrow, lime-green leaves topped, from late spring to early summer, by clusters of greeny-yellow flowers. In autumn, the leaves turn various shades of yellow and orange. Choose a site in full sun. Avoid skin contact with the milky sap.

☼ ◊ ✿ ✿ ✿

‡↔ to 90cm (36in)

Fremontodendron '**California Glory**' ♥

EVERGREEN SHRUB

While not completely hardy, this shrub will survive most winters if it is trained against a sheltered, south-facing wall. The large golden-yellow flowers bloom from late spring to mid-autumn, and are set off by dark green, five-lobed foliage, making this plant a valuable addition to any garden. It grows happily on chalky, free-draining soil, and can be pruned lightly in early spring. Contact with the foliage may cause an allergic reaction.

☼ ◊ ❀ ❀

‡ to 6m (20ft) ↔ to 4m (12ft)

Genista lydia ♥

DECIDUOUS SHRUB

Ideally suited to the well-drained conditions of a rock garden or raised bed, this dome-shaped, low-growing shrub will trail over sunny walls and rocks. In early summer, its prickle-tipped, grey-green, arching branches are covered in bright yellow, pea-like flowers. It prefers hot sites in poor, light soils that have not been enriched. Take semi-ripe cuttings in summer or sow seed in autumn. Pruning is unnecessary and straggly plants are best replaced.

☼ ◊ ❀ ❀ ❀

‡↔ to 60cm (24in)

Geum 'Lady Stratheden' ♀
PERENNIAL

Geums are especially suitable for the front of a herbaceous border. They form clumps of arching, kidney-shaped leaves that have a covering of fine hairs. The cup-shaped, semi-double, golden-yellow flowers are carried on branching stems. Plant in full sun, in moist but well-drained, soil. Divide large clumps in autumn. Unlike many geums, 'Lady Stratheden' will come true from seed.

☼ ◊ ◑ ✿ ✿ ✿
‡ to 60cm (24in) ↔ to 45cm (18in)

Halimium 'Susan' ♀
EVERGREEN SHRUB

A small, spreading, evergreen shrub valued for its single or semi-double summer flowers, which are bright yellow with deep purple markings. They have a nice quality against the greyish foliage. 'Susan' grows well in any light, well-drained soil, and would suit a rock garden in a warm, coastal area. Provide shelter at the foot of a warm wall where winters are cold, and trim lightly in spring, if necessary. The flowers are best during long, hot summers. *H. ocymoides* is similar but more upright.

☼ ◊ ✿ ✿
‡ to 45cm (18in) ↔ to 60cm (24in)

Helichrysum italicum subsp. *serotinum*

PERENNIAL

The curry plant is grown for its aromatic, evergreen, sage-green foliage and clusters of yellow flowers. Despite its common name, the leaves of this plant are not used in curry powder, however, they are edible and their savoury tang can be used to enliven cream cheese, egg, or chicken dishes. It can suffer during wet winters and should be planted in a raised bed or open, sunny situation in very well-drained soil.

☼ ◊ ❀❀ *f*

↕ to 40cm (16in) ↔ to 75cm (30in)

Hemerocallis lilioasphodelus ♀

PERENNIAL

There are thousands of cultivated daylilies to choose from but this species is up there with the best of them. It is vigorous and easy to grow, with funnel-shaped, fragrant flowers that only last for a day or two, but are soon replaced. They open in the afternoon and last through the night, so plant a clump close to the patio or other area in the garden that you use in the evening. Plant in full sun, in moist, but well-drained, soil. Divide large clumps in spring.

☼ ◊ ◊ ❀❀❀ *f*

↕↔ to 1m (3ft)

Hemerocallis 'Stella de Oro'

PERENNIAL

Daylilies are perfect herbaceous border plants. Their narrow, arching leaves quickly form an attractive clump; and while their colourful flowers may only last a day or so, they appear in rapid succession over several weeks. Happiest in full sun, in moist, but well-drained, soil, daylilies will tolerate the damp margins of a pond. 'Stella de Oro' is a compact form that is very free-flowering and powerfully fragrant. Propagate by division in spring.

☼ ◊ ◊ ❀ ❀ ❀ *f*
‡ to 30cm (12in) ↔ to 45cm (18in)

Humulus lupulus 'Aureus' ♀

CLIMBER

A herbaceous climber that will quickly clothe a pergola or fence. Male and female flowers grow on separate plants, with the female producing the hops. The yellow colour of 'Aureus' – which is far less vigorous than commercially grown hops – is transitory because the leaves turn green later in the year. Grow in moist, but well-drained, soil. Full sun will enhance leaf colour. Remove remains of old growth in early spring. Dry hops for decoration.

☼ ◊ ◊ ❀ ❀ ❀
‡ to 6m (20ft)

Iris 'Brown Lasso' ♥

PERENNIAL

Bearded irises come in a wide range of colours. 'Brown Lasso' is a lovely combination of yellow upper petals and lilac lower petals edged with butterscotch. Each stem carries 6–12 of these three-toned flowers. Plant in fertile, well-drained, neutral to acid soil, in full sun. Divide clumps when they become congested, usually after 3–5 years. The upright, sword-shaped leaves remain after the flowers have faded to add form to the herbaceous border.

☼ ◊ ❁❁❁

‡ to 55cm (22in) ↔ indefinite

Iris innominata

PERENNIAL

This attractive Pacific Coast iris originates from the West coast of the United States. It has pale yellow to cream flowers with bold brown veining. Other colours include purple and pale lavender. It is quite a small plant, rarely exceeding a height of 25cm (10in), with narrow, dark green, evergreen leaves that flush to purple at their base. Easily swamped in a border, it is best appreciated in a raised bed or trough. Plant in full sun or partial shade, in neutral or slightly acid soil.

☼ ◐ ◊ ❁❁❁

‡ to 25cm (10in) ↔ to 30 (12in)

Jasminum humile 'Revolutum' ♀

EVERGREEN SHRUB

This variety of jasmine is treasured for its fragrant, rich yellow flowers from late spring to early summer. It is fairly versatile and can be trained against a wall or support; it will tolerate shade, although it flowers more freely in sun. After flowering, shorten flowered shoots to a strong bud; when mature, remove one in five of the oldest, flowered stems. It is also good in a border, or as ground cover in sun. The flowers are good for cutting.

☼ ❋ ◊ ◔ ❋ ❋ ❋ *f*

‡ to 2.5m (8ft) ↔ to 3m (10ft)

Kniphofia 'Buttercup' ♀

PERENNIAL

A robust red hot poker, 'Buttercup' will hold its own in a busy herbaceous border. It forms a large clump of narrow, strappy leaves and, in early summer, produces several tall spikes of clear yellow flowers that open from green buds. They are very attractive to bees. For best results, plant in full sun or light shade, in fertile, moist but well-drained soil. Old foliage offers protection over winter; remove it in spring and divide large clumps.

☼ ❋ ◊ ◔ ❋ ❋ ❋

‡↔ to 75cm (30in)

Ligularia przewalskii ♀
PERENNIAL

Tall, narrow spikes of yellow flowers on purple-green stems rise in stately fashion above a robust clump of deeply divided leaves. A lover of deep, moist soil, this plant would look wonderful beside a large pond. Another situation it would suit is tucked towards the back of a permanently moist, mixed or herbaceous border where, sheltered among other plants, it is less vulnerable to strong, gusting winds. Although it is happy in full sun, light shade during the middle of the day would be ideal.

☼ ☀ ◊ ● ❁ ❁ ❁
‡ to 2m (6ft) ↔ to 1m (3ft)

Limnanthes douglasii ♀
ANNUAL

The two-tone petals of this fast-growing, hardy annual inspired its common name of poached-egg plant. It has deeply divided, slightly succulent, glossy green leaves, and stays in flower over a long period right through summer. Sow seed *in situ* during spring or late summer in moist, but well-drained, fertile soil. Use it to edge a path or dot it among rows of vegetables where it will attract hoverflies which help control aphids.

☼ ◊ ❁ ❁ ❁
‡ to 15cm (6in) ↔ to 10cm (4in)

Lupinus arboreus ♀
EVERGREEN SHRUB

Tree lupins are strong shrubs, often evergreen in mild winters, with sprawling branches of greyish-green leaves. They make wonderful specimen plants in a hot, dry border. The species has fragrant, sulphur-yellow flowers, but there are also lavender or white forms. The tree lupin is not fully hardy and may be damaged by hard frost, so plant it in a sunny position, in sandy, well-drained soil, preferably by the coast where it grows very well. Propagate by seed in spring.

☼ ◊ ❀❀❀ *f*
‡↔ to 2m (6ft)

Luzula sylvatica 'Aurea'
PERENNIAL

This golden form of greater woodrush is a clump-forming evergreen rush, with narrow, grass-like leaves. They are a bright golden yellow in winter, fading to yellow-green in summer. It is happy in deep or partial shade, in humus-rich, moist but well-drained, poor to moderately fertile soil. It tolerates dry soils. Use as ground cover or in a woodland garden. It can be increased by division in autumn and spring.

☀ ◑ ◊ ◊ ❀❀❀
‡ to 80cm (32in) ↔ to 45cm (18in)

Mimulus guttatus

PERENNIAL

The monkey flower is at home in the deep, moist soil beside a stream or pond where it forms a spreading mat of toothed, mid-green leaves. Through summer until autumn it produces tall, narrow spikes of deep yellow flowers, which are often freckled with reddish brown spots. Their shape resembles the intricate flowers of the snapdragon (*Antirrhinum*). Plant in full sun or in dappled shade. Monkey flowers tend to be shortlived, so propagate plants by dividing them in spring.

☼ ☀ ◐ ◊ ◆ ❄❄❄

‡ to 30cm (12in) ↔ to 60cm (24in)

Oenothera fruticosa 'Fyrverkeri' ♀

PERENNIAL

The scented, deep yellow flowers of the evening primrose open at dusk and are pollinated by night-flying insects. While they may last only a day or so, the flowers are produced in abundance all summer long. The plant has striking red stems and, when young, the lance-shaped leaves are flushed red, too. It is a good plant for a raised bed, gravel garden, or the front of a herbaceous border. Grow it in full sun or partial shade, in well-drained, sandy soil.

☼ ☀ ◊ ❄❄❄ *f*

‡↔ to 38cm (15in)

Phlomis fruticosa ♀
EVERGREEN SHRUB

Jerusalem sage forms a mound of aromatic, felted, grey-green leaves. From early to midsummer, short stems of golden-yellow, hooded flowers are produced in bunches. A massed planting would suit a sunny border or a gravel garden with well-drained, light soil. Although generally hardy, there is a risk it may be killed by particularly cold, damp winters – in cold areas, give it the shelter of a warm wall. Propagate by taking cuttings in summer.

‡ to 1m (3ft) ↔ to 1.5m (5ft)

Primula florindae ♀
PERENNIAL

The giant Himalayan cowslip is one of the largest primulas, with a handsome basal rosette of mid-green, toothed leaves. The freshly fragrant, sulphur-yellow, bell-shaped flowers are borne on tall stems up to 1.2m (4ft) high. It should be planted in full sun or partial shade in moist, humus-rich, neutral or slightly acid soil. Plant in swathes along a stream bank, or in large groups in a bog or woodland garden, or around the margins of a natural pond.

‡ to 1.2m (4ft) ↔ to 1m (3ft)

Ranunculus constantinopolitanus 'Plenus'

PERENNIAL

This cultivated buttercup has neat, double, yellow-green pompon flowers in early summer. It has deeply divided leaves, which are often dotted with greyish-white spots. It is a well-behaved plant that would suit a rock garden or mixed border. Plant it in full sun in moist, but well-drained soil. Propagate by dividing the woody roots after flowering has finished.

☼ ◐ ◊ ✿ ✿ ✿

‡ to 50cm (20in) ↔ to 30cm (12in)

Rhodiola rosea

PERENNIAL

The waxy-covered, triangular-shaped leaves of roseroot clump together to form a neat mound of stiffly erect stems. In early summer it produces large heads of pink buds that open to greenish-yellow, star-shaped flowers. Give it a sunny spot in well-drained, moderately fertile soil in a rock garden, dry walls, or at the front of a raised bed or herbaceous border.

☼ ◊ ✿ ✿ ✿

‡↔ to 30cm (12in)

Rosa GRAHAM THOMAS ('Ausmas') ♀
DECIDUOUS SHRUB

This superb modern shrub rose forms
a nicely rounded bush. It never gets
out of hand and is one of the best yellow
roses available. All through summer
until autumn, it has deep golden-yellow,
cup-shaped, fragrant flowers. If space
allows, plant in a group of 4–5, in full
sun in well-drained, humus-rich, fertile
soil. Shrub roses are suitable for growing
in mixed borders and need less rich
growing conditions than bush roses
such as Mountbatten.

☀ ◊ ❀❀❀ *f*

‡ to 1.2m (4ft) ↔ to 1.5m (5ft)

Rosa MOUNTBATTEN ('Harmantelle') ♀
DECIDUOUS SHRUB

A very vigorous, repeat-flowering
floribunda rose, with double, fragrant,
deep yellow flowers. It forms a nice
bush with plenty of glossy green foliage.
Plant it in a sunny position in well-
drained soil, enriched with plenty of
organic matter. Remove dead flowers to
encourage the production of new buds.
Prune main stems to about 30cm (12in)
above the ground in early spring, then
apply a balanced fertilizer and a thick
mulch of well-rotted manure.

☀ ◊ ❀❀❀ *f*

‡ to 1.2m (4ft) ↔ to 75cm (30in)

Rosa xanthina 'Canary Bird' ♀

DECIDUOUS SHRUB

This is a very decorative, but rather large, shrub rose suitable for a wild garden, as it needs a lot of space to develop well. It produces long, arching branches covered in early summer with single, saucer-shaped, lightly fragrant, deep-yellow flowers. A smattering of flowers may appear until autumn. In exposed areas it is vulnerable to severe frost and the young buds may be damaged by cold winds. Grow in moist, but well-drained, fertile soil, in full sun.

☼ ◊ ✿✿✿ *f*

‡↔ to 2.1m (7ft)

Sedum acre 'Aureum'

PERENNIAL

A mat-forming plant, with upright or sprawling stems that are covered with small fleshy, green leaves with yellow variegated tips. The bright yellow, star-shaped flowers are borne throughout the summer. Given the right conditions – full sun and a very well-drained soil – it may become invasive, but it is easily controlled. It makes a colourful plant for a trough filled with gritty compost, a raised bed, or a rock garden. Take cuttings in spring or late summer.

☼ ◊ ✿✿✿

‡ to 5cm (2in) ↔ to 23cm (9in)

Thermopsis rhombifolia var. montana

PERENNIAL

An upright plant with divided leaves and tall spikes of bright yellow, pea-like flowers that are attractive to bees. Although tolerant of a wide range of conditions, it prefers a sunny spot in fertile, light, sandy soil. Often used to provide vertical accents in a herbaceous border, it is perhaps best suited to an informal wildlife garden where its invasive tendencies are more easily accommodated. Propagate by division in spring or sow seed in autumn.

☼ ☀ ◐ ◊ ✿✿✿

‡ to 90cm (36in) ↔ to 60cm (24in)

Verbascum 'Gainsborough' ♀

PERENNIAL

This mullein is one of the Cotswold hybrids and overwinters as a large rosette of downy, greyish-green leaves. In early summer it springs into action and produces a stately spire of saucer-shaped, pale-yellow flowers. Further flowers often appear on side branches. A long-flowering plant for a herbaceous border, it is, sadly, rather short-lived. Plant in a sunny position, in well-drained fertile soil.

☼ ◊ ✿✿✿

‡ to 1.2m (4ft) ↔ to 60cm (24in)

Calendula officinalis
ANNUAL

An old favourite, the pot marigold is a vigorous, erect plant with hairy, aromatic, spoon-shaped leaves. The bright orange-yellow, daisy-like flowers are produced from summer to autumn. Superb as bedding, it can also be used in pots, or as a cut flower. Sow seed in fertile soil *in situ* in spring. For strong orange shades choose 'Fiesta Gitana' (a dwarf cultivar), 'Orange King' (double blooms) or 'Indian Prince' (reddish flowers). Deadhead to keep the show going.

☼ ◊ ❋ ❋ ❋ *f*
‡ to 75cm (30in) ↔ to 45cm (18in)

Eccremocarpus scaber
CLIMBER

The Chilean glory flower is a vigorous evergreen, with tubular bright orange-red flowers, which appear early in summer and continue to autumn. A short-lived, tender perennial, it will only survive the winter outside if planted in a sunny, sheltered position, such as against a south-facing wall that is protected from hard frosts. Alternatively, grow it as an annual. Use it to clothe a trellis, or pergola, or train it on wires up a house wall. Plant it in full sun in well-drained, fertile soil.

☼ ◊ ❋
‡ to 3m (10ft)

Eremurus x *isabellinus* 'Cleopatra'

PERENNIAL

This is a dramatic foxtail lily, with tall, stately spikes of deep orange flowers, held above mid-green, lance-shaped leaves. It needs to be grown in very well-drained, fertile, sandy soil in full sun. The fleshy roots will quickly rot if the soil becomes too wet, so it is advisable to plant it in a raised bed, where any excess water will quickly drain away. Mulch them over in winter with straw, bracken or fleece to protect the emerging shoots.

☼ ◊ ❀❀❀
‡ to 1.5m (5ft) ↔ to 50cm (20in)

Geum coccineum 'Cooky'

PERENNIAL

Geums are sturdy, clump-forming perennials for the herbaceous border or cottage garden. They bear pretty, five-petalled flowers in warm colours, from yellow to red. 'Cooky' has bright orange flowers from early to midsummer above bunches of hairy, fresh green foliage. The flowers last well when cut. Most garden soils are suitable.

☼ ◊ ◊ ❀❀❀
‡ to 50cm (20in) ↔ to 30cm (12in)

Gladiolus 'Solveiga'

PERENNIAL CORM

If you are looking for a show-stopping gladiolus, 'Solveiga' is one of a few. It can be hard to come by, but the effort is worthwhile. It bears tall spires of large, ruffled yellow flowers with orange centres and rosy marking on the lower petals – a very pleasing combination. The flowering time is from early to midsummer. 'Solveiga' is also a good variety for displaying as a cut flower. Choose a sunny site with good drainage, and sprout the corms on a sunny windowsill before planting in spring.

☼ ◊ ❀

‡ to 1m (3ft) ↔ to 8cm (3in)

Iris 'Blue Eyed Brunette'

PERENNIAL

The name of this bearded iris accurately brings to mind the colour of its distinctive flowers. The petals are tinted orange-brown, with the lower set highlighted with a bright lilac spot, surmounted by a golden-yellow "beard". Use it in a mixed or herbaceous border and combine it with bronze grasses, such as *Carex flagellifera*, to create an unusual colour theme. Plant in a sunny situation in well-drained, fertile, neutral to acid soil (*see* 'Bold Print' *p.159*).

☼ ◊ ❀ ❀ ❀

‡ to 1m (3ft) ↔ indefinite

Kniphofia 'Bees' Sunset' ♀
PERENNIAL

A beautiful red hot poker, 'Bees' Sunset'
produces tall spikes of pale orange,
tubular flowers over a long period from
early summer. Grow it in groups in a
fiery colour-themed border or gravel
garden. It complements pale yellow
and bright red flowers, such as dahlias.
Plant it in moist, well-drained soil in
full sun or partial shade. Leave the
remains of the old foliage over winter
for protection and remove it in spring,
when large clumps can also be divided.

☼ ☀ ◑ ◊ ◊ ✲ ✲ ✲
‡ to 90cm (36in) ↔ to 60cm (24in)

Lonicera x *tellmanniana*
CLIMBER

This twining, deciduous, woody-
stemmed honeysuckle bears clusters of
coppery orange, tubular flowers, which
open from late spring to midsummer.
They are a pleasing shade against the
deep green, oval leaves with blue-white
undersides. Train the climbing growth
onto a fence or wall, or up into a large
shrub, and after flowering, trim shoots
back by one-third. This honeysuckle
will grow in any moist but well-drained,
humus-rich soil, with the best flowering
displays in light shade.

☼ ☀ ◑ ◊ ◊ ✲ ✲
‡ to 5m (15ft)

Papaver nudicaule Gartenzwerg Group

PERENNIAL

Iceland poppies are short-lived perennials, best in neutral to acid soils. In appearance, they are much like the common field poppy, but with flowers in very bright and cheerful shades of orange, pink, red, peach, yellow, and white. Mixtures like Gartenzwerg Group are very popular and can either be bought as plug plants or as seed, which can be sown in autumn or spring, in beds or containers. Unlike field poppies, their flowers last well when cut.

☼ ◊ ◐ ❀ ❀ ❀

‡ to 60cm (24in) ↔ to 30cm (12in)

Rosa FLOWER CARPET AMBER ('Noa97400a')

DECIDUOUS SHRUB

This compact, low-growing shrub rose features pale orange, lightly fragrant flowers from early summer into autumn. Relatively disease resistant and tolerant of heat and humidity, this low maintenance rose is well suited to containers and planting in small groupings as a ground cover. Grow in full sun in well drained soil amended with organic matter. Apply slow release fertilizer or top dress with compost in early spring.

☼ ◐ ❀ ❀ ❀ *f*

‡ to 60cm (24in) ↔ to 90cm (36in)

Tagetes 'Tangerine Gem'
ANNUAL

An upright Signet marigold with
ferny, dark green leaves. It is very free
flowering, producing vast numbers
of single, orange flowers throughout
the summer. These marigolds make
excellent edging and bedding plants,
or use them in hanging baskets and
containers. Plant them in full sun, in
fertile, well-drained soil and deadhead
regularly. They are easily rasied from
seed sown in early spring in pots on
a windowsill or under glass.

‡ to 20cm (8in) ↔ to 30cm (12in)

Tropaeolum majus
CLIMBER

Nasturtiums are colourful annuals
with rounded, pale green leaves, held
on climbing or scrambling stems. They
are very free flowering and bear orange,
yellow, and red long-spurred flowers.
Plant nasturtiums in containers and
hanging baskets, or use them in an
annual or herbaceous border trained
up a tripod. They prefer a sunny
situation and moist, well-drained soil.
Check plants regularly for caterpillars
and black fly, and remove them before
the plants become infested.

‡ to 30cm (12in)

LATE SUMMER

Many of the plants that bless the hottest and driest time of year are annuals. Sweet peas, sunflowers, marigolds, and nasturtiums are just a few that can make a cheerful show in a border. Other plants, used as annuals, can join them, like salvias and *Ricinus communis* 'Carmencita'. Unlike most annuals, which are sun-lovers, tobacco plants (*Nicotiana*) also thrive in shade where their pastels and lime-greens glow alluringly. As with sweet peas, not all are scented, so check the variety if fragrance is required.

Fuchsias bloom continuously; the large frilly flowers of many are favourites for pots and hanging baskets, along with pelargoniums. As temperatures soar, water containers on a daily basis. It is also vital to water new plants in dry periods. Give priority to trees, shrubs, and climbers planted less than a year ago, and water generously so that moisture penetrates deep below the soil surface.

Borders and gravel gardens are aglow with coneflowers (*Echinacea* and *Rudbeckia*) and red-hot pokers (*Kniphofia*), but for sheer elegance a white colour theme is hard to beat. Combine *Anemone* x *hybrida* 'Honorine Jobert', *Epilobium angustifolium* f. *album*, and tall white dahlias, hollyhocks, and lilies for a display that takes on a luminous quality at dusk. To extend the show into autumn, keep deadheading and fill any gaps with fast growers like penstemon.

HOT TROPICAL STYLE

Mirror the heat of summer days with vibrant combinations of red and orange flowers. *Phygelius* x *rectus* 'African Queen' and dahlias like 'Hillcrest Royal' and 'Wootton Impact' will set the garden alight. Punctuate them with red-hot pokers, and choose *Ensete ventricosum*, cannas, agaves, and yuccas to increase the tropical flavour with their flamboyant foliage.

Abelia × *grandiflora* ♀

EVERGREEN SHRUB

This large rounded plant has arching
branches, and glossy dark green leaves.
It flowers from mid- to late summer
and produces fragrant, funnel-shaped,
pink-flushed white flowers. Plant in
a sunny site in a sheltered position,
or against a west-facing wall, where it
will be protected from cold, damaging
winds. Grow it in fertile, well-drained
soil, and to rejuvenate established
plants, cut out some of the older stems
after flowering.

☼ ◊ ❀ ❀ *f*
‡ to 3m (10ft) ↔ to 4m (12ft)

Achillea ageratum '**W.B. Childs**'

PERENNIAL

This variety of yarrow makes a clump
of feathery foliage as it emerges from
the ground in spring. From midsummer,
these clumps are topped by flat heads
of long-lasting, small white daisy
flowers with darker centres. Apart from
needing to be tidied up each winter,
like most herbaceous perennials, it
is relatively trouble free and is a good
choice for any partially shaded border.

◐ ◊ ❀ ❀ ❀
‡↔ to 60cm (24in)

Agapanthus 'Snowy Owl'

PERENNIAL

This white-flowered agapanthus is good for late borders or large containers. With its large, round heads of tubular flowers, it makes an excellent late-summer perennial, and established clumps can be very impressive when in flower, although they may take up a lot of room. The lush green, strap-shaped foliage dies back in winter. In pots, grow in soil-based compost, and water and fertilize weekly in summer. Divide large clumps in spring, and protect the roots with a mulch in cold winters.

☼ ◐ ◊ ❄ ❄ ❄
‡ to 1.2m (4ft) ↔ to 60cm (24in)

Anemone x *hybrida* 'Honorine Jobert' ♥

PERENNIAL

The Japanese anemone is a popular late-flowering plant, perfect for growing in a summer or autumn herbaceous border. It is also good for cutting. This is one of the prettiest varieties, bearing single, pure white flowers, with bright green centres surrounded by golden-yellow stamens. Plant it in sun or light shade in moist, fertile, well-drained soil. It spreads quickly to form large clumps and can be invasive. Divide the plants in early spring.

☼ ☀ ◊ ◑ ❄ ❄ ❄
‡ to 1.5m (5ft) ↔ to 60cm (24in)

Campanula alliariifolia

PERENNIAL

Ivory bells is an elegant, herbaceous plant which forms clumps of greyish-green, hairy, heart-shaped leaves. The white, bell-shaped, pendent flowers are held on branched, wiry stems. It prefers a slightly shaded situation, and is ideal for planting beneath a light canopy of deciduous trees or shrubs in a mixed border. It blooms from summer to early autumn, and can be cut to the ground after flowering to prevent self-seeding. Grow it in moist, well-drained, fertile, neutral or alkaline soil.

☼ ◐ ◊ ◊ ❈ ❈ ❈

‡ to 60cm (24in) ↔ to 50cm (20in)

Clerodendrum trichotomum var. *fargesii* ♀

DECIDUOUS SHRUB

In late summer this upright large shrub or small tree produces clusters of very fragrant, white flowers with persistent green sepals. The flowers are followed later in the year by bright blue berries. The young leaves are also a feature, opening bronze before turning green. In cold areas, plant it against a west- or south-facing wall in moist, well-drained, fertile soil. Pruning is rarely required, except to remove crossing branches.

☼ ◊ ◊ ❈ ❈ ❈ *f*

‡↔ to 6m (20ft)

Dahlia 'Angora'

PERENNIAL

This dahlia has double, white flowers, and creates a stunning display when planted in front of a dark background, or in a white border. The blooms also make excellent cut flowers. Dahlias need a sunny position in fertile, moist, well-drained soil. Plant it in spring and insert a supporting cane when planting. Lift the tubers after the first frost, allow them to dry, and then store them in boxes of dry sand or compost in a frost-free, cool place.

☀ ◊ ◑ ❋ ❋

‡ to 90cm (36in) ↔ to 60cm (24in)

Echinacea purpurea 'White Swan'

PERENNIAL

Coneflowers originate from the prairies of North America, and have daisy-like flowers with raised cone-like centres. The flowers of 'White Swan' are borne on tall, erect stems above lance-shaped leaves, and are composed of white petals, with an orange-brown cone. Plant it in a sunny site in a herbaceous border, in deep, well-drained soil. It will also tolerate a little shade. Cut the stems back after flowering to encourage a second flush of blooms.

☀ ◊ ❋ ❋ ❋

‡ to 60cm (24in) ↔ to 45cm (18in)

Epilobium angustifolium f. *album*

PERENNIAL

The common rosebay willow herb is an invasive thug of a plant, and is not suitable for growing in the garden. However, this beautiful white form is less aggressive and perfect for a wild area of the garden or the herbaceous border. Narrow, lance-shaped leaves provide a foil for the tall spikes of white summer flowers. It is not fussy about soil conditions, and will grow in full sun or partial shade. It self-seeds, so deadhead it after flowering.

☼ ◐ ♢ ♦ ♦ ❄❄❄

↕ to 1.5m (5ft) ↔ to 50cm (20in)

Erica tetralix 'Alba Mollis' ♀

EVERGREEN SHRUB

The cross-leaved heath is a spreading bush, with small, silvery-grey leaves, which are arranged in the shape of a cross. In late summer, it is covered with small, bell-shaped, white flowers. It grows naturally on wet moorland, and needs damper soil conditions than other species of heather. It also requires an acid soil, and should be grown in full sun for the best results. Clip over the plant in spring to keep it neat.

☼ ♦ ❄❄❄

↕ to 20cm (8in) ↔ to 30cm (12in)

Eucomis bicolor ♀
PERENNIAL BULB

An exotic-looking bulb, the pineapple lily has large, strap-like, light green leaves, and purple-spotted flower stems. In late summer it bears dense spikes of purple-edged white flowers, topped by a rosette of small leaves that inspired its common name. Plant bulbs about 15cm (6in) deep, in full sun in fertile, well-drained soil. The bulbs may survive the winter in mild areas, but in cold climates, lift them and store in a frost-free place, then replant them in spring. Alternatively, grow them in pots.

☼ ◊ ❀❀
 to 50cm (20in) ↔ to 60cm (24in)

Fallopia baldschuanica
CLIMBER

The mile-a-minute plant, or Russian vine, is a rampant climber which grows rapidly up to a height of 12m (40ft). It has woody, twining stems, covered with heart-shaped, pale green leaves. In late summer, it bears masses of small, pink-flushed, creamy-white flowers. Although unsuitable for a small garden, it is useful for covering an ugly wall or a dead tree. Grow it in full sun or partial shade, in poor or slightly fertile, well-drained soil. Don't be afraid to cut it back hard in the spring.

☼ ◑ ◊ ❀❀❀
 to 12m (40ft)

Fuchsia 'Annabel' ♀

EVERGREEN SHRUB

'Annabel' is a free-flowering, trailing fuchsia that produces delicate white flowers, and is well suited to hanging baskets and tall containers. It can also be trained as a standard, if provided with a permanent supporting stake. Feed it regularly throughout its growing season. This fuchsia is not hardy, so move it indoors for the winter into a frost-free greenhouse. To propagate it, take softwood cuttings in the spring.

☼ ☀ ◊ ◊ ❄

‡↔ to 60cm (24in)

Galtonia candicans ♀

PERENNIAL BULB

Valued for its late summer blooms, this bulbous plant has long greyish-green, strap-like leaves, and white, pendent, slightly fragrant, tubular flowers, which are produced on tall spikes. It is quite hardy, but in areas that experience very cold winters, the bulbs should be dug up in autumn and stored in a frost-free place, or covered with a deep mulch. Plant the bulbs in spring in full sun and fertile, moist soil that never dries out.

☼ ◊ ❄❄ *f*

‡ to 1.2m (4ft) ↔ to 23cm (9in)

Gaura lindheimeri ♀
PERENNIAL

This graceful, clump-forming perennial with tall and slender stems will more than earn its keep in any sunny garden. Not only is it easy to grow, it flowers over a very long period in summer up until the first frosts of autumn. These flowers are carried in loose spires and open from pinkish white buds each morning to display white flowers. It is a graceful plant for a mixed flower border, tolerating both heat and drought, and some part-day shade. Divide clumps in spring, if necessary.

‡ to 1.5m (5ft) ↔ to 90cm (36in)

Hydrangea macrophylla 'Veitchii' ♀
DECIDUOUS SHRUB

Lacecap hydrangeas have flat-topped flowerheads composed of a cluster of small fertile blooms, surrounded by larger sterile flowers. 'Veitchii' has white sterile flowers that become pink as they age, and forms a mound of dark green foliage. The flowerheads can be cut and dried, or left over the winter and removed in spring, when a few of the oldest stems can also be pruned to the ground. Plant in sun or partial shade, in moist, well-drained, fertile soil.

‡ to 2m (6ft) ↔ to 2.5m (8ft)

Hydrangea quercifolia 'Snowflake'
DECIDUOUS SHRUB

This double-flowered variety of the oak-leaved hydrangea is a mound-forming, deciduous shrub bearing arching clusters of white flowers that fade to pink, from midsummer to autumn. The very distinctive, oak-like, mid-green leaves turn bronze-purple in autumn. This shrub is useful in a range of garden sites, including large containers, but the leaves may become yellow if grown in shallow, chalky soil. Keep any pruning to a minimum, in spring if necessary.

☼ ☀ ◊ ❀❀❀

‡ to 2m (6ft) ↔ to 2.5m (8ft)

Jasminum officinale 'Argenteovariegatum' ♥
CLIMBER

This jasmine is semi-evergreen, with cream-edged, green leaves. The highly fragrant, pure white flowers appear in clusters from early summer to early autumn. Grow it in full sun or partial shade, in fertile, well-drained soil. Once flowering is over, thin old or congested stems. During summer, take semi-ripe cuttings. It is not fully hardy, so plant it in a sheltered position or by a warm wall. It can also be grown in containers of loam-based compost.

☼ ☀ ◊ ❀❀ *f*

‡ to 12m (40ft)

Lathyrus latifolius 'Albus' ♀
CLIMBER

The everlasting pea is a herbaceous perennial, which can be used to climb up a support or as ground cover. 'Albus' produces white to creamy-white flowers that appear from summer to early autumn. It grows well in full sun or light shade in well-drained, fertile soil, which has been enriched with well-rotted manure. Cut back any dead stems in the spring, but otherwise leave it undisturbed.

☼ ◐ ◊ ❀❀❀
↕ to 2m (6ft)

Lilium regale ♀
PERENNIAL BULB

One of the best lilies for perfume, the regal lily is a vigorous plant with erect or arching stems, clothed with shiny, greyish-green leaves. In midsummer it produces up to 25, intensely fragrant, trumpet-shaped, white flowers. The petals have purple streaks on the back and golden-yellow throats. Regal lilies grow well in containers, although they need the support of tall canes. Plant them in well-drained, fertile soil in full sun, with the lower part of the plant shaded by other planting.

☼ ◊ ❀❀❀ *f*
↕↔ to 2m (6ft)

Lonicera periclymenum 'Graham Thomas' ♀

CLIMBER

A vigorous climber with white flowers that turn yellow with age and are followed by glossy, red berries. Grow it through trees and over pergolas or trellis, or it can be used as gound cover and over banks. The flowers are highly fragrant and attract night-flying moths and insects. Bear this in mind if you are considering planting it near the house. Plant in sun or partial shade in any reasonable soil. Cut established plants back by up to a third after flowering.

☼ ☀ ◌ ◊ ❀ ❀ ❀ *f*
↕ to 7m (23ft)

Magnolia grandiflora

EVERGREEN TREE

Given a warm, sheltered position, the bull bay eventually makes a large tree, with glossy, leathery, dark green leaves. In late summer it bears large, creamy-white flowers, up to 25cm (10in) across. Flowers may also appear sporadically at other times of the year. It is not fully hardy, and in cold areas it should be grown against a west- or south-facing wall in moist, well-drained soil. Grow it in full sun or partial shade. 'Exmouth' is one of the hardiest cultivars, and will flower at an earlier age.

☼ ☀ ◌ ◊ ❀ ❀ *f*
↕ to 18m (60ft) ↔ to 15m (50ft)

Myrtus communis ♀
EVERGREEN SHRUB

Myrtle has an upright habit and bears rounded, glossy, dark green, aromatic leaves. The attractive, fragrant white flowers have frothy centres, created by long white stamens. It blooms from the middle of the summer to the beginning of the autumn. A Mediterranean plant, myrtle is not completely hardy and is more likely to survive cold winters if planted against a sunny wall. Grow it in slightly fertile, moist, well-drained soil.

☼ ◊ ◑ ❀❀ *f*
↕↔to 3m (10ft)

Nicotiana sylvestris ♀
PERENNIAL

A vigorous, short-lived perennial, the tobacco plant is frequently grown as an annual in cool climates. The flowers of this species are borne on long stems above a rosette of elliptic, dark green, sticky leaves. The long, white, highly fragrant flowers resemble shooting stars and are produced from midsummer. It is easily damaged by frost, but may survive a mild winter if protected by a thick layer of mulch. Plant it in a sunny or partially shaded site in moist, well-drained soil.

☼ ☀ ◊ ◑ ❀ *f*
↕ to 1.5m (5ft) ↔to 75cm (30in)

Rhododendron 'Polar Bear' ♀

EVERGREEN SHRUB

'Polar Bear' is unusual for a rhododendron – instead of flowering in spring like most, it bears its huge trusses of fragrant, waxy white flowers in late summer. It makes a sturdy, tree-like shrub with large, oval leaves. In a medium to large garden, it is ideal for adding colour to a shaded area, being spectacular if grown in groves or avenues, and it will also grow in a large container. Acid soils are essential. Little pruning is required.

☀ ◗ ❀ ❀ ❀ *f*
‡ to 5m (15ft) ↔ to 4m (12ft)

Rodgersia aesculifolia ♀

PERENNIAL

A sizeable, clump-forming plant, with creeping roots and large, dark, bronzy-green leaves that are similar in shape to a horse-chestnut tree. In summer it produces tall plumes of fragrant, white or pinkish-white flowers. Plant in moist, fertile soil in full sun. A perfect pond-side plant, it will also grow well in a bog garden, but tolerates slightly drier soil in partial shade. Propagate by dividing established plants in autumn.

☼ ☀ ◗ ❀ ❀ ❀ *f*
‡↔ to 1m (3ft)

Schizophragma hydrangeoides

CLIMBER

Japanese hydrangea vine is cloaked in oval to heart-shaped, dark green leaves. In mid- to late summer, creamy white flowers bloom in terminal clusters. It attaches to surfaces by aerial roots and is ideal for planting at the base of a large tree or a wall. Grow in moderately fertile, well-drained soil in part or dappled shade; it may tolerate full sun in cool regions.

☼ ☀ ◊ ◊ ❀ ❀
‡ to 12m (40ft)

Yucca filamentosa ♀

EVERGREEN SHRUB

The Spanish dagger is an architectural plant, and bears stiff, lance-shaped, spiky leaves with razor-sharp points. Cut off these points if growing yuccas in gardens used by children. In late summer it produces a tall spike of bell-shaped, creamy-white flowers. Plant it in well-drained soil in a sunny position, such as in a gravel garden, where it has space to grow to its full size. Protect young plants during cold, wet winters with a straw mulch or fleece.

☼ ◊ ❀ ❀
‡ to 2m (6ft) ↔ to 1.5m (5ft)

Achillea 'Cerise Queen'

PERENNIAL

This pretty, pink-flowered yarrow is ideal for a sunny herbaceous border. Its flat, dish-like flowerheads appear through midsummer and are very attractive to many flying insects, such as butterflies. They are also good cut for indoor display. The flowerheads may flop over, so place a support over the plant in spring. Divide large clumps in spring or autumn, and remove old flowerheads to promote reflowering. This is a tough plant that can tolerate drought and hot weather.

☼ ◌ ◗ ✿ ✿ ✿
↕↔ to 60cm (24in)

Agrostemma githago 'Milas'

ANNUAL

Corn cockle used to be a cornfield annual weed, but the widespread use of herbicides has made it a rare plant in the wild. It has lance-shaped, greyish-green leaves, and in the summer 'Milas' has vibrant plum-pink flowers with white centres. Plant corn cockles in full sun in poor, well-drained soil. They can be grown in a cottage-style garden, in containers, or planted in a summer flower meadow. The species self-seeds freely.

☼ ◌ ✿ ✿ ✿
↕ to 90cm (36in) ↔ to 30cm (12in)

Alcea rosea

PERENNIAL

Hollyhocks are tall, vigorous plants, with rounded, slightly hairy leaves. In summer they produce a long spike of funnel-shaped pink, white, purple or creamy-yellow flowers. 'Chater's Double' is a beautiful double form. Hollyhocks need a sunny position and well-drained, fertile soil. They look good grown by a wall. Rust can be a problem, so look out for resistant types; they are often grown as biennials to reduce the effects of this disease. They may need staking in open positions.

☼ ◊ ✿ ✿ ✿

↕ to 2m (6ft) ↔ to 60cm (24in)

Androsace lanuginosa ♀

PERENNIAL

The fine, silky hairs that clothe the evergreen leaves of this low-growing perennial give the plant a soft-textured appearance. The primrose-like, pink flowers appear in mid- to late summer or early autumn. Rosettes of tiny, deep grey-green leaves are arranged along the length of the trailing stems. It needs a sunny position and very well-drained soil. Add plenty of grit to heavy clay soils to improve drainage. Good for a rock garden, trough or along the top of a dry-stone wall.

☼ ◊ ✿ ✿ ✿

↕ to 4cm (1½in) ↔ to 18cm (7in)

Anemone hupehensis 'Hadspen Abundance' ♀

PERENNIAL

This late-flowering anemone produces deep pink flowers over a long period that are good for cutting. The edges of the petals fade to white as the flower ages. The long-stalked leaves have three leaflets. This anemone enjoys a sunny or partially shaded site. Plant it in moist soil in a herbaceous border. In cold areas, mulch it well in the autumn.

☼ ☀ ◊ ❀ ❀ ❀

‡ to 1.2m (4ft) ↔ to 45cm (18in)

Anemone x *hybrida* 'Elegans'

PERENNIAL

The Japanese anemone is a vigorous late-flowering plant with upright, branched stems. From late summer to mid-autumn, 'Elegans' produces masses of beautiful single, light pink flowers, which become darker as they age. It looks superb in a herbaceous border, and is good for cutting. It does best in a moist, fertile soil in full sunshine or partial shade. 'Margarete' has double, pale pink flowers.

☼ ☀ ◊ ◊ ❀ ❀ ❀

‡ to 1.5m (5ft) ↔ indefinite

Begonia 'Roy Hartley'

PERENNIAL

The glossy leaves provide the perfect foil for this tuberous begonia's large, salmon-pink flowers, which are borne from midsummer. Its upright growth makes it an excellent bedding plant. Tubers can be planted in the garden when all risk of frost has passed; it flowers better in a partially shaded site and moist, well-drained soil. For an indoor display, plant 'Roy Hartley' in a large container of loam-based compost in bright light, away from direct sun.

☀ ◊ ◗ ❀

‡ to 60cm (24in) ↔ to 45cm (18in)

Callistephus chinensis Ostrich Plume Series

ANNUAL

China aster flowers resemble chrysanthemums with double blooms. The Ostrich Plume Series are tall plants, with flowers in shades of pink, purple, and red. They bloom from late summer until the middle of autumn, and can be deadheaded to prolong flowering. Plant them in a sunny, sheltered site in moist, well-drained soil. China asters make good bedding plants and cut flowers.

☀ ◊ ◗ ❀

‡ to 60cm (24in) ↔ to 30cm (12in)

Calluna vulgaris 'County Wicklow' ♀

EVERGREEN SHRUB

There are over 500 different cultivars of ling, or heather. All are evergreen shrubs and can be used in heather gardens or as ground cover. 'County Wicklow' is compact, with slightly prostrate stems and mid-green foliage. It bears spikes of small, double shell-pink flowers, and blooms from late summer to late autumn. Plant it in full sun in well-drained, acid (lime-free) soil. Clip it over in spring to keep it neat and bushy.

☼ ◊ ❀❀❀

‡ to 30cm (12in) ↔ to 35cm (14in)

Chelone obliqua

PERENNIAL

The turtlehead plant bears stiff stems sparsely covered with lance-shaped, mid-green leaves. From late summer to mid-autumn it produces clusters of pink flowers with turtle mouth-like openings, which explain its common name. It will perform well planted in a sunny border or partial shade in deep, fertile, moist soil. To propagate it, divide clumps in spring.

☼ ◑ ◊ ❀❀❀

‡ to 1m (3ft) ↔ to 50cm (20in)

Chrysanthemum 'Clara Curtis'

PERENNIAL

Unlike many chrysanthemums, this variety has simple, single daisy-like flowers, with pale pink petals and greeny-yellow centres. Their perfume comes as something of a surprise, because many chrysanthemums are unscented. Plant it in well-drained soil that has previously been enriched with well-rotted manure. It is hardy, but in cold, wet areas it should be dug up and overwintered in a frost-free place.

 ☼ ◊ ❀❀❀ *f*

‡ to 75cm (30in) ↔ to 45cm (18in)

Cleome hassleriana 'Rose Queen'

ANNUAL

Spider flowers are tall, handsome plants with hand-like leaves. They flower in late summer, producing large clusters of spidery, pink, white, or purple blooms that are good for cutting. They are ideal for the back of a herbaceous border as they do not need staking, and for filling spaces created when spring flowering perennials are over. Sow seed in spring, in a heated propagator, and plant out after all risk of frost has passed, in full sun and fertile, well-drained soil.

☼ ◊ ❀

‡ to 1.5m (5ft) ↔ to 45cm (18in)

Cosmos bipinnatus Sensation Series

ANNUAL

This elegant hardy annual is perfect for an annual or mixed border where it is valued for its feathery, mid-green leaves and large, showy blooms. The long-stemmed, daisy-like flowers come in a range of pinks and whites and are good for cutting. Prolong flowering with regular deadheading. It prefers a sunny position in moist but well-drained soil. For early flowering, sow seed in autumn.

☼ ◊ ◑ ✿✿✿

‡ to 90cm (36in) ↔ to 60cm (24in)

Crinum x *powellii* ♥

PERENNIAL BULB

From late summer to autumn, tall stems of large, slightly fragrant, funnel-shaped, pale pink flowers appear on this vigorous, clump-forming perennial. The strap-like leaves can measure up to 1.5m (5ft) in length. Crinums are not completely hardy, and in cold areas protect them with a thick mulch during the winter. They should be planted with the neck of the bulb just above the ground, preferably in the shelter of a sunny wall, in fertile, moist, well-drained soil.

☼ ◊ ◑ ✿✿ *f*

‡ to 1m (3ft) ↔ to 60cm (24in)

Dahlia 'Fascination' ♀

PERENNIAL

Dahlias provide a late burst of colour after early-flowering perennials are past their best. 'Fascination' is a dwarf form, with bronze-tinged leaves, and purple-pink flowers. It can be used as a bedding plant at the front of a border, and makes a good cut flower. Grow it in full sun in fertile, well-drained soil. Dig up the tubers after the first frost, pack them in boxes of dry sand, or compost, and overwinter them in a frost-free place. Plant out in late spring.

☼ ◊ ✿✿

↕ to 45cm (18in) ↔ to 30cm (12in)

Dianthus gratianopolitanus ♀

PERENNIAL

The Cheddar pink is a compact, low-growing evergreen that forms a carpet of waxy, narrow, grey-green leaves. In late summer solitary, very fragrant, pink or red flowers with toothed petals are borne on short stems. It will flourish in a rock garden, raised bed or trough, and should be planted in well-drained, gritty soil in full sun.

☼ ◊ ✿✿✿ *f*

↕ to 15cm (6in) ↔ to 30cm (12in)

Diascia barberae '**Blackthorn Apricot**' ♀

PERENNIAL

This mat-forming plant produces masses of apricot-pink flowers in summer and autumn, and is ideal for the front of a herbaceous border, a rock garden, or a container. Diascias grow well in full sun, in moist, well-drained, fertile soil, and need protection in cold, wet winters. Other excellent forms include 'Salmon Supreme', with larger, pale apricot flowers, and 'Ruby Field', which produces deep salmon-pink flowers.

☼ ◊ ◊ ❀ ❀

‡ to 25cm (10in) ↔ to 50cm (20in)

Echinacea purpurea

PERENNIAL

The coneflower has tall, erect stems that bear slightly hairy, lance-shaped leaves. In the late summer and early autumn it produces large, purplish-pink, daisy-like flowerheads, with cone-shaped centres comprised of tiny golden-brown flowers. It is ideal for the middle or back of a border, and to grow well, needs full sun and a deep, well-drained soil. Good for cutting.

☼ ◊ ❀ ❀ ❀

‡ to 1.5m (5ft) ↔ to 45cm (18in)

Erica ciliaris 'Corfe Castle'

EVERGREEN SHRUB

The Dorset heath 'Corfe Castle' bears rose-pink flowers from midsummer to the middle of autumn. In winter the mid-green foliage has a bronze tone, and its spreading stems make good ground cover. *Erica ciliaris* and its cultivars should be planted in an open, sunny situation in acid (lime-free), well-drained soil. Although hardy, it may suffer during very cold winters. Clip over the plants in spring to keep them neat, and remove dead flowers.

☼ ◊ ❀ ❀ ❀

‡ to 22cm (9in) ↔ to 35cm (14in)

Erica vagans 'Birch Glow' ♀

EVERGREEN SHRUB

This summer-flowering heather is a low and spreading, evergreen shrub, looking good on its own in a container or trough filled with bark-based ericaceous compost. Its deep pink flowers continue well into autumn. In the open garden choose a sunny site and grow in acid soil, although it will tolerate chalk. It can be grown as ground cover and is tolerant of coastal conditions. Trim in early spring.

☼ ◊ ◊ ❀ ❀ ❀

‡ to 30cm (12in) ↔ to 50cm (20in)

Erigeron karvinskianus ♥

PERENNIAL

This carpeting plant produces spreading stems and greyish-green, lance-shaped leaves. The pretty, daisy-like flowers, which appear in summer, are solitary or produced in groups of up to five white or pink blooms, which darken to reddish-purple as they age. It should be planted in full sun, in moist but well-drained soil. The blooms will liven up a rock garden or the front of a border, and it is ideal for planting in cracks and crevices in walls and paving. Once established it spreads freely.

☼ ◊ ❀ ❀ ❀

‡ to 15cm (6in) ↔ indefinite

Eupatorium maculatum **Atropurpureum Group** ♥

PERENNIAL

Joe Pye weed is tall, with very strong, reddish-purple stems, and pointed, lance-shaped, purple-tinged green leaves. The large heads of pinkish-purple flowers appear from midsummer to early autumn. It is a useful plant for the back of a large, late summer border and blends well with grasses such as *Miscanthus*. It enjoys damp, slightly alkaline soil, in full sun or partial shade.

☼ ☽ ◊ ❀ ❀ ❀

‡ to 2.2m (7ft) ↔ to 1m (3ft)

Filipendula purpurea ♀

PERENNIAL

This close relative of meadowsweet is a pretty perennial for moist or wet ground. It forms upright clumps of elegant, dark green foliage that is topped by feathery clusters of red-purple flowers on purple-tinged stems in summer. It looks good planted in groups to form drifts and would be suitable for a waterside planting or a bog garden. It can also be naturalized in damp woodland. The plant will tolerate full sun provided the soil is reliably moist.

☼ ☀ ◗ ♦ ❀ ❀ ❀

‡ to 1.2m (4ft) ↔ to 60cm (24in)

Fuchsia 'Leonora'

DECIDUOUS SHRUB

A free-flowering, upright fuchsia that has bell-shaped, soft pink flowers with reflexed outer sepals. It is a good choice for a patio container; use loam-based potting compost and position it in full sun or light shade. In summer, water well, and feed regularly with a balanced fertilizer, or use a slow-release fertilizer when planting. Keep it frost-free over winter, moving it outside after frosts are over. New plants are easy to raise from softwood cuttings in spring.

☼ ☀ ◗ ♦ ❀

‡ to 1.5m (5ft) ↔ to 1m (3ft)

Gaura lindheimeri 'Siskiyou Pink'

PERENNIAL

This robust plant has branched stems and forms a clump of narrow lance- or spoon-shaped leaves. The flowers of 'Siskiyou Pink' are white, but heavily flushed with deep pink. They first appear in late spring, but reach their peak in late summer, and continue into the early autumn. This long-flowering plant is perfect for the front of a sunny border and needs a fertile, moist, well-drained soil. It will tolerate partial shade and dry soil during the summer.

☼ ☀ ◊ ◑ ❀ ❀
‡ to 1.2m (4ft) ↔ to 1m (3ft)

Hebe 'Great Orme' ♀

EVERGREEN SHRUB

There are over 75 species of hebe, all suitable for coastal gardens. This one forms a rounded bush, with purple shoots and glossy leaves. From midsummer to mid-autumn it produces spikes of pink flowers, which fade to white as they age. It is a medium-sized shrub, and will add year-round interest to a mixed border. Plant it in a sunny or partially shaded position, sheltered from cold winds and frost, in well-drained soil. No pruning is necessary.

☼ ☀ ◊ ◑ ❀ ❀
‡↔ to 1.2m (4ft)

Hemerocallis 'Jolyene Nichole'
PERENNIAL

The daylily is so called because its flowers open for just one day. 'Joylene Nichole' is unusual in that it unfurls its flowers late in the afternoon and they stay open throughout the night. It has large, pink flowers with a yellowish-green throat, lined with deep pink veins. The flowers are borne above a large clump of almost evergreen, bluish-green leaves. Plant in moist but well-drained soil, in a sunny border near the house or patio to enjoy its blooms fully.

‡ to 50cm (20in) ↔ to 1m (3ft)

Hydrangea paniculata
PINK DIAMOND ('Interhydia') ♡
DECIDUOUS SHRUB

In late summer and early autumn this spreading hydrangea bears large, cone-shaped flowerheads, that open creamy-white but then turn deep pink as they age. It should be planted in a moist, well-drained, fertile soil in sun or partial shade. It will also benefit from some protection against cold, drying winds. No pruning is necessary, but flowering is improved by cutting back stems in early spring to a permanent framework of branches.

‡ to 7m (22ft) ↔ to 2.5m (8ft)

Hydrangea serrata 'Rosalba'

DECIDUOUS SHRUB

This upright yet compact, deciduous shrub is valued for its flat flowerheads, which appear from summer to autumn. These are made up of tiny pink flowers in the centre, surrounded by larger white flowers that become red-marked as they age. The leaves are oval, mid-green and pointed. 'Rosalba' is ideal as a specimen plant or in a shrub border. Grow in sun or partial shade in moist soil; the flowers may turn blue in acid conditions. Very little pruning is necessary.

☼ ☼ ◊ ❋ ❋ ❋
‡↔ to 1.2m (4ft)

Indigofera dielsiana

DECIDUOUS SHRUB

The dark green leaves of this medium-sized bush are composed of small opposing leaflets, and contrast well with the pea-like, pale reddish-pink flowers that are produced from summer to early autumn. *Indigofera* is not fully hardy and should be grown in full sun in a sheltered shrub border, or against a warm, south- or west-facing wall. It will do well when planted in fertile, moist, well-drained soil. The stems produce an orange-yellow latex when they are cut, which may irritate the skin.

☼ ◊ ❋ ❋
‡↔ to 1.5m (5ft)

Lathyrus latifolius ♥

CLIMBER

The everlasting pea is a herbaceous climber with branched stems and pairs of blue-green leaflets. The leaves terminate in tendrils, which allows it to scramble or climb over banks or through shrubs. In late summer and early autumn, it bears clusters of pea-like, magenta-purple flowers. Plant it in fertile, well-drained soil in full sun or partial shade, and prune it to the ground in spring to encourage new stems, otherwise leave undisturbed. Sow seed in the autumn.

☼ ☀ ◊ ❀❀❀
‡ to 2m (6ft)

Lavatera maritima ♥

EVERGREEN PERENNIAL

This shrubby perennial has rounded, greyish-green leaves with shallow lobes. In summer it bears solitary, saucer-shaped, pink flowers with deep magenta veins radiating out from the centre. It prefers a spot in full sun, in fertile, well-drained soil, sheltered or staked against the wind. To encourage healthy growth the following year, after flowering cut back to a strong bud close to the base. Mallows are good choices for seaside gardens, although they tend to be short-lived.

☼ ◊ ❀❀❀
‡ to 1.5m (5ft) ↔ to 1m (3ft)

Lilium Pink Perfection Group ♀

PERENNIAL BULB

These Asiatic lilies have large, slightly nodding, trumpet-shaped flowers, held on tall, robust stems. The blooms are fragrant, and have deep pinkish-purple petals with swept-back tips. Plant Asiatic lilies in well-drained, fertile soil which has been enriched with leafmould or well-rotted garden compost. They need a sunny position to thrive, with the base of the plant in shade. If using them as cut flowers, snip off the orange anthers as the pollen stains.

☼ ◊ ❋❋❋ *f*

‡ to 2m (6ft)

Lonicera periclymenum 'Serotina' ♀

CLIMBER

The late Dutch honeysuckle has woody, twining stems, and greyish-green leaves. In mid- to late summer it produces clusters of pink buds opening to display highly perfumed, creamy-white and purple-pink flowers. It is very hardy and can be grown over fences and pergolas, or through trees and shrubs, or as ground cover over a bank. Plant it in full sun or partial shade, in fertile, moist, but well-drained soil. Prune back after flowering to keep within bounds.

☼ ◐ ◊ ◑ ❋❋❋ *f*

‡ to 7m (22ft)

Lychnis coronaria ♀
BIENNIAL

The rose campion has lance-shaped, soft, downy, silver-grey leaves and stems, which in mid- to late summer contrast beautifully with the bright magenta, rounded, flat-topped flowers. It self-seeds with abandon, and is a welcome addition to any garden bed or border. Plant rose campion in full sun in slightly fertile, well-drained soil. Sow seed in spring to flower the following year.

☼ ◊ ❀❀❀
↕ to 60cm (24in) ↔ to 45cm (18in)

Monarda 'Croftway Pink' ♀
PERENNIAL

This pink-flowered variety of bergamot is a clump-forming, herbaceous perennial primarily grown for its round heads of tubular pink flowers that appear in late summer. These are carried above the small and deliciously aromatic, light green leaves, which betray the plant's use as a herb. Bergamot would suit a mixed or herbaceous border, or even a kitchen garden. Another common name for the plant is bee balm, as the flowers are attractive to bees.

☼ ☼ ◊ ❀❀❀ *f*
↕ to 1m (3ft) ↔ to 45cm (18in)

Morina longifolia

PERENNIAL

A spiny-toothed, evergreen perennial with dark-green, aromatic leaves that overwinter as a thistle-like rosette. In early summer it produces a spike of small, dangling, tubular flowers – these open white, turn pink after they have been fertilized, then eventually change to red before falling. Plant in a sunny position, in poor, very well-drained soil. The roots will rot if the soil is wet during the winter months, so mulch with grit or gravel.

☼ ◊ ✾ ✾ ✾ *f*

↕ to 75cm (30in) ↔ to 30cm (12in)

Nicotiana 'Domino Salmon-pink'

ANNUAL

This tobacco plant is grown as an annual in cooler climates. It has large, sticky basal leaves and narrow, lance-shaped stem leaves. In mid- to late summer, 'Domino Salmon-pink' is clothed with star-shaped, salmon-pink flowers that open up in the early evening and emit a delicate scent. Grow tobacco plants in full sun or partial shade in fertile, moist, well-drained soil, near a window or path where the fragrance can be enjoyed.

☼ ◑ ◊ ◑ ✾ *f*

↕ to 45cm (18in) ↔ to 40cm (16in)

Nymphaea 'René Gérard'

PERENNIAL

Waterlilies are aquatic perennials grown for their showy flowers and rounded, floating leaves. The shade cast by the leaves is useful in reducing growth of pond algae and providing shelter for fish and other pond creatures. The star-shaped flowers of 'René Gérard' are rosy red. Plant in aquatic planting baskets in still water, and divide plants in spring if necessary. The plants retreat underwater in winter.

☼ ♦ ❀❀❀
↔ to 1.5m (5ft)

Origanum 'Kent Beauty'

DECIDUOUS SHRUB

A semi-evergreen herb with creeping roots and a prostrate habit, with aromatic, rounded, bright green leaves. From midsummer it produces masses of small, tubular, pale-pink or mauve flowers, surrounded by deep pink bracts. Oregano is perfect for a herb or gravel garden, patio pot, or the front of a herbaceous border. Plant it in full sun in slightly fertile, well-drained soil.

☼ ◊ ❀❀❀ *f*
↕ to 20cm (8in) ↔ to 30cm (12in)

Pelargonium '**Bird Dancer**' ♀

PERENNIAL

This frost-tender plant bears decorative rounded green leaves, with wavy edges and a darker zone in the centre. The flowers are pale salmon-pink and borne on long stems in ball-headed clusters from summer to autumn. Its compact, neat habit makes it ideal for a patio container or a sunny window box. Plant it in fertile, well-drained potting compost or bed out in free-draining garden soil. Move under cover for the winter and keep fairly dry.

☼ ☀ ◊ ❋

‡ to 20cm (8in) ↔ to 15cm (6in)

Pelargonium '**Clorinda**'

PERENNIAL

This vigorous scented-leaved pelargonium has crinkled evergreen foliage that smells of cedar. Rounded clusters of deep rose-pink flowers appear from summer to autumn. Grow it in containers in well-drained potting compost, in a position in sun or light shade. A tender plant, this pelargonium must be overwintered in a frost-free greenhouse or indoors. Alternatively, take softwood cuttings of non-flowering shoots from spring to autumn.

☼ ☀ ◊ ❋ *f*

‡ to 50cm (20in) ↔ to 25cm (10in)

Penstemon 'Apple Blossom' ♀

PERENNIAL

This penstemon bears spikes of elegant, tubular, light pink flowers with white throats from midsummer right through to autumn, if the blooms are deadheaded regularly. It prefers a moist but free-draining soil in full sun or light shade, and is perfect for a border with a pastel colour theme. Although it may survive the winter in a sheltered site, it is not fully frost hardy. As a precaution, it is a good idea to take softwood cuttings from the middle of summer.

☼ ☀ ◊ ❀❀

↕↔ to 60cm (24in)

Persicaria affinis 'Donald Lowndes' ♀

EVERGREEN PERENNIAL

This vigorous plant is popular for its dense spikes of long-lasting, pale pink flowers that appear in midsummer on long, slender stems. These will enliven any herbaceous border in late summer, and as the flowers age to dark pink, a range of lovely pink shades continues until autumn. The mats of lance-shaped, deep green leaves turn rich brown in autumn. Plant in groups or use as ground cover. Dig out any invasive or spreading roots in spring or autumn.

☼ ☀ ◊ ❀❀❀

↕↔ to 15cm (6in)

Phlox paniculata '**Windsor**' ⚘

PERENNIAL

The dense, conical heads of carmine-rose flowers with distinctive, deep red eyes are borne on this phlox in late summer above oval, mid-green leaves. Grow it in full sun or partial shade in well-drained, moist soil, and stake where necessary. Plant groups of this tall phlox in a herbaceous border or behind shorter plants in a gravel garden. Deadhead regularly in summer, and thin out weak shoots in spring for improved flowering.

☼ ◑ ◊ ❀ ❀ ❀

‡ to 1.2m (4ft) ↔ to 1m (3ft)

Physostegia virginiana '**Variegata**'

PERENNIAL

The obedient plant is unusual because its flower stalks are hinged, so that when the blooms are moved they stay in position. In summer, tall spikes bear small, mauve-pink, tubular flowers, which will brighten up a border and are also good for cutting. The leaves are lance-shaped and mid-green, edged with white. Plant in sun or partial shade in a moist soil.

☼ ◑ ◊ ❀ ❀ ❀

‡ to 1.2m (4ft) ↔ to 60cm (24in)

Physostegia virginiana 'Vivid' ♀

PERENNIAL

Commonly known as the obedient plant because the flowers will remain in position after they are moved on their stalks. Tall spikes of small, tubular, vivid purple-pink flowers appear from midsummer to autumn and are ideal for cutting. The mid-green leaves are lance-shaped and toothed and form dense clumps. Grow in full sun in well-drained, moisture-retentive soil. Overcrowded clumps can be divided in spring.

☀ ◊ ◊ ❀ ❀ ❀

↔ to 60cm (24in)

Rodgersia pinnata 'Superba'

PERENNIAL

This impressive, clump-forming plant bears upright clusters of star-shaped, bright pink flowers. These are borne in mid- to late summer above the equally attractive, heavily veined and palmately divided, large, dark green foliage. Each leaf can measure up to 90cm (36in) across and bears a purplish bronze tint when young. It is good near water, such as in a bog garden, or for naturalizing at a woodland margin, as long as the soil is moist – it will not tolerate drought. Shelter from cold, drying winds.

☀ ☀ ◊ ❀ ❀ ❀

↕ to 1.2m (4ft) ↔ to 75cm (30in)

Sanguisorba obtusa

PERENNIAL

Burnet is a clump-forming plant with bold, greyish-green leaves. In summer, thin wiry stems, tipped with spikes of tiny pink flowers like bottle-brushes, are produced. Grow them in a border, or next to a pond in moist but well-drained soil, in full sun or partial shade. Both the flowers and leaves are good for cutting.

☼ ☀ ◊ ◐ ❀ ❀ ❀
‡ to 1.2m (4ft) ↔ to 60cm (24in)

Saponaria officinalis 'Rosea Plena'

PERENNIAL

Before commercial detergents became available, soapwort was used as a soap substitute for washing delicate fabrics. Today it is still often used in natural shampoos. A robust plant with rough, rounded leaves, this form has double, pale pink flowers. It can spread rapidly and may need to be kept in check in a border to prevent it smothering other plants. It is best in well-drained neutral to alkaline soils in a sunny position.

☼ ◊ ❀ ❀ ❀
‡ to 60cm (24in) ↔ to 50cm (20in)

Spiraea japonica 'Anthony Waterer'

DECIDUOUS SHRUB

This medium-sized, twiggy shrub has small, lance-shaped leaves that emerge red and gradually turn dark green as they age. The foliage is occasionally tinged with cream or pink, too. The flat heads of purple buds open to frothy, dark pink flowers from mid- to late summer. Grow this spiraea in a shrub or mixed border in full sun and any moderately fertile soil that does not completely dry out. Cut back lightly after flowering.

☼ ◊ ◑ ❀ ❀ ❀
‡↔ to 1.5m (5ft)

Tamarix ramosissima 'Pink Cascade'

DECIDUOUS SHRUB

This tamarisk is an attractive small tree with graceful, arching branches and feathery foliage. In summer it is covered with tiny pink flowers. It makes a superb windbreak or hedge in coastal areas; in inland areas it will need a more sheltered position. To prevent plants becoming straggly, cut back shrubs and hedges in early spring. It grows best in sandy, well-drained soil in full sun.

☼ ◊ ❀ ❀ ❀
‡ to 4m (12ft) ↔ to 3.5m (11ft)

Achillea 'Summerwine' ♀

SEMI-EVERGREEN PERENNIAL

This yarrow has beautiful wine-red, flat flowerheads which are alive with insects in mid- to late summer, who seem to use them as landing platforms. They look striking in a border and are also good for cutting, which encourages further blooms. The lovely feathery foliage is greyish green. Place a support over the emerging clump in spring to prevent the flowers flopping, and divide large clumps in spring or autumn. This tough plant can tolerate periods of drought and hot weather.

☼ ◊ ◊ ❀❀❀
‡↔ to 80cm (32in)

Aster novae-angliae 'Andenken an Alma Pötschke'

PERENNIAL

New England asters are clump-forming perennials, with erect, woody stems covered with mid-green, narrow, lance-shaped leaves. This variety bears dense sprays of salmon-red, daisy-like flowers and is a superb plant for a late summer border. It is also good for cutting. New England asters also benefit from support with twiggy sticks, or canes and string. Divide clumps regularly in the spring.

☼ ◑ ◊ ◊ ❀❀❀
‡ to 1.2m (4ft) ↔ to 60cm (24in)

Begonia Nonstop Series ♀

PERENNIAL

These compact tuberous begonias have heart-shaped, mid-green leaves and double flowers, measuring up to 8cm (3in) across. They are available in a wide range of bright colours, including red, pink, yellow, and orange. Use them as bedding plants or in pots, and grow them in full sun in fertile, moist, well-drained soil. They are not hardy and the tubers must be dug up before the first frosts. Store them in dry sand in a cool room indoors.

‡↔ to 30cm (12in)

Campsis radicans

CLIMBER

The common trumpet creeper has dark green leaves, divided into many leaflets, and in late summer produces clusters of orange-red, trumpet-shaped flowers. It is not fully hardy and is best planted in full sun against a warm wall, to which it will cling with aerial roots. Plant it in fertile, moist, well-drained soil. In warm areas it will grow vigorously to cover a large area within a few seasons, and it suits a tropical-style garden. Keep it clear of roofs and gutters, and hard prune it in winter to keep it in check.

‡ to 10m (30ft)

Canna 'Assaut'

PERENNIAL

The Indian shot plant is grown for its large, broad leaves and exotic-looking flowers. 'Assaut' has impressive purple-brown foliage, and spikes of scarlet blooms. Cannas grow quickly and make a dramatic addition to a late summer border, tropical-style garden, or they can be grown in pots. Plant them in late spring in full sun and moist, well-drained soil. They are not hardy and the rhizomes should be overwintered in just-moist compost in a frost-free place.

☼ ◊ ◊ ❄

↕ to 1.2m (4ft) ↔ to 60cm (24in)

Chrysanthemum 'Cherry Chintz'

PERENNIAL

'Cherry Chintz' produces huge double blooms, composed of many red petals, in late summer. Plant it in a sheltered site in fertile, moist, well-drained soil, with well-rotted manure incorporated into it before planting. It is mostly grown for cutting and needs staking. Often grown in pots of loam-based compost under glass, it is also suitable for a sheltered, sunny patio or terrace. Remove all but the terminal bud for the largest flowers for exhibition.

☼ ◊ ◊ ❄ ❄

↕ to 1.3m (4½ft) ↔ to 75cm (30in)

Cosmos atrosanguineus

PERENNIAL

This Mexican plant has green, deeply-lobed leaves, and from midsummer to early autumn produces masses of dark red, chocolate-scented, single flowers on reddish-brown stems. While it is not completely hardy, it should survive most winters if covered with a thick layer of mulch. In very cold locations, dig up the tubers in the autumn and store them during the winter in trays of slightly damp sand or compost. Plant it in full sun in moist, well-drained soil.

‡ to 60cm (24in) ↔ to 45cm (18in)

Crocosmia 'Lucifer'

PERENNIAL

This widely-grown plant has dramatic mid-green leaves, and from mid- to late summer produces arching stems bearing clusters of bright-red flowers. For maximum effect, plant it in groups in a gravel garden or herbaceous border. It prefers full sun or partial shade and a moist, well-drained soil. When clumps become congested after a few years divide them in the autumn and replant the corms elsewhere. In cold gardens, apply a protective mulch in winter.

‡ to 1m (3ft) ↔ to 25cm (10in)

Dahlia 'Hillcrest Royal' ♥

PERENNIAL

The red-purple, cactus-type flowers of this striking dahlia are held on strong stems, and make a dramatic statement in the middle of a herbaceous border. It needs a sunny site and fertile, moist, well-drained soil. Deadhead it regularly to promote the development of more flowers, and in summer feed it with a general-purpose fertilizer. Lift the tubers after the first frost and store them over winter in a frost-free place. Plant in mid- to late spring, and insert a stake at the same time.

☼ ◊ ◑ ❀ ❀

‡ to 1.1m (3½ft) ↔ to 60cm (24in)

Dahlia 'Whale's Rhonda'

PERENNIAL

A dark purple-red pompon dahlia, the petals of 'Whales Rhonda' have silver undersides, giving them a two-tone appearance. It is often grown for cut flower arrangements or for exhibitions, and should be planted in full sun in a moist, well-drained soil. It can also be planted in a large container. Lift and store the tubers as described for 'Hillcrest Royal' (*see above*).

☼ ◊ ❀ ❀

‡ to 1m (3ft) ↔ to 60cm (24in)

Escallonia rubra 'Woodside'

EVERGREEN SHRUB

This dwarf escallonia is a small-leaved shrub that produces abundant clusters of miniature red flowers in summer amid the attractively glossy foliage. It thrives in relatively mild, coastal sites, but it would just as easily suit an inland garden as a low, formal or informal, evergreen hedge, or as part of a mixed border. Clip annually in spring for a formal shape. Overly vigorous shoots should be cut out as they appear; this is the plant reverting to the larger species form, which can reach 5m (15ft) tall.

‡ to 75cm (30in) ↔ to 1.5m (5ft)

Fuchsia 'Golden Marinka' ♀

DECIDUOUS SHRUB

From midsummer to early autumn this trailing fuchsia produces bright red flowers, set off by variegated green and yellow foliage. Grow it in full sun or partial shade. It can be used as ground cover, or planted in hanging baskets in soil-less potting compost, or containers of loam-based compost. In the garden, grow it in moist, well-drained soil. Feed fuchsias in containers every fortnight with a balanced liquid fertilizer, or mix in slow-release fertilizer when planting.

‡ to 30cm (12in) ↔ to 45cm (18in)

Fuchsia magellanica 'Thompsonii' ♀

DECIDUOUS SHRUB

A hardy fuchsia with small red flowers that appear in midsummer, this plant can be grown as a hedge, or a shrubby specimen in a border. In cold areas, mulch it over winter, as the top growth may be damaged by frost. Cut out dead stems in spring, and pinch out the soft tips of the stems to encourage bushy growth. It can also be trained as a standard or grown in a large pot. Plant it in a sheltered site in moist, free-draining soil, in sun or partial shade.

☼ ☀ ◊ ◐ ✿✿

‡ to 3m (10ft) ↔ to 2m (6ft)

Gaillardia x *grandiflora* 'Dazzler' ♀

PERENNIAL

As the name suggests, the flowers of this plant will certainly catch the eye in a bed or border. Their petals are deep orange-red, tipped with yellow, while the centres resemble a maroon pincushion. The blooms appear from early summer and continue up until the early autumn. Grow 'Dazzler' in a sunny position, in fertile, well-drained soil, and remove the dead flowers to prolong blooming. Good for cutting.

☼ ◊ ✿✿✿

‡ to 60cm (24in) ↔ to 50cm (20in)

Helenium 'Moerheim Beauty' ♀

PERENNIAL

This undemanding, yet very rewarding summer perennial is a firm favourite for its beautiful, rich coppery red, daisy-like flowers that appear towards the end of summer when many other flowers are fading. Combined with ornamental grasses and coneflowers, it can bring a late summer garden to life. Deadhead regularly and divide large clumps in spring or autumn to maintain vigour.

☼ ◊ ◊ ❁ ❁ ❁

↕ to 1m (3ft) ↔ to 60cm (24in)

Hemerocallis 'Stafford'

PERENNIAL

A beautiful daylily, this form produces deep red flowers with golden-yellow centres, borne above a clump of strap-like, mid-green leaves. It flowers from early to midsummer, and will help to fire up a gravel garden or the front of a border. Alternatively, it can be grown in a large container if well watered in the summer. Plant it in full sun in moist, well-drained soil.

☼ ◊ ◊ ❁ ❁ ❁

↕ to 70cm (28in) ↔ to 1m (3ft)

Knautia macedonica

PERENNIAL

This clump-forming, often short-lived plant forms a rosette of hairy, lobed, basal leaves, and in summer produces branched stems that bear deeply divided leaves, and small, pincushion-shaped heads of tiny dark red flowers. Attractive to bees, it is perfect for a wild garden, herbaceous border, or cottage garden. It will flourish in full sun, in a well-drained, preferably alkaline soil.

☼ ◊ ❀❀❀

‡ to 75cm (30in) ↔ to 60cm (24in)

Lathyrus odoratus 'Red Ensign'

CLIMBER

This sweet pea carries sweetly scented, scarlet-red flowers from the summer to late autumn. It can be grown up a cane pyramid in a border for instant height, or train it against a trellis. Cut the flowers regularly for the home and to stimulate more to develop. Grow sweet peas in full sun in moist, well-drained soil with well-rotted manure incorporated into it. Sow the seeds in pots in autumn to overwinter in a cold frame for planting out in spring, or sow *in situ* in spring.

☼ ◊ ❀❀❀ *f*

‡ to 2m (6ft)

Lilium speciosum var. *rubrum*

PERENNIAL BULB

This tall lily has erect, purple-flushed stems, and lance-shaped, dark green leaves. In late summer it produces up to a dozen fragrant, slightly pendent, turk's-cap flowers with swept-back petals. The deep carmine-red blooms are marked with darker red spots, and have very long stamens. This lily grows well in moist, well-drained, slightly acid soil in partial shade, and will thrive in a woodland garden.

 ❀ ◊ ◊ ✽✽✽ *f*

↕ to 1.7m (5½ft)

Lobelia 'Cherry Ripe'

PERENNIAL

'Cherry Ripe' has narrow, deep green leaves, and in summer, spikes of bright cherry-red flowers. It will bring a splash of colour to a damp herbaceous border, woodland, or the margins of a pool. For a spectacular effect, plant a group of five or more, in moist soil and full sun. Lobelias are very vulnerable to damage by slugs and snails in spring – sharp grit around the new shoots may deter these pests.

 ❀ ◊ ✽✽

↕ to 1m (3ft) ↔ to 23cm (9in)

Lychnis chalcedonica ♀
PERENNIAL

The Jerusalem cross forms a clump of evergreen basal leaves, above which domed heads of small, scarlet flowers appear in summer, borne on tall, hairy flower stems. The stems of this hardy plant are rather weak and will need to be staked if it is grown in an exposed site. It is ideal for a herbaceous border, or a gravel or wild garden, and should be planted in moist, well-drained soil, in full sun or dappled shade.

☼ ☽ ◊ ◑ ❀❀❀
‡ to 1.2m (4ft) ↔ to 45cm (18in)

Monarda '**Cambridge Scarlet**' ♀
PERENNIAL

Bergamot, or bee balm, is a clump-forming herb with aromatic, toothed leaves. 'Cambridge Scarlet' has vivid red, hooded, spidery-looking flowers and, like all bergamot, it is attractive to bees. Perfect for a border or prairie-style garden, it spreads quickly in a moist but well-drained soil that does not dry out in summer, or become waterlogged in winter, and a sunny situation. It can be divided in spring.

☼ ◊ ◑ ❀❀❀ *f*
‡ to 1m (3ft) ↔ to 45cm (18in)

Penstemon 'Chester Scarlet' ♀

PERENNIAL

In late summer and up to the first frosts this beautiful penstemon produces tall spikes of bell-shaped, scarlet flowers. It should be planted in full sun or partial shade in fertile, well-drained soil, and is suitable for a warm herbaceous border. Deadhead it regularly to prolong the flowering period. As this plant is not reliably hardy, protect it during winter with a thick layer of mulch. It is easy to propagate from softwood cuttings taken in early summer.

☼ ☀ ◊ ❀ ❀

‡ to 90cm (36in) ↔ to 75cm (30in)

Persicaria amplexicaulis 'Firetail' ♀

PERENNIAL

This Himalayan bistort is a vigorous clump-forming plant with decorative, large, dark green, lance-shaped leaves. From midsummer to autumn 'Firetail' produces tall spikes of small, bright red flowers. It likes moist soil conditions and offers a long season of interest in a damp border, or an area partially shaded by deciduous trees. Its foliage also makes good ground cover.

☼ ☀ ◊ ❀ ❀ ❀

‡↔ to 1.2m (4ft)

Phygelius x *rectus* 'African Queen' ♀

EVERGREEN SHRUB

In late summer, this upright plant bears tall spires of pendent, pale red flowers above lance-shaped, dark green leaves. It should be planted in fertile, free-draining soil in a border among hardy shrubs, or against a sunny wall. In cold locations, it is best to treat this frost tender shrub as a herbaceous perennial. To protect it in the winter, cover with a thick mulch in autumn, and cut the stems down to the ground in spring.

☼ ◊ ◊ ❀ ❀

‡ to 1m (3ft) ↔ to 1.2m (4ft)

Ricinus communis 'Carmencita' ♀

ANNUAL

The castor oil plant is usually grown for its large, architectural, palm-shaped leaves. This variety has dark bronzy-red foliage, and in late summer it may produce tall spikes of small, bright red flowers. It should be planted in full sun in fertile, well-drained soil, and is useful in bedding schemes and tropical-style gardens. It can also be grown in a large container. All parts of this plant are highly toxic.

☼ ◊ ❀

‡ to 1.5m (5ft) ↔ to 1m (3ft)

Salvia coccinea 'Lady in Red' ♀

PERENNIAL

This tender South American perennial is usually treated as an annual in colder countries. It has erect stems and oval or heart-shaped dark green leaves, and in the summer and autumn it produces spikes of bright red flowers. Plant it in a sunny position in light, well-drained soil. This bushy salvia works well at the front of a herbaceous border, or use it as a bedding or container plant. The seeds should be sown in spring for flowers the same year.

☼ ◊ ❀ ❀

‡ to 60cm (24in) ↔ to 30cm (12in)

Salvia x jamensis 'Hot Lips'

EVERGREEN SHRUB

This eye-catching salvia has extremely pretty red and white flowers that appear throughout summer. Unlike many salvias, it is reasonably hardy to frost, but in areas with cold winters it is sensible to restrict it to a very sheltered position. Plant in early summer to allow the roots to establish well before winter. The aromatic leaves smell of mint when crushed.

☼ ◊ ❀ ❀ *f*

‡↔ to 75cm (30in)

Solenostemon scutellarioides

PERENNIAL

Better known as coleus, the flame nettle is a tender plant, grown primarily for its foliage. The most decorative varieties have toothed, hairy variegated leaves in a range of bright colours, including red, yellow, burgundy, and green. They bear spikes of small blue or white flowers, which should be removed before they open to retain the foliage effect. Plant them in light shade, in pots of loam-based compost, or as part of a bedding scheme in moist, well-drained soil.

☀ ◊ ◊ ❁

↕ to 45cm (18in) ↔ to 30cm (12in)

Tagetes 'Cinnabar'

ANNUAL

One of many varieties of fast-growing French marigold, this has feathery, deeply-divided, dark green leaves. From midsummer to early autumn it bears rusty-red, single flowers with bright yellow eyes. Usually grown as a half-hardy annual bedding plant or for containers, it should be planted in a sunny location in fertile, well-drained soil. Easy to raise from seed, it can be sown under glass in early spring, or *in situ* in late spring.

☀ ◊ ❁

↕↔ to 30cm (12in)

Zauschneria californica 'Dublin' ♀

PERENNIAL

The Californian fuchsia forms a clump of slightly hairy, greyish-green, lance-shaped leaves, and in late summer bears large numbers of bright red, tubular flowers on slightly arching stems. Plant it in a gravel or rock garden, at the front of a mixed border, or in the gaps of a dry-stone wall, in full sun and reasonably fertile, well-drained soil. It is quite hardy, but needs a protected site, out of cold winds.

☼ ◊ ❀❀

‡ to 30cm (12in) ↔ to 45cm (18in)

Zinnia elegans 'Ruffles'

ANNUAL

A striking, upright, bushy plant with egg- or lance-shaped, mid-green leaves, 'Ruffles' lives up to its name, bearing frilly, pompon, fully double flowers in a wide range of colours, including red. Plant it in sun, in any well-drained soil. Use it as bedding, or plant it in groups in a herbaceous border. Zinnias are also good for cutting for use in the home.

☼ ◊ ❀

‡ to 60cm (24in) ↔ to 30cm (12in)

Allium sphaerocephalon

PERENNIAL BULB

The round-headed leek sends up table-tennis-ball-sized flowerheads in midsummer. They are a rich, bright purple and are a magnet to bees. These bulbs are tremendous value and worth mixing into any perennial border, as they take up no space at all, yet rise above most other plants to add an extra dimension to displays. They come up year after year requiring little or no effort from the gardener. They are also ideal for wildlife gardens.

☼ ◊ ◊ ❀❀❀

‡ to 90cm (36in) ↔ to 5cm (2in)

Angelica gigas

PERENNIAL

The double pleasures of purple flowers and burgundy flower stems make this short-lived perennial well worth growing in a large border. Closely related to culinary angelica, be sure to give its lush, mid-green leaves plenty of room to spread. It is ideally suitable for an informal woodland garden and, as a lover of moist, but well-drained, fertile soil, it is at home around the margins of a large pond. It will tolerate sun and partial shade. Grow from seed because mature plants resent being moved.

☼ ◑ ◊ ❀❀❀

‡ to 2m (6ft) ↔ to 1.2m (4ft)

Aster x *frikartii* 'Mönch' ♀
PERENNIAL

Considered by many people to be
one of the best of the perennial asters,
this form has bright lavender-blue,
daisy-like flowers, held on tall sturdy
stems that rarely need staking. It
flowers over a very long period from
midsummer until the first frosts. An
excellent addition to a herbaceous
border, this aster needs a sunny site
and well-drained, fertile soil. It can
be propagated by division in spring.

☼ ◊ ❀❀❀
‡ to 70cm (28in) ↔ to 40cm (16in)

Buddleja crispa
DECIDUOUS SHRUB

The arching stems of this attractive, late-
flowering shrub are clothed in toothed,
white-felted leaves. From midsummer to
early autumn it produces large, fragrant,
clustered spikes of lilac flowers. It is
very attractive to beneficial insects and
butterflies. Grow in a mixed border or in
a shrub border. It is not completely hardy
and is sometimes damaged by hard
frosts, so plant in a sheltered position in
cold or exposed gardens. Plant it in full
sunshine, in fertile, well-drained soil.

☼ ◊ ❀❀ *f*
‡↔ to 3m (10ft)

Buddleja davidii 'Dartmoor' ♀

DECIDUOUS SHRUB

This butterfly bush has long, arching branches and grey-green leaves. From mid- to late summer, it produces large conical clusters of small, magenta-purple, fragrant flowers. Its flowers attract butterflies, and it is ideal for a wildlife garden. Alternatively, plant it close to a path or the house where the butterflies can be seen. It prefers full sun and a well-drained soil. Prune it hard in the spring, to the ground or to a low permanent framework.

☼ ◊ ❀ ❀ ❀ *f*

‡ to 3m (10ft) ↔ to 5m (15ft)

Campanula latiloba 'Hidcote Amethyst' ♀

PERENNIAL

The pale mauve of this rosette-forming bellflower is a good mixer in the busy colour palette of the herbaceous border. Tall flower stems carry the large, bell-shaped flowers well above the bed of broad, lance-shaped leaves. Plant in any fertile, neutral to alkaline soil, which is also moist but well drained. Light shade is preferable, although a spot in full sun is fine but the flower colour may fade. Divide large clumps in autumn.

☼ ☀ ◊ ◊ ❀ ❀ ❀

‡ to 90cm (36in) ↔ to 45cm (18in)

Cercis canadensis '**Forest Pansy**' ♀

DECIDUOUS TREE

The eastern redbud, or Judas tree, is remarkable for its pale pink flowers that adorn the bare tree in spring before the heart-shaped leaves emerge. This variety is chosen for its red-purple, velvety foliage that turns purple and gold in autumn. Standing alone, the tree will develop a rounded shape, but it can be trained against or wall or as a foliage plant in a mixed border, making it suitable for a small to medium garden. Prune after flowering, if necessary.

☼ ☀ ◊ ❋ ❋ ❋
 ↔ to 5m (15ft)

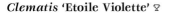

Clematis '**Etoile Violette**' ♀

CLIMBER

'Etoile Violette' is one of the Viticella Group of clematis, which are known for their late summer displays. This old variety is truly tried and tested, freely bearing good-sized, very fetching, violet-purple flowers for many weeks. The growth can be quite vigorous, and as it should be cut back to ground level each year in late winter to a pair of strong buds, it can be allowed to grow into and over large shrubs and trees where it will never pose a risk of taking over.

☼ ☀ ◊ ◊ ❋ ❋ ❋
 ↕ to 5m (15ft) ↔ to 1.5m (5ft)

Clematis 'Jackmanii' ♀

CLIMBER

From midsummer to the middle of autumn, this widely grown clematis bears an abundance of large, single, velvety, purple-violet flowers. Team it with roses on a pergola or arch, or train it up trellis for late summer colour. It will flourish in full sun or partial shade, in fertile, moist, well-drained soil, with the roots in shade. Flowering on the current year's stems, it should be pruned back to about 20cm (8in) from the ground in early spring.

☼ ☀ ◊ ◊ ❀ ❀ ❀
‡ to 3m (10ft)

Clematis 'Purpurea Plena Elegans' ♀

CLIMBER

This variety of clematis has leathery, lobed leaves. In late summer, it produces double, reddish-mauve flowers with unusual ruffled petals. Plant it in full sun or partial shade in fertile, moist, well-drained soil, and train it over a pergola or arch, or grow it through a large shrub. It flowers on the current year's stems and should be cut back to just above the ground in early spring.

☼ ☀ ◊ ◊ ❀ ❀ ❀
‡ to 4m (12ft)

Cynara cardunculus ♀
EVERGREEN PERENNIAL

Closely related to the globe artichoke, the cardoon is a fast-growing, large architectural plant with greyish-green, deeply divided, arching evergreen leaves. The purple, thistle-like flowers are borne on tall, robust stems from summer until autumn. If space allows, for real impact plant it in groups of 3–4 in a sheltered, sunny spot by a wall or fence in fertile, well-drained soil. A useful plant, it is attractive to bees, the flowers dry well and, when blanched, the leaf stalks and midribs are edible.

☼ ◊ ❀ ❀ ❀
‡ to 2m (6ft) ↔ to 1m (3ft)

Fuchsia 'Auntie Jinks'
DECIDUOUS SHRUB

From midsummer to mid-autumn this trailing plant produces flowers with deep pink tubes, pink-edged white sepals, and purple petals. For hanging baskets, use a soil-less compost, while plants in containers are better grown in loam-based compost. Feed fortnightly with a balanced fertilizer. It is happy in full sun or partial shade, but it is not hardy and should be overwintered in a light, frost-free place. Easy to raise from softwood cuttings in spring.

☼ ☀ ◊ ◑ ❀
‡ to 20cm (8in) ↔ to 40cm (16in)

Fuchsia 'La Campanella' ♀
DECIDUOUS SHRUB

The trailing branches of this fuchsia bear mid-green leaves and masses of blooms from midsummer up to the first frosts. The semi-double flowers are pale pink and deep purple. In summer, plant it outside in full sun or partial shade, in hanging baskets filled with soil-less compost. It can also be grown in a container filled with a loam-based compost. Feed fortnightly with a balanced fertilizer. It should be overwintered in a cool greenhouse.

☼ ☀ ◊ ◊ ❄

‡ to 30cm (12in) ↔ to 45cm (18in)

Hemerocallis 'Prairie Blue Eyes'
PERENNIAL

The majority of daylilies have yellow or orange blooms, but this one has deep lavender-blue flowers, produced from early to midsummer. Semi-evergreen, it forms a clump of narrow mid-green leaves, which add structure and form to a sheltered border throughout the year. It can also be used in a large container or in gravel beds, and prefers a sunny site and fertile, moist, well-drained soil.

☼ ◊ ◊ ❄ ❄ ❄

‡ to 70cm (28in) ↔ to 75cm (30in)

Hydrangea villosa
DECIDUOUS SHRUB

This delightful spreading plant is much loved by garden designers for its lance-shaped, velvety, mid-green leaves, and large, flat flowerheads. In summer, masses of tiny, bluish-purple fertile flowers are borne, surrounded by larger, lilac-pink sterile blooms. It can be grown as a specimen plant, or in a mixed border. This hydrangea will thrive when grown in sun or partial shade, and moist, well-drained soil. Little pruning is needed apart from deadheading in spring.

☼ ◐ ◑ ◊ ❀ ❀ ❀
‡↔ to 3m (10ft)

Liatris spicata
PERENNIAL

Gayfeather is an attractive plant from the prairies of North America. It forms a tuft of narrow leaves, measuring up to 40cm (16in) in length, and in late summer and early autumn it produces tall spikes of feathery, pinkish-purple flowers that are attractive to bees. The flower buds at the top of the spike open before those further down. Plant it in full sun and very well-drained, reasonably fertile soil. It is not suitable for heavy clay soils, as the roots will rot if they get too wet.

☼ ◊ ❀ ❀ ❀
‡ to 60cm (24in) ↔ to 30cm (12in)

Limonium platyphyllum

PERENNIAL

Sea lavender forms a rosette of large, elliptic- or spoon-shaped, dark green leaves, and in late summer it produces dense, wiry, branched stems, covered with clusters of tiny, tubular, lavender-blue flowers. It grows well in coastal areas, but the frothy sprays of flowers are a valuable addition to any mixed or herbaceous border. Plant four or five plants together for maximum impact, and grow them in full sun and sandy, well-drained soil. The cultivar 'Violetta' has deep violet flowers.

☼ ◊ ❉ ❉ ❉

‡ to 60cm (24in) ↔ to 45cm (18in)

Lobelia erinus 'Cascade Blue'

PERENNIAL

This small, trailing lobelia flowers from summer to the middle of autumn. It is grown as an annual. It produces hundreds of tiny, two-lipped, dark blue flowers, although similar plants with white, pink, red, purple, and violet flowers are available. All lobelias make superb plants for hanging baskets and trailing over the edges of containers or window boxes. Plant them in full sun, or in partial shade, which they last longer in, and do not let them dry out.

☼ ◑ ◊ ❉

‡↔ to 15cm (6in)

Lobelia x *gerardii* 'Vedrariensis'

PERENNIAL

This tall, stately plant forms a rosette of elliptic- or lance-shaped deep green leaves. The flower spikes appear in late summer and bear small, violet-purple, tubular flowers. Position four or five plants together in a group to maximize their impact, and plant them in moist, fertile soil that does not dry out, in full sun or partial shade. This lobelia is perfect for a late-summer border, or for the margins of a water garden.

☼ ◊ ✿✿✿

‡ to 1m (3ft) ↔ to 30cm (12in)

Monarda 'Prärienacht'

PERENNIAL

A member of the mint family, this vigorous clump-forming beebalm selection has square stems and lance-shaped leaves. Its lilac-purple flowers bloom from midsummer into early autumn, attracting butterflies and other pollinators. It is drought tolerant once established and is a good choice for a mixed border. Powdery mildew can develop in humid regions. Grow in moderately fertile, well drained soil in full sun.

☼ ◊ ✿✿✿

‡ to 1.2m (4ft) ↔ to 60cm (24in)

Passiflora 'Amethyst' ♀

CLIMBER

This fast-growing passion flower bears
distinctive purple-blue flowers in late
summer, followed by large, oval, orange
fruits. It is not hardy, and in cold
areas, it is best to grow this climber in
a warm greenhouse or a conservatory
where it will form a leafy canopy when
trained on wires or support. Plant
it in a container filled with loam-based
compost, and water well in summer.
Prune back the vigorous growth in
spring to keep within bounds.

☼ ◊ ◐ ❄
↕ to 4m (12ft)

Passiflora caerulea ♀

CLIMBER

The blue passion flower has woody
stems and dark green divided foliage.
The exotic-looking flowers have white
petals, which are sometimes tinged with
pink, and a ring of purple-blue banded
strands that radiate out from the centre.
In hot summers the blooms may be
followed by round, yellow fruit. Plant
it in a sunny, sheltered site in moist,
well-drained soil. It is not fully hardy
and may be killed by hard frosts, but
young shoots often appear from the base
if the root area is mulched over winter.

☼ ◊ ◐ ❄ ❄
↕ to 10m (30ft)

Penstemon '**Stapleford Gem**' ♀
PERENNIAL

The bell-shaped flowers of this lilac-purple penstemon are suffused with shades of mauve, pink, and purple, giving a multi-coloured effect. It blooms from midsummer to early autumn, and needs full sun and a well-drained soil. Penstemons are wonderful plants for a herbaceous border, and this one works well as part of a pastel colour scheme. 'Stapleford Gem' is one of the hardiest penstemons, but will need a sheltered spot and winter mulch in cold areas.

☼ ◑ ◊ ❀❀

‡ to 60cm (24in) ↔ to 45cm (18in)

Stachys officinalis
PERENNIAL

Wood betony is an attractive perennial which produces ground-covering rosettes of deeply veined leaves with scalloped edges. From early summer to early autumn it is adorned with spikes of tubular, reddish-purple flowers. Its long flowering season makes it an ideal candidate for the front of a herbaceous border, or use it in a wild garden. Easy to grow, this betony prefers a sunny or lightly shaded position in well-drained, slightly fertile soil. Divide in autumn or spring.

☼ ◑ ◊ ❀❀❀

‡ to 60cm (24in) ↔ to 45cm (18in)

Thalictrum delavayi 'Hewitt's Double' ♥

PERENNIAL

This upright, clump-forming perennial produces upright sprays of long-lasting, pompom-like, rich mauve flowers from midsummer to early autumn. Its finely divided, mid-green leaves are carried on slender, purple-tinted stems. 'Hewitt's Double' makes an excellent foil in a herbaceous border to plants with bolder leaves and flowers. Divide large clumps and replant every few years to maintain vigour.

☼ ☀ ◊ ◕ ❋ ❋ ❋

‡ to 1.5m (5ft) ↔ to 60cm (24in)

Tradescantia 'Purple Dome'

PERENNIAL

This clump-forming, hardy plant belongs to the Andersoniana group of tradescantias, and has branching stems and narrow, strappy leaves. In summer to early autumn, it produces clusters of small, deep purple flowers with three triangular petals and fluffy purple stamens. Plant it *en masse* in a mixed or herbaceous border, in full sun or partial shade, and a moist, fertile soil. Divide large clumps in autumn or spring.

☼ ☀ ◕ ❋ ❋ ❋

‡ to 60cm (24in) ↔ to 45cm (18in)

Tulbaghia violacea

PERENNIAL BULB

This South African plant forms clumps of narrow, greyish-green leaves, and from midsummer to early autumn it produces stout stems that bear clusters of fragrant, star-shaped, lilac-blue flowers. In mild areas it can be grown outside in a sunny position in slightly fertile, well-drained soil. In cold countries where temperatures dip well below freezing for long periods, pot it up in a container filled with loam-based compost, and overwinter it in a cool greenhouse or conservatory.

☼ ◊ ❀ ❀ *f*

‡ to 60cm (24in) ↔ to 30cm (12in)

Verbena bonariensis ♀

PERENNIAL

The tall, airy, branched stems of this verbena hold aloft small, domed clusters of tiny, lilac-purple, scented flowers, which appear from midsummer to early autumn. Individual plants come into their own when planted in a group, and can be positioned at the front, as well as the back, of the border or in a gravel garden. They need full sun and fertile, well-drained soil, and a sheltered position. In cold gardens, mulch with bracken or garden compost for winter protection.

☼ ◊ ❀ ❀ *f*

‡ to 1.5m (5ft) ↔ to 60cm (24in)

Aconitum '**Bressingham Spire**' ♀

PERENNIAL

Monkshood is a tall, striking plant that thrives in woodland gardens and in herbaceous borders. It has glossy, dark green, deeply-lobed leaves, and in late summer and early autumn produces large spikes of deep violet-blue flowers. It can be grown in full sun, but will perform better in partial shade and moist soil. To maintain its vigour, dig it up and divide it after 3–4 years. All parts of this plant are very toxic.

☼ ☀ ◊ ❄ ❄ ❄
‡ to 1m (3ft) ↔ to 50cm (20in)

Agapanthus '**Blue Giant**'

PERENNIAL

The African blue lily is impossible to overlook in the late summer garden. It forms a clump of arching, deep green, strap-shaped leaves, and large spherical flowerheads, held on tall, stiff stems. 'Blue Giant' is exceptionally large, with huge balls of deep blue, bell-shaped flowers. It should be grown in a sunny, sheltered position, in fertile, moist, well-drained soil. It is borderline hardy, so in cold areas, protect it with a thick layer of mulch in winter.

☼ ◊ ◊ ❄ ❄ ❄
‡ to 1.2m (4ft) ↔ to 60cm (24in)

Aster amellus 'King George' ♀

PERENNIAL

This species prefers drier conditions than the popular New England and New York asters, and thrives in alkaline soil. It has small, mid-green leaves, and from late summer to late autumn produces loose clusters of light violet-blue, daisy-like flowers. Plant it in groups in a sunny herbaceous or mixed border, in reasonably fertile, well-drained soil. Divide clumps every three to four years in spring to rejuvenate and to keep plants growing vigorously.

☼ ◊ ❄❄❄

↕↔ to 50cm (20in)

Campanula cochleariifolia ♀

PERENNIAL

Known as fairies' thimbles, this dwarf campanula forms rosettes of toothed, bright green leaves, and in summer produces masses of slightly pendent, pale blue or white flowers. It will add colour and interest to a rock garden, or the gaps in paving or a dry-stone wall, flourishing in the well-drained soil both these sites afford. It can be grown in full sun or partial shade, and although it may become rather invasive, it is easy to control by pulling up surplus growth.

☼ ◐ ◊ ❄❄❄

↕ to 8cm (3in) ↔ indefinite

Caryopteris x *clandonensis* 'Heavenly Blue'
DECIDUOUS SHRUB

This free-flowering plant with aromatic, greyish-green foliage forms clusters of deep blue flowers in late summer. It provides colour and form in a mixed border or gravel garden, and needs full sun and a sheltered site in well-drained soil. In cold gardens, plant by a sunny wall to give some extra protection during winter. Prune it back hard in spring, taking care not to cut into old wood, from which it may not regrow.

☼ ◊ ❀ ❀ *f*
‡↔ to 1m (3ft)

Catananche caerulea 'Major' ♀
PERENNIAL

Cupid's dart is a short-lived perennial, which is often grown as biennial. It looks rather like a cornflower, with oblong, lilac-blue petals with serrated tips and a dark blue centre. Plant it in a sunny position in well-drained soil at the front or in the middle of a flower or herbaceous border. It does not grow very well in heavy soils, and may die at the end of the year.

☼ ◊ ❀ ❀ ❀
‡ to 60cm (24in) ↔ to 30cm (12in)

Ceratostigma plumbaginoides ♀

PERENNIAL

This rhizomatous, spreading plumbago features upright, wiry red stems and bright green leaves that develop a reddish hue in autumn. From late summer until the first frosts, clusters of blue flowers appear above the foliage. It is good for ground cover, edging, or for a rock garden, but it may spread aggressively in ideal conditions. Grow in moderately fertile, well drained soil in full sun to part shade.

☼ ☀ ◊ ❀ ❀ ❀

‡ to 45cm (18in) ↔ to 20cm (8in)

Clematis 'Perle d'Azur'

CLIMBER

This late-flowering clematis has very pretty sky blue, open bell-shaped flowers approximately 10cm (4in) in diameter. They are carried in profusion on vigorous growth, which benefits from the support of a large bush, such as a shrub rose. This growth should be cut back to ground level each year in late winter, to a pair of healthy-looking buds. Specimens often take a year or two to become established. During this time, give the young stems some support and protect them from slugs and snails.

☼ ☀ ◊ ◊ ❀ ❀ ❀

‡ to 3m (10ft) ↔ to 1m (3ft)

Echinops ritro 'Veitch's Blue'

PERENNIAL

Grown partly for its architectural, spiny, greyish-green leaves, in summer this vigorous plant also produces spherical dark blue flowerheads on woolly grey stems. The lollipop-shaped flowerheads contrast well with flat-headed blooms, such as those of achillea, in a gravel garden or a herbaceous border. The flowers are frequently used, fresh or dried, in floral arrangements. Plant it in groups of four or five in poor, well-drained soil, in full sunshine.

☼ ◑ ◊ ✽✽✽
‡ to 1.2m (4ft) ↔ to 75cm (30in)

Eryngium x *oliverianum* ♀

PERENNIAL

This striking sea holly forms a clump of heart-shaped, mid-green, spiny leaves with distinctive silver veining. In the summer and early autumn, branched stems produce lavender-blue, thistle-like flowers, surrounded by spiny, linear, leaf-like bracts. The whole plant is suffused with a steel-blue colouration. Plant in a sunny position in well-drained soil, and use in a gravel garden or herbaceous border. The flower stems make excellent cut flowers, too, or can be left to stand in winter.

☼ ◊ ✽✽✽
‡ to 90cm (36in) ↔ to 45cm (18in)

Felicia amelloides 'Santa Anita' ♀

EVERGREEN SHRUB

The tender blue daisy is often grown as an annual in cooler climates. It is bushy and compact, with oval, deep green leaves. From the middle of summer to autumn, it bears bright blue, daisy-like flowers with yellow centres. It can be grown in containers or is mostly used as bedding, although it may survive in mild, sheltered areas in the garden. Plant it in full sun in any well-drained soil. Pinch out the shoot tips in the spring to promote side shoots.

☼ ◊ ❀

↕↔ to 60cm (24in)

Geranium ROZANNE ('Gerwat') ♀

PERENNIAL

The summer-long display of this geranium makes it one of the best. From clumps of prettily divided foliage emerge the most perfect saucer-shaped, vibrant violet-blue flowers. As it keeps on flowering from early summer right until the first frosts in autumn, this has to be one of the best value for money plants on the market. The foliage dies back in winter, and it suits most well-drained soils.

☼ ◊ ◐ ❀❀❀

↕↔ to 50cm (20in)

Hibiscus syriacus '**Oiseau Bleu**' ♀

DECIDUOUS SHRUB

This hardy hibiscus makes an exotic-looking addition to a shrub or mixed border. It has upright branches and toothed, lobed, mid-green leaves that appear late in the spring. In late summer it produces large, deep blue, trumpet-shaped flowers. Plant it in full sun and moist, well-drained, fertile soil. It will survive most winters, but in very cold areas plant it against a warm wall, and cover the root area with a thick mulch during the winter.

☼ ◊ ◊ ◊ ❀ ❀ ❀
‡ to 3m (10ft) ↔ to 2m (6ft)

Hydrangea macrophylla '**Blue Wave**'

DECIDUOUS SHRUB

This lacecap hydrangea makes a rounded shrub with large green leaves, and flat flowerheads that appear from mid- to late summer. The blooms are made up of small, dark blue fertile flowers, surrounded by large pale blue sterile flowers. In acid soil the flowers turn a rich shade of gentian-blue but in alkaline soil they are mauve-pink. Plant it in full sun or partial shade in moist, well-drained, fertile soil, rich in organic matter. Suitable for coastal gardens.

☼ ☼ ◊ ◊ ❀ ❀ ❀
‡ to 2m (6ft) ↔ to 2.5m (8ft)

Hydrangea serrata 'Bluebird' ♀

DECIDUOUS SHRUB

This compact hydrangea has bright green leaves. From late summer to early autumn it bears large flat flowerheads of tiny, deep blue fertile flowers, surrounded by larger, pale blue, infertile flowers, which may become pink in alkaline soil. Ideal for a shrub or mixed border in a small garden, it grows well in full sun or partial shade and moist, but well-drained, fertile soil, preferably neutral, or slightly acid for the best flower colour.

☼ ◐ ◊ ◊ ❋ ❋

‡↔ to 1.2m (4ft)

Hyssopus officinalis

SEMI-EVERGREEN SHRUB

Hyssop is a pretty garden plant, which can also be used for medicinal and culinary purposes. It has small, aromatic leaves, and the flowers vary in colour from blue to violet, pink and white. It blooms from early or midsummer to early autumn, and will add colour and form to a herb bed or the front of a border. It can also be grown in a large container or a gravel garden. Plant it in a sunny situation in well-drained soil.

☼ ◊ ❋ ❋ ❋ *f*

‡ to 60cm (24in) ↔ to 1m (3ft)

Ipomoea tricolor 'Heavenly Blue' ♀

CLIMBER

Morning glory, grown as an annual, has fast-growing twining stems and heart-shaped, light green leaves. In late summer it produces large sky-blue, funnel-shaped flowers with white throats. Plant this eye-catching climber outside in late spring or early summer, in full sun and well-drained soil. Provide support in the form of a tripod. Use ipomeas to clothe an arch or a trellis or grow in a large container.

☼ ◊ ❀ ❀
↕ to 3m (10ft)

Lathyrus nervosus

CLIMBER

Lord Anson's blue pea, a perennial, is often grown as an annual. In late summer it bears fragrant, indigo-blue flowers. Each leaf is split into a pair of greyish-green leaflets. It will quickly ascend a support when grown in full sun and a well-drained, fertile soil. This pea is not fully hardy and will be killed by winter wet and hard frosts unless protected with a cloche and a deep dry mulch. Grow it from seed in early spring and plant it out in late spring or early in the summer.

☼ ◊ ❀ ❀ *f*
↕ to 5m (15ft)

Lathyrus odoratus 'Noel Sutton' ♀

ANNUAL

'Noel Sutton' is a vigorous sweet pea, which can be grown up supporting canes or a trellis. If shoot tips are pinched out while the plant is young, it will form a much smaller bush suitable for a container. In summer the stems are covered with sweetly perfumed, mauve-blue flowers, which should be picked regularly for the home to promote new blooms. Plant it in sun or light shade in moist, well-drained soil, rich in organic matter.

☼ ☀ ◊ ◐ ❀❀❀ *f*

‡ to 2.5m (8ft)

Lobelia siphilitica

PERENNIAL

The blue cardinal flower forms a rosette of egg-shaped, light green leaves. In summer it produces tall stems that bear tubular, bright blue blooms with double lips. It needs permanently moist, fertile soil, and is happy in full sun or partial shade. It adds grace and elegance to a damp border, or an area beneath deciduous trees, or plant it beside a pool. To propagate this lobelia, divide it in spring.

☼ ☀ ◐ ❀❀❀

‡ to 1m (3ft) ↔ to 23cm (9in)

Nemesia strumosa 'Blue Gem'

ANNUAL

This vigorous, compact, bushy annual has spoon- or lance-shaped, toothed, and slightly hairy leaves. In late summer it bears vast numbers of small, bright blue flowers, and makes a colourful bedding or container plant. It needs a site in full sun and moist, well-drained soil. It must be watered regularly during the summer if it is to produce a good display of flowers. Nemesias come in other colours including red, yellow, and pink.

☼ ◊ ◊ ❄

↕ to 30cm (12in) ↔ to 15cm (6in)

Nepeta sibirica

PERENNIAL

This relative of catmint is a vigorous plant, with branched, upright stems and dark green, lance-shaped, toothed, aromatic foliage. In late summer lavender-blue flowers appear on tall spikes, and make a bold statement in a gravel garden or a herbaceous bed. As its name suggests, this plant comes from Siberia and is very hardy. It should be planted and divided in spring in a sunny position, in well-drained soil.

☼ ◊ ❄❄❄ *f*

↕ to 90cm (36in) ↔ to 45cm (18in)

Perovskia 'Blue Spire' ♀

DECIDUOUS SHRUB

This is an attractive, late flowering shrub with tall stems and silver, deeply dissected, aromatic foliage. In the late summer it produces branched spikes of small lavender-blue flowers. It prefers a sunny position and should be planted in very well-drained soil in a gravel bed or a herbaceous border, or use it in a low hedge to edge a path. To keep it bushy, cut back stems in spring. It will tolerate chalk soil and coastal conditions.

☼ ◊ ❀❀❀ *f*

‡ to 1.2m (4ft) ↔ to 1m (3ft)

Platycodon grandiflorus ♀

PERENNIAL

The balloon flower is often mistaken for a campanula, to which it is related. The leaves appear late in the spring, but eventually grow to form a clump of toothed, blue-green foliage. In late summer, bell-shaped, purplish-blue flowers open from balloon-shaped buds. Ideal for a rock garden or the front of a border, it does not like to be disturbed and should not be divided. Plant it in full sun or partial shade in moist, well-drained soil.

☼ ☀ ◊ ◊ ❀❀❀

‡ to 60cm (24in) ↔ to 45cm (18in)

Salvia patens 'Cambridge Blue' ♀

PERENNIAL

From summer to autumn this form of sage produces delicate pale blue flowers. Beneath the flower stems, it forms a clump of oval, mid-green leaves. Plant it in a sunny, sheltered border, or by a wall, in well-drained soil. Not fully hardy, this salvia is unlikely to survive a hard frost and is better treated as an annual in cold areas. Sow seed under glass in spring, or overwinter mature plants in a frost-free greenhouse.

☼ ◊ ❀ ❀

‡ to 60cm (24in) ↔ to 45cm (18in)

Salvia uliginosa ♀

PERENNIAL

The bog sage prefers damp conditions. It forms a clump of lance-shaped mid-green leaves, above which tall flower spikes bear clusters of pale blue flowers. A good source of colour for the back of a damp late summer border, it should be planted in full sun and moist soil. The bog sage is not totally hardy, but it can survive winters in mild areas if protected with a thick layer of mulch or grown in a pot and moved under glass.

☼ ◊ ❀ ❀

‡ to 2m (6ft) ↔ to 90cm (36in)

Scabiosa caucasica 'Clive Greaves' ♀

PERENNIAL

A beautiful scabiosa, 'Clive Greaves' has grey-green basal leaves, and violet-blue flowers with cream-coloured centres, which attract bees and butterflies. It is perfect for a wild-flower garden or a herbaceous border, and needs a sunny position and well-drained, reasonably fertile, neutral to alkaline soil to thrive. Young plants flower most freely, so divide and replant them every spring to ensure a good display each summer. Deadhead the plants regularly, too.

☼ ◊ ❀ ❀ ❀

↔ to 60cm (24in)

Scaevola aemula 'Saphira'

EVERGREEN PERENNIAL

The fairy fan flower is a vigorous trailing plant ideal for the edge of a container or basket. It bears a profusion of pretty blue flowers, but purplish and mauve varieties are also available. In frost-free areas, scaevolas grow as short-lived evergreen perennials, but in cold climates they are treated as bedding annuals, fed fortnightly to maintain a prolific flowering display. Grow in moist but well-drained, fertile soil in a well-lit position.

☼ ◊ ◊ ❀

↔ to 50cm (20in)

Stokesia laevis
EVERGREEN PERENNIAL

Stokes' aster is an evergreen, clump-forming plant, with long, lance-shaped leaves with a distinctive pale green midrib. From midsummer to early autumn, it bears solitary cornflower-like blooms on stout stems. The outer petals are purplish-blue, pink or white – the pale varieties exhibit a darker centre, while the dark forms have pale centres. 'Blue Star' has deep blue petals and a pale blue eye. Plant Stokes' asters in a sunny border in well-drained soil.

☼ ◊ ❀ ❀ ❀
↕↔ to 45cm (18in)

Symphyandra wanneri
PERENNIAL

As the pretty, hanging clusters of deep violet-blue flowers suggest, the ring bellflower is a close relative of the true bellflowers (*Campanula*). These flowers are carried in profusion over a long period in summer amid the toothed, mid-green leaves. The plants may not flower in their first year, and will usually die once the display is over and the seed has set. Collect the seed for sowing again, or allow to self seed. This plant is good for a rock garden.

☼ ◐ ◊ ❀ ❀ ❀
↕↔ to 30cm (12in)

Tradescantia 'J.C. Weguelin' ♀

PERENNIAL

This clump-forming, hardy plant has narrow, lance-shaped, mid-green leaves, held on branching stems. The blooms appear in late summer, and are composed of pale blue petals that surround fluffy stamens. It can be used at the front of a mixed or herbaceous border, and should be planted in full sun or partial shade in moist, well-drained, fertile soil. It can be divided in the spring or autumn.

↕ to 60cm (24in) ↔ to 45cm (18in)

Veronica longifolia

PERENNIAL

The long-leaf veronica is a tall perennial that makes upright spikes of bright blue flowers in late summer. It is ideal for a mixed or herbaceous border, planted in groups of three or five. The pointed, mid-green leaves are carried in twos or threes along the stems. Cut the plant back in late winter to prepare for the new growth in spring.

☼ ◑ ◊ ◕ ❀ ❀ ❀

↕ to 1.2m (4ft) ↔ to 30cm (12in)

Agave americana 'Variegata' ♀

PERENNIAL

This plant, ideal for a patio or tropical-style garden, forms a basal rosette of fleshy, lance-shaped, cream-edged leaves, with spiny margins and pointed tips. The leaves grow upright, then arch over and finally lie flat on the ground. Plant in a large container of loam-based compost. Place it outside in summer, and move it indoors in winter. It may survive outside in mild, very well-drained, sheltered conditions provided it is protected when young.

☼ ◊ ❀

↕↔ to 1.5m (5ft)

Deschampsia cespitosa 'Goldtau'

PERENNIAL GRASS

Tussock grass is a robust, evergreen plant with rigid, rough-edged green leaves. In late summer 'Goldtau' bears arching stems of yellow-green that turn golden-brown as they age. This form is much more compact than other tussock grasses, and is perfect for a herbaceous or wildflower garden. It is happy in full sun or partial shade, and a moist or well-drained soil. Leave the dried flowerheads to decorate a winter garden, but remove them in spring.

☼ ☼ ◊ ◊ ❀ ❀ ❀

↕ to 70cm (28in) ↔ to 50cm (20in)

Ensete ventricosum ♀
PERENNIAL

The Ethiopian banana is a tender plant, and bears huge, paddle-shaped leaves. Grow it in a large pot of loam-based compost. It will inject an exotic look when moved outside and plunged in a late summer border or tropical-style garden, placed in full sun or light shade. It also needs to be fed and watered regularly when in growth. At the end of the summer it must be moved indoors and overwintered in a heated greenhouse or conservatory with a minimum temperature of 7°C (45°F).

‡ to 6m (20ft) ↔ to 3m (10ft)

Melianthus major ♀
EVERGREEN SHRUB

The honey bush is usually treated as a herbaceous perennial. Grown for its foliage, it has beautiful, bluish-green, feather-like leaves, which are divided into several sharply-toothed leaflets. The brown flowers are rather uninspiring. Plant it in a sunny position, sheltered from cold winds, in moist, well-drained, fertile soil. Frost destroys the upper growth, but if it is protected during the winter with a thick mulch it should resprout again in spring.

‡↔ to 3m (10ft)

Moluccella laevis

ANNUAL

Bells of Ireland bears deeply-veined, rounded, pale green leaves, and in summer and autumn it produces stems of tiny white flowers, surrounded by large, pale green cups. Its architectural flower spikes make a dramatic statement in a herbaceous border, and are very useful in flower arrangements, fresh or dried. Plant it in full sunshine, in fertile, moist, well-drained soil. It is easy to grow from a spring sowing of the seed.

☼ ◊ ◖ ❀ *f*

‡ to 60cm (24in) ↔ to 20cm (8in)

Nicotiana langsdorffii ♀

ANNUAL

This tobacco plant forms a rosette of large egg-shaped leaves at the base, and in summer produces apple-green flowers that dangle like slender bells from the tall, branched, sticky stems. It adds interest to the middle of a herbaceous border and is ideal for disguising the space left by spring bulbs. Plant it in a sunny or lightly shaded position in fertile, moist, well-drained soil, and stake if necessary.

☼ ☀ ◊ ◖ ❀

‡ to 1.5m (5ft) ↔ to 30cm (12in)

Pennisetum macrourum

PERENNIAL GRASS

Well-drained soil is vital for this pretty grass, with its foxtail-like, fluffy plumes of seedheads that appear in late summer and last well into autumn. They fade from green to pale brown as they age, with a straw-like quality that gives a long season of interest. Cut back plants in late winter to allow for the new growth. Grow in a sunny, mixed border in a sheltered position. The flowerheads are also good for cutting.

☼ ◊ ❋❋

‡ to 1.8m (6ft) ↔ to 1.2m (4ft)

Zinnia elegans 'Envy'

ANNUAL

Most zinnias stand out because of their brightly coloured flowers, but 'Envy' is more subtle, with semi-double, yellow-green blooms. It makes a good bedding or container plant, and will perform well when grown in a sunny or lightly shaded position and fertile, moist, well-drained soil. The seed should be sown indoors in early spring, or *in situ* outside in late spring. Useful in flower arrangements because of its unusual colour.

☼ ☀ ◊ ❋

‡ to 60cm (24in) ↔ to 30cm (12in)

Achillea filipendulina 'Cloth of Gold' ♥

PERENNIAL

Although this plant grows nearly double the height of 'Coronation Gold' (*see p.256*), it is actually less vigorous. It has attractive, feathery, light green leaves and bears large, golden-yellow flowerheads, up to 12cm (5in) across, from early summer right through until early autumn. It is ideal for growing in a herbaceous border and will thrive in any well-drained soil. By late spring, the tall stems will need supporting with canes. Good for cutting fresh or for drying.

☼ ◊ ◖ ❋ ❋ ❋
↕↔ to 1.5m (5ft)

Catalpa bignonioides 'Aurea' ♥

DECIDUOUS TREE

The golden form of the Indian bean tree has spreading branches, and large, heart-shaped leaves. The foliage is bronze in spring, but turns golden-yellow by the time the flowers appear in midsummer. The candle-shaped spikes of fragrant, white flowers with yellow and purple marks are followed by dangling pods that last through winter and give this tree its name. Plant it in full sun, away from strong winds, in deep, fertile, moist, well-drained soil.

☼ ◊ ◖ ❋ ❋ ❋ *f*
↕↔ to 10m (30ft)

Celosia argentea 'Century Yellow'

ANNUAL

From summer to frost, this vigorous cockscomb cultivar produces large, golden yellow, feathery plumes that attract bees and butterflies. The flowers make excellent cut or dried flowers. It will self-sow readily. It works well as a container plant or in a mixed annual bed. Grow in full sun in moist, well-drained soil.

☼ ◐ ◑ ❀

↕ to 90cm (36in) ↔ to 60cm (24in)

Chrysanthemum 'Mary Stoker'

PERENNIAL

In late summer and early autumn this hardy chrysanthemum bears single, apricot-yellow, daisy-like flowers, with green centres that turn yellow as they mature. The flowers are set off by the lobed, deep green leaves that have a slight silvery sheen. Plant it in a sunny, sheltered herbaceous or mixed border, in well-drained soil. It will benefit from a protective, thick mulch in the winter.

☼ ◐ ❀ ❀ ❀

↕ to 1.2m (4ft) ↔ to 75cm (30in)

Crocosmia 'Solfatare' ♀

PERENNIAL CORM

The bronzy-green leaves and clusters of apricot-yellow flowers that appear on slender, arching stems make this a very desirable plant for a border or gravel garden. It will grow well in full sun or partial shade, and prefers moist, well-drained soil. The individual plants are quite small and are best planted in groups of three or five. It is not fully hardy and needs a sheltered site and thick mulch to survive a harsh winter.

☼ ☀ ◊ ◗ ❀❀
↕ to 70cm (28in) ↔ to 8cm (3in)

Cytisus battandieri ♀

DECIDUOUS SHRUB

In summer, the pineapple broom produces tight clusters of fruit-scented, bright yellow, lupin-like flowers. Its silvery-green leaves are carried on arching, spreading branches, giving the bush an open shape. Although not fully hardy, it should overwinter successfully if it is planted in a sunny, sheltered spot by a wall, in well-drained, sandy, moderately fertile soil. Other than to remove shoots that spoil the symmetry of the bush – do this in early spring – it does not really need pruning.

☼ ◊ ❀❀❀ *f*
↕↔ to 5m (15ft)

Dahlia 'Yellow Hammer' ♛

PERENNIAL

This tender perennial is usually grown as an annual bedding plant, and has bronze-green leaves and clear yellow flowers. For a dazzling bedding display, plant it with other dwarf dahlias, such as the scarlet-flowered 'Preston Park', or use it in a herbaceous border, or in containers. Providing it is deadheaded regularly, 'Yellow Hammer' will flower continuously up to the first frosts. Plant it in full sun in fertile, well-drained soil, or loam-based compost.

‡ to 60cm (24in) ↔ to 45cm (18in)

Euphorbia sikkimensis ♛

PERENNIAL

This spreading perennial is recommended for its heads of yellow flowers that appear from midsummer, but the spring growth, which is bright pink, is just as attractive. These upright shoots are clothed in narrow leaves, which become paler with red veins and margins as they age. The flowers are followed by blue-green pods, which are also attractive. Ideal for a shady border. When handling this plant, wear gloves as the milky sap can irritate the skin.

☀ ◊ ❄ ❄ ❄
‡ to 1.2m (4ft) ↔ to 45cm (18in)

Genista aetnensis ♀
DECIDUOUS TREE

The Mount Etna broom forms a large shrub or medium-sized tree with green, arching, almost leafless branches. In summer it explodes into colour, producing masses of fragrant, yellow, pea-like flowers. It makes a spectacular specimen tree for a sunny situation, with a canopy that is light enough to allow underplanting. Pruning is unnecessary, except to remove damaged stems. Plant in well-drained, light, poor to moderately fertile soil.

☼ ◊ ❀❀ *f*
‡↔ to 8m (25ft)

Helenium 'Butterpat' ♀
PERENNIAL

Unlike many heleniums, which tend to have muddy-coloured flowers, those of 'Butterpat' are a clear, bright yellow. Very free flowering, it is a good clump-forming plant for a herbaceous border. The blooms, which are usually crowded with bees, are held on tall stems and make excellent cut flowers. Remove the deadheads to encourage more blooms. Grow it in sun, in moist, well-drained, fertile soil, and divide it in early spring every 2–3 years to maintain its vigour.

☼ ◊ ◊ ❀❀❀
‡ to 90cm (36in) ↔ to 60cm (24in)

Helianthus annuus

ANNUAL

A fast-growing, unfussy flower that is a favourite with children. The growth spurt of some of the giant sunflowers is spectacular – in one season they can reach 3m (10ft). The large daisy-like flowers have long yellow petals and a dark purply-brown centre. If left to dry, the seedhead will provide valuable food for the bird table over winter. Sunflowers need a sunny position, in well-drained, fertile soil. Grow them from seed each year. Tall-growing plants will need staking and a sheltered site.

☼ ◊ ❀❀❀
‡ to 3m (10ft) ↔ to 45cm (18in)

Helianthus 'Lemon Queen'

PERENNIAL

In late summer 'Lemon Queen' bears large quantities of acid yellow, daisy-like flowers with darker centres. This is a vigorous, herbaceous perennial with erect stems and slightly hairy, lance-shaped, dark green leaves. Plant it in a sunny position in fertile, moist, but well-drained, neutral or alkaline soil. A good plant for cutting, it also combines well with other plants in a herbaceous border. To maintain its vigour, divide plants in early spring every 2–4 years.

☼ ◊ ◊ ❀❀❀
‡ to 1.5m (5ft) ↔ to 60cm (24in)

Helichrysum 'Schwefellicht'

PERENNIAL

Clusters of small, fluffy, sulphur-yellow flowers that turn orange-yellow as summer progresses, make this an interesting plant for a well-drained rock, gravel, or scree garden. Its spreading stems, which are covered with white hairs and narrow, silvery white leaves, form an attractive, weed-suppressing mound. Plant it in a sunny situation, in reasonably fertile, well-drained, neutral to acid soil.

☼ ◊ ❀ ❀ ❀

‡ to 60cm (24in) ↔ to 30cm (12in)

Heliopsis helianthoides 'Sommersonne'

PERENNIAL

A superb plant for the herbaceous border, the ox eye is a clump-forming perennial with erect, branched stems and egg- or lance-shaped, mid-green leaves. In late summer it produces semi-double flowerheads, which look rather like small sunflowers, with deep-golden petals and a brownish centre. Grow it in full sun, in fertile, moist, but well-drained soil. Established clumps need dividing in early spring every 2–3 years to maintain vigour.

☼ ◊ ◊ ❀ ❀ ❀

‡ to 90cm (36in) ↔ to 60cm (24in)

Hemerocallis 'Corky' ♀
PERENNIAL

One of the more compact daylilies, 'Corky' is suitable for planting in a small garden or in containers. Clusters of reddish-brown buds appear on long, erect stems among the evergreen, mid-green leaves. These buds open one or two at a time to reveal bright yellow flowers. Although each flower lasts only for one day, they are quickly replaced. Plant it in full sun, in fertile, moist, but well-drained soil. Propagate daylilies by dividing large clumps in the spring.

‡ to 70cm (28in) ↔ to 40cm (16in)

Hypericum calycinum
EVERGREEN SHRUB

Through summer to mid-autumn, the rose of Sharon produces yellow, cup-shaped flowers with showy stamens. It is a low-growing shrub that quickly spreads by means of trailing stems. It is unfussy, and not surprisingly, it makes excellent ground cover for a bank or area where little else will grow. It can become invasive; to keep it neat and bushy, cut it back to the ground in spring. Plant in full sun, or partial shade, any well-drained soil. It is easily propagated by division in spring.

‡ to 60cm (24in) ↔ indefinite

Hypericum 'Hidcote' ♀
EVERGREEN SHRUB

The arching, spreading branches of 'Hidcote' are covered with handsome, lance-shaped, dark green leaves. Through summer to early autumn clusters of bright golden-yellow flowers, up to 6cm (2½in) across, are produced in profusion. Plant in a reasonably fertile, moist, but well-drained soil, in full sun. This is a good choice for a shrub or mixed border.

☼ ◊ ◖ ❀ ❀ ❀
‡ to 1.2m (4ft) ↔ to 1.5m (5ft)

Inula hookeri
PERENNIAL

A superb plant for a shady border, this perennial from the Himalayas will soon form large clumps where conditions suit. It has slender, erect, softly hairy stems, and lance-shaped, mid-green leaves. From late summer to autumn, it produces clusters of pale yellow flowers with a darker, brownish-yellow centre. Plant it in partial shade, in fertile, moist, but well-drained, soil. To propagate, divide established clumps in spring or autumn.

☼ ◊ ◖ ❀ ❀ ❀
‡ to 75cm (30in) ↔ to 45cm (18in)

Kniphofia 'Royal Standard' ♀

PERENNIAL

Although 'Royal Standard' has been around for a long time, it is still one of the best red hot pokers for the herbaceous border. Green, strappy leaves form a large clump from which rise tall, robust, flower spikes. These are studded with scarlet-red buds that open to bright yellow, tubular flowers. Kniphofias are a favourite of bees. Plant them in fertile, moist but well-drained soil in sun.

☼ ◊ ◊ ❄ ❄

‡ to 1.2m (4ft) ↔ to 60cm (24in)

Kniphofia 'Wrexham Buttercup'

PERENNIAL

A yellow red hot poker, 'Wrexham Buttercup' bears tapering spikes of tubular flowers, lightly tipped with orange. It is similar to, but rather larger than, 'Buttercup' (*see p.273*). Grow in full sun or light shade, in fertile, moist, but well-drained, soil. Red hot pokers are classic herbaceous border plants and a favourite of bees. Leave remains of old foliage in place over winter for protection and remove in spring, when large clumps can also be divided.

☼ ◐ ◊ ◊ ❄ ❄ ❄

‡ to 1.2m (4ft) ↔ to 60cm (24in)

Koelreuteria paniculata ♀
DECIDUOUS TREE

The golden-rain tree deserves a rest over winter because for the other three seasons it puts on an amazing show. In late summer, this wonderful specimen tree produces spikes of small yellow flowers followed, in autumn, by pink or red seed capsules. Early spring foliage is a bright pinkish-red, turning through mid-green to a rich, buttery yellow in late summer and early autumn. Plant it in full sun, in fertile, well-drained soil. No pruning is needed.

☼ ◊ ✿✿
‡↔ to 10m (30ft)

Ligularia 'Gregynog Gold' ♀
PERENNIAL

In late summer, from a base of large, heart-shaped leaves, 'Gregynog Gold' throws up pyramids of daisy-like golden flowers on very tall, stiff stems. Each flower is delicately flecked with chocolate brown filaments. Choose a site where the soil is moderately fertile and permanently damp – around the margins of a natural pond would be ideal – in full sun or partial shade.

☼ ☀ ◊ ♦ ✿✿✿
‡ to 1.8m (6ft) ↔ to 1m (3ft)

Lilium Golden Splendor Group ♀

PERENNIAL BULB

In midsummer, stout stems bear long, plump buds that open to large, trumpet-shaped, rich yellow flowers. Like many lilies, the scent is exquisite and they are ideal for cutting, but take care not to get the bright orange pollen on your clothes. Lilies are wonderful plants to dot about in borders, ideally close to paths where they can be really appreciated. Remove lily beetle frass from the mid-green leaves on sight. Plant bulbs in autumn or spring.

☼ ◊ ✺✺✺ *f*

‡ to 2m (6ft) ↔ to 30cm (12in)

Linaria dalmatica

PERENNIAL

The bright yellow, spurred flowers of this toadflax bear more than a passing resemblance to those of the snapdragon (*Antirrhinum*). The slightly erect, lance-shaped, waxy, green leaves grow up to 18cm (7in) long. Plant it in full sun, in a light, preferably sandy, fertile, well-drained soil. Its upright stature will ensure it stands out in the middle of a busy herbaceous border; it would also do well in a gravel garden.

☼ ◊ ✺✺✺

‡ to 1m (3ft) ↔ to 60cm (24in)

Lysimachia nummularia '**Aurea**' ♀

PERENNIAL

The golden form of creeping Jenny is a vigorous evergreen that readily roots when its stems touch the soil. It can become rampant and may need to be controlled by weeding. The leaves are a bright yellow, lime green in shade, and during summer it has small, yellow, upright, cup-shaped flowers. Choose a spot in full sun or partial shade, in a moist, well-drained soil that won't dry out during summer. Propagate by division in spring or autumn.

☼ ☽ ◐ ◊ ❋ ❋ ❋

‡ to 5cm (2in) ↔ indefinite

Lysimachia punctata

PERENNIAL

This is an extremely vigorous perennial which quickly spreads by means of underground rhizomes. The upright stems have tiers of lance-shaped leaves and numerous bright yellow, cup-shaped flowers. It makes an attractive plant for a damp border; but take care, because it can become invasive. It grows best in partial shade, but will tolerate full sun. Plant it in fertile, moist, but well-drained soil.

☼ ☽ ◊ ◊ ❋ ❋ ❋

‡ to 75cm (30in) ↔ to 60cm (24in)

Nymphaea 'Marliacea Chromatella' ♀

PERENNIAL

'Marliacea Chromatella' is a beautiful waterlily, with canary yellow flowers that appear among the rounded, floating leaves in summer. The shade cast by its leaves is useful in reducing growth of pond algae and providing shelter for fish and other pond creatures. It is an aquatic perennial and should be grown in aquatic planting baskets where the water is reliably tranquil. The plants retreat underwater in winter. Divide plants in spring if necessary.

☼ ● ✿ ✿ ✿
↔ to 1.5m (5ft)

Oenothera biennis

BIENNIAL

The clear yellow, cup-shaped flowers of the evening primrose are a true delight, as their name would suggest, on late summer evenings when they seem to glow with the warmth of the day in the failing light. The plants are biennial, which means that they form a large rosette of foliage in their first year, then sending up a tall flowering stem in the second. After this, the plant dies, but from the seeds new plants will usually come up again on their own in successive years.

☼ ◊ ✿ ✿ ✿
↕ to 1.5m (5ft) ↔ to 60cm (24in)

Robinia pseudoacacia '*Frisia*' ♀

DECIDUOUS TREE

Dramatic leaf colour is what makes this fast-growing, spreading tree so special. In spring, the leaves are bright yellow, in early summer they take on a dash of lime, then, in late summer, they turn a rich orange-yellow. The tree has fragrant, white flowers in spring, and spiny branches. A wonderful specimen tree, with a canopy light enough for underplanting. Give it a spot in full sun, in fertile, moist, but well-drained, soil. No pruning is required.

☼ ◊ ◑ ❀❀❀ *f*

‡ to 15m (50ft) ↔ to 8m (25ft)

Rudbeckia fulgida '*Goldsturm*' ♀

PERENNIAL

The dark-centred flowers of the black-eyed Susan are produced in abundance from late summer to mid-autumn. The deep green leaves are lance-shaped. It will grow in any reasonably fertile, well-drained soil as long as it does not dry out in the summer; it also suits clay soil. A good mixer in a herbaceous or woodland border, it is also perfect for naturalistic plantings with ornamental grasses.

☼ ☀ ◊ ◑ ❀❀❀

‡ to 75cm (30in) ↔ to 30cm (12in)

Rudbeckia laciniata 'Herbstsonne' ♀
PERENNIAL

The cheerful coneflower is one of the
mainstays of the late-summer garden.
'Herbstsonne' has yellow, daisy-like
flowers with conical greeny-brown
centres that are carried aloft on tall,
upright stems. The rich, glossy green
leaves are deeply veined. It does best
in fertile, moist, but well-drained, soil,
including clay. This clump-forming
plant is perfect for the back of a
herbaceous border where it will act as a
foil for smaller plants. Good for cutting.

☼ ☀ ◊ ◖ ✽ ✽ ✽
‡ to 2.3m (7ft) ↔ to 75cm (30in)

Silphium perfoliatum ♀
PERENNIAL

From summer through to early autumn,
the upright, branching stems of the cup
plant are crowned with sunny-yellow,
daisy-like flowers. Its deeply toothed
leaves are attractive too, if a little
bristly to touch. This clump-forming
herbaceous perennial prefers a rather
heavy, neutral or alkaline soil, including
clay, that is moist but well-drained. It
would be at home in a partially shaded
wild or woodland garden.

☼ ☀ ◊ ◖ ✽ ✽ ✽
‡ to 2.5m (8ft) ↔ to 1m (3ft)

Solidago 'Goldenmosa' ♀
PERENNIAL

With its upright, yellow-stalked golden flowerheads and wrinkled, mid-green leaves, this is a select form of golden rod. Compact and bushy, it is much less invasive than the species. Plant it in a late-summer border, in full sunshine, in well-drained, slightly fertile, sandy soil. It is an ideal plant for a wild garden and is also good for cutting.

☼ ◊ ❀❀❀

↕ to 1m (3ft) ↔ to 60cm (24in)

Solidago rugosa 'Fireworks'
PERENNIAL

From late summer to mid-autumn, this goldenrod cultivar's long, arching stems bear dense panicles of tiny yellow blooms in such a way that they resemble fireworks. The flowers attract bees and butterflies. It works well in a mixed perennial border or in a wild garden, meadow, or naturalized area. Plant in full sun in average soil.

☼ ◊ ❀❀❀

↕↔ to 90cm (36in)

Tropaeolum peregrinum
CLIMBER

The Canary creeper is a vigorous
annual climber with deeply lobed, grey-
green leaves. In summer it produces
clusters of bright yellow flowers. These
have three small lower petals and two
larger, deeply fringed, upper petals,
which give it a bird-like appearance.
Plant it in a sunny position, in moist,
but well-drained, slightly fertile soil.
Canary creeper is ideal for growing
against a trellis, over a fence or pergola,
or through a deciduous tree. Sow seed
in situ in early spring.

☼ ◊ ◑ ❄
‡ to 4m (12ft)

Verbascum nigrum
PERENNIAL

The elegant dark mullein bears 50cm
(20in) tall flower spikes dotted with
yellow, saucer-shaped blooms that have
purple filament hairs. The heart-shaped
leaves are fuzzy and grey beneath, and
form a rosette at the base, gradually
becoming smaller as they grow up the
stem. Grow in poor, well-drained,
alkaline soils; in richer soils the plant
grows larger and needs staking. Ideal
for planting in gravel or naturalizing in
a wild garden, this mullein also mixes
well in a sunny herbaceous border.

☼ ◊ ❄ ❄ ❄
‡ to 1m (3ft) ↔ to 60cm (24in)

Antirrhinum majus 'Trumpet Serenade'

PERENNIAL

In a range of jolly colours, including this rich gold, the freesia-like blooms of 'Trumpet Serenade' are very different to the usual "squeeze-open, snap-shut" flowers of most snapdragons. As short-lived, tender perennials, they are usually grown as annual bedding plants, filling gaps at the front of a herbaceous border or used as a cut flower. Plant in full sun, in fertile, preferably sandy soil. Avoid wet soil as it encourages rust, although this is a resistant variety.

☼ ◊ ❄

‡↔to 30cm (12in)

Arctotis fastuosa

PERENNIAL

The deeply lobed leaves of the African daisy are silvery white and covered with hairs. In late summer, it bears orange, daisy-like flowers with a black or dark maroon centre. It is a tender perennial, and it is usually treated as a half-hardy annual used in bedding schemes, gravel gardens, and containers. Outside it needs a moist but very well-drained soil, in an open, sunny site. It can be kept from year to year in a pot of gritty, well-drained compost and overwintered under glass.

☼ ◊ ❄

‡ to 60cm (24in) ↔to 30cm (12in)

Begonia 'City of Ballarat'
PERENNIAL

Bright orange flowers, up to 18cm (7in) across, adorn this tuberous begonia. Grow it in containers of loam-based compost as a houseplant, and move it outside in summer. It can be used as bedding if the tubers are lifted in autumn before the first frost and stored in trays of dry sand in a cool place. In early spring, moisten the trays of tubers and move them to a warm place before planting out in late spring, in moist but well-drained soil in partial shade.

☀ ◊ ❄

‡ to 60cm (24in) ↔ to 45cm (18in)

Campsis x *tagliabuana* 'Madame Galen' ♥
CLIMBER

The trumpet creeper is a vigorous, self-clinging climber with long, divided leaves. From late summer to autumn it produces clusters of orange-red, trumpet-shaped flowers. It can quickly cover a trellis or clamber through an old tree. Keep it clear of the roof and gutters and hard prune in winter to keep within bounds. Vulnerable to frost damage, in colder areas grow the vine against a sunny wall. The soil should be fertile and moist but well drained.

☀ ◊ ◐ ❄ ❄

‡ to 10m (30ft)

Canna 'Striata' ♀

PERENNIAL

In late summer, this striking plant pushes up tall spikes of gladiolus-like orange flowers. The real scene-stealer, though, is the flamboyant foliage, marked with green and yellow stripes. It makes a superb plant for a border among other red or orange flowers, or can be grown in pots. Plant out in late spring in sun and well-drained soil. It is tender, so lift rhizomes before the first frosts, place in a tray of moist compost, and overwinter under glass.

☼ ◊ ❀

‡ to 1.5m (5ft) ↔ to 50cm (20in)

Crocosmia 'Star of the East' ♀

PERENNIAL CORM

With its large, orange flowers, 'Star of the East' is a particularly attractive crocosmia. A vigorous plant with erect, sword-shaped, deep green leaves, it looks wonderful planted among shrubs or with other late-flowering perennials. If the corms become overcrowded they will lose their vigour, so dig them up in spring, and replant them on a fresh site. Crocosmia prefer a spot in full sun, in fertile, moist but well-drained soil.

☼ ◊ ◊ ❀ ❀

‡ to 70cm (28in) ↔ to 8cm (3in)

Dahlia 'Hamari Gold' ♀

PERENNIAL

Golden-yellow blooms and deeply divided, dark green leaves make this an attractive border plant. Dahlias are not hardy, so when the foliage has been blackened by the first frosts, dig up the tubers and store them in dry compost over winter. Wait until all risk of frost has past before replanting in full sun, in well-drained soil. It benefits from a stake, best inserted at planting time to avoid damaging the tubers. Feed regularly in the growing season.

☼ ◊ ❄

‡ to 1.2m (4ft) ↔ to 60cm (24in)

Dahlia 'Wootton Impact' ♀

PERENNIAL

This attractive, semi-cactus dahlia is ideal for a sunny border where space is limited. Strong stems of medium-sized, bronze-coloured flowers, which are good for cutting, are held well above the main bulk of the plant. They need early staking. Like all dahlias, it requires a sunny spot in fertile, well-drained soil, while in winter the tubers need to be lifted and stored (*see* 'Hamari Gold' *above*).

☼ ◊ ❄

‡ to 1.2m (4ft) ↔ to 60cm (24in)

Fuchsia 'Coralle'
DECIDUOUS SHRUB

The tubular bells of 'Coralle', which are borne in tight clusters, will appeal to those who prefer less artificial-looking fuchsias. Upright in habit, this shrub has strong stems with velvety, olive-green leaves. It is superb for growing in a container, use a loam-based compost and choose a spot in full sun or light shade. Feed regularly throughout the summer with a balanced fertilizer, and move under glass during the winter as it is not hardy.

☼ ◐ ◊ ◊ ❄

↕ to 90cm (36in) ↔ to 60cm (24in)

Helenium 'Septemberfuchs'
PERENNIAL

Heleniums are invaluable for providing areas of warm colour in the late-summer border. This particularly tall variety benefits from early staking with canes or hazel twigs. It has dark green leaves and burnt-orange flowers streaked with yellow. Bees find the domed centres irresistible. For best effect, plant them in groups of three or more in a sunny position, in moist but well-drained fertile soil. Established clumps need dividing every couple of years.

☼ ◊ ◊ ❄ ❄ ❄

↕ to 1.5m (5ft) ↔ to 60cm (24in)

Helianthus annuus 'Music Box'
ANNUAL

From late summer this small sunflower produces an abundance of bright orange, yellow, or red flowers, each bloom measuring up to 12cm (5in) across. The markings on the petals subtly darken towards the black central disc. Wonderful as cut flowers, and short enough to grow in a pot, they also blend well among other plants in a sunny herbaceous or annual border. Sow the seed *in situ* in spring, in fertile, moist but well-drained soil.

☀ ◊ ◖ ✿✿✿

‡ to 70cm (28in) ↔ to 60cm (24in)

Kniphofia rooperi ♀
PERENNIAL

Living up to its common name of red hot poker and torch lily, this dazzling plant is guaranteed to brighten up the herbaceous border or gravel garden. Its globe-shaped spikes of reddish-orange flowers turn a golden colour as they mature. It is a very robust, clump-forming plant with shapely, pointed, evergreen leaves. Plant it in late spring, in full sun or partial shade, in fertile, well-drained, preferably sandy soil. Mulch over winter in the first year. Divide large clumps in spring.

☀ ◐ ◊ ✿✿✿

‡ to 1.2m (4ft) ↔ to 60cm (24in)

Lilium henryi ♀

PERENNIAL BULB

Vigorous and clump-forming, this tall lily has erect stems and narrow, dark green, lance-shaped leaves. In late summer, it develops clusters of ten or more delicately scented flowers, with black-spotted, swept-back petals. It is happiest in partial shade, in neutral or slightly alkaline, well-drained soil. Tall lilies, like this one, are ideal for brightening up the back of a shrub or herbaceous border.

☀ ◊ ❀❀❀ *f*
‡ to 3m (10ft)

Lonicera sempervirens ♀

CLIMBER

The beautiful trumpet honeysuckle is semi-evergreen in mild winters, and in summer produces clusters of tubular, orange-red flowers with a yellow throat. The oval, paired leaves help to frame the flowers, and highlight their intense colour. In autumn, the plant is covered with bright red berries, giving it a long season of interest. Use it to cover a warm wall, or to brighten up a sheltered position in the garden. Plant it in full sun or partial shade in fertile, well-drained soil.

☀ ☀ ◊ ❀❀
‡ to 4m (12ft)

Mimulus aurantiacus ♀
EVERGREEN SHRUB

The shrubby musk is an attractive,
small plant for a warm, sunny border.
The dark green, sticky, lance-shaped
leaves are the perfect foil for the orange,
trumpet-shaped flowers, which appear
from late summer through to autumn.
Plant it in fertile, well-drained soil and,
as it is not completely hardy, somewhere
sheltered in full sunshine. In cold areas
it is best grown in a conservatory.

☼ ◊ ❀❀
‡↔ to 1m (3ft)

Xerochrysum bracteatum
Monstrosum Series

ANNUAL

Everlasting flowers are erect annuals
with greyish-green, lance-shaped leaves.
The Monstrosum Series has vibrant
orange, double flowers that measure
8cm (3in) across. Other colours are
available, including yellows and reds.
Use it as a bedding plant, to fill spaces
in a herbaceous border or in containers.
Plant in full sunshine, in slightly fertile,
moist, but well-drained soil. Everlasting
flowers dry well and retain their colour
for a long time.

☼ ◊ ◗ ❀
‡ to 90cm (36in) ↔ to 30cm (12in)

AUTUMN

As the days begin to shorten and night temperatures fall, many plants have completed their annual cycles and retreat underground. The end of the growing season is signalled by the brilliant colour displays of deciduous trees before they drop their leaves and enter their dormancy. The vibrance of the show varies each year but most of the maples (*Acer*) give rich, reliable autumnal tints. There is also plenty of choice for gardens that are too small to accomodate large trees: shrubs, such as *Euonymus alatus* and the stag's horn sumach (*Rhus typhina*), can provide dramatic foliage displays of crimson, scarlet, and gold.

Ornamental vines *Vitis* 'Brant' and *V. coignetiae* are among the climbers with bright red foliage in autumn, and vigorous Boston ivy, *Parthenocissus tricuspidata*, transforms the appearance of walls as it turns from green and becomes a glowing sheet of scarlet.

FRUIT AND FLOWERS

Decorative fruits are much in evidence now and some of the best crops are carried on cotoneasters, rowans (*Sorbus*), and crab apples (*Malus*). And there are shrub roses, such as *Rosa rugosa*, which produce masses of shining scarlet hips.

Although the annual border has been cleared and many perennials have begun to die down, some flowering plants come into their own at this time – notably autumn crocuses and colchicums. Michaelmas daisies (*Aster*), Monkshood (*Aconitum*), and chrysanthemums of every colour will continue to flower as long as the weather permits. Do not be in too much of a hurry to clear away all remnants of summer; decorative seedheads can stay until they collapse, and allow the graceful flowerheads and foliage of ornamental grasses to stand through winter, not only so you can enjoy them, but for the protection it offers the plant.

Ageratina altissima 'Chocolate'

PERENNIAL

Formerly classified under *Eupatorium*, white snakeroot is a clump-forming perennial that is good in shade, even dry shade, and bears clusters of small white flowers in late summer. The variety name refers to the colour of the toothed leaves, which are an attractive deep brown colour through spring and summer, gradually greening with age, before the whole plant dies back over winter. Plants may wilt in hot sun if not watered. Divide in spring, as necessary.

☼ ☀ ◊ ◊ ◆ ❀ ❀ ❀
‡ to 1m (3ft) ↔ to 60cm (24in)

Aralia elata 'Variegata' ♀

DECIDUOUS TREE

The Japanese angelica tree is upright in habit with stout, spreading, thorny branches arranged in tiers. In mild areas it forms a small tree, but elsewhere may only be a large shrub up to 3m (10ft) tall. The leaflets, which are edged with creamy-white, turn gold in autumn. Abundant clusters of small white flowers are borne in late summer and early autumn. It prefers fertile, moist but well-drained soil in sun but tolerates light, dappled shade.

☼ ☀ ◊ ◆ ❀ ❀ ❀
‡↔ to 10m (30ft)

Arbutus x *andrachnoides*
EVERGREEN TREE

The Grecian strawberry tree is a shrubby, spreading evergreen with peeling, red-brown bark and oval, glossy, dark green leaves. From autumn through to spring, it bears hanging clusters of small, almost spherical, white flowers; occasionally it produces small, bright red fruits at the same time. Grow it in a site sheltered from cold winds, in full sun in humus-rich, well-drained soil. It tolerates alkaline soils so long as they are deep and rich in leafy organic matter.

☼ ◊ ❀❀

‡↔ to 8m (25ft)

Aster ericoides 'White Heather'
PERENNIAL

Asters are invaluable for autumn colour in herbaceous and mixed borders. This bushy perennial has wiry, upright stems smothered in tiny, long-lasting, white daisies from late summer to late autumn. The slender stems need staking. Grow in sun or partial shade in fertile, well-drained soil that does not dry out during the growing season; moisture helps reduce the risk of mildew, although this variety shows some resistance to the disease.

☼ ◑ ◊ ◐ ❀❀❀

‡ to 1m (3ft) ↔ to 30cm (12in)

Cimicifuga simplex

PERENNIAL

The tiny, star-shaped autumn flowers of this herbaceous perennial, also known as *Actea simplex*, appear brilliant white against their dark stems. The tall, arching flower spikes are seen at their best if the stems are supported by an unobtrusive, grow-through support, positioned in spring. The leaves are glossy, finely divided, and fresh green. Good for late colour in a woodland garden or shady border. Grow in moist, humus-rich soil in light shade to prevent the sun scorching the delicate leaves.

☀ ◊ ❀❀❀

‡ to 1.5m (5ft) ↔ to 60cm (24in)

Cortaderia richardii ♀

PERENNIAL

Commonly known as toe toe, *Cortaderia richardii* is native to New Zealand. The arching, fluffy flowerheads, up to 60cm (2ft) long, first appear in summer, high above the tussocks of long, narrow, olive-green leaves. If left on the plant, the slender creamy-white plumes will persist through autumn and winter. They can also be cut for fresh or dried-flower arrangements. Grow in well-drained soil in sun. Cut out the dead foliage and flowerheads in early spring – protect your hands with gloves.

☼ ◊ ❀❀

‡ to 2.5m (8ft) ↔ to 1m (3ft)

Cortaderia selloana 'Sunningdale Silver' ♀

PERENNIAL GRASS

Large, dense, evergreen tussocks of sharp-edged, deep greyish-green leaves are topped by tall upright stems of long-lasting, silvery-white flowerheads in late summer and autumn. It makes an impressive specimen plant where space is available. Leave dead foliage in place over winter to protect the crown from frosts then, wearing stout gloves, cut and comb it out in spring. Grow in sun in well-drained soil. Cut back every two or three years in spring to rejuvenate.

☼ ◊ ❀❀

 to 2.1m (7ft) ↔ to 1.2m (4ft)

Crocus ochroleucus ♀

PERENNIAL CORM

This crocus bears slender, creamy-white flowers with yellow throats in late autumn, when most other autumn-flowering crocus are over. The leaves usually emerge with or just after the flowers, and are green with a central white stripe. It is very easy to grow in well-drained soil in sun, and will naturalize if planted in drifts in short grass. Overcrowded clumps can be divided after flowering. Plant corms in late summer.

☼ ◊ ❀❀❀

 to 5cm (2in) ↔ to 2.5cm (1in)

Galanthus reginae-olgae

PERENNIAL BULB

This snowdrop flowers from mid-autumn to early winter, with petals up to 2.5cm (1in) long. The narrow leaves appear after flowering and are dark green with a central grey stripe. Grow in sun or light dappled shade in well-drained, neutral to alkaline soil. It prefers drier soils and more sun than other snowdrops. Overcrowded clumps can be divided as the leaves start to wither. Plant bulbs in autumn.

☼ ◗ ◊ ❀ ❀

↕ to 20cm (8in) ↔ to 5cm (2in)

Leucojum autumnale

PERENNIAL BULB

The autumn snowflake is a beautiful plant with narrow, dark green, grass-like leaves. The nodding white flowers, tinged with pink at the base, are borne on slender stems in late summer and early autumn. A native of the stony slopes of the western Mediterranean, it prefers a warm, sunny spot in light, free-draining soil. It is ideal for rock gardens, sunny banks and terraces. Plant bulbs in late summer.

☼ ◊ ❀ ❀

↕ to 15cm (6in) ↔ to 5cm (2in)

Sorbus cashmiriana ♀

DECIDUOUS TREE

The Kashmir rowan forms a spreading, open-branched small tree. The white or blush-pink flowers open in late spring or early summer. The finely divided, rich green leaves turn gold and russet in autumn, forming a backcloth to the clusters of white, marble-sized berries that appear from late summer and early autumn onwards. Grow in sun or light dappled shade, in fertile, well-drained but moisture-retentive soil. It is most easily propagated by seed, sown as soon as it is ripe in autumn.

☼ ☀ ◊ ◑ ❀ ❀ ❀
‡ to 8m (25ft) ↔ to 7m (22ft)

Symphoricarpos albus var. *laevigatus*

DECIDUOUS SHRUB

Snowberry is a densely upright, robust shrub with rounded, dark green leaves. It carries tiny pink flowers in summer, followed by its most notable feature: eye-catching, pure white berries in autumn. It grows on a range of sites, including dry shade, but can be invasive, so it is best as a boundary plant, where it could be included in a mixed hedge. Prune out old shoots to the base in spring.

☼ ☀ ◊ ◑ ❀ ❀ ❀
‡↔ to 2m (6ft)

Amaryllis belladonna ♀

PERENNIAL BULB

This South African bulb is grown for its late-summer and early-autumn flowers. The fragrant, trumpet-shaped, pink blooms are borne in clusters on long, purple-tinted stems. The dark green, strap-like leaves appear after the flowers and last until the following summer. In cold areas, protect the leaves from frost with a cloche. Grow in a warm, sheltered, sunny site in very well-drained soil enriched with organic matter. Plant in summer, with the tip of the bulb just below the soil surface.

☼ ◊ ❈ ❈ *f*
‡ to 80cm (32in) ↔ to 45cm (18in)

Camellia sasanqua

EVERGREEN SHRUB

Autumn camellias always stand out in a garden, since the majority flower in spring. They make upright shrubs or small trees and are valued for their fragrant, single-petalled white flowers in mid- to late autumn, although many pink varieties are also available. The foliage is dark green. In mild areas, *C. sasanqua* can be grown as a hedge, but otherwise it prefers the shelter of a warm, sunny wall. Moist, humus-rich, acid soil is essential. The plant will tolerate hard pruning after flowering.

☼ ☀ ◊ ◊ ❈ ❈ *f*
‡ to 6m (20ft) ↔ to 3m (10ft)

Chrysanthemum 'Rose Yvonne Arnaud'

PERENNIAL

The fully double flowers of this florist's chrysanthemum are produced in abundance in late summer and autumn. The deep rose-pink petals are neatly backswept. The plant should be lifted in autumn after flowering and over-wintered in frost-free conditions. New shoots can be planted out after the last frost or used for basal cuttings in early spring to produce new plants. Grow in fertile, well-drained soil, in full sun.

‡ to 1.2m (4ft) ↔ to 75cm (30in)

Clerodendrum bungei

DECIDUOUS SHRUB

This suckering shrub is not fully frost-hardy, but if the woody stems die back in cold winters, they often grow again from the base in spring if given a deep winter mulch. The fragrant flowers are deep pink and, although tiny, are borne in large clusters throughout late summer and early autumn. The large, heart-shaped, serrated-edged leaves emit a pungent odour when brushed against. Grow in a warm, sunny, sheltered site, in a humus-rich, well-drained soil.

‡↔ to 2m (6ft)

Colchicum byzantinum ♀

PERENNIAL CORM

C. byzantinum produces up to 20 large, funnel-shaped, pale mauve-pink flowers in autumn. The broad leaves, which are ribbed or pleated, appear in spring and last until early summer. As they fade they can look rather untidy, so hide the foliage by growing them among other plants. Plant the corms, which resemble a tiny clenched fist, in late summer, in a sunny position in soil that is moist but free draining. This colchicum establishes quickly and will spread where the conditions suit it.

☼ ◊ ◐ ❀❀❀
‡ to 12cm (5in) ↔ to 10cm (4in)

Colchicum 'The Giant'

PERENNIAL CORM

The flowers of this autumn-flowering corm are very large. Mauve-pink with white throats, they are lightly chequered and crocus-like. This is one of the easiest colchicums to grow, and it will increase rapidly. Broad leaves appear in winter and die back in summer. The corms are best grown among other plants to conceal the leaves. Plant the corms in late summer in fertile, free-draining soil in sun. Plants tolerate light or partial shade.

☼ ◊ ❀❀❀
‡↔ to 20cm (8in)

Crocus kotschyanus ♀
PERENNIAL CORM

In autumn, this fully hardy crocus bears delicate, lilac-pink flowers with yellow centres and white stamens. The flowers open out fully in sun to display the glossy surface of the petals. They are followed, in winter through to spring, by narrow, semi-erect leaves with white lines along the centre. It is ideal for naturalizing in drifts in well-drained soil in a warm, sunny position. Overcrowded clumps can be divided after flowering. Plant corms in late summer.

☼ ◊ ❀❀❀
‡ to 8cm (3in) ↔ to 5cm (2in)

Cyclamen hederifolium ♀
PERENNIAL

This small cyclamen has ivy-shaped leaves that are intricately patterned in shades of grey-green. Appearing after the flowers in autumn, they can provide a foil for other winter-flowering bulbs until they fade by early summer. The pink flowers appear from late summer to autumn. Grow in light shade in a well-drained soil that is rich in leafy organic matter. Plant tubers in late summer about 2.5cm (1in) deep. Clumps are best left undisturbed, but self-sown seedlings can be lifted and moved.

☼ ◐ ◊ ❀❀❀
‡ to 10cm (4in) ↔ to 15cm (6in)

Euonymus phellomanus
DECIDUOUS SHRUB

The corkbush makes a medium-sized shrub with a reliable and wonderfully vivid display of bright pink seed capsules in autumn. Each capsule splits as it ripens, to reveal bright orange seeds. The plant is named for its corky-winged stems, which are highly unusual and particularly noticeable in winter. The oval leaves redden in autumn before they fall. It would also make a lovely tree for a wildlife garden. Please note that the fruits are toxic to humans.

☼ ☼ ◊ ✿✿✿
‡ to 2m (6ft) ↔ to 3m (10ft)

Nerine bowdenii ♀
PERENNIAL BULB

Stout stems bear umbrella-like clusters of rose-pink flowers with wavy-edged petals from early to mid-autumn. The strap-shaped leaves appear with, or just after, the flowers. Grow in sun in very free-draining soil; they are best at the foot of a warm, sunny wall and left to multiply undisturbed. Plant in spring with the tip of the bulb at, or just below, the soil surface. In winter in colder areas, cover over with a mulch of leafmould or bracken.

☼ ◊ ✿✿
‡ to 60cm (24in) ↔ to 15cm (6in)

Nerine bowdenii f. *alba*
PERENNIAL BULB

This robust perennial is one of the best
late-flowering bulbs. In autumn, it bears
open sprays of five to ten trumpet-
shaped, faintly scented, bright pink
flowers with curled, wavy-edged petals.
The strap-like, fresh green leaves appear
after the flowers, at the base of the
plant. Despite its exotic appearance, it
will survive winter cold with protection
at the base of a warm, sunny wall. The
flowers are good for cutting. Lay a mulch
over the dormant bulbs in winter.

☼ ◊ ❀❀❀ *f*

‡ to 60cm (24in) ↔ to 15cm (6in)

Schizostylis coccinea 'Sunrise' ♀
PERENNIAL

The kaffir lily produces tall spikes of
delicate, cup-shaped, soft pink flowers
in late summer and autumn. The mid-
green, narrow leaves are sword-shaped,
and both flowers and foliage are
excellent for indoor arrangements.
In the garden, it is suited to sunny
borders, waterside plantings, or it can
be planted against a sunny wall. Grow
in fertile, moist, well-drained soil in
full sun. Divide regularly in the spring
to maintain the plant's vigour.

☼ ◊ ❀❀❀

‡ to 60cm (24in) ↔ to 30cm (12in)

Sedum spectabile ♀

PERENNIAL

The ice plant is deservedly popular and flowers over long periods from late summer to autumn. It is ideal for the front of a sunny border, where its densely packed, flat heads of tiny star-shaped, soft-pink flowers will attract butterflies and bees. The leaves are fleshy and pale grey-green. Grow in any well-drained soil in full sun. The flowerheads can be cut and dried or left to stand until winter, adding interest to the border.

☼ ◊ ❀❀❀

‡↔ to 45cm (18in)

Sorbus hupehensis var. *obtusa* ♀

DECIDUOUS TREE

This rowan has a narrow, compact habit. The young foliage is followed by trusses of white flowers in late spring and early summer. Pink berries form during late summer and become deeper pink as they mature. The leaves are divided into many leaflets that turn fiery orange and red in autumn. The berries remain long after the leaves have fallen. Grow in moisture-retentive, well-drained neutral or slightly acid (lime-free) soil in sun or light dappled shade.

☼ ☀ ◊ ◑ ❀❀❀

‡ to 12m (40ft) ↔ to 8m (25ft)

Sorbus vilmorinii ♀

DECIDUOUS TREE

The delicate-looking, fern-like leaves of Vilmorin's rowan are dark green, turning shades of orange to bronze-red in autumn. This large shrub or small tree has a rounded crown with slender, arching branches and is suitable for a small garden. White flowers in late spring are followed by fruits in autumn that ripen through shades of deep red-pink to white flushed with pink. Plant in moisture-retentive but well-drained neutral or slightly acid soil in full sun or light dappled shade.

☼ ☀ ◊ ◊ ✽✽✽
‡↔ to 5m (15ft)

Zephyranthes grandiflora ♀

PERENNIAL BULB

Soft pink, funnel-shaped flowers open to a starry shape between late summer and early autumn above clumps of very slender leaves. Plant bulbs 10cm (4in) deep in spring in a sheltered, sunny site, in well-drained, moisture-retentive soil. In cold areas, lift after flowering and overwinter in a frost-free place. It can also be grown in containers of gritty compost and moved under glass in winter, or grown permanently in the greenhouse or conservatory.

☼ ◊ ◊ ✽
‡ to 30cm (12in) ↔ to 10cm (4in)

Acer palmatum 'Dissectum Atropurpureum'

DECIDUOUS TREE

This small tree is one of the most popular forms of Japanese maple. It has wide-spreading branches clothed with ferny, deeply divided, red-purple leaves that turn red in autumn. Grow in full sun or partial shade, in fertile, moist, but well-drained soil, in a sheltered position; the leaves may be damaged by frosts and cold or dry winds. Grow it with other Japanese maples, or in a large container of loam-based compost (John Innes No. 3).

☼ ◐ ◊ ◑ ❀ ❀ ❀

↕ to 1.5m (5ft) ↔ to 1m (3ft)

Acer palmatum 'Osakazuki' ♥

DECIDUOUS TREE

This Japanese maple has large, bright green leaves that are divided into seven lobes, each drawn out into a finely tapered tip. In autumn they turn a vivid scarlet. Plant it in full sun or partial shade, in fertile, moist but well-drained soil, with shelter from hard frosts and cold, dry winds. To fully appreciate its autumn foliage, it is best grown as a specimen tree.

☼ ◐ ◊ ◑ ❀ ❀ ❀

↕↔ to 6m (20ft)

Acer rubrum 'October Glory' ♀

DECIDUOUS TREE

The red maple dons its bright red autumn colours early in the season and retains its leaves for several weeks, even in windy weather. The dark green summer leaves will develop their most vibrant colours if the tree is grown in acid (lime-free) soil. Plant it in full sun or partial shade, in fertile, moist but well-drained soil. This tree has a spreading habit.

☼ ☀ ◊ ◊ ❀ ❀ ❀

‡ to 20m (70ft) ↔ to 10m (30ft)

Acer rubrum 'Scanlon'

DECIDUOUS TREE

There are few trees that colour up as vividly in autumn as this one – the dark green leaves turn a vivid shade of deep reddish orange. Plant it in full sunshine, in moist but well-drained, fertile soil. The best autumn colours appear when grown in acid (lime-free) soil. This tree has a narrow columnar form, making it more suitable for smaller gardens than 'October Glory'.

☼ ◊ ◊ ❀ ❀ ❀

‡ to 15m (50ft) ↔ to 5m (15ft)

Amelanchier lamarckii ♀
DECIDUOUS TREE

Often shrubby, this attractive small tree has upright branches and downy young shoots. It bears hanging clusters of white flowers in mid-spring, which are followed by edible, purplish-black fruit in summer. The leaves are flushed bronze as they emerge in spring, then turn dark green, before becoming orange and finally red in autumn. Plant in full sun or partial shade, in acid (lime-free), fertile, moist but well-drained soil. Thin out main stems if necessary to improve the appearance.

☼ ☽ ◊ ◖ ❄ ❄ ❄
‡ to 10m (30ft) ↔ to 12m (40ft)

Arbutus unedo ♀
EVERGREEN TREE

The strawberry tree has a bushy, spreading habit and attractive, peeling, reddish-brown bark. The oval leaves are dark green and glossy. From late autumn to spring, it bears hanging sprays of small, waxy-textured white flowers accompanied by small, strawberry-like red fruits – these result from the previous year's flowers. Grow in full sun, in a fertile, well-drained soil enriched with leafy organic matter. It is best in a sheltered spot with some protection from strong, cold winds.

☼ ◊ ❄ ❄ ❄
‡↔ to 8m (25ft)

Aronia x *prunifolia*
DECIDUOUS SHRUB

The bright green, oval leaves of this relatively large, fan-shaped shrub turn a rich wine red in autumn before they fall in winter. It is commonly known as purple chokeberry, named for the deep purple berries that mature over the summer from the white flowers in mid-spring. The fruits ripen just before the autumn leaves turn, making this a fine autumn plant. The plant grows best in neutral to acid soil. The variety 'Brilliant' has particularly fine leaf colour.

 ☼ ☼ ◊ ◑ ❀ ❀ ❀

‡ to 3m (10ft) ↔ to 2m (6ft)

Berberis x *ottawensis* 'Superba' ♥
DECIDUOUS SHRUB

A large shrub with gracefully arching, spiny branches bearing red berries. The rounded leaves open purplish red and turn a brilliant crimson-red in autumn. In spring, it bears clusters of pale yellow flowers. It is a tough shrub that can be planted in almost any well-drained soil and will grow happily in full sun or partial shade. Use it in a shrub or mixed border or as an intruder-proof hedge. Prune hard for the best foliage effects.

 ☼ ☼ ◊ ❀ ❀ ❀

‡↔ to 2.5m (8ft)

Cercidiphyllum japonicum ♀

DECIDUOUS TREE

The Katsura tree is pyramid-shaped when young, becoming more rounded with maturity. It has rounded, fresh green leaves that turn yellow, orange, and red in autumn, with a scent like burnt sugar when they fall. It makes a beautiful specimen tree. Plant it in full sun or dappled shade, in humus-rich, moist but well-drained, neutral to acid (lime-free) soil. The best autumn colour is obtained when it is planted in acid soil.

☼ ☀ ◊ ◑ ✿ ✿ ✿ *f*
↕ to 20m (70ft) ↔ to 15m (50ft)

Chrysanthemum 'George Griffiths' ♀

PERENNIAL

Chrysanthemums should be planted in a sheltered position in full sun. They need a fertile, moist but well-drained soil that is enriched with well-rotted manure. The flowerheads of 'George Griffiths' are heavy and the stems should be tied in to a cane for support. Lift plants after flowering and overwinter in frost-free conditions. Plant out in spring after the final frost, or raise new plants from basal cuttings. This chrysanthemum is often grown for exhibition.

☼ ◊ ◑ ✿ ✿
↕ to 1.5m (5ft) ↔ to 75cm (30in)

Cotinus 'Grace'

DECIDUOUS SHRUB

This is an extremely beautiful form of smoke bush, with rich purple, oval leaves. In summer, it bears plumes of small flowers that are followed by sprays of tiny purplish-pink fruits. In autumn, the leaves turn a vivid shade of scarlet. Plant it in full sun or light shade, in moisture-retentive but well-drained soil. To obtain the best autumn colour, do not plant it in too rich a soil and choose a sunny position; it does not colour as well in shade.

☼ ☀ ◊ ◑ ❀ ❀ ❀
‡ to 6m (20ft) ↔ to 5m (15ft)

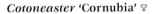

Cotoneaster 'Cornubia' ♧

SEMI-EVERGREEN SHRUB

This vigorous shrub or small tree has arching branches clothed in dark green leaves; some of them turn bronze in autumn. It is one of the tallest of the cotoneasters. The clusters of small, white spring flowers produce an abundance of bright red fruits in autumn. Plant it in full sunshine or partial shade, in moisture-retentive but well-drained soil. It can be planted as a screen, in a large shrub border, or can be trained to form a standard tree.

☼ ☀ ◊ ◑ ❀ ❀ ❀
‡↔ to 10m (30ft)

Cotoneaster horizontalis ⚜

DECIDUOUS SHRUB

A low-growing shrub, with flattened, wide-spreading branches covered with small, oval, dark green leaves. The branches are arranged in a distinctive herringbone pattern. Small white, pink-flushed flowers appear in spring and are followed, in autumn, by bright scarlet-red fruit. The leaves also turn red in autumn, creating an outstanding display. Grow it against a wall or use it as ground cover. Plant it in full sun in any moderately fertile, well-drained soil.

☼ ◊ ❀❀❀
‡ to 1m (3ft) ↔ to 1.5m (5ft)

Euonymus alatus ⚜

DECIDUOUS SHRUB

There are few plants that can compete with the winged spindle for dramatic autumn colour. It has dark green leaves that are borne on curious, corky-winged shoots. In autumn the leaves turn a brilliant crimson-red. The purple-red autumn fruits open to reveal seeds with bright orange coats. Plant it in full sun or light shade, in any well-drained soil. It can be grown in a shrub border, but it also makes a beautiful specimen, planted alone so that its beauty can be fully appreciated.

☼ ◑ ◊ ❀❀❀
‡ to 2m (6ft) ↔ to 3m (10ft)

Euphorbia dulcis

PERENNIAL

This spreading perennial has upright
stems with oblong-shaped green leaves.
The upper part of the stem is branched
and covered with triangular leaves.
In autumn, the stems turn purple and
the leaves take on various shades of
red, yellow, and orange. Yellow-green
flowerheads are produced in early
summer. It is best in a moist, humus-
rich soil in light shade, but it does
tolerate drier soils. It self-seeds freely.
Good for a shady border and excellent
for a woodland garden.

☀ ◊ ◊ ❀❀❀

‡↔ to 30cm (12in)

Fothergilla gardenii

DECIDUOUS SHRUB

The witch alder is a small, bushy
shrub, with dark green, oval leaves.
In the summer, it produces cylindrical
spikes of small white flowers. It is
mainly grown for its autumn colour,
when the leaves become infused
with intense shades of red, yellow,
and orange. It should be grown in a
sunny position, in moisture-retentive
but well-drained, humus-rich, acid
(lime-free) soil. It can be grown in
partial shade but the colour of the
autumn foliage will be less vibrant.

☀ ◊ ◊ ❀❀❀ *f*

‡↔ to 1m (3ft)

Gaultheria tasmanica
EVERGREEN SHRUB

Originating in Tasmania, this is a dwarf, mat-forming shrub, with small, glossy, dark green leaves. In spring, it produces bell-shaped, white flowers that are followed, in autumn, by bright red fruits. It is best planted in partial shade, in moist, neutral or acid (lime-free) soil, but it will tolerate some sun if the soil does not dry out. It is suitable for the front of a shady border or a woodland garden. It can also be planted in containers; use ericaceous compost and do not let it dry out.

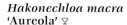

☼ ◊ ✴ ✴ ✴
‡ to 7cm (3in) ↔ to 25cm (10in)

Hakonechloa macra 'Aureola' ♡
PERENNIAL

This clump-forming Japanese grass has arching, slender, bright yellow leaves which are narrowly striped with green. They become red tinted in autumn. In late summer and early autumn, it bears spiky flowerheads. Plant it in partial shade, in fertile, moist but well-drained, humus-rich soil. It is ideal for a woodland garden or for planting at the front of a mixed or herbaceous border. It also looks good in containers.

☼ ◊ ◊ ✴ ✴ ✴
‡ to 40cm (16in) ↔ to 60cm (24in)

Helenium 'Bruno'

PERENNIAL

This upright perennial forms dense clumps of mid-green leaves. From late summer to autumn, it produces abundant heads of deep red-crimson, daisy-like flowers with chocolate-brown centres. Although the flower stems are sturdy, they may need staking on exposed sites. Grow it in a sunny border, in any moisture-retentive but well-drained fertile soil. To keep clumps vigorous and productive, divide them every two or three years.

‡ to 75cm (30in) ↔ to 50cm (20in)

Imperata cylindrica 'Rubra'

PERENNIAL

Japanese blood grass forms clumps of narrow green leaves that turn wine-red as the season progresses. By autumn, when fluffy, silvery flowerheads appear, the leaves have become crimson-scarlet. Grow in full sun or light shade, in humus-rich, moist but well-drained soil. Protect young plants with a winter mulch. Overcrowded clumps can be divided in early spring. It is a good plant for woodland gardens, herbaceous borders or containers.

‡↔ to 50cm (20in)

Liquidambar styraciflua

DECIDUOUS TREE

Sweet gum trees are often mistaken for maples because of their very similar foliage and wonderful autumn colours that range from yellow to orange, purple, and crimson. They are narrowly conical, deciduous trees that also have an attractive bark, but as they grow quite tall, they are best for medium to large gardens. There are a number of varieties on the market: 'Worplesdon' is one of the most reliable for its intense red, orange, and yellow leaves; 'Palo Alto' also has very fine autumn colour.

☼ ◐ ◊ ✿✿✿

↕ to 25m (80ft) ↔ to 12m (40ft)

Lonicera periclymenum 'Belgica'

CLIMBER

Early Dutch honeysuckle is a vigorous climber with bright red berries for autumn interest. It has mid-green leaves and flowers in spring and again in late summer. The tubular flowers, white on the inside and red outside, are highly scented. It is ideal for growing through a tree or over a trellis; if given space to scramble, it seldom needs pruning. Grow it in full sun or partial shade, in humus-rich, moist but well-drained soil.

☼ ◑ ◊ ◊ ✿✿✿ *f*

↕ to 7m (22ft)

Malus 'Evereste'

DECIDUOUS TREE

Crab apples are appreciated in autumn for their ornamental fruit, which often lasts right through winter, acting as a sustaining food supply for hungry birds. 'Evereste' has cherry-sized, orange-red fruit. In spring, the whole tree is covered in white blossom that develops from pink buds. Its tidy habit and year-round interest makes this a good choice for small gardens; the blossom will also pollinate eating apples. Trim crowded and untidy shoots in late winter to keep an open, pleasing shape.

‡↔ to 4m (12ft)

Malus x *schiedeckeri* 'Red Jade'

DECIDUOUS TREE

An attractive small tree with weeping branches, 'Red Jade' has bright pink buds that open in the spring to semi-double, pink-flushed white flowers. These are followed, in autumn, by a profusion of bright red, cherry-sized fruit. The leaves are bright green and glossy. Grow it in full sun, in moist but well-drained, moderately fertile soil. It makes a beautiful specimen tree that is suitable for small gardens.

‡ to 4m (12ft) ↔ to 6m (20ft)

Nyssa sylvatica ♀

DECIDUOUS TREE

The tupelo is a broad, cone-shaped tree, with slightly drooping lower branches, an interesting textured bark, and exuberant autumn colour. The dark green leaves turn vibrant yellow, orange and finally red-crimson shades in mid- to late autumn. Plant it in a sheltered site in full sun or partial shade, in neutral to slightly acid (lime-free) soil that is fertile and moisture retentive but well drained. It makes a glorious specimen tree.

☼ ☽ ◊ ◊ ❀❀❀
‡ to 20m (70ft) ↔ to 10m (30ft)

Parrotia persica ♀

DECIDUOUS TREE

The Persian ironwood is a shrubby tree with peeling grey and brown bark. The large glossy leaves put on a glorious autumn display in shades of red, orange, and yellow. In late winter or early spring, small, spidery red flowers appear on the bare branches. Plant in full sun or partial shade, in a good depth of fertile, moist but well-drained soil. The best autumn colour occurs on acid (lime-free) soil, but it also tolerates alkaline conditions. A fine specimen tree, it develops great character with age.

☼ ☽ ◊ ◊ ❀❀❀
‡ to 8m (25ft) ↔ to 10m (30ft)

Parthenocissus tricuspidata ♀

CLIMBER

Boston ivy is a vigorous woody climber, with glossy, dark green leaves that are toothed and divided into three lobes. In autumn, these turn gold, brilliant red and purple before falling. It is superb for covering a large, unattractive or featureless wall, or for growing through a tall, sturdy tree. Grow it in full sun or shade, in fertile, well-drained soil that is rich in humus. Provide young plants with support until they are established.

☼ ☼ ☀ ◊ ◊ ❀ ❀ ❀

‡ to 20m (70ft)

Prunus avium ♀

DECIDUOUS TREE

The wild cherry, or gean, is a large, spreading tree with dark green leaves that are tinted bronze in spring and turn red and gold in autumn. In the middle of spring it bears clusters of white flowers, followed, in late summer and autumn, by small, dark red fruit, which the birds love to eat. Plant it in full sunshine or partial shade, in fertile, moist but well-drained soil. It is a fine specimen tree and is also useful in a larger garden for attracting wildlife.

☼ ☼ ◊ ◊ ❀ ❀ ❀

‡ to 20m (70ft) ↔ to 10m (30ft)

Rhus typhina 'Dissecta' ♀
DECIDUOUS TREE

The stag's horn sumach gets its common name from the upright, velvet-covered branch tips that resemble antlers. In summer, upright spikes of small, yellow-green flowers turn dark crimson as they fruit. The ferny leaves turn shades of brilliant red, gold, and orange in autumn. Plant in full sun, in fertile, moist but well-drained soil. If its spreading suckers are a nuisance, they can be dug out over winter when the plant is dormant.

☼ ◊ ◊ ✿ ✿ ✿
‡ to 2m (6ft) ↔ to 3m (10ft)

Rosa x *odorata* 'Mutabilis' ♀
DECIDUOUS SHRUB

This slender shrub has purple-red stems and purple flushed, dark green leaves. The single, cup-shaped flowers open pale yellow, turning first pink and then carmine-red; they are borne over a long period from summer to autumn and have a wonderful fragrance. Plant it in a sheltered position in fertile, humus-rich, moist but well-drained soil. It is normally grown as a shrub rose but will climb if it is provided with some support.

☼ ◊ ◊ ✿ ✿ ✿ *f*
‡↔ to 2m (6ft)

Rosa rugosa
DECIDUOUS SHRUB

Easy-going and vigorous, this repeat-flowering rose has robust, prickly stems and wrinkled, bright green leaves that turn yellow in autumn. The single, fragrant, carmine-red flowers are borne from early summer to autumn. From late summer they are accompanied by large, spherical, orange-red hips. Tolerant of a wide range of conditions, it prefers full sun or light shade and a moist but well-drained soil. It makes a superb, intruder-proof hedge. Trim or prune to shape in late winter or early spring.

☼ ☀ ◊ ◖ ❀ ❀ ❀ *f*
↕↔ to 2m (6ft)

Ruscus aculeatus
EVERGREEN SHRUB

Butcher's broom is a clump-forming plant with upright stems that bear very tough, spine-tipped, leaf-like modified stems. From late summer to winter, female plants produce small, round, bright red berries. Male and female or hermaphrodite plants are needed to ensure fruiting. It grows in sun, deep shade and in any but waterlogged soil; it also tolerates dry soil. The cut stems can be used in flower arrangements.

☼ ☀ ☀ ◊ ◖ ❀ ❀ ❀
↕ to 75cm (30in) ↔ to 1m (3ft)

Schizostylis coccinea

PERENNIAL

From late summer to autumn, this cheerful plant produces shiny, bright red flowers on strong but slender stems, which are held above green, strap-shaped, almost evergreen leaves. Remove flowers as they fade. Grow in a sunny, sheltered position in fertile, moist soil and protect the crowns with a mulch in winter in cold or exposed gardens. It spreads freely; divide overcrowded clumps in spring. Plant it in a herbaceous border or beside water. It is also good for cutting.

☼ ◊ ❀❀❀
‡ to 50cm (20in) ↔ to 30cm (12in)

Sorbus aucuparia

DECIDUOUS TREE

The rowan is a small or medium-sized tree, with mid-green leaves divided into small leaflets. In spring, it bears clusters of creamy-white flowers that are followed by bright red berries in autumn. They are very attractive to birds. The foliage turns red or yellow in autumn. Plant in full sun or dappled shade, in moderately fertile, humus-rich, well-drained soil. It is tolerant of a wide range of conditions and will grow happily on both acid (lime-free) and slightly alkaline soils.

☼ ☼ ◊ ❀❀❀
‡ to 15m (50ft) ↔ to 7m (22ft)

Sorbus commixta

DECIDUOUS TREE

Slightly smaller than *Sorbus aucuparia*, this tree has dark green leaves divided into many small, lance-shaped leaflets. The autumn colour is outstanding as the leaves become infused with brilliant shades of vivid red, yellow, and purple. In late spring, it bears clusters of white flowers that are followed by bright orange-red or red autumn fruits. It should be planted in full sunshine or dappled shade, in moderately fertile, humus-rich, moist but well-drained soil.

☼ ☀ ◐ ◊ ✿ ✿ ✿
‡ to 10m (30ft) ↔ to 7m (22ft)

Sorbus sargentiana ♀

DECIDUOUS TREE

The large leaves of this slow-growing tree are divided into lance-shaped green leaflets that take on brilliant shades of red and orange in autumn. In winter, distinctive, bright red, sticky buds form. In early summer, it produces clusters of white flowers, followed by broad sprays of small, scarlet autumn fruits. Plant it in a sunny position, in humus-rich, fertile, moist but well-drained soil. It makes a beautiful specimen tree and, like other sorbus, has several seasons of interest.

☼ ◊ ◊ ✿ ✿ ✿
‡↔ to 10m (30ft)

Taxus baccata 'Fastigiata' ♀
EVERGREEN TREE

Irish yew is a dense, upright conifer that becomes columnar with age, adding structure to the garden and useful during bare winter months. Dark, needle-like leaves give it an imposing presence and make it a good specimen plant. This is a female variety, so reliably bears fleshy, berry-like, bright red fruits in late summer. Leave the berries to birds, as this is a poisonous plant. Slow-growing, it takes many years to outgrow its position; trim out any wayward shoots in spring.

☀ ◐ ◖ ❀ ❀ ❀
‡ to 10m (30ft) ↔ to 4m (12ft)

Viburnum opulus
DECIDUOUS SHRUB

The guelder rose is a vigorous deciduous shrub that bears maple-like, lobed, mid-green leaves that turn red in autumn. It is valued particularly for its large bunches of spherical bright red berries that appear from late summer to autumn and are much-loved by birds. These develop from the flat heads of showy white flowers in late spring; like the berries these also have a wildlife value as they attract pollinating insects. 'Compactum' is a much smaller, denser variety which grows up to 1.5m (5ft) tall.

☀ ◑ ◐ ◖ ❀ ❀ ❀
‡ to 5m (15ft) ↔ to 4m (12ft)

Vitis 'Brant' ♀

CLIMBER

This vigorous, woody-stemmed vine is
grown for its autumn colour and edible,
blue-black grapes that ripen in autumn.
The deeply lobed leaves are green
throughout summer, but in autumn,
take on vibrant shades of deep red and
purple, with yellow veins. It can be
trained against a wall on supporting
wires, and is excellent on a pergola.
Grow it in a warm, sheltered spot in
full sun, in well-drained, preferably
neutral to alkaline soil.

☼ ◊ ❀ ❀ ❀
‡ to 7m (22ft)

Vitis coignetiae ♀

CLIMBER

Possibly one of the best vines for
autumn colour. This rampant climber
has large, heart-shaped green leaves
that turn vivid shades of bright red
and crimson in autumn. It is ideal for
clothing a pergola, growing through
a big tree, or for disguising a large
featureless wall. Plant it in full sun or
partial shade, in well-drained, neutral
to alkaline soil. If it gets too large,
prune it back to strong buds in winter,
to within 5cm (2in) of the previous
year's growth.

☼ ◑ ◊ ❀ ❀ ❀
‡ to 15m (50ft)

Aster 'Little Carlow' ♀

PERENNIAL

This is an upright, clump-forming aster selection that bears oval to heart-shaped, dark green leaves. In early to mid-autumn, violet blue flowers with yellow centres bloom in loose clusters 15–20cm (6–8in) wide. Ideal for the outer edge of a woodland garden or, in cooler regions, in a sunny mixed border. Grow it in part shade to full sun in moist but well-drained soil. In early summer, trim off the top third of the plant with shears to encourage a more compact, bushier shape.

☼ ☼ ◊ ✿✿✿

‡ to 90cm (36in) ↔ to 45cm (18in)

Aster novi-belgii 'Peace'

PERENNIAL

This vigorous Michaelmas daisy produces large, mauve-purple flowerheads from late summer to autumn. It is best planted at the back or middle of the herbaceous border, in full sunshine and in very fertile, moist soil. It has strong stems so supports are not essential. It should be cut back to the ground after flowering and covered with a layer of mulch for the winter. Divide every three years in spring.

☼ ◊ ✿✿✿

‡ to 90cm (36in) ↔ to 75cm (30in)

Berberis thunbergii 'Rose Glow' ♀

DECIDUOUS SHRUB

This is a vigorous, dense, spiny shrub with small, rounded, reddish-purple leaves. Later in autumn, white and pink flecks appear on the leaves, spreading so the outer leaves become variegated. In late spring it bears small clusters of red-tinged, yellow flowers. In autumn the leaves turn orange and red. It makes a dense hedge that grows to medium height; pruning should be delayed until after flowering. Plant in full sun or partial shade in well-drained soil.

☼ ☀ ◊ ❋ ❋ ❋
↕↔ to 2m (6ft)

Billardiera longiflora ♀

CLIMBER

The climbing blueberry has rather wiry stems that will climb over any suitable support. It has narrow, lance-shaped dark green leaves. The green, bell-shaped flowers of summer are followed by purplish-blue, egg-shaped fruit in autumn; some plants bear pink, red, or white fruit. Grow in a warm, sheltered site in full sun or light shade, in humus-rich, neutral to acid (lime-free) soil. In very cold areas, grow in a conservatory in containers of ericaceous compost.

☼ ☀ ◊ ❋ ❋
↕ to 2m (6ft)

Callicarpa bodinieri 'Profusion' ♀

DECIDUOUS SHRUB

The beauty berry is a striking shrub with upright branches and large, pale green leaves that are tinted bronze in spring. It produces pale pink flowers in midsummer, but is grown mainly for its colourful fruit that look just like clusters of shining, bright violet beads. These are retained on the bare branches after leaf fall. Grow in full sunshine or light, dappled shade, in well-drained, fertile soil. Planting in groups will maximize fruiting.

☀ ◐ ◊ ◊ ❀ ❀

‡ to 3m (10ft) ↔ to 2.5m (8ft)

Cercidiphyllum japonicum 'Rotfuchs'

DECIDUOUS TREE

The katsura tree is a fast-growing, spreading tree with small, heart-shaped, mid-green leaves. These emerge bronze when young, but the tree is grown mainly for its autumn colour, with the leaves turning to pale yellow, orange, red, or pink before they fall. At this time, the tree also exudes a "burnt-sugar" perfume. The best foliage colours are seen on neutral to acid soils. Grow in fertile, moist but well-drained ground, with plenty of depth for the roots.

☀ ◐ ◊ ◊ ❀ ❀ ❀

‡ to 20m (70ft) ↔ to 15m (50ft)

Colchicum agrippinum ♀

PERENNIAL CORM

This autumn-flowering colchicum has
funnel-shaped, purplish-pink flowers
that are marked with a conspicuous
chequerboard pattern. It has upright,
slightly wavy, strap-shaped leaves that
appear in early spring but disappear by
summer. The corms should be planted
10cm (4in) deep in summer or early
autumn. Grow in an open situation in
full sun, in deep, fertile, well-drained
soil. It is suitable for a rock garden, a
trough or can be grown in a container.

☼ ◊ ✽✽✽

‡ to 15cm (6in) ↔ to 10cm (4in)

Crocus medius ♀

PERENNIAL CORM

This is an attractive dwarf crocus, with
funnel-shaped, bright purple flowers in
late autumn. The narrow leaves, which
are green with a silvery-white line down
the centre, appear with or just after the
flowers. It is suitable for naturalizing in
grass, or for planting on a rock garden.
Grow it in full sunshine, in gritty, very
well-drained, poor to moderately fertile
soil. It prefers dry conditions during the
summer when it is dormant.

☼ ◊ ✽✽✽

‡ to 8cm (3in) ↔ to 2.5cm (1in)

Gaultheria mucronata 'Mulberry Wine' ♀

EVERGREEN SHRUB

This bushy shrub has shining, spine-tipped, dark green leaves. In late spring and summer, it bears small white flowers that are followed, in autumn, by glossy fruits that ripen to dark purple. Grow in partial shade, in acid (lime-free), humus-rich, moist soil. Grow male and female plants together to ensure fruiting. Gaultherias associate well with heathers and are suitable for woodland gardens. There are also varieties with pink, red, or white fruits.

☀ ◊ ❀❀❀

‡↔ to 1.2m (4ft)

Liriope muscari ♀

PERENNIAL

Lilyturf is a densely clump-forming, evergreen perennial, with narrow, strap-shaped, dark green leaves. In late summer and early autumn, it produces long, slender spikes of small violet-mauve flowers. Plant it in partial or full shade, in acid to neutral, preferably moist but well-drained soil. It will tolerate dry, shady conditions. Use it as ground cover, in a woodland garden, or for planting towards the front of a border. Overcrowded clumps can be divided in spring.

☀ ◊ ◊ ❀❀❀

‡ to 30cm (12in) ↔ to 45cm (18in)

Sorbus reducta ♀
DECIDUOUS SHRUB

The upright, suckering stems of this unusual shrubby rowan spread to form a dense, low thicket. The finely divided leaves turn red and purple in autumn. In spring, it bears clusters of small white flowers, followed by pink-flushed white berries. Plant in an open site in full sun, in humus-rich, moderately fertile, well-drained soil. It is good for small town gardens and roadside situations as it tolerates pollution. Pull out unwanted stems when still young and soft.

☼ ◊ ❀❀❀
‡↔ to 30cm (12in)

Tricyrtis formosana ♀
PERENNIAL

This vigorous perennial spreads by means of underground stems. In autumn, it produces small pinkish-purple flowers, patterned with purple spots. It has slightly hairy, branched stems and glossy, dark green leaves. Plant it in a sheltered, shady situation, in moist but well-drained, humus-rich soil. In cold gardens it needs a deep mulch of straw, leafmould, or dry bracken to protect it from hard frost. It is an excellent plant for a damp woodland garden or a shady border.

☼ ☽ ◊ ◑ ❀❀❀
‡ to 1m (3ft) ↔ to 45cm (18in)

Aconitum carmichaelii 'Arendsii' ♥

PERENNIAL

This monkshood makes a striking display with its tall spikes of deep blue flowers that appear from early to mid-autumn. An upright plant with deeply lobed, dark green leaves, it is suitable for a woodland garden, and is also successful in a shaded mixed or herbaceous border. Plant in partial shade and in moist, fertile soil. It is best in a site sheltered from strong winds; support the stems with canes. All parts are toxic.

☀ ◊ ◆ ❀❀❀

‡ to 1.5m (5ft) ↔ to 30cm (12in)

Aster x *frikartii* 'Wunder von Stäfa' ♥

PERENNIAL

A superb plant for the middle of a border, this tall aster has dark green leaves and stiffly upright stems. Bright blue flowers with yellow centres are produced from late summer until early autumn. Plant in moderately fertile, well-drained, preferably alkaline soil, in full sun. After flowering, cut stems back to the ground and apply a layer of mulch. It can be increased quickly by division in spring.

☀ ◊ ❀❀❀

‡ to 70cm (28in) ↔ to 40cm (16in)

Ceanothus '**Autumnal Blue**' ♀

EVERGREEN SHRUB

The majority of Californian lilacs flower during spring or early summer, but this one produces clusters of small, vivid blue flowers in late summer to early autumn. It has broadly oval, glossy, dark green leaves. Plant it in full sun, with some protection from cold winds, in fertile, well-drained soil. It rarely needs pruning, but if wayward shoots spoil the symmetry of the shrub, they should be removed when it has finished flowering.

☼ ◊ ❀❀
↕↔ to 3m (10ft)

Gentiana sino-ornata ♀

PERENNIAL

The beautiful autumn gentian overwinters as a rosette of glossy, dark green leaves. Low, spreading shoots appear in spring, each developing at its tip an upward-pointing, deep blue flower in autumn. The base of the flower's throat is greenish white, marked with distinct purplish-blue lines radiating from the centre. Plant it in humus-rich, moist but well-drained, acid (lime-free) or neutral soil with some shade from strong summer sunshine. It is suitable for a rock garden or trough.

❉ ◊ ◊ ❀❀❀
↕ to 5cm (2in) ↔ to 30cm (12in)

Hordeum jubatum
PERENNIAL

The squirrel-tail grass is a tufted grass with arching, narrow, green leaves. The attractive, nodding flowerheads, with their long, feathery bristles, appear in summer. They are green when young, turning pale buff-beige in autumn. Plant in full sun, in well-drained, moderately fertile soil in a herbaceous border or wild garden. It is also grown for cutting, which should be done before the flowerheads have set seed.

☼ ◊ ✿✿✿

‡ to 60cm (24in) ↔ to 30cm (12in)

Kniphofia 'Percy's Pride'
PERENNIAL

This red-hot poker forms clumps of tough, slender, arching leaves and produces stout-stemmed heads of tubular flowers in late summer and early autumn. Green in bud, the flowers open greenish yellow and become cream with age. Grow in a sunny or partially shaded site, in deep, fertile, moist but well-drained soil. Cover young plants with a protective mulch in their first winter, and cut back old growth in spring.

☼ ☀ ◊ ◖ ✿✿

‡ to 1m (3ft) ↔ to 50cm (20in)

Miscanthus sinensis 'Silberfeder' ♀

PERENNIAL

This tall grass forms a large clump of arching, mid-green leaves and, in early and mid-autumn, upright stems bearing silvery-buff flowerheads. Suitable for most soils, it grows best in full sun, in moderately fertile, moist but well-drained soil. The flowerheads can be left in place during winter but should be cut down to the ground, together with any dead growth, in early spring. This grass is easily increased by dividing established clumps in spring.

☼ ◊ ◖ ❀❀❀

‡ to 2.5m (8ft) ↔ to 1.2m (4ft)

Miscanthus sinensis 'Zebrinus' ♀

PERENNIAL

Zebra grass will bring drama and height to a mixed or herbaceous border, or a gravel bed. It bears tall, strap-like foliage marked with yellow horizontal bands. This grass forms a large clump and produces spikes of silky, maroon flowerheads in the autumn. Leave the foliage and flowers to dry to a buff colour during the autumn and winter, and then cut them down in spring to make way for new growth.

☼ ☀ ◊ ◖ ❀❀

‡ to 1.2m (4ft) ↔ to 45cm (18in)

Panicum virgatum 'Heavy Metal'

PERENNIAL

This is a particularly upright-growing switch grass. In late summer it produces beautiful, nodding spikes of small, purple-green flowers. The metallic, bluish-green leaves turn golden yellow in late autumn and finally light brown in winter. It has a beautiful winter presence in the garden, especially when the flowerheads are left in place. Grow in a sunny site, in well-drained, moderately fertile soil. Cut back before growth begins in early spring.

☼ ◊ ❀ ❀ ❀
‡ to 1m (3ft) ↔ to 75cm (30in)

Pennisetum alopecuroides 'Hameln'

PERENNIAL

Fountain grass is a clump-forming plant with flat, pointed, dark evergreen leaves. 'Hameln' is compact and, in summer and early autumn, it bears long, arching spikes of pale green flowers. The leaves turn yellow before they die down and the flowers age to a warm, pale grey-brown. Grow in full sun, in moderately fertile, well-drained soil. Provide a protective winter mulch in cold areas or grow in containers. Cut back in spring before growth begins.

☼ ◊ ❀ ❀
‡ to 1.5m (5ft) ↔ to 1.2m (4ft)

Prunus laurocerasus 'Caucasica'

EVERGREEN SHRUB

This reliable cherry laurel is a broad-leaved shrub with dense, glossy dark green foliage. Dependable all year round, it is particularly nice in autumn for the small red fruits that ripen to black, and also in mid- to late spring for its abundant spikes of white flowers, which sometimes repeat in autumn. Plant as a specimen shrub or boundary hedge. It establishes quickly and will tolerate hard pruning. 'Otto Luyken' is a smaller variety which grows up to 1m (3ft) tall.

☼ ☀ ◐ ◑ ❀ ❀ ❀
‡↔ to 8m (25ft)

Woodwardia radicans

PERENNIAL FERN

The European chain fern is a tall, architectural plant with large and arching, dark green, feathery fronds. It is evergreen, with the overwintering leaves taking on coppery tints. It makes an impressive plant for a large pot, performing best in a bark-based compost with added grit and leafmould. In the garden, site in a damp, shady place. It should survive outdoors easily in mild areas, otherwise mulch with straw and bracken. The arching fronds may take root at their tips, making new plants.

☼ ◑ ❀ ❀
‡ to 2m (6ft) ↔ to 3m (10ft)

Ajania pacifica

PERENNIAL

Related to chrysanthemums, this low-growing, mound-forming perennial or small shrub has attractive lobed green leaves highlighted by a silver line around the outer edges. In early autumn, small yellow flowers bloom in dense clusters. It spreads slowly and makes good ground cover in mixed borders or rock gardens. It thrives in well-drained soil in full sun and tolerates poor soil and drought, once established.

☼ ◊ ◖ ◗ ✿ ✿ ✿

‡ to 30cm (12in) ↔ to 90cm (36in)

Betula pendula 'Tristis' ♀

DECIDUOUS TREE

This elegant, fast-growing tree has white bark and cascading branches bearing diamond-shaped, dark green leaves that turn bright golden-yellow in autumn. It bears long, hanging yellow catkins in early spring. With its narrow crown, it is ideal for a small garden and casts little shade. Plant it as a specimen tree or in a group, in full sun or light, dappled shade. It tolerates a range of soils but prefers it moist but well-drained and moderately fertile.

☼ ☀ ◊ ◖ ✿ ✿ ✿

‡ to 25m (80ft) ↔ to 10m (30ft)

Calluna vulgaris 'Robert Chapman' ♀

EVERGREEN SHRUB

This heather has dense, golden-yellow foliage and bears spikes of purple-pink flowers in late summer. In winter, the leaves take on orange and red shades, retaining the colour until the new growth emerges the following spring. Plant in a group to maximize its effect; it associates well with other heathers with different foliage tints. Grow in sun, in well-drained, acid (lime-free) soil that is humus-rich. Shear off flowered shoots in spring to keep it compact.

☼ ◊ ❀❀❀

‡ to 25cm (10in) ↔ to 65cm (26in)

Chrysanthemum 'Pennine Alfie' ♀

PERENNIAL

In early autumn, this chrysanthemum has bright yellow, semi-double flowers, with spoon-shaped petals and bright red bases. Plant it in a sunny border, in fertile, moist but well-drained soil. Support the stems with canes. Lift plants after flowering and overwinter in frost-free conditions. Plant out in spring after the final frost and raise new plants from basal cuttings.

☼ ◊ ◗ ❀❀

‡ to 1.2m (4ft) ↔ to 75cm (30in)

Chrysanthemum 'Wendy' ♀
PERENNIAL

A spray chrysanthemum with light bronze, double flowers in early autumn. The outer petals point downwards, rather like an umbrella. For extra large flowers, remove all but four of the buds. Support stems with canes. Lift plants after flowering and overwinter in frost-free conditions. Plant out in spring once frosts are finished, or raise new plants from basal cuttings taken in winter. Grow in reasonably fertile, moist but well-drained soil in a sunny position.

☼ ◊ ◊ ✿ ✿

‡ to 1.2m (4ft) ↔ to 75cm (30in)

Clematis 'Bill MacKenzie' ♀
CLIMBER

In late summer and early autumn, this vigorous climber produces hanging, bell-shaped flowers up to 8cm (3in) across. The blooms are yellow with red anthers and are followed by feathery, silvery seedheads. Plant in fertile, humus-rich, moist but well-drained soil, with the plant's base in shade and the upper growth in sun or light shade. Provide support. In spring, cut back the previous year's growth to a pair of strong buds, about 20cm (8in) from the base.

☼ ☼ ◊ ◊ ✿ ✿ ✿

‡ to 7m (22ft)

Clematis rehderiana ♀
CLIMBER

One of the more unusual species of clematis, with clusters of small, nodding, primrose-yellow flowers that smell like cowslips. It flowers from the middle of summer to autumn. Plant in fertile, humus-rich, moist but well-drained soil, in full sun or partial shade, but with the roots shaded and kept cool with a gravel mulch. Grow it on supports against a fence or wall, over a pergola or into a tree. Cut back hard in spring and trim each shoot to a pair of strong buds, 20cm (8in) from the base.

☼ ◑ ◊ ◐ ❁ ❁ ❁ *f*
‡ to 7m (22ft)

Clematis tangutica
CLIMBER

This late-flowering clematis has bluish green, divided leaves and from midsummer to autumn, produces large numbers of hanging, bell-shaped, bright yellow flowers. They are followed by silky seedheads that last into winter. Grow it up a trellis, through a small tree, or allow it to scramble over a bank as ground cover. Plant in fertile, humus-rich, moist but well-drained soil, in full sun or partial shade with the roots in cool shade. Cut back hard in spring to within 20cm (8in) of the base.

☼ ◑ ◊ ◐ ❁ ❁ ❁
‡ to 6m (20ft)

Cotoneaster frigidus 'Fructu Luteo'

DECIDUOUS SHRUB

The upright stems of this shrubby or tree-like cotoneaster arch gracefully as it matures. The narrow leaves are dull green but develop golden tints in autumn. In summer, the branches are wreathed with white flowers that give rise to creamy-yellow fruit in autumn. Grow in sun or light dappled shade, in any well-drained, moderately fertile soil. Use as an ornamental screen, for the back of a shrub border, or as a specimen.

☼ ☀ ◊ ❀❀❀
‡↔ to 10m (30ft)

Cotoneaster 'Rothschildianus' ♥

EVERGREEN SHRUB

This vigorous, spreading shrub has narrow, pale green leaves and clusters of white flowers along the arching branches in early summer. In autumn, it produces clusters of attractive golden-yellow fruit. It is an extremely beautiful shrub for the back of a mixed or shrub border and, where there is room, makes an attractive specimen. Plant it in full sun or partial shade, in any moderately fertile, well-drained soil.

☼ ☀ ◊ ◊ ❀❀❀
‡↔ to 5m (15ft)

Ginkgo biloba ♀
DECIDUOUS TREE

The maidenhair tree makes an elegant addition to medium to large gardens, particularly urban front gardens as it tolerates air pollution. It is valued for its unmistakable, butterfly-shaped, wavy-edged, bright green leaves, which take on lovely buttery yellow tints in autumn before they fall. People are often surprised to learn that it is a conifer, and so bears no flowers. Tolerant of most well-drained, fertile soils. Prune out dead, diseased, crossing, or wayward shoots in late winter.

☼ ◐ ◊ ✲✲✲

‡ to 30m (100ft) ↔ to 8m (25ft)

Gleditsia triacanthos '**Sunburst**' ♀
DECIDUOUS TREE

This golden-leaved honey locust is a conical tree with an open tracery of spreading branches. The delicate, ferny leaves are golden yellow in spring, later turning green, then brilliant yellow in autumn. 'Sunburst' is less vigorous and thorny than the species and makes a beautiful specimen for smaller gardens, especially in urban situations as it tolerates pollution. Plant it in full sun, in any well-drained, fertile soil.

☼ ◊ ✲✲✲

‡ to 12m (40ft) ↔ to 10m (30ft)

Hamamelis virginiana
DECIDUOUS SHRUB

The Virginian witch hazel is an upright shrub with oval green leaves that turn bright yellow in autumn. As they begin to fall, small clusters of spidery yellow flowers are produced. Plant it in full sunshine or partial shade, in moderately fertile, moist but well-drained, neutral to acid (lime-free) soil. It will grow in deep soils over chalk. It prefers an open site but with some shelter from strong wind. Grow it as a specimen, at the back of a shrub border or in a woodland garden.

☼ ☀ ◊ ◑ ❀ ❀ ❀
‡↔ to 4m (12ft)

Helichrysum splendidum ♀
EVERGREEN SHRUB

This clump-forming shrub has white-woolly stems and masses of tiny, silver-grey leaves. The deep yellow flowerheads appear at the tips of upright stems from late summer to autumn. They can be cut and dried for winter arrangements. It is drought tolerant and excellent for a hot, sunny bank or a mixed or herbaceous border. Grow in full sun, in very well-drained, poor to moderately fertile soil. Trim each year in spring to keep it compact. It may not survive cold wet winters.

☼ ◊ ❀ ❀ ❀
‡↔ to 1.2m (4ft)

Ilex x *altaclerensis* 'Golden King' ♀

EVERGREEN SHRUB

This variegated holly is a compact, evergreen shrub with glossy, dark green leaves edged in gold; the leaf margins may be smooth or softly toothed. The flowers are insignificant but develop into red berries in autumn. It is a wonderful shrub, ideal during the colder months when it provides important structure; birds love hollies for their fruit and for the shelter they provide. Clipped each spring, hollies can also be transformed into interesting shapes.

☼ ☽ ◊ ◊ ❁ ❁ ❁

‡ to 30m (20ft) ↔ to 4m (12ft)

Kirengeshoma palmata ♀

PERENNIAL

This is a clump-forming perennial with dark stems bearing deeply lobed, slightly hairy, pale green leaves. In late summer and early autumn, it produces nodding, tubular, pale yellow flowers that have a waxy texture. Plant it in a shady situation, in moist, acid (lime-free) soil enriched with leafmould. It is an elegant plant for a shady border or woodland garden and looks especially beautiful at the sides of streams or pools.

☽ ◊ ❁ ❁ ❁

‡ to 1m (3ft) ↔ to 60cm (24in)

Liquidambar styraciflua 'Golden Treasure'

DECIDUOUS TREE

A slow-growing tree, the variegated sweet gum is grown mainly for its foliage. The deeply lobed, maple-like leaves are margined with rich yellow, and in late autumn, they take on dramatic tints as they turn red and purple with golden margins. It tolerates partial shade but the best autumn colour develops in full sun. Plant in neutral to acid (lime-free), moderately fertile soil that is moist but well-drained.

☼ ◐ ◊ ● ❀ ❀ ❀

‡ to 10m (30ft) ↔ to 6m (20ft)

Malus 'Golden Hornet' ♀

DECIDUOUS TREE

An attractive crab apple, 'Golden Hornet' is valued for its spherical golden-yellow fruits that appear in autumn and remain on the bare branches well into winter. In spring, it bears masses of white flowers that open from pink buds. Plant it in full sun, in fertile, moist but well-drained soil. It is best grown as a specimen tree, sited where its pretty fruit can be fully appreciated. The slightly smaller variety, *M. calocarpa*, has bright red fruits.

☼ ◊ ● ❀ ❀ ❀

‡ to 10m (30ft) ↔ to 8m (25ft)

Phygelius x *rectus* 'Moonraker'

EVERGREEN SHRUB

This is a long-flowering, small shrub with glossy, dark green leaves and long, upright spikes of hanging, creamy yellow flowers from midsummer to autumn. Plant in full sun, in fertile, moist but well-drained soil. Deadhead regularly to prolong flowering. Excellent in a mixed or herbaceous border and also good against a warm, sunny wall. In cold areas, it may lose its leaves and die back, but usually grows from the base in spring.

☼ ◊ ◊ ❀ ❀ ❀
‡ to 1m (3ft) ↔ to 1.2m (4ft)

Sambucus racemosa 'Plumosa Aurea'

DECIDUOUS SHRUB

The deeply cut, yellow leaves of this red-berried elder flush bronze when young. The creamy flowers are borne in clusters in spring and are followed by red fruits in summer. Plant this bushy shrub in a lightly shaded site as the foliage may scorch in bright sun. Grow in moderately fertile, moist but well-drained soil. For the best foliage effects, prune it hard in spring to within a few buds of the base, then feed and mulch.

☼ ◊ ◊ ❀ ❀ ❀
‡↔ to 3m (10ft)

Sorbus 'Joseph Rock'
DECIDUOUS TREE

Suitable for the smaller garden, 'Joseph Rock' grows quickly once established, forming a crown of upright branches. The finely divided, bright green leaves turn brilliant shades of orange, red, and purple during autumn, when it also bears crops of particularly attractive, creamy-yellow berries that age to golden yellow. There are clusters of white flowers in spring. Plant it in full sunshine or partial shade, in fertile, moist but well-drained, humus-rich soil.

☼ ☀ ◊ ◊ ✲ ✲ ✲

‡ to 10m (30ft) ↔ to 7m (22ft)

Sternbergia lutea
PERENNIAL BULB

The autumn daffodil bears deep yellow, goblet-shaped flowers in autumn. The narrow, dark green leaves appear with, or just after, the flowers. Plant bulbs in late summer, in a warm, sunny site, in gritty, moderately fertile, very well-drained soil. It is a beautiful plant for a rock garden, but is also suitable for a container or a trough filled with gritty compost. If conditions are suitable, it will spread to form clumps; leave bulbs undisturbed and do not divide unless overcrowding impairs flowering.

☼ ◊ ✲ ✲

‡ to 15cm (6in) ↔ to 10cm (4in)

Tricyrtis ohsumiensis
PERENNIAL

The toad lily is a clump-forming perennial with arching, slightly hairy stems and pale green leaves. In early autumn, it produces star-shaped, primrose-yellow flowers, covered with numerous tiny brown spots. Plant in a sheltered position in deep or partial shade and in moist, leafy, humus-rich, well-drained soil. It is excellent for damp woodland or a shady border. In cold areas, mulch with leafmould, straw, or dried bracken in winter.

‡ to 50cm (20in) ↔ to 23cm (9in)

Ulmus glabra 'Lutescens'
DECIDUOUS TREE

With its resistance to Dutch elm disease, the golden elm is a viable garden tree. Left to grow, it forms a large, round canopy with spreading branches, but it can easily be pollarded every two to three years (cut back to a stump) to keep it within bounds for a smallish garden. It responds to frequent cutting by sending out long branches clothed in its fine golden leaves, which take on lovely yellow shades in autumn before falling; the foliage contrasts well with other trees. It is tolerant of coastal conditions.

‡ to 40m (130ft) ↔ to 25m (80ft)

Acer campestre ♀

DECIDUOUS TREE

The field maple is a very underused tree that is ideal for planting in medium-sized gardens. It has a rounded crown of lobed, dark green leaves that take on autumn tints of apricot yellow and, in frosty autumns, shades of orange and red. It is very hardy and tolerates pollution, clay and shallow, chalky soils. It can also be included in mixed hedges and wildlife gardens. Plant it in full sun or partial shade, in any fertile, moist but well-drained soil.

☼ ☀ ◊ ◑ ❀ ❀ ❀
‡ to 8m (25ft) ↔ to 4m (12ft)

Acer platanoides 'Palmatifidum'

DECIDUOUS TREE

An attractive form of Norway maple, this tree has five-lobed leaves, with the lobes drawn out into fine points. In autumn, the leaves turn brilliant shades of orange and red. The conspicuous clusters of small flowers emerge in spring before the leaves. It is a large tree and needs plenty of space. Plant it in larger gardens, in an open situation in full sunshine or partial shade, in any fertile, moist but well-drained soil.

☼ ☀ ◊ ◑ ❀ ❀ ❀
‡ to 20m (70ft) ↔ to 10m (30ft)

Chrysanthemum 'Amber Enbee Wedding' ♀

PERENNIAL

From late summer to mid-autumn, this upright chrysanthemum produces warm golden-amber flowers with yellow-green centres. It is excellent for late colour in a mixed or herbaceous border. Grow in full sun in moist but well-drained, neutral to slightly acid soil that has been enriched with well-rotted organic matter. Support the stems with stakes to prevent them falling over in wind and heavy rain.

☼ ◊ ◐ ❀❀

‡ to 1.2m (4ft) ↔ to 75cm (30in)

Cotinus 'Flame' ♀

DECIDUOUS SHRUB

Primarily grown for its stunning autumn colour, this bushy shrub or small tree has oval, light green leaves that turn a brilliant orange-red. In hot summers, its sprays of tiny flowers hover like a smoky haze above the foliage. Grow in a shrub border or as a specimen in sun or light shade, in moist but well-drained, moderately fertile soil. Cut back hard in spring for the best foliage effects, and feed and mulch after pruning.

☼ ☼ ◊ ◐ ❀❀❀

‡ to 6m (20ft) ↔ to 5m (15ft)

Euphorbia griffithii 'Fireglow'

PERENNIAL

The upright stems of this spurge are red when young and clothed with dark green, red-veined leaves. In early summer, it produces clusters of yellow flowerheads surrounded by orange-red bracts. The leaves turn fiery orange and red in autumn. Plant in light dappled shade, in moist, humus-rich soil. It is good for woodland gardens or large shady borders. It can become invasive. The milky sap may cause an allergic skin reaction.

☀ ◐ ❀ ❀ ❀
‡ to 1m (3ft) ↔ to 50cm (20in)

Hamamelis vernalis 'Sandra' ♀

DECIDUOUS SHRUB

This Ozark witch hazel has young purple leaves that gradually turn green as spring progresses, then, in autumn, they assume glorious shades of orange and red. The spidery yellow or reddish-yellow flowers appear on the bare shoots during late winter and early spring. Plant it in full sun or partial shade, in neutral to acid (lime-free), moist but well-drained soil. Best in a site that is not exposed to strong winds. It will grow on deep soils over chalk.

☀ ☼ ◐ ◐ ❀ ❀ ❀
‡↔ to 5m (15ft)

Hippophae rhamnoides ♀
DECIDUOUS SHRUB

Sea buckthorn is a vigorous shrub with narrow, silvery grey-green leaves and spiny branches. Inconspicuous spring flowers are followed in autumn, on female plants, by clusters of shining orange fruit. Grow male and female plants together to ensure fruiting. Grow in a mixed border or as an intruder-proof hedge. Plant in full sun, in moist but well-drained soil. It thrives by the sea and tolerates exposed sites. If it becomes too large, it can be pruned hard back in late summer or when dormant.

☼ ◊ ◊ ✴✴✴
↔ to 6m (20ft)

Malus tschonoskii ♀
DECIDUOUS TREE

Prized for its autumn colour, this vigorous tree has a flame-shaped crown of rounded, glossy green leaves. It flowers in spring, bearing pink-flushed white flowers, followed by red-tinged, yellow-green fruit. In autumn, the leaves take on spectacular shades of orange, scarlet, and purple. Plant it in full sun, in moderately fertile, moist but well-drained soil. It makes a beautiful specimen tree for small to medium-sized gardens.

☼ ☀ ◊ ◊ ✴✴✴
‡ to 12m (40ft) ↔ to 7m (22ft)

Physalis alkekengi ♀
PERENNIAL

The Chinese lantern is a vigorously spreading perennial with triangular to diamond-shaped green leaves on upright stems. The nodding, creamy-white flowers appear in midsummer and are followed by orange-red, papery pods that enclose orange fruits. Plant it in full sun or partial shade in fertile, well-drained soil. It can be grown in a potager – the fruits are edible when ripe – or a border and cut for dried arrangements. It can be invasive.

☼ ☀ ◊ ❀❀

‡ to 75cm (30in) ↔ to 90cm (36in)

Rosa moyesii 'Geranium'
DECIDUOUS SHRUB

'Geranium' is a more compact form of a rather vigorous species. It has strong, arching stems and delicately divided green leaves. In summer, it bears single, cup-shaped, sealing-wax-red flowers, that are followed by spectacular bright orange-red, flask-shaped hips in autumn. It is good for a sunny mixed border or wild garden. Plant it in fertile, humus-rich, moist but well-drained soil. To keep it compact, shorten the main stems by up to a third after flowering.

☼ ◊ ◗ ❀❀❀

‡ to 3m (10ft) ↔ to 2.5m (8ft)

Stipa arundinacea

PERENNIAL

Pheasant's tail grass is an evergreen that forms a loose tussock of arching, rather leathery, dark green leaves. As the season progresses, the leaves begin to exhibit orange streaks and by winter, the whole clump has turned russet-brown. In summer, arching spikes of purplish-green flowers appear that also turn golden orange as they mature. Plant in full sun or partial shade, in moderately fertile, well-drained soil. Cut back dead foliage and flowerheads in spring.

☼ ◑ ◊ ❀❀❀

‡ to 1.5m (5ft) ↔ to 1.2m (4ft)

Zelkova serrata ♥

DECIDUOUS TREE

The Japanese zelkova is an elegant tree with wide-spreading branches that makes a fine specimen for a large garden. At maturity, the grey bark peels to reveal paler orange bark beneath. The coarsely toothed, dark green leaves rustle in the breeze and have wonderful autumn colour in shades of yellow, orange, and red. Plant it in full sun or partial shade, in deep, fertile, moist but well-drained soil. Choose a site that will lend some protection from cold, dry winds when young.

☼ ◑ ◊ ◊ ❀❀❀

‡ to 30m (100ft) ↔ to 25m (80ft)

WINTER

The dark, cold months of winter need not be without cheer. Many plants flower in winter, and while few have large and exuberant blooms, several are unsurpassed for scent – the witch hazels (*Hamamelis*), wintersweet (*Chimonanthus*), and shrubby honeysuckles are among them. Mahonias produce large sprays of highly fragrant flowers in the very depths of winter and the scented white flowers of *Viburnum farreri* appear in all but the coldest spells.

Consider too the many brightly foliaged evergreens that bring living colour to the winter garden – and provide a backdrop all year round – such as the variegated hollies, *Euonymus fortunei*, and skimmias bedecked with buds and berries. Some, such as the heaths and heathers (*Erica* and *Calluna*), assume the most vivid shades of orange, gold, and red in winter, often prompted or enhanced by periods of very intense cold.

BARK AND SEEDHEADS

This is the best time to appreciate the branch structure of deciduous trees and enjoy the colour and texture of their bark, so often overlooked when trees are in full leaf. The snake bark maples, such as *Acer grosseri* var. *hersii*, are striped green and white and the peeling papery bark of *A. griseum* glows coppery red in low winter light. Young stems of dogwoods also look dramatic at this time: vibrant red in *Cornus sanguinea* 'Winter Beauty' and *C. alba* 'Sibirica', while those of *C. alba* 'Kesselringii' are purple.

The dried seedheads of many plants also have their part to play, notably the silvery heads of pampas grass (*Cortaderia*). Leave them to stand after the autumn clear up, they look stunning when rimmed with winter frost. Any seeds will be appreciated by the birds, which will also be lured into the garden by berries lingering on pyracanthas and cotoneasters.

Abeliophyllum distichum
DECIDUOUS SHRUB

The white forsythia has spreading branches clothed with oval, dark green leaves in summer. In late winter and early spring, on bare branches, it carries clusters of small, white flowers that are invaluable for bringing fragrance into the winter garden. It performs best if trained against a sunny wall in a sheltered site, but it can also be planted in a mixed border or as a free-standing shrub. Grow it in full sun, in fertile, well-drained soil.

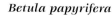

☼ ◊ ❀❀❀ *f*
‡↔ to 1.5m (5ft)

Betula papyrifera
DECIDUOUS TREE

The paper birch has pure white bark that peels off in large sheets to expose the new, pale orange-brown bark beneath. Yellow, hanging catkins appear in spring and the oval, dark green leaves turn attractive shades of yellow and orange in autumn. Plant it as a specimen tree; the white bark is seen at its best against a warm red brick wall or a dark background of evergreen shrubs. Grow in full sun or light shade, in moderately fertile, moist but well-drained soil.

☼ ◑ ◊ ◑ ❀❀❀
‡ to 20m (70ft) ↔ to 10m (30ft)

Galanthus elwesii ♀

PERENNIAL BULB

This is bigger than the common snowdrop in all its parts. It bears large, honey-scented white flowers, with green blotches, in late winter. It is a robust plant with broad, slightly twisted, waxy, bluish green leaves. Plant bulbs in early autumn in partial shade, in humus-rich, moist but well-drained soil. It does particularly well on alkaline soil. Grow in a woodland garden, naturalized in grass or at the front of a mixed or herbaceous border. Divide large clumps after flowering while still in leaf.

‡ to 30cm (12in) ↔ to 8cm (3in)

Galanthus nivalis ♀

PERENNIAL BULB

The common snowdrop is a small plant with narrow, waxy leaves and hanging, sweetly scented flowers in winter. Plant the bulbs in early autumn. It can be used beneath trees or shrubs, naturalized in grass, or on a rock garden. It grows best in partial shade, in humus-rich, moist but well-drained soil, including alkaline soil. In suitable conditions, it will self-seed freely to form extensive colonies. Divide large clumps after flowering while still in leaf.

‡ to 15cm (6in) ↔ to 8cm (3in)

Helleborus niger ⚜
PERENNIAL

The Christmas rose is a clump-forming perennial with thick, leathery, dark green leaves that remain green over winter. The large, white, saucer-shaped flowers appear in early winter and remain until early spring; they have green centres and yellow stamens, and turn pink as they age. Plant in heavy, neutral to alkaline soil, in dappled or partial shade. It suits a woodland garden and can be appreciated fully in a container placed close to the house. Slugs and snails can be a problem.

☀ ◊ ❀❀❀
‡↔ to 30cm (12in)

Lonicera fragrantissima
DECIDUOUS SHRUB

This honeysuckle is a bushy, spreading shrub. In late winter and early spring, it produces clusters of fragrant, creamy-white flowers on bare branches, followed by dull red berries. In mild gardens the oval leaves may be held through winter. Plant it in full sun or partial shade, in any well-drained soil. It is suitable for planting in a shrub border and can be grown as a screen or in a mixed hedge. It is also effective flanking a frequently used entrance to make the most of its winter scent.

☀ ☀ ◊ ❀❀❀ *f*
‡ to 2m (6ft) ↔ to 3m (10ft)

Narcissus cantabricus

PERENNIAL BULB

The white hoop-petticoat is one of
the earliest flowering narcissus. The
blooms have a white, funnel-shaped
trumpet surrounded by smaller outer
petals. The leaves are narrow, dark
green and almost cylindrical. It needs
sharp drainage, and dry conditions
for its summer dormancy. Grow it in
a raised bed or rock garden in very
gritty soil, or in pots of one part grit
to two parts loam-based compost and
keep it in a cold frame during the
summer months.

☼ ◊ ❋ ❋ ❋
‡ to 20cm (8in) ↔ to 5cm (2in)

Rubus cockburnianus

DECIDUOUS SHRUB

This is an outstanding ornamental
ghost bramble with prickly, deep purple
stems that are covered with a striking,
waxy white bloom. The dark green
leaves are covered beneath with greyish
white hairs. Plant it in full sun, in
well-drained, fertile soil. It can be
grown in a wild garden or mixed border;
the winter stems stand out best against
a dark background. Cut canes to the
ground each year in spring to ensure
plenty of new young stems. Feed and
mulch after pruning.

☼ ◊ ❋ ❋ ❋
‡↔ to 2.5m (8ft)

Sarcococca hookeriana 'Purple Stem'

EVERGREEN SHRUB

The modest white flowers, tinted pink in this variety of Christmas box, emit a rich honey-like scent. The glossy, dark green leaves grow from purple shoots. The flowers are followed by blue-black fruit. It thrives in deep or partial shade, in humus-rich, moist but well-drained soil; it tolerates sun in reliably moist soil. Excellent in a woodland garden or in a sheltered niche where the fragrance intensifies in the still air.

☀ ❂ ○ ◊ ◊ ❋ ❋ ❋ *f*

↕ to 1.5m (5ft) ↔ to 2m (6ft)

Skimmia japonica 'Wakehurst White'

EVERGREEN SHRUB

An attractive shrub with oval, glossy, dark green leaves. Clusters of small, fragrant white flowers open in spring. They are followed by spherical white fruit that persist into winter. Grow in a mixed border or woodland garden and plant a male form nearby to ensure fruit, as male and female flowers are usually borne on separate plants. It prefers some shade, but tolerates sun. Grow in moderately fertile, humus-rich, moist but well-drained soil.

❂ ○ ◊ ❋ ❋ ❋ *f*

↕↔ to 6m (20ft)

Viburnum farreri ♀
DECIDUOUS SHRUB

This upright shrub has highly fragrant,
white or pink-tinged flowers, which
appear on bare branches in late autumn
and winter. The leaves emerge bronze-
green, turn dark green as the season
progresses, then colour in shades of
red-purple in autumn before they fall.
Plant this viburnum in full sun or
partial shade, in fertile, moist but
well-drained soil. Use it in a mixed or
shrub border or as a specimen, for its
shape improves with age.

☼ ❂ ◊ ◖ ✿ ✿ ✿ *f*
↕ to 3m (10ft) ↔ to 2.5m (8ft)

Viburnum tinus 'Eve Price' ♀
EVERGREEN SHRUB

This is a justifiably popular shrub with
large, oval, dark green leaves. It has
dense clusters of pink buds, deep pink
in 'Eve Price', which open in winter and
early spring to white flowers. During
summer, it bears small bluish-black
fruit. Plant in fertile, moist but well-
drained soil, in sun or light shade. Use
it as a flowering hedge or screen, in a
woodland garden or in a mixed border.
Trim hedges after flowering.

☼ ❂ ◊ ◖ ✿ ✿ ✿
↕↔ to 3m (10ft)

Clematis cirrhosa '**Freckles**' ♀

CLIMBER

This evergreen climber has deeply divided leaves that turn bronze-green during winter. In late winter and early spring, it bears pale pink flowers that are heavily spotted and streaked with red within. They are followed by silky seedheads. Grow in full sun, with the roots in shade, in humus-rich, fertile, moist but well-drained soil. It is ideal for training over a pergola or wall, or through an old tree. Cut back after flowering to keep within bounds.

☼ ◑ ◊ ◗ ❁ ❁

‡ to 3m (10ft)

Cyclamen coum **Pewter Group** ♀

PERENNIAL

This tuberous perennial has dark green leaves with a pewter-silver sheen that covers almost the entire surface. The flowers appear from late winter to early spring, they range in colour from pure white to pink and carmine. Plant tubers 5cm (2in) deep, in sun or partial shade in humus-rich, rather gritty, moderately fertile, well-drained soil with added leafmould. Excellent when grown beneath deciduous trees or shrubs.

☼ ◑ ◊ ❁ ❁ ❁

‡ to 8cm (3in) ↔ to 10cm (4in)

Daphne mezereum

DECIDUOUS SHRUB

Mezereon is a compact, upright shrub, bearing masses of small, purplish-pink, fragrant flowers at the stem tips in late winter and early spring, before the narrow bluish-green leaves. They are followed by bright red, rather fleshy, toxic fruits. Plant it in full sun or partial shade, in moderately fertile, humus-rich, neutral to alkaline soil. Mezereon thrives in chalky soil. Grow it in a woodland garden, in a mixed or shrub border, or on a sunny bank.

☼ ☀ ◊ ❀❀❀ *f*
‡ to 1.2m (4ft) ↔ to 1m (3ft)

Daphne odora 'Aureomarginata' ♥

EVERGREEN SHRUB

This is an extremely attractive, rounded shrub with rather leathery, dark green leaves, set off by an irregular yellow margin. In late winter and early spring, it produces small clusters of highly fragrant white flowers that are deep pinkish-purple on the outside. It is not completely hardy, so plant in a site with shelter from cold winds. It grows best in partial shade, in neutral to slightly alkaline soil that is moist but well-drained and rich in organic matter.

☀ ◊ ❀❀ *f*
‡↔ to 1.5m (5ft)

Erica carnea 'Vivellii' ♀
EVERGREEN SHRUB

An attractive heather with dark bronze-green leaves that become completely bronzed in winter. It is very free flowering – the spikes of deep purplish pink flowers age to magenta and appear from the middle of winter to mid-spring. Plant it in full sun or partial shade, in peaty, well-drained soil. It will tolerate atmospheric pollution and also grows in alkaline soil. Clip over after flowering to keep compact.

☼ ☼ ◊ ❀❀❀

‡ to 15cm (6in) ↔ to 35cm (14in)

Prunus x *subhirtella* 'Autumnalis Rosea' ♀
DECIDUOUS TREE

This is a superb flowering cherry for the winter garden. Clusters of delicate, semi-double, blush-pink flowers appear on a skeleton of bare, spreading branches during periods of mild weather from autumn and throughout the winter until spring. The foliage is bronze-green when new in spring and turns yellow in the autumn. Plant it as a specimen tree in full sun, in fertile, moist but well-drained soil.

☼ ◊ ◊ ❀❀❀

‡↔ to 8m (25ft)

Rhododendron 'Christmas Cheer'

EVERGREEN SHRUB

This is a compact rhododendron with clusters of pink buds that open to pale pink flowers. It flowers in mild weather in winter, but it will bloom in early spring if it is cold. It is an old cultivar that was often pot-grown and forced under glass for flowers at Christmas, hence its name. Plant it in humus-rich, acid (lime-free), moist but well-drained soil in a sheltered niche in light dappled shade. Mulch annually with leafmould or chipped bark.

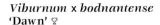
‡↔ to 2m (6ft)

Viburnum x *bodnantense* 'Dawn' ♀

DECIDUOUS SHRUB

This is one of the most reliable of all winter-flowering shrubs. The fragrant, deep pink flowers are produced on bare branches from late autumn to early spring. The oval, toothed leaves are bronze as they emerge in spring, gradually turning to dark green, then red-bronze in autumn. Plant in full sun or partial shade, in moderately fertile, moist but well-drained soil. It is ideal as a specimen or in a mixed border.

‡ to 3m (10ft) ↔ to 2m (6ft)

Acer capillipes ♀
DECIDUOUS TREE

The snake-bark maple takes on strong red tints as autumn turns to winter, first with its three-lobed leaves turning to orange and red, and then as they fall, leaving the coral-red young shoots. The striated, white-veined, greenish-grey bark is also a key feature of this small tree. In spring, long, hanging clusters of yellow flowers appear that soon develop to tiny, pink-winged fruit. Little pruning is necessary. *A.* × *conspicuum* 'Phoenix' is also valued for its red winter colour.

☼ ☀ ◊ ◖ ❀ ❀ ❀
↕↔ to 10m (30ft)

Acer griseum ♀
DECIDUOUS TREE

The paper-bark maple is an elegant tree with a spreading crown of dark green leaves that turn to vivid shades of crimson, gold, and scarlet during autumn. When leafless in winter, it reveals the beauty of its attractive bark – a rich mahogany red, peeling away on older trees to reveal the orange-red younger bark beneath. Plant it as a specimen tree or at the back of a mixed border, in full sun or partial shade, in fertile, moist, but well-drained soil.

☼ ☀ ◊ ◖ ❀ ❀ ❀
↕↔ to 10m (30ft)

Acer pensylvanicum 'Erythrocladum'

DECIDUOUS TREE

The moosewood maple is a beautiful tree with greenish, white-striped bark that becomes a vivid salmon-pink in winter; the young shoots are an especially bright red-pink. It has three-lobed, green leaves that turn to a warm shade of clear butter-yellow in autumn. Plant it in full sun or dappled shade, in fertile, moist but well-drained soil. It makes a wonderful specimen tree and its beautiful bark is a highly distinctive winter feature.

☼ ☀ ◊ ◔ ❀ ❀ ❀

‡ to 12m (40ft) ↔ to 10m (30ft)

Arbutus menziesii ♀

EVERGREEN TREE

The madroño is a broad, spreading tree with glossy, dark green, long-oval leaves. Its main attraction during the winter months is the bright reddish-brown bark, which peels away to reveal the younger, smooth olive-green bark beneath. In early summer, it bears upright clusters of waxy, creamy-white flowers, which are sometimes followed in autumn by orange-red fruit. Plant it in full sun or dappled shade, in a sheltered position on acid (lime-free), humus-rich, moist but well-drained soil.

☼ ☀ ◊ ◔ ❀ ❀ ❀

‡↔ to 15m (50ft)

Bergenia 'Ballawley' ♀
PERENNIAL

This vigorous evergreen has large, leathery, dark green leaves, flushed with red and bronze-purple in winter. In spring, upright stems bearing clusters of bright crimson flowers appear. Plant in a sheltered site, in full sun or partial shade, in humus-rich, moist but well-drained soil. It is a superb ground cover plant for a woodland garden, or for the front of a herbaceous border. Remove tatty leaves in spring. Divide clumps every 4–5 years to maintain vigour.

☀ ◑ ◊ ◑ ✽✽✽
↕↔ to 60cm (24in)

Brassica oleracea Acephala Group
BIENNIAL

The ornamental cabbages are grown for their attractive foliage, with different combinations of green, red, pink, and white leaves. Extremely useful as a winter bedding plant, they attain their deepest colouration during the cold winter months. Plant in a sunny site, preferably in lime-rich, fertile, well-drained soil, or in containers. Sow seed in spring or buy in as young plants.

☀ ◊ ✽✽✽
↕↔ to 45cm (18in)

Camellia sasanqua 'Crimson King' ♥

EVERGREEN SHRUB

One of the earliest camellias to flower, 'Crimson King' has glossy, dark green leaves and single, crimson-red flowers from late autumn through winter; it is often in bloom at Christmas. Grow in a sheltered spot, in dappled shade or sun, but away from early morning sun, in humus-rich, acid (lime-free), moist but well-drained soil. In cold areas, grow in containers of ericaceous compost and flower under glass.

☼ ☀ ◊ ◔ ❄❄

‡ to 6m (20ft) ↔ to 3m (10ft)

Cornus alba 'Sibirica' ♥

DECIDUOUS SHRUB

The red-barked dogwood is an upright shrub, usually grown for its striking red winter stems, but the dark green leaves also turn bright red before falling in autumn. Plant it in full sun, in any reasonably fertile soil. It is the new young growth that produces the brightest and longest lasting winter stem colour. Cut all stems back in the early spring, just before growth begins, to within two or three buds from the ground. Feed and mulch after pruning.

☼ ◊ ◔ ❄❄❄

‡↔ to 3m (10ft)

Cornus sanguinea 'Winter Beauty'

DECIDUOUS SHRUB

The oval green leaves of this vigorous shrub turn bright red in the autumn and, as they fall, they reveal the vivid red and orange winter shoots. Prune hard in early spring to stimulate new growth, which has the best colour. Cut back to within 2–3 buds from the base of the plant, then feed and mulch. The colour develops fully when the shrub grows in full sun. It thrives in any reasonably fertile, well-drained soil.

☼ ◊ ❀❀❀

‡ to 3m (10ft) ↔ to 2.5m (8ft)

Cotoneaster cashmiriensis ♥

EVERGREEN SHRUB

A low, mound-forming shrub with glossy, dark green leaves. Pink buds open in the summer to small white flowers. They are followed by spherical, deep red berries that persist into winter. It is one of the smaller prostrate cotoneasters, and makes a compact ground cover plant for a rock garden or sunny bank. Plant it in full sun or partial shade, in any moderately fertile, well-drained soil, including chalk. This plant is often sold as *C. cochleatus*.

☼ ◑ ◊ ❀❀❀

‡ to 30cm (12in) ↔ to 2m (6ft)

Cotoneaster conspicuus '**Decorus**' ♀

EVERGREEN SHRUB

This is an attractive, low-growing, spreading shrub with small, narrow, dark green leaves. The tiny white flowers appear in early summer and are followed by large quantities of conspicuous, spherical, bright red berries that last for most of the winter. Plant it in full sun or partial shade, in moderately fertile, well-drained soil. It is ideal for planting on a dry, sunny bank, where it will provide colour throughout the winter.

☼ ☀ ◊ ❀❀❀

‡ to 1.5m (5ft) ↔ to 2.5m (8ft)

Cotoneaster lacteus ♀

EVERGREEN SHRUB

This is a substantial shrub with large, deeply veined, oval, dark green leaves with a yellowish white, woolly undersurface. The milky white flowers appear in large clusters in summer and are followed in autumn by large bunches of bright red berries that last well into winter. It makes a dense, ornamental hedge, or can be grown in a mixed border. Trim lightly in late summer to keep in shape. Plant it in full sun or partial shade, in any well-drained, moderately fertile soil.

☼ ☀ ◊ ❀❀❀

‡↔ to 4m (12ft)

Gaultheria procumbens ♀
EVERGREEN SHRUB

Wintergreen is a creeping shrub with underground stems and glossy, dark green leaves that smell strongly of wintergreen when crushed. The white or pink, urn-shaped flowers appear in summer and are followed in autumn by bright red, aromatic fruit. It prefers partial shade, but will grow in full sun if provided with soil that is reliably moist. Grow in neutral to acid (lime-free), peaty soil. It is an excellent plant for providing ground cover in damp woodland or shady borders.

☼ ◐ ◊ ❀❀❀ *f*
‡ to 15cm (6in) ↔ indefinite

Hamamelis x *intermedia* 'Diane' ♀
DECIDUOUS SHRUB

This elegant shrub is grown for its clusters of fragrant flowers that appear on bare branches in late winter. They have thread-like, dark red petals. The rounded, bright green leaves turn red and yellow in autumn. Plant in full sun or partial shade, in moderately fertile, neutral to acid (lime-free) moist but well-drained soils rich in leafy organic matter. Grow in a shrub border or use as a specimen.

☼ ◐ ◊ ◊ ❀❀❀ *f*
‡↔ to 4m (12ft)

Ilex aquifolium 'J.C. van Tol' ♀

EVERGREEN TREE

This is a form of common holly without any prickles. The leaves are dark green and very glossy and are carried on purple stems. It is a self-fertile female plant that produces its bright red berries through the winter without the need for a male plant nearby. Plant it in full sun or partial shade, in fertile, moist but well-drained soil. It grows happily in a woodland garden and can be used as a hedge or a specimen tree. Clip hedges in summer.

☼ ◐ ◊ ❀❀❀

‡ to 6m (20ft) ↔ to 4m (12ft)

Ilex x *meserveae* BLUE PRINCESS ('Conapri')

EVERGREEN SHRUB

An attractive hybrid holly, with spiny, bluish green leaves and tiny white or pink flowers in late spring. It needs a male plant nearby to produce the glossy red fruit of autumn and winter. Grow in a woodland garden or use it to make an impenetrable hedge. Plant it in full sun or partial shade, in fertile, humus-rich, moist but well-drained soil. If it is grown as a hedge, it should be trimmed annually in summer.

☼ ◐ ◊ ❀❀❀

‡↔ to 3m (10ft)

Leucothoe SCARLETTA ('Zeblid')

EVERGREEN SHRUB

This small to medium-sized, upright shrub has lance-shaped, rather leathery leaves. They are dark red-purple in the spring, becoming dark green in summer before finally assuming red and bronze tints in the winter. In spring, it has clusters of tiny, white, narrowly pitcher-shaped flowers. It should be grown in a shady position, in acid (lime-free), humus-rich, moist soil. It is ideal for planting in a woodland garden or shady border.

☀ ☀ ◊ ❀ ❀ ❀
↕ to 2m (6ft) ↔ to 3m (10ft)

Prunus serrula ♀

DECIDUOUS TREE

This attractive flowering cherry is grown mainly for its tactile, rich coppery-red bark. This is very shiny and particularly striking on a sunny winter's day. It has narrow, dark green leaves that turn yellow in autumn and small, single, bowl-shaped white flowers in spring. It should be planted in full sun, in moderately fertile, moist but well-drained soil. It looks particularly dramatic when grown as an avenue tree, but it also makes a handsome specimen in a smaller garden.

☀ ◊ ◊ ❀ ❀ ❀
↕↔ to 10m (30ft)

Skimmia japonica 'Nymans' ♀

EVERGREEN SHRUB

This low-spreading shrub with dark green leaves is a female plant noted for its large, red winter fruits that are borne very freely if the plant is grown with a male plant nearby. They arise from the dense clusters of white spring flowers. Grow it in partial to deep shade, in moderately fertile, moist but well-drained soil. Plant in a shrub border or woodland garden. Like most skimmias, it is good in coastal and urban gardens and tolerates most soils.

☀ ☀ ◊ ◊ ❋ ❋ ❋
‡ to 1m (3ft) ↔ to 2m (6ft)

Skimmia japonica 'Rubella' ♀

EVERGREEN SHRUB

This skimmia is a compact, dome-shaped shrub with red-edged, dark green leaves. It is a male plant that produces dense clusters of deep red buds from autumn to winter. In early spring, the buds open to reveal small, fragrant white flowers. It is a good pollinator for female skimmias. Grow it in partial to deep shade, in moderately fertile, moist but well-drained soil. Plant in a shrub border or woodland garden. Also good in containers.

☀ ☀ ◊ ◊ ❋ ❋ ❋ *f*
‡↔ to 6m (20ft)

Bergenia cordifolia 'Purpurea' ♀

PERENNIAL

During late winter this evergreen produces dark, stout stems of deep magenta-purple flowers. It has substantial, leathery, mid-green leaves that turn reddish purple during the winter; the colour is most intense in very cold weather. Plant it in full sun or partial shade, in humus-rich, moist but well-drained soil. It is suitable for the front of a herbaceous border or for a woodland garden. Remove tatty leaves in spring.

☼ ◐ ◊ ◑ ❋ ❋ ❋
↕↔ to 50cm (20in)

Cornus alba 'Kesselringii'

DECIDUOUS SHRUB

This striking shrub is especially valuable for its dramatic, purplish black winter stems. Bronzed leaves open in spring, turning green and then reddish-purple in autumn. In spring, it bears clusters of white flowers that are followed in autumn by white fruit. Cut back in early spring to within a few buds from the ground to stimulate the growth of new, more deeply coloured shoots, then feed and mulch. Plant in sun any well-drained, reasonably fertile soil.

☼ ◊ ❋ ❋ ❋
↕↔ to 3m (10ft)

Cryptomeria japonica Elegans Group

EVERGREEN TREE

Japanese cedars are well worth planting as an alternative to other conifers. Not only are they reliable, but they are unusual in that their leaf colour varies with the seasons. Those of the Elegans Group take on coppery bronze-purple tints in autumn and winter. A good evergreen specimen tree for a medium to large garden, it can also be kept clipped to shape for a smaller site or planted as a hedge – choose a sheltered site. No formal pruning is necessary.

☼ ☀ ◐ ◊ ◊ ❋ ❋ ❋
‡↔ to 2m (6ft)

Iris unguicularis ♥

PERENNIAL

A wonderful winter-flowering iris with large, fragrant, pale lavender-purple or deep violet-blue blooms, marked by a large patch of yellow on the lower petals. It has upright stems and tough, grass-like evergreen leaves. Grow it in a rock garden, raised bed, on a terrace, or at the foot of a warm, sunny wall. Plant it in full sun, in gritty, very well-drained, neutral to alkaline soil. Good for cutting.

☼ ◊ ❋ ❋ ❋ *f*
‡ to 30cm (12in) ↔ indefinite

Acer grosseri var. *hersii* ♀

DECIDUOUS TREE

The snake-bark maple is an extremely attractive tree with upright, green-barked branches heavily marked with white striations with an appearance reminiscent of snake's skin. The mid-green leaves are shallowly lobed and turn yellow and orange in autumn. Clusters of pale yellow flowers hang beneath the shoots in spring, followed by pink-brown autumn fruit. Plant it as a specimen, in sun or partial shade, in fertile, moist but well-drained soil.

☼ ☀ ◊ ◑ ✿ ✿ ✿

↕↔ to 15m (50ft)

Acer pensylvanicum ♀

DECIDUOUS TREE

The moosewood maple looks equally attractive in winter and summer. In spring, it produces long clusters of small, yellow-green flowers. The lobed, bright green leaves turn clear butter-yellow in autumn, revealing the white striped, jade-green bark when they fall. Plant it in full sun or partial shade, in moist but well-drained, fertile soil. Plant close to a footpath, where the bark can be fully appreciated during the winter.

☼ ☀ ◊ ◑ ✿ ✿ ✿

↕ to 12m (40ft) ↔ to 10m (30ft)

Arum italicum 'Marmoratum' ♀

PERENNIAL

The upright, dark green, arrow-shaped leaves, heavily mottled with paler green markings, last through the winter. In early summer, greenish-white hooded flowers appear, followed by spikes of bright orange-red berries. Grow in light shade or in sun with some shade from the hottest summer sunshine. Plant tubers in spring or autumn, in humus-rich, well-drained soil. It makes good ground cover beneath deciduous shrubs, or in a woodland garden.

☀ ◊ ❋❋

‡ to 25cm (10in) ↔ to 30cm (12in)

Garrya elliptica

EVERGREEN SHRUB

The silk-tassel bush is a dense shrub with wavy-edged, leathery, greyish-green leaves. Male and female flowers are borne on separate plants; the male plants are more attractive, with longer, dangling, grey-green catkins, measuring 20cm (8in) or more, that are borne in midwinter and early spring. Plant it in full sun or partial shade, in fertile, well-drained soil. Excellent on a shady wall or shrub border and good as a specimen or as hedging in coastal gardens.

☀ ◑ ◊ ❋❋❋

‡↔ to 4m (12ft)

Helleborus viridis
PERENNIAL

The green hellebore is a deciduous, clump-forming hellebore with very deeply divided, rather leathery, dark green leaves. In late winter and early spring, it produces tall stems adorned with nodding, bright green flowers. It looks best when planted against a dark background and will grow in deep shade. Plant it in a woodland garden or a shrub border. It grows best in rather heavy, neutral or alkaline soil, in dappled shade. It often self-seeds.

☀ ☀ ◊ ❁ ❁ ❁

↕↔ to 30cm (12in)

Ribes laurifolium
EVERGREEN SHRUB

This is a low-growing shrub, with spreading branches bearing leathery, dark green leaves. In late winter and early spring, it produces substantial, hanging clusters of greenish-yellow flowers. Male and female flowers are borne on separate plants; if grown together, females produce black fruits. Plant it in a shrub border in full sun or partial shade, in moderately fertile, well-drained soil. In cold areas, plant in a sheltered spot away from cold, dry winter winds.

☀ ☀ ◊ ❁ ❁ ❁

↕ to 1m (3ft) ↔ to 1.5m (5ft)

Stachyurus praecox ♀

DECIDUOUS SHRUB

The gracefully arching branches of this spreading shrub produce hanging chains of small, pale yellow flowers in late winter and early spring. The similar *S. chinensis* flowers about two weeks later. Plant in full sun or partial shade, in fertile, humus-rich, acid (lime-free), well-drained soil, ideally against a wall or in a woodland garden. When mature, cut out the oldest flowered shoots at the base after flowering; this ensures the production of strong, new flowering stems.

☼ ◑ ◊ ❀ ❀ ❀
‡ to 4m (12ft) ↔ to 3m (10ft)

Thuja occidentalis 'Hetz Midget'

EVERGREEN SHRUB

This dwarf conifer is a slow-growing selection of the white cedar that forms a dense, rounded mound of golden green foliage that smells of apples when crushed. It is ideal as a specimen in a rock garden and associates particularly well with heathers. Grow in full sun in deep, moisture-retentive but well-drained, fertile soil. In cool gardens, plant in a sheltered place, away from cold, dry winds.

☼ ◊ ◑ ❀ ❀ ❀
‡↔ to 50cm (20in)

Azara microphylla ♀
EVERGREEN TREE

An upright, often shrubby small tree with oval, glossy, dark green leaves. In late winter and early spring, it bears clusters of small, vanilla-scented, yellow flowers. Plant it in full sun or partial shade, in humus-rich, well-drained, fertile soil. It can be grown in a shrub border but flowers best against a sheltered, sunny wall. When grown on a wall, train in the shoots when young to ensure good coverage. Then prune back after flowering to within 2–4 buds of the woody framework of main stems.

☼ ◑ ◊ ❀❀❀ *f*

‡ to 10m (30ft) ↔ to 4m (12ft)

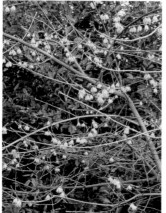

Chimonanthus praecox 'Grandiflorus' ♀
DECIDUOUS SHRUB

The wintersweet is an upright shrub with lance-shaped green leaves. It is especially valuable for the highly fragrant, nodding, deep yellow flowers that are stained red within. They appear on bare stems in winter and are excellent for cutting for winter posies. Plant it in full sun, in fertile, well-drained soil in a warm, sheltered place. Grow as a specimen or train it against a sunny wall. If wall-trained, shorten any outward-growing shoots after flowering.

☼ ◊ ❀❀❀ *f*

‡ to 4m (12ft) ↔ to 3m (10ft)

Cornus mas

DECIDUOUS SHRUB

The cornelian cherry is a vigorous shrub or small tree with spreading branches and mid-green leaves that turn red-purple in the autumn. It is most dramatic in late winter when it produces an abundance of small, yellow flowers in clusters on bare branches. Bright red fruit ripen in late summer or early autumn, often as the foliage assumes its autumn tints. Grow as a specimen, in a shrub border or woodland garden. Plant in full sun or partial shade, in any moderately fertile, well-drained soil.

‡↔ to 5m (15ft)

Cornus sericea 'Flaviramea' ♀

DECIDUOUS SHRUB

This vigorous dogwood forms a thicket of bright yellow stems that create a brilliant winter display. In summer, small white flowers are followed by white fruit in autumn, when the leaves turn vivid orange and red before falling. It looks beautiful at the side of pools or streams, especially if planted with the red-stemmed *C. sanguinea*. Grow in wet or moist soil in full sun. Cut back to the base each year in early spring, and then feed and mulch.

‡ to 2m (6ft) ↔ to 4m (12ft)

Coronilla valentina subsp. *glauca* ♀
EVERGREEN SHRUB

A dense, bushy plant with divided, blue-green leaves. In late winter, early spring, and often again in late summer, it produces clusters of bright yellow, pea-like flowers. It is suitable in a shrub border or on a sheltered wall, as it is not completely hardy and needs protection from cold winds. Plant it in full sun in sandy, moderately fertile, well-drained soil. In very cold areas, grow in a container as a conservatory plant and move outdoors in summer.

☼ ◊ ❀❀

‡ to 1.5m (5ft) ↔ to 1.5m (5ft)

Hacquetia epipactis ♀
PERENNIAL

This is a low-growing spreading perennial that produces tiny yellow flowers, surrounded by a collar of bright emerald-green, leaf-like bracts, in late winter and early spring. The brilliant green leaves only develop fully after flowering. It is suitable for planting in moist, shady situations, such as by poolsides or in a damp woodland garden. Plant it in humus-rich, moist but well-drained, acid or neutral soil. It is easily increased by dividing the clumps in the spring.

◑ ◊ ◊ ❀❀❀

‡ to 6cm (2½in) ↔ to 23cm (9in)

Hamamelis x *intermedia* '**Arnold Promise**' ♥

DECIDUOUS SHRUB

This attractive late winter-flowering shrub produces a profusion of spidery, bright yellow flowers on bare, upright branches. It is excellent in a shrub border or as a specimen, as the vivid green leaves turn red and gold in autumn. Plant in full sun or partial shade, in fertile, neutral to acid (lime-free), moist but well-drained soil.

☼ ◐ ◊ ◑ ❄ ❄ ❄

↕↔ to 4m (12ft)

Hamamelis japonica '**Sulphurea**'

DECIDUOUS SHRUB

The Japanese witch hazel is an upright, branched shrub with rounded, glossy green leaves that turn gold in autumn. In late winter the bare branches are studded with small, sulphur-yellow flowers with very narrow petals. Plant it in full sun or partial shade, in fertile, neutral to acid (lime-free), moist, but well-drained soil. Plant it in groups in a woodland garden or as a specimen. It can also be grown on deep, humus-rich soil over chalk.

☼ ◐ ◊ ◑ ❄ ❄ ❄

↕↔ to 4m (12ft)

Ilex aquifolium 'Bacciflava'

EVERGREEN TREE

'Bacciflava' is a female form of common holly with spiny, glossy, dark green leaves. With a male pollinator nearby, the tiny, insignificant flowers of spring and early summer will give rise to yellow berries that last into winter. It forms an erect, pyramidal tree that is good as a specimen and is also suitable for hedging. Trim hedges in summer. Plant in full sun or partial shade, in moist but well-drained, moderately fertile soil.

☼ ☀ ◑ ◊ ❁ ❁ ❁

‡ to 20m (70ft) ↔ to 6m (20ft)

Ilex aquifolium 'Ferox Argentea' ♀

EVERGREEN TREE

Hedgehog hollies are noted for their unusual, spine-covered leaves. This variegated type is ideal for the winter garden because it provides excellent structure when much of the garden is bare, and the foliage is bright and pretty. There are no berries as it is a male plant, but its flowers would pollinate female hollies nearby. It is ideal as a free-standing specimen, as hedging, or clipped to any shape. Remove any green foliage as it appears, as it may take over.

☼ ☀ ◑ ◊ ❁ ❁ ❁

‡ to 8m (25ft) ↔ to 4m (12ft)

Jasminum nudiflorum ♀
DECIDUOUS SHRUB

The winter jasmine is one of the most popular of winter-flowering shrubs. It has arching, scrambling, dark green stems and dark green leaves, each divided into three leaflets. It is very free flowering, bearing bright yellow, six-petalled flowers in late winter. It looks best when planted against a fence or trellis, but needs tying in to a support. Plant in full sun or partial shade, in fertile, well-drained soil. Trim after flowering to keep it dense, cutting back to strong buds.

☼ ☀ ◊ ❀ ❀ ❀
↕↔ to 3m (10ft)

Mahonia japonica ♀
EVERGREEN SHRUB

A beautiful winter-flowering shrub with upright branches clothed in spiny, divided, dark green leaves. It bears drooping spikes of strongly fragrant, lemon yellow flowers from late autumn to early spring. These are followed by an abundant crop of bluish-black berries. It provides a long season of interest in a shrub border or woodland garden. Plant it in a slightly shaded position, in humus-rich, moist but well-drained soil.

☀ ◊ ◊ ❀ ❀ ❀ *f*
 ↕ to 2m (6ft) ↔ to 3m (10ft)

Mahonia x *media* 'Charity'

EVERGREEN SHRUB

This is one of the most attractive forms of the Oregon grape. It has large, dark green leaves divided into sharply toothed leaflets. Masses of sweetly scented, bright yellow flowers are borne in dense spikes from late autumn into winter. Plant it in partial shade and moderately fertile, humus-rich, moist but well-drained soil. It makes an architectural specimen for planting in front of a wall, in a shrub border or woodland garden.

☀ ◐ ◊ ◊ ❀ ❀ ❀ *f*

↕ to 5m (15ft) ↔ to 4m (12ft)

Narcissus 'Rijnveld's Early Sensation' ♥

PERENNIAL BULB

This golden-yellow daffodil flowers in late winter, well before the other early flowering daffodils, such as 'February Gold'. It makes a valuable, long-flowering addition to the winter garden and should be planted in a bold group or naturalized in grass. Plant bulbs at one-and-a-half times their own depth in late summer. Grow in full sun, in fertile, well-drained soil. It often produces several flowers on each stem. Remove the dead flowers regularly.

☀ ◊ ❀ ❀ ❀

↕ to 35cm (14in)

Pyracantha 'Soleil d'Or'

EVERGREEN SHRUB

Pyracanthas have several seasons of interest. This one has spiny red shoots and glossy green leaves. In summer, it produces sprays of small white flowers, followed by yellow fruit that last well into winter. Plant in full sun or shade, in fertile, well-drained soil. It can be trained against a wall or fence, grown as a free-standing shrub and also makes an excellent dense, impenetrable hedge. Trim hedges in mid-spring and summer.

‡ to 3m (10ft) ↔ to 2.5m (8ft)

Viola x wittrockiana Universal Series

PERENNIAL

Universal pansies are among the most prolific of all winter-flowering plants, flowering almost non-stop from early winter to mid-spring. The colour range includes yellow, blue, mauve, maroon, red, and white, some with darker patches at the centre. Plant in sun in fertile, moist but well-drained soil. Although perennial, they are usually grown as annuals or biennials for bedding. Use in borders, containers, or hanging baskets.

‡↔ to 20cm (8in)

Calluna vulgaris 'Boskoop'

EVERGREEN SHRUB

This dense and compact heather bears spikes of lilac-pink flowers from mid-summer to late autumn. Then, the foliage, which is golden throughout the summer, begins to assume vibrant orange-red winter tints that persist until the new growth emerges in spring. Grow in full sun in humus-rich, well-drained acid soil. Clip plants lightly in spring to keep them shapely. Excellent for a rock garden, it associates well with conifers and other heathers.

☼ ◊ ❀ ❀ ❀

‡ to 30cm (12in) ↔ to 40cm (16in)

Ilex aquifolium 'Amber' ♀

EVERGREEN TREE

This is one of the most attractive forms of the common holly, with virtually spine-free, glossy, bright green leaves. The tiny, spring and early summer flowers give rise to profuse clusters of amber-yellow fruit. The tree is female and needs a male to be planted nearby to produce fruit. Plant it in full sun, in well-drained, fertile soil. It can be grown as a hedge or as an attractive specimen tree. Trim in summer, if grown as a hedge.

☼ ◊ ❀ ❀ ❀

‡ to 6m (20ft) ↔ to 2.5m (8ft)

Iris foetidissima ♀
PERENNIAL

The stinking gladwyn is so called
because the leaves smell unpleasantly
when crushed. It forms clumps of
evergreen leaves and, in early summer,
bears dull-purple, yellow-tinged flowers.
It really comes into its own, however,
when the seed pods ripen in autumn.
They split to reveal glistening orange-
red seeds that remain in place until
winter. Grow in well-drained, moderately
fertile, neutral to acid soil. It is one of
the toughest and most useful plants
for dry shade.

‡ to 90cm (36in) ↔ indefinite

Pyracantha 'Orange Glow' ♀
EVERGREEN SHRUB

This is a vigorous, upright shrub with
spiny stems and glossy, dark green
leaves. In late spring, clusters of small
white flowers are followed by masses
of orange berries that last until winter.
Plant in full sun or shade, in well-
drained, moderately fertile soil. After
flowering, shorten sideshoots back to
two or three leaves to show off the
berries. It can be trained against a wall,
but also makes an intruder-proof hedge.
Trim hedges in spring and summer.

‡↔ to 3m (10ft)

ALL SEASONS

It is a good idea to include a few reliable, undemanding plants that remain attractive in every season. They give the garden shape and structure, and provide a backdrop for transient seasonal displays. Use them to liven up a border, or to create focal points: for example, shapely conifers can serve as topiary – without the work. The cabbage palm (*Cordyline*) and New Zealand flax (*Phormium*) may appear as tender exotics but are tougher than they look. Their spiky shapes are portable in containers, and in borders they enhance a colourful display.

Climbers like ivy (*Hedera*) can be used to disguise fences and sheds, to shield an unsightly compost heap by training along a trellis, or for ground cover. Evergreen ground cover plants play a valuable role in helping to suppress weeds; low-growing junipers, silvery artemisias, and heathers are all good choices as, with minimal care, their foliage provides interest all year round.

More visual punctuation may be obtained using grasses and bamboos, especially if you have plenty of space. Bamboos are normally grown as an elegant, rustling screen, but some, like *Phyllostachys flexuosa*, grace the garden with the changing colour of their stems.

A STRUCTURAL BACKBONE

Evergreen hedges and screens can surround the entire garden or divide it into sections. Box (*Buxus sempervirens*) and yew (*Taxus baccata*) are traditional choices for clipped formal hedging and topiary, but hollies (*Ilex*) and pyracanthas form superb impenetrable hedges, and may also reward you with flowers and berries. Other conifers, apart from yew, will create a tall screen, but choose with care, as some become a nuisance if they are allowed to grow too large. Leyland cypress can reach 35m (120ft); there many more suitable alternatives for domestic situations.

Artemisia arborescens ♀

EVERGREEN SHRUB

This small, aromatic evergreen plant has very finely divided, silver-grey leaves that provide a foil for stronger flower colours in a sunny border or gravel garden. It also produces small yellow flowerheads in late summer and autumn. Plant it in a sunny situation, in moderately fertile, well-drained soil. It can become leggy and should be pruned hard in spring to keep it neat and compact. It dislikes cold, wet winters and in very cold areas is best grown close to a warm, sheltered wall.

☼ ◊ ✽✽✽ *f*

‡ to 1m (3ft) ↔ to 1.5m (5ft)

Artemisia stelleriana 'Boughton Silver'

PERENNIAL

This attractive evergreen forms a low, spreading clump of silver-grey leaves. It looks superb when planted against a background of darker foliage at the front of a border, or it can be used as path edging or in a gravel garden. The foliage looks better if the insignificant yellow flowers are removed before they open in late summer. It prefers a position in full sun, and well-drained, moderately fertile soil.

☼ ◊ ✽✽✽

‡ to 15cm (6in) ↔ to 45cm (18in)

Ballota acetabulosa ♀
EVERGREEN SHRUB

The upright, white-woolly stems of this compact, woody plant are clothed all year with rounded, greyish-green leaves. In summer, it produces spires of small, purple-pink flowers. It grows well in hot, dry sites in full sun, and poor, very well-drained soil. It may not survive cold, wet winters, but where it does, cut it back hard in spring to keep it bushy. Grow it as a backdrop for bright flower colours in a raised bed, sunny border, or in gravel and Mediterranean-style gardens. *Ballota pseudodictamnus* is hardier.

 ☼ ◊ ❀❀ *f*
‡ to 60cm (24in) ↔ to 75cm (30in)

Betula utilis 'Silver Shadow' ♀
DECIDUOUS TREE

Birch trees are a year-round asset to a garden. They are valued for their graceful winter skeleton, attractive bark, yellow catkins in spring, and leaves that colour yellow in the autumn. 'Silver Shadow' has silvery bark and makes a beautiful specimen tree, especially against a dark background of evergreen trees or shrubs. Plant it in sun or dappled shade in fertile, moist, well-drained soil.

 ☼ ☀ ◊ ◊ ❀❀❀
‡ to 18m (60ft) ↔ to 10m (30ft)

Cortaderia selloana '**Silver Comet**'

PERENNIAL GRASS

The arching clumps of tough, leathery evergreen leaves of pampas grass create an architectural presence throughout the year. The soft, silvery plumes arise in late summer and persist through the winter. Grow it as a specimen in well-drained, fertile soil in full sun. Remove the old flowerheads and dead foliage before growth begins in spring. The leaves are sharp-edged, so wear tough gloves to protect the hands.

☼ ◊ ❀ ❀ ·

‡ to 1.5m (5ft) ↔ to 1m (3ft)

Eucalyptus pauciflora subsp. *niphophila* ♀

EVERGREEN TREE

The alpine snow gum is fast-growing once established, and has attractive bark that peels to form a patchwork of green, grey, and cream. The leaves are blue-green and rounded in the juvenile form, lance-shaped when mature. Plant it in full sun in fertile, moist, well-drained soil. Grow it as a specimen tree or, in small gardens and borders, prune it hard every year in spring to produce a shrub with colourful young foliage. Feed and mulch after pruning.

☼ ◊ ◊ ❀ ❀ ❀

‡↔ to 6m (20ft)

Euonymus fortunei 'Silver Queen'

EVERGREEN SHRUB

Valued for its year-round foliage, this compact shrub scrambles upwards if given support. The oval, leathery leaves are pale yellow when young, later becoming green with an irregular white margin that flushes pink during cold weather. Excellent for brightening a dull corner, it is also very effective when grown against a wall. Plant it in full sun or light shade in any but waterlogged soil. Trim shrubs in mid-spring to keep them within bounds.

☼ ☀ ◐ ◊ ❀ ❀ ❀

‡ to 2.5m (8ft) ↔ to 1.5m (5ft)

Hebe pinguifolia 'Pagei' ♥

EVERGREEN SHRUB

The purple stems of this tough hebe are clothed in silvery, blue-grey leaves that remain attractive throughout the year. It produces short spikes of small white flowers over a long period, from late spring to summer. Plant it in full sun or partial shade, in moderately fertile, moist, well-drained soil. Use it at the front of a mixed border, in a rock garden, or as ground cover.

☼ ☀ ◊ ◊ ❀ ❀

‡ to 30cm (12in) ↔ to 60cm (24in)

Sedum spathulifolium 'Cape Blanco' ♔

PERENNIAL

This evergreen stonecrop forms dense, low-growing mats of silvery-green foliage, comprised of rosettes of fleshy leaves covered in a waxy white bloom. The mats are spangled in summer with tiny, star-shaped yellow flowers. It is ideal for raised beds, troughs, and the tops of dry-stone walls. Grow it in gritty, poor to moderately fertile, very well-drained soil. The silvery foliage develops best in full sun, but the plant tolerates light shade.

☼ ◊ ❀ ❀ ❀

‡ to 5cm (2in) ↔ indefinite

Sempervivum arachnoideum ♔

PERENNIAL

The cobweb houseleek is an evergreen mat-former with rosettes of fleshy, dark green, red-tipped leaves covered with a fine web of white hairs. In late summer it may produce sturdy stems with rose-red, star-shaped flowers at the tips. Each rosette dies after flowering, but new ones are readily formed to fill the gap. Plant it in full sun, in poor to moderately fertile, very well-drained soil. Grow it in a trough, pot, rock garden, or on a dry stone wall.

☼ ◊ ❀ ❀ ❀

‡ to 12cm (5in) ↔ to 10cm (4in)

Senecio cineraria 'Silver Dust' ♀

EVERGREEN SHRUB

This attractive shrub has deeply divided leaves, which are covered with greyish-white felt. It produces mustard-yellow, daisy-like flowers in summer, although these should be removed before they open to maintain its foliage effect. Plant it in full sun and slightly fertile, well-drained soil. It is reasonably hardy, but dislikes winter wet, and semi-ripe cuttings should be taken at the end of the summer to guarantee new plants the following year.

☼ ◊ ❀❀

↕↔ to 30cm (12in)

Stachys byzantina

EVERGREEN PERENNIAL

Lambs' ears form an evergreen, soft-textured mat of bright, silvery white-woolly leaves. In summer, it produces upright, hairy stems of pinkish purple flowers, but for the best foliage effect remove these before the blooms open. It makes an excellent ground cover plant beside a path, at the front of a border, or in a gravel garden. It can become rather straggly, and old growth should be cut back in early spring. Grow it in a sunny situation in moderately fertile, well-drained soil.

☼ ◊ ❀❀❀

↕ to 38cm (15in) ↔ to 60cm (24in)

Ajuga reptans 'Atropurpurea'

PERENNIAL

This evergreen, mat-forming perennial is grown for its glossy, bronze-purple leaves, rather than the late spring spikes of blue flowers. The creeping stems root where they touch the soil, making this a superb ground-cover plant that is relatively easy to control. Grow it in a partially shaded or sunny site, in moist, moderately fertile soil. It is excellent in a woodland garden or shady border. 'Multicolor' has bronze-green and white leaves, heavily suffused with purple.

☼ ☽ ◊ ❄ ❄ ❄

↕ to 15cm (6in) ↔ to 90cm (36in)

Cordyline australis Purpurea Group

EVERGREEN TREE

The New Zealand cabbage palm is an architectural specimen with narrow, purplish-green leaves. It develops a trunk as it matures and may produce creamy-white summer flowers. It will survive outdoors in mild climates, and sheltered urban gardens. Elsewhere, grow it in a container of loam-based compost and move under cover in winter. Outdoors, grow it in sun or light shade in fertile, well-drained soil, and protect it over winter in its early years.

☼ ☽ ◊ ❄ ❄

↕ to 3m (10ft) ↔ to 1m (3ft)

Ophiopogon planiscapus '**Nigrescens**' ♀

PERENNIAL

The black lilyturf is a clump-forming, grass-like perennial with dark purple, almost black leaves. It looks superb when planted as edging or in pale-coloured gravel. It is also suitable for raised beds. In summer, it produces spikes of tiny, bell-shaped, purple-flushed white flowers. Plant it in full sun or partial shade, in slightly acid, moist but well-drained soil.

‡ to 23cm (9in) ↔ to 30cm (12in)

Phormium tenax **Purpureum Group** ♀

PERENNIAL

New Zealand flax is an evergreen with large, leathery, sword-shaped leaves in a rich copper or deep purple-red hue. In summer, tall, upright, architectural spikes of tubular, dark red flowers arise on plum-purple stems. Grow it as a specimen plant or in a border, in full sun and deep, fertile, moisture-retentive soil, with shelter from cold, dry winds. In cold, wet areas, provide a deep, dry mulch in winter. Phormiums do well in coastal gardens.

‡ to 2.5m (8ft) ↔ to 1m (3ft)

Phyllostachys nigra ♀
EVERGREEN BAMBOO

The black bamboo is quite well known for its darkly coloured, upright canes. It forms a gently arching clump, clothed with lance-shaped, dark green leaves. The canes emerge green and gradually turn to black in their second or third years. For the best effect, strip off some of the lower leaves to expose the canes, and occasionally remove a few of the older canes so that they remain nicely spaced. Use as a screen or as a large feature plant.

☼ ☀ ◊ ◖ ❀❀
‡ to 8m (25ft) ↔ indefinite

Pittosporum tenuifolium 'Purpureum'
EVERGREEN SHRUB

The kohuhu is an evergreen shrub or small tree, with black stems and wavy-edged, leathery, purple leaves. In late spring, it has tiny, scented, dark red, bell-shaped flowers. Plant it in full sun or partial shade in fertile, moist, well-drained soil. The leaf colour is most intense in full sun, and the plant should be protected from cold winds. It is a superb hedge for coastal gardens, and the foliage is used in floral displays. Trim hedges in spring and early autumn.

☼ ◊ ◖ ❀❀ *f*
‡ to 10m (30ft) ↔ to 5m (15ft)

Salvia officinalis '**Purpurascens**' ♥

EVERGREEN SHRUB

The purple sage forms a shrubby mound of aromatic, red-purple leaves, with spikes of purple summer flowers which are very attractive to bees. It can be grown in a herb garden for culinary use, and it is also a useful foliage foil in a sunny border or gravel garden, where it associates well with silver-leaved plants. Grow it in full sun in moderately fertile, light, well-drained soil. Clip it over in spring and after flowering to keep it shapely.

☼ ◊ ❀❀❀ *f*

‡ to 80cm (32in) ↔ to 1m (3ft)

Sedum spathulifolium '**Purpureum**' ♥

EVERGREEN PERENNIAL

This low-growing evergreen forms tight, dense mats of ground-covering foliage, studded with starry yellow flowers in summer. The rosettes of fleshy, silvery-grey leaves are flushed with purple and covered in a thick, waxy bloom. Grow it in a rock garden, a trough, on top of a dry-stone wall, or in a raised bed. It grows best in full sun in gritty, very well-drained, poor to moderately fertile soil. It can easily be trimmed back occasionally to restrict its spread.

☼ ◊ ❀❀❀

‡ to 10cm (4in) ↔ to 60cm (24in)

Festuca glauca 'Elijah Blue'

PERENNIAL GRASS

This densely tufted evergreen grass forms a rounded clump of narrow, blue leaves with matching spikes of flowers in early summer. It makes a valuable colour foil at the front of a border, or in a gravel or rock garden. The best effects are achieved by planting it in drifts of 3–5 plants. Grow it in full sun, in poor to slightly fertile, well-drained, rather dry soil. Divide and replant it every 2–3 years in spring.

☼ ◊ ❀ ❀ ❀

↕ to 30cm (12in) ↔ to 25cm (10in)

Juniperus squamata 'Blue Star' ♀

EVERGREEN SHRUB

This low-growing conifer forms dense, compact mounds of sharply pointed greyish-blue leaves that retain their colour throughout the year. The older stems have attractive reddish-brown bark. It is ideal for growing as ground cover on a bank or in a gravel garden, and combines well with other dwarf conifers and heathers. Plant it in full sun or dappled shade, in fertile, well-drained soil. It seldom needs pruning.

☼ ◑ ◊ ❀ ❀ ❀

↕ to 40cm (16in) ↔ to 1m (3ft)

Leymus arenarius
PERENNIAL GRASS

This robust, tufted grass forms loose clumps of rather stiff, bright steel blue leaves, adorned in summer by strong-stemmed heads of blue-grey flowers that age to buff. It spreads rapidly but can be confined in a container. It will develop the best colour when grown in full sun in light, well-drained, slightly fertile soil, and it is ideal for creating foliage contrasts in a herbaceous or mixed border. Cut down the faded growth in spring, and trim back before flowering for improved foliage.

☼ ◊ ❀❀❀

‡ to 1.5m (5ft) ↔ indefinite

Ruta graveolens 'Jackman's Blue'
EVERGREEN SHRUB

This rounded shrub is grown for its deeply lobed, aromatic, blue-green leaves. In summer, it produces small yellow flowers, but these should be removed before they bloom for the best foliage effect. It will grow well in a sunny position in a gravel garden, when planted in moderately fertile, well-drained soil. It can also be grown in a herb garden, or in a mixed or herbaceous border. Contact with the sap can cause a severe skin reaction.

☼ ◊ ❀❀❀ *f*

‡↔ to 60cm (24in)

Asplenium scolopendrium ♀

PERENNIAL FERN

The hart's tongue fern forms
shuttlecock-like clumps of emerald
green, lance-shaped fronds, which
often have wavy margins. In summer,
rust-coloured spore cases are arranged
herringbone-fashion on the undersides
of the fronds. A beautiful fern for a
damp, shady wall, crevice, or border,
it is also suitable for a woodland garden.
Grow it in partial shade in a moist,
preferably alkaline, well-drained soil.
Divide large clumps in spring.

☀ ◊ ◑ ❀ ❀ ❀
‡ to 75cm (30in) ↔ to 45cm (18in)

Blechnum penna-marina ♀

PERENNIAL FERN

A tough but delicate-looking fern, this
variety has long, slender fronds with
many small, triangular, glossy, dark
green leaflets. It spreads by means of
underground stems and can form large,
extensive colonies in ideal conditions.
It forms good year-round ground cover
in a woodland garden or a damp border,
or plant it in a shady niche by a wall.
Grow it in partial shade in moist, fertile,
slightly acid soil.

☀ ◑ ❀ ❀ ❀
‡ to 30cm (12in) ↔ to 45cm (18in)

Buxus sempervirens ♀

EVERGREEN SHRUB

The common box is a slow-growing shrub with small, dark green leaves. It is widely grown as a hedge, planted in pots, or trimmed into balls, pyramids or other topiary shapes. If left unpruned, it eventually forms a small bushy tree. 'Suffruticosa' is best for dwarf hedges or for edging beds. Box prefers partial shade, but will tolerate full sun as long the soil does not dry out. Grow it in moist, well-drained soil; it thrives on chalky soil, or in pots of loam-based compost. Trim once a year in summer.

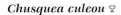

‡↔ to 5m (15ft)

Chusquea culeou ♀

EVERGREEN BAMBOO

This useful slow-growing bamboo is less invasive than most, and forms a fountain-shaped clump of cylindrical yellowish green stems, with whiskery sheaves of narrow leaves arising at intervals on the stems. Plant it in sun or partial shade, in moist but well-drained soil. Grow it in a sheltered site, where it is protected from cold, dry winds, such as in a woodland garden or to disguise a fence. Old canes can be cut out and used for staking other plants.

☼ ☀ ◐ ◊ ❁ ❁ ❁

‡ to 5m (15ft) ↔ to 2.5m (8ft)

Cupressus sempervirens
EVERGREEN TREE

The Italian cypress is unmistakable due to its narrow, pencil-thin shape so reminiscent of Mediterranean gardens. Its foliage comprises of dark green, feathery fronds and it also bears attractive round grey cones, which are distinctive of the genus. It is a valuable, evergreen structural tree, probably best in a sheltered position. Slow-growing, it is tolerant of both dry soils and coastal conditions, and needs no pruning. 'Stricta' is an even narrower variety. 'Swane's Gold' has yellowish foliage.

☼ ◊ ◊ ❀ ❀ ❀

‡ to 20m (70ft) ↔ to 1.5m (5ft)

Fargesia nitidia
EVERGREEN BAMBOO

The fountain bamboo is slow-growing and produces erect, purplish-green canes, topped by narrow, lance-shaped, dark green leaves. It can be grown in a wild garden, but its spread may need to be restricted elsewhere. To achieve this, plant it in a large, bottomless container plunged up to its rim in the ground. Alternatively, chop back the rootstock using a sharpened spade every couple of years. Plant this bamboo in dappled shade in fertile, moist soil, and protect it from cold, drying winds.

☼ ◊ ❀ ❀ ❀

‡ to 5m (15ft) ↔ to 1.5m (5ft)

Fatsia japonica ♀

EVERGREEN SHRUB

A superb architectural shrub with huge, deeply lobed leaves. In the summer, it produces large heads of creamy-white flowers. Plant it in full sun or partial shade in fertile, moist but well-drained soil. It is hardy but needs a sheltered position away from cold drying winds, which can damage the large leaves. It also benefits from a deep mulch to give some winter protection in the early years. Tolerant of pollution, it is suitable for urban gardens, and can be grown successfully by the coast too.

☼ ☀ ◌ ◌ ❀ ❀ ❀
‡↔ to 4m (12ft)

Griselinia littoralis ♀

EVERGREEN SHRUB

This vigorous shrub can become tree-like in mild areas, but is more often grown as a hedge, valued for its rather leathery, glossy, emerald-green leaves. Plant it in full sunshine, in well-drained, fertile soil. Cold, drying winds can damage it in exposed inland gardens, but it makes a good windbreak in mild coastal areas. Clip hedges in spring, or for a more informal effect, prune back with secateurs.

☼ ◌ ❀ ❀ ❀
‡ to 8m (25ft) ↔ to 5m (15ft)

Hebe cupressoides 'Boughton Dome'

EVERGREEN SHRUB

A compact, dwarf hebe, this variety forms a dense, rounded mound of bright green leaves. Mature plants may produce small spikes of white flowers. It makes a neat specimen that needs no pruning, or can be used in a container, rock garden or raised bed. Plant it in full sun or partial shade, in poor to slightly fertile, moist, well-drained, neutral to alkaline soil. It is also tolerant of coastal conditions and salt spray.

☼ ☼ ◊ ◊ ❄ ❄ ❄

‡ to 30cm (12in) ↔ to 60cm (24in)

Hedera colchica 'Dentata' ♥

CLIMBER

This Persian ivy is a vigorous climber or spreader with dark green, heart-shaped leaves that have serrated margins. The leaves are aromatic if crushed or bruised and have purplish stems. Because of its vigorous spread, this ivy is best used on a large wall or as a ground cover in an area where it can be easily contained. Grow in part to near full shade in well-drained, humus-rich soil.

☼ ☼ ◊ ❄ ❄ ❄

‡↔ to 10m (30ft)

Hedera helix '**Erecta**' ♀

EVERGREEN SHRUB

'Erecta' is an unusual ivy in that it is a non-climbing form. It is shrub-like, with stiffly upright, spire-like stems clothed in arrow-shaped, dark green leaves. It can be grown in a shrub border or as ground cover between trees, and looks especially effective at the foot of tree stumps or boulders. Plant it in fertile, preferably alkaline, moist, well-drained soil, in sun or partial shade. It needs very little pruning.

☼ ☀ ◐ ◊ ❀ ❀ ❀
‡ to 1m (3ft) ↔ to 1.2m (4ft)

Juniperus communis '**Hibernica**' ♀

EVERGREEN SHRUB

This juniper forms a narrow, tapering column of dense, prickly, bluish-green foliage. It will grow happily in most well-drained soils, including chalky conditions. While many junipers tolerate some degree of shade, 'Hibernica' may become misshapen if not provided with a sunny position. It suits formal gardens or plant it as a vertical accent in a large rock garden or a gravel garden. It does not need to be pruned.

☼ ◊ ❀ ❀ ❀
‡ to 5m (15ft) ↔ to 30cm (12in)

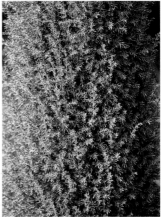

Juniperus procumbens
EVERGREEN SHRUB

The Bonin Island juniper is a creeping, low-growing conifer that forms a ground-hugging mound of yellowish-green, needle-like leaves. It makes a superb ground-cover plant for a bank, or for the edge of a gravel garden or a patio. It associates well with heathers and more upright dwarf conifers, and will grow well in full sun or partial shade in any well-drained soil; it thrives in sandy, chalky and dry soils. It needs no pruning and should be given space to spread.

☼ ◑ ◊ ❀ ❀ ❀

‡ to 75cm (30in) ↔ to 2m (6ft)

Lonicera pileata
EVERGREEN SHRUB

The privet honeysuckle has glossy, dark green, oval- to lance-shaped leaves. In late spring, it produces clusters of creamy-white, funnel-shaped flowers, which are followed by small, violet, translucent berries in summer. Plant it in full sun or partial shade, in any well-drained soil. It makes a good ground-cover plant that requires little attention, and is suitable for coastal gardens since it tolerates salt spray. In cold winters it may lose some of its leaves.

☼ ◑ ◊ ❀ ❀ ❀

‡ to 60cm (24in) ↔ to 2.5m (8ft)

Phyllostachys flexuosa

EVERGREEN BAMBOO

The zigzag bamboo forms clumps of slender, arching canes. The canes are bright green when they emerge, later becoming golden brown and finally almost black as they mature. Grow in a sheltered situation, such as a woodland garden, and plant it in fertile, humus-rich, moist, well-drained soil, in sun or dappled shade. In mild areas clumps will grow fast and require cutting back with a sharp spade every 2–3 years.

‡ to 8m (25ft) ↔ indefinite

Picea mariana 'Nana' ♀

EVERGREEN SHRUB

This is a slow-growing, dwarf form of the black spruce, and bears bluish-grey leaves. It forms a neat, rounded bush that is suitable for growing in a gravel or rock garden, on a patio, or with heathers. Plant it in full sun, in neutral to slightly acid, moderately fertile, well-drained soil. It occasionally produces vigorous upright shoots, which mar the appearance of the plant. Cut them back to the base as soon as they appear.

‡↔ to 50cm (20in)

Pinus mugo 'Mops' ♀

EVERGREEN SHRUB

A diminutive selection of the Japanese dwarf mountain pine, 'Mops' forms a small, almost spherical shrub with upright branches covered in deep green, needle-like leaves. It produces tiny, oval, dark brown cones. Very slow growing, it is suitable for planting in a rock garden or with heathers and other dwarf conifers. Choose a site in full sun with well-drained soil. It requires very little or no pruning.

☼ ◊ ❀❀❀

‡ to 1m (3ft) ↔ to 2m (6ft)

Pittosporum tobira ♀

EVERGREEN SHRUB

The Japanese mock orange forms an upright shrub or small tree that bears leathery, shiny, dark green leaves. In the late spring and early summer, it produces clusters of scented, creamy-white flowers. In mild areas, grow it outdoors in a sunny, sheltered site in fertile, moist, well-drained soil, and mulch in winter with straw or bracken. In colder gardens, grow it in a large container of loam-based compost, and move it to a cool conservatory or greenhouse over winter.

☼ ◊ ◖ ❀❀ *f*

‡ to 10m (30ft) ↔ to 3m (10ft)

Polystichum setiferum
Divisilobum Group

PERENNIAL FERN

One of the most beautiful of all hardy ferns, this variety forms a spreading, evergreen plant with soft, feathery fronds, divided several times into tiny pale green leaflets. It will flourish when planted in full or partial shade in fertile, moist but well-drained soil. Grow it in a mixed border beneath shrubs, a dark, shady corner, or in a woodland garden.

☼ ☀ ◊ ◖ ✿ ✿ ✿
‡ to 60cm (24in) ↔ to 45cm (18in)

Sasa veitchii

EVERGREEN BAMBOO

This spreading bamboo needs plenty of space. Its purple canes bear dark green leaves during summer, but later in the year, the margins dry out so that they appear variegated. Grow it in fertile, moist, well-drained soil in partial to deep shade; it tolerates sun in reliably moist soil. It is suitable for a woodland garden; elsewhere, to restrict it, plant it in a large bottomless container, plunged in the ground to the rim. Alternatively, chop back clumps with a sharp spade every couple of years.

☼ ☀ ◊ ◖ ✿ ✿ ✿
‡ to 1.5m (5ft) ↔ indefinite

Stipa gigantea ♀
PERENNIAL GRASS

Golden oats is a magnificent, evergreen grass that forms dense clumps of very narrow, dark green leaves. In summer, tall, slender but strong stems appear bearing clouds of tiny, glistening, purple-green flowers that age to gleaming gold. They make an attractive feature in the garden over winter, so wait until early spring to cut them down, along with any dead leaves. Grow as a specimen or as a gauzy screen at the back of a border. Best in full sun in fertile, well-drained soil.

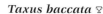

‡ to 2.5m (8ft) ↔ to 1m (3ft)

Taxus baccata ♀
EVERGREEN TREE

The common yew makes a large specimen tree but it is also one of the finest species for hedging and topiary. It forms a dense, dark green hedge and impenetrable barrier. Wherever possible, use plants grown from cuttings, because seedlings can vary slightly in colour. Plant in full sun or partial shade, in fertile, moist but well-drained soil. Yew also grows well on chalk. Trim hedges once a year in late summer; renovate overgrown or misshapen hedges by cutting back hard in late summer.

‡ to 20m (70ft) ↔ to 10m (30ft)

Thuja orientalis 'Aurea Nana'

EVERGREEN SHRUB

This is a dwarf, globe-shaped conifer, with upright sprays of yellowish-green leaves that become bronzed in autumn and winter. It is ideal for a raised bed or rock garden, for planting with heathers and for growing as part of a collection of dwarf conifers. Plant it in full sun, in moderately fertile, moist but well-drained soil. It needs little or no pruning.

☼ ◊ ◊ ❋❋❋
‡↔to 60cm (24in)

Vinca minor

EVERGREEN SHRUB

This scrambling plant has glossy, dark green leaves and violet-blue flowers from spring to autumn. A few flowers often appear in the colder months of the year. It makes an excellent ground-cover plant, with spreading stems that root wherever they touch the ground– it is, however, fairly easy to control. It grows well in any moderately fertile, well-drained soil, in partial or dappled shade, but it flowers most freely in sun. *V. major* is more invasive.

☼ ◊ ❋❋❋
‡ to 20cm (8in) ↔indefinite

Abies nordmanniana 'Golden Spreader' ♀

EVERGREEN SHRUB

The common Nordmann fir forms a very large ornamental tree, but 'Golden Spreader' is a dwarf, slow-growing form with spreading branches. The leaves on the inner parts of the plant are green, but those on the tips are bright golden-yellow, giving a very attractive two-tone effect. It is suitable for growing in a rock or gravel garden. Plant in full sun, in fertile, moist but well-drained, neutral or acid (lime-free) soil.

☼ ◊ ◊ ✻ ✻ ✻
‡ to 1m (3ft) ↔ to 1.5m (5ft)

Aucuba japonica 'Gold Dust'

EVERGREEN SHRUB

The spotted laurel is a rounded shrub with glossy green leaves variably spotted and splashed with golden yellow. If grown with a male plant, this female plant bears bright red berries in the autumn. Aucubas are happy in most soils and tolerant of pollution and salt spray. It prefers partial shade but will tolerate deep shade and grows in any soil, except waterlogged. It can be planted as a hedge, which should be pruned with secateurs in spring.

☀ ◊ ◊ ✻ ✻ ✻
‡↔ to 3m (10ft)

Buxus sempervirens 'Elegantissima' ♀

EVERGREEN SHRUB

This variegated form of the common box makes a neat, dome-shaped bush that can also be used for hedging and topiary. It grows best in dappled shade, but will also tolerate full sun. Grow in any well-drained, fertile soil, or as trimmed shapes in pots of loam-based compost. Trim hedging in summer. If older bushes become untidy, they can be rejuvenated by hard pruning in spring, followed by an application of general-purpose fertilizer.

☀️ ◐ ◊ ❀❀❀

‡↔ to 1.5m (5ft)

Calluna vulgaris 'Gold Haze' ♀

EVERGREEN SHRUB

There are several forms of ling or Scots heather with golden-yellow foliage. 'Gold Haze' retains its brilliant colour all year and in summer produces long spikes of pure white flowers. 'Ruth Sparkes' is more compact, with double white flowers. The golden leaves of 'Spitfire' turn red during winter. All three are useful ground-cover plants. Plant in full sun, in acid, moist but well-drained, fertile soil. Clip over in spring to keep compact and bushy.

☀️ ◊ ◊ ❀❀❀

‡ to 45cm (18in) ↔ 60cm (24in)

Carex oshimensis 'Evergold' ♀

PERENNIAL

This sedge forms tussocks of narrow, arching, brightly variegated leaves. The leaves are dark green with a central stripe of rich golden yellow. In mid- to late spring, it also produces spikes of dark brown flowers. Plant it in full sun or partial shade, in fertile, moist but well-drained soil, although it tolerates dry conditions. It looks very good in containers, near water and towards the front of a mixed or herbaceous border.

☼ ☀ ◐ ◊ ❀ ❀ ❀
↕↔ to 20cm (8in)

Chamaecyparis obtusa 'Crippsii' ♀

EVERGREEN TREE

A slow-growing form of the Hinoki cypress, this lovely specimen tree forms a broad column. The rich golden-yellow colour of its leaves is most strongly emphasized if it is planted against a background of darker foliage, such as a yew hedge. Plant it in full sun, in fertile, moist but well-drained, neutral or slightly acid soil. It will also grow on deep chalky soil. Pruning is unnecessary.

☼ ◊ ◊ ❀ ❀ ❀
↕ to 15m (50ft) ↔ to 8m (25ft)

Chamaecyparis pisifera 'Sungold'

EVERGREEN TREE

A form of Sawara cypress, this irregularly conical conifer has tiers of slightly drooping, thread-like, golden-yellow shoots. There are several other cultivars with golden-yellow foliage, but they tend to be scorched by cold winds and strong sunshine. Plant 'Sungold' in fertile, moist but well-drained, neutral to slightly acid soil. A pretty specimen tree, it looks its best when planted against the dark background of an evergreen hedge, such as yew.

☼ ☀ ◊ ◊ ✿ ✿ ✿
‡ to 12m (40ft) ↔ to 5m (15ft)

Choisya ternata
SUNDANCE ('Lich') ♀

EVERGREEN SHRUB

With its bright yellow leaves boldly divided into three leaflets, SUNDANCE is one of the most dramatic evergreen shrubs for a mixed or shrub border. The colour is more vibrant if it is planted in full sun, as the leaves become yellowish green in shade. Plant in well-drained, fertile soil and provide shelter from cold, drying winds – against a warm wall is ideal.

☼ ◊ ✿ ✿
‡↔ to 2.5m (8ft)

Cordyline australis 'Torbay Dazzler' ♈

EVERGREEN TREE

A decorative form of New Zealand cabbage palm, 'Torbay Dazzler' develops a slender trunk that bears a large cluster of creamy-white variegated, sword-shaped leaves. In summer, it may produce creamy-white flowers. Plant it in fertile, well-drained soil in full sun or partial shade. Dry mulch for winter protection in its early years. In cold areas it is better grown as a container plant and over-wintered in a frost-free conservatory or greenhouse.

☼ ◐ ◊ ❀ ❀

↕ to 3m (10ft) ↔ to 1m (3ft)

Cryptomeria japonica 'Sekkan-sugi'

EVERGREEN SHRUB

This is a slow-growing type of Japanese cedar with creamy-yellow foliage that turns almost white in winter. It is best planted in partial shade because the pale foliage is easily scorched in strong sunshine. Plant it in fertile, moist but well-drained soil. It is best planted as a specimen tree. Unusually for a conifer, if it is cut back hard it will sprout again, so it can be safely pruned if it outgrows its allotted space.

☼ ◊ ◊ ❀ ❀ ❀

↕ to 8m (25ft) ↔ to 5m (15ft)

Cupressus macrocarpa 'Goldcrest' ♀

EVERGREEN TREE

'Goldcrest' is a striking conifer that forms a narrow, column-shaped tree with bright golden-yellow leaves. Suitable for a coastal garden, plant it in full sun, in any well-drained soil. Although it is fully hardy, in its early years it needs protection from severe frost. It also needs shelter from cold, drying winds which may scorch the foliage. It makes an attractive hedge that needs only gentle trimming in late summer – take care not to cut back into old wood.

☼ ◊ ❈❈❈
‡ to 5m (15ft) ↔ to 2.5m (8ft)

Elaeagnus pungens 'Maculata'

EVERGREEN SHRUB

This vigorous shrub has dark green, glossy, leathery leaves with a bold, central yellow blotch. In autumn, it bears clusters of small white flowers. Remove any shoots that revert to plain green as soon as they appear and, in spring, trim any stray stems that spoil the shape of the plant. Suitable for hedging, it is also tolerant of coastal conditions. If grown as a hedge, trim it in summer. Plant it in full sun or partial shade, in fairly fertile, well-drained soil.

☼ ◐ ◊ ❈❈❈
‡ to 4m (12ft) ↔ to 5m (15ft)

Erica carnea 'Foxhollow' ♀

EVERGREEN SHRUB

Some heaths have especially attractive foliage, such as 'Foxhollow' which is yellow-green and has bronze-tipped young shoots. In cold winters, its leaves are infused with shades of pinkish orange and red. In late winter and early spring it bears purple-pink flowers. Plant in full sun, in moist but well-drained, fertile, acid soil. It will also tolerate slightly alkaline soil. A lovely ground-cover plant, give it a light clipping after flowering to keep it neat.

☼ ◊ ◗ ❀ ❀ ❀

‡ to 15cm (6in) ↔ to 40cm (16in)

Euonymus fortunei 'Emerald 'n' Gold' ♀

EVERGREEN SHRUB

This robust and easily grown, bushy shrub has glossy green leaves with bright yellow margins; during the cold winter months they take on pinkish tints. It grows in any soil, except waterlogged, and while it will tolerate shade, the leaf colour is richer and stronger in full sun. A superb ground-cover plant, it can also be grown in containers, or as a low hedge needing only a light trim in summer to keep it in shape.

☼ ◊ ◗ ❀ ❀ ❀

‡ to 60cm (24in) ↔ to 90cm (36in)

Hebe ochracea
'James Stirling' ♀
EVERGREEN SHRUB

The tiny, scale-like leaves of the whipcord hebe give it the appearance of a dwarf conifer. The rich ochre-yellow leaves look particularly attractive in winter. In late spring and early summer it bears clusters of small white flowers. Plant it in a raised bed or on a rock garden in full sun or partial shade, in moderately fertile, moist but well-drained soil. It is a tough shrub that is ideally suited to the conditions in a coastal garden.

☼ ☀ ◊ ◊ ❄ ❄ ❄
‡ to 45cm (18in) ↔ to 60cm (24in)

Hedera colchica
'Sulphur Heart' ♀
CLIMBER

Persian ivy is a vigorous, self-clinging climber with large, glossy, evergreen leaves that are marked with a central blotch of soft sulphur yellow. It provides excellent, fast-growing cover for a shady wall and can also be used as a ground-cover plant. Grow it in full sun or partial shade, in fertile, moist but well-drained, preferably alkaline soil. It develops the most intense leaf colour in a sunny position. Clip back at any time of year if necessary.

☼ ☀ ◊ ◊ ❄ ❄ ❄
‡ to 5m (15ft)

Hedera helix 'Buttercup'

CLIMBER

An extremely attractive form of the common ivy, this self-clinging evergreen climber has large, lobed, bright butter-yellow leaves. In full sun the leaves really colour up, while in shade they are a pale green. This makes for some interesting colour effects as the leaves overlap each other. Grow in fertile, moist but well-drained, preferably alkaline soil. An excellent wall plant, trim it back at any time of year if it exceeds its allotted space.

☼ ☀ ◊ ◐ ❀ ❀ ❀
‡ to 2m (6ft)

Ilex aquifolium 'Golden Milkboy'

EVERGREEN TREE

A dense, upright tree, this striking holly makes a fine specimen or hedge. Its spiny, dark green leaves have irregular, golden-yellow markings in the centre. 'Golden Milkboy' is a male plant and does not produce berries, but it makes a good pollinator for female, berrying hollies. Plant in full sun or partial shade, in fertile, moist but well-drained soil. For best leaf colour, plant in full sun. Trim hedges in summer.

☼ ☀ ◊ ◐ ❀ ❀ ❀
‡ to 6m (20ft) ↔ to 4m (12ft)

Osmanthus heterophyllus 'Aureomarginatus'

EVERGREEN SHRUB

This rounded, slow-growing shrub
has spiny, toothed leaves that resemble
those on a holly bush, and in mild
areas it makes a good hedging plant.
'Aureomarginatus' has glossy, bright
green, mottled foliage, edged in golden-
yellow. In late summer it bears small
clusters of highly fragrant, small, white,
tubular flowers. It is not totally hardy,
and should be grown in full sun or
partial shade in a sheltered position,
and planted in fertile, well-drained soil.

☼ ☀ ◊ ❀❀ *f*

‡↔ to 5m (15ft)

Phormium 'Yellow Wave' ♥

PERENNIAL

The arching, sword-shaped leaves of this
large clump-forming evergreen make
a bold focal point. They are a vibrant
yellow-green with a broad, central green
stripe. In summer, tall spikes of red-
purple flowers may appear. Plant in full
sun, in moist but well-drained, fertile
soil. During winter in colder areas,
protect the crown by tucking in a thick
layer of dry mulch among the leaves.
Use as a specimen plant or in a mixed
border. Suitable for coastal gardens.

☼ ◊ ◑ ❀❀

‡ to 3m (10ft) ↔ to 2m (6ft)

Pinus sylvestris 'Gold Coin'

EVERGREEN SHRUB

A diminutive, slow-growing version of the Scots pine, this dwarf conifer has greenish yellow, needle-like leaves that turn an intense shade of golden yellow in winter. A small rounded shrub, it is a good choice for an urban garden where space is limited; it is also ideally suited to a rock or gravel garden. Plant it in full sun, in any moderately fertile, well-drained soil. It needs no pruning.

☼ ◊ ❀❀❀
‡↔ to 2m (6ft)

Pittosporum tenuifolium 'Abbotsbury Gold'

EVERGREEN SHRUB

This kohuhu is valued for its green-margined, golden leaves. A bushy shrub or small tree, it is suitable for smaller gardens where it will thrive against a sunny wall. It can also be used for hedging, especially in coastal gardens, needing a trim once only in spring to keep it in shape. Grow in fertile, moist but well-drained soil. Provide shelter from cold, drying winds; in areas where winters are severe, grow in containers and bring in under cover.

☼ ◑ ◊ ◊ ❀❀
‡ to 3m (10ft) ↔ to 1.5m (5ft)

Pittosporum tenuifolium 'Irene Patterson' ♀

EVERGREEN SHRUB

The emergent spring foliage of this attractive shrub is cream, gradually becoming marbled with dark green. Slow-growing and mound-forming, it makes an attractive specimen but it is also suitable as a hedging plant, especially in wild and coastal gardens. Trim to shape in spring. Plant in moist but well-drained, fertile soil, in full sun or partial shade. Protect from cold, drying winds and mulch young plants over winter.

☼ ☽ ◊ ◊ ❀ ❀
‡ to 1.2m (4ft) ↔ to 60cm (24in)

Thuja plicata 'Stoneham Gold' ♀

EVERGREEN SHRUB

A small cone-shaped bush, this is a dwarf form of the Western red cedar. The irregularly arranged sprays of foliage are coppery bronze, becoming golden yellow and then green as it ages. It is slow-growing and makes a good plant for a rock garden. Plant in moist but well-drained, fertile soil in full sun. It needs to be protected from cold, drying winds to avoid foliage scorch, especially in its early years.

☼ ◊ ◊ ❀ ❀ ❀
‡↔ to 2m (6ft)

INDEX

A

PICTURE CREDITS

The publisher would like to thank the following for their kind permission to reproduce their photographs: (Key: a-above; b-below t-top)

17 Dorling Kindersley: Andrew Butler (b). **20 GAP Photos:** John Glover (b). **34 Dorling Kindersley:** Juliette Wade (t). **37 GAP Photos:** Martin Hughes-Jones (b). **39 Garden and Wildlife Matters Photo Library:** (b). **42 A-Z Botanical Collection:** Andrew Ackerley (b); Adrian Thomas (t). **43 Garden Picture Library:** Sunniva Harte (b). **56 Caroline Reed:** (t). **58 Garden Picture Library:** Brian Carter (b). **68 Garden World Images:** Trevor Sims (b). **106 Garden Picture Library:** Jacqui Hurst (b). **107 Martin Page:** (t). **109 James Young:** (t). **110 Garden and Wildlife Matters Photo Library:** (t). **118 Garden Picture Library:** Sunniva Harte (b). **119 Photolibrary:** Garden Picture Library / Michael Howes (t). **122 GAP Photos:** Neil Holmes (b). **123 Photolibrary:** Garden Picture Library / Jerry Pavia (b). **124 A-Z Botanical Collection:** Adrian Thomas (b). **125 Andrew Lawson:** (b). **127 Photos Horticultural:** (b). **128 GAP Photos:** Howard Rice (b). **130 Garden Picture Library:** Jacqui Hurst (t). **136 GAP Photos:** Martin Hughes-Jones (t). **140 The Garden Collection:** Torie Chugg (b). **143 A-Z Botanical Collection:** Jack Coulthard (t). **149 Garden World Images:** (b). **154 Marianne Majerus Garden Images:** MMGI (t). **160 Photolibrary:** JS. Sira (t). **162 Garden World Images:** (t). **164 GAP Photos:** Martin Hughes-Jones (b). **165 Garden Picture Library:** Christopher Fairweather (t). **166 Dorling Kindersley:** Andrew Butler (t). **167 GAP Photos:** Rob Whitworth (b). **168 Dorling Kindersley:** Juliette Wade (b). **173 GAP Photos:** Julie Dansereau / RHS Wisley (t). **174 Martin Page:** (b). **176 GAP Photos:** Martin Hughes-Jones (b). **187 Garden World Images:** Trevor Sims (b). **192 Martin Page:** (t). **194 Dorling Kindersley:** Roger Smith (b). **Photos Horticultural:** (t). **196 Dorling Kindersley:** Roger Smith (b). **199 Garden World Images:** (b). **Marianne Majerus Garden Images:** MMGI (t). **200 Photos Horticultural:** (b). **202 Garden World Images:** Trevor Sims (b). **204 GAP Photos:** Howard Rice (b). **205 Garden World Images:** Martin Hughes-Jones (b). **Eric Crichton Photos:** (t). **207 GAP Photos:** FhF Greenmedia (t).

ACKNOWLEDGMENTS

FIRST EDITION
Project editor: Helen Fewster
Art editor: Ann Thompson
Project art editor: Alison Donovan
Managing editor: Anna Kruger
Managing art editor: Lee Griffiths
DTP design: Louise Waller
Production: Mandy Inness
Picture research: Samantha Nunn
Picture library: Richard Dabb,
Lucy Claxton, Charlotte Oster
Index: Michèle Clarke

NEW EDITION 2011
Editors Caroline Reed, Becky Shackleton
Editorial assistance: Rukmini Chawla
Kumar, Eva Young, Neha Pande, Archana
Ramachandran, Neha Samuel, Suefa Lee
DTP Assistance: Tarun Sharma
Picture research: Rob Nunn
Picture library: Lucy Claxton